Grassroots Elections in China

Twenty years after the launch of village elections, the time is ripe to assess the progress and impact of China's most notable political reform. Where have elections been conducted well and where have they been conducted poorly? How have procedures changed over the years and have elections truly transformed how power is exercised in the countryside? What methods are researchers employing to study elections and how have scholars from different disciplines contributed to our knowledge of grassroots politics in China?

This book carefully examines the implementation and effects of China's village, township, and people's congress elections, both in terms of democratizing the polity and spurring other changes in state-society relations.

The chapters in this book, except for the introduction, were previously published in the *Journal of Contemporary China,*.

Kevin J. O'Brien is Alann P. Bedford Professor of Asian Studies and Professor of Political Science at the University of California, Berkeley, USA.

Suisheng Zhao is Editor of the *Journal of Contemporary China,* and Professor and Executive Director at the Center for China-US Cooperation, Josef Korbel School of International Studies, University of Denver, USA.

Grassroots Elections in China

Edited by
Kevin J. O'Brien and Suisheng Zhao

Routledge
Taylor & Francis Group

LONDON AND NEW YORK

First published 2011
by Routledge
2 Park Square, Milton Park, Abingdon, Oxon, OX14 4RN

Simultaneously published in the USA and Canada
by Routledge
711 Third Avenue, New York, NY 10017

Routledge is an imprint of the Taylor & Francis Group, an informa business

First issued in paperback 2013

This book is a reproduction of a selection of articles from the *Journal of Contemporary China*. The Publisher requests to those authors who may be citing this book to state, also, the bibliographical details of the special issues on which the book was based.

Typeset in Times New Roman by Taylor & Francis Books

British Library Cataloguing in Publication Data
A catalogue record for this book is available from the British Library

ISBN13: 978-0-415-57157-9 (hardback)
ISBN13: 978-0-415-84805-3 (paperback)

Disclaimer
The publisher would like to make readers aware that the chapters in this book are referred to as articles as they had been in the special issue. The publisher accepts responsibility for any inconsistencies that may have arisen in the course of preparing this volume for print.

Contents

CONTENTS

Part II: Studies of Village Elections

Part III. Elections and the Local Economy

Part IV: Township and People's Congress Elections

CONTENTS

Notes on contributors

Björn Alpermann is Assistant Professor for Contemporary Chinese Studies at the University of Würzburg, Germany. His publications include *The State in the Village: Rural Self-Administration in China* (Hamburg, 2001, in German), *China's Cotton Industry: Economic Transformation and State Capacity* (London and New York, 2010) and the edited volume *Politics and Markets in Rural China* (London and New York, forthcoming).

Thomas P. Bernstein is Professor Emeritus of Political Science at Columbia University in New York. His books include *Taxation without Representation in Contemporary Rural China*, co-authored with Lü Xiaobo (Cambridge, 2003); *China Learns from the Soviet Union, 1949-Present*, co-edited with Li Hua-yu (Lexington Books, 2010).

Siu Fung Chung is Lecturer at the School of Health, University of New England, Australia. She also teaches research methods in the Education, Health & Professional Studies Programs. She has diverse research interests across the social sciences, public policy and management, health care and public health.

Dong Lisheng is Professor of Political Science at the Graduate School of the Chinese Academy of Social Sciences, China. His books include *The Provision of Public Goods in China* (China Society Press, 2007), *Combating Vote-Buying in Village Committee Elections* (China Society Press, 2005) and *A Comparative Study of the Central-Local Government Relations in EU Member States* (Press of China University of Political Science and Law, 2000).

Guo Zhenglin is Professor of Political Science at Zhongshan University, Guangzhou, and director of the Institute for Local Government.

Rongbin Han is a Ph.D. student in the Department of Political Science at the University of California, Berkeley.

He Junzhi is Associate Professor of Political Science at the School of International Relations and Public Affairs and Vice Director of the Center for Electoral and Parliamentary Systems Studies at Fudan University, Shanghai. His research interests include comparative electoral systems and parliamentary systems, especially China's People's Congress System.

Jude Howell is Professor and Director of the Centre for Civil Society at the London School of Economics and Political Science. She is the author and co-author of five books and over 45 articles and book chapters on the related themes of governance, civil society, development and gender, both generally and specifically on China. Her latest publications include *Governance in China* (Rowman and Littlefield, 2004), *Gender and Civil Society* (with Diane Mulligan) (Routledge, 2004), and *Civil Society and Development* (with Jenny Pearce) (Lynne Rienner Inc., 2001).

Rong Hu is Mingjiang Chair Professor of Sociology at Xiamen University, China. His books include Sociology: An Analysis of Social Unities (Xiamen, 1995), Rational Choice and Institutional Implementation: Village Elections in Rural China (Shanghai, 2001) and Social Capital and Local Governance (Beijing, 2009).

Zongze Hu received his Ph.D. in Social Anthropology from Harvard University. His dissertation entitled, "Keeping Hope: Encountering and Imagining the National State in a North China Village" focused on ways in which local residents experience and view the nation-state in a Chinese village.

John James Kennedy is Associate Professor in the Department of Political Science at the University of Kansas. His research focuses on rural, social and political development including village elections, tax reform and rural education. He teaches classes on contemporary China and has published several book chapters as well as articles in journals such as *Asian Survey, The China Quarterly, Journal of Chinese Political Science, Journal of Contemporary China*, and *Political Studies*.

Melanie Manion is Professor of Political Science and Public Affairs at the University of Wisconsin, Madison. Her recent books include *Corruption by Design: Building Clean Government in Mainland China and Hong Kong* (Harvard, 2004) and *Contemporary Chinese Politics: New Sources, Methods, and Field Strategies* (co-edited, Cambridge, 2010).

Kevin J. O'Brien is Alann P. Bedford Professor of Asian Studies and Professor of Political Science at the University of California, Berkeley. His books include *Engaging the Law in China: State, Society and Possibilities for Justice* (Stanford, 2005), *Rightful Resistance in Rural China* (Cambridge, 2006), and *Popular Protest in China* (Harvard, 2008).

Gunter Schubert is Chair Professor of Greater China Studies at the Department of Chinese and Korean Studies, Institute of Asian and Oriental Studies, University of Tuebingen. His recent books include *Asian European Relations: Building Blocks for Global Governance?* (Routledge 2008), *Regime Legitimacy in Contemporary China: Institutional Change and Stability* (Routledge 2009), *Political Participation and Regime Legitimacy in the PRC. Vol II: Rural China* (Wiesbaden 2009; in German).

Tianjian Shi is Associate Professor of Political Science at Duke University where he specializes in comparative politics with an emphasis on political culture and political participation in Chinese politics. He is the author of *Political Participation in Beijing* (Harvard, 1997).

Qingshan Tan is Director of Asian Studies and Professor of Political Science at the Cleveland State University. He has published many works on village elections and governance, including his latest book entitled *Village Elections in China: Democratizing the Countryside*.

Xin Qiushui is Senior Research Fellow at the Anhui Academy of Social Sciences.

NOTES ON CONTRIBUTORS

David Zweig is Chair Professor, Division of Social Science at Hong Kong University of Science and Technology, and Director of its Center on China's Transnational Relations. He has written four books, including *Internationalizing China: Domestic Interests and Global Linkages* (Cornell, 2002) and has edited four books, including *Globalization and China's Reforms* (Routledge, 2007). He writes on China's Returned Students, Hong Kong-Mainland ties, and China's "Resource Diplomacy."

Rong Hu is Mingjiang Chair Professor of Sociology at Xiamen University, China. His books include *Sociology: An Analysis of Social Unities* (Xiamen, 1995), *Rational Choice and Institutional Implementation: Village Elections in Rural China* (Shanghai, 2001) and *Social Capital and Local Governance* (Beijing, 2009).

Introduction: understanding China's grassroots elections

Kevin J. O'Brien

In his widely-read book, *The China Fantasy*, James Mann argues that a 'soothing scenario' of gradual, inevitable democratization dominates American views of China's future. In this sunny outlook, grassroots elections enjoy a special place. They are a 'panacea' that reassures us that China is heading in the right direction and a reason we need not be too dismayed about China's authoritarian present: better days are to come. Although Mann rejects nearly everything associated with this scenario, he maintains that many China watchers and influential Americans – from a string of US presidents, to business elites and consultants, to pundits and leading academic experts – subscribe to it.[1]

Mann has clearly not been reading the chapters in this volume. All of them were originally published from 1999–2010 as articles of the *Journal of Contemporary China,*. Like most works on grassroots elections, they present a sober, not overly soothing view of what has been happening on the ground and what it adds up to. Some of the authors consider the implications of elections for regime-level transformation but none deem democratization 'inevitable' or 'automatic.' Instead, the spread of local balloting is understood to have brought about a significant adjustment in state-society relations that may have as much to do with authoritarian resilience[2] as with democracy.

Elections, in these accounts, reflect the stop-and-go progress of political reform itself. Not a sham, they are, like other liberal institutions in an illiberal polity, part of a strategy designed to help one-party rule endure. Big, unintended consequences may yet emerge, but to this point, local elections operate in a limited context and have local effects. From their beginnings, elections arose out of a state-building as much as a democratizing impulse,[3] and, several decades later, they may be legitimating the current regime rather than serving as a harbinger of systemic change.[4]

Beyond their unblinkered view of political reform and its implications, what else do the authors in this volume share? And what future do they suggest for the next generation of election studies?

Methods and approaches

In this remarkably busy field, a number of trends are apparent. For one, research methods are changing. Quantitative studies, based on surveys, are increasingly common. At least two or three survey teams are in the field at any time and both local and national surveys of election procedures and popular attitudes toward elections have been completed.[5] This research is a welcome addition to a literature that at first depended on findings from a handful of locations visited for a short time, supplemented by archival materials. As the chapters by Tan and Xin (chapter 8), Zweig and Chung (chapter 11), Rong Hu (chapter 12), and Shi (chapter 13) show, survey-based analyses are very much the wave of the present and, taken together, are making headway on an issue that case studies cannot: how to generalize about all (or a subset) of the hundreds of thousands villages and urban locations where elections take place. Moreover, as Melanie Manion explains in chapter 2, much remains to be done, even if nationally representative samples cannot always be drawn and local probability sampling must be relied on to illuminate 'patterns and trends' and 'temporal and cross-sectional variation.' Beyond competitive elections and their relationship to economic development, which is examined in Part III of this collection, Manion reminds us that surveys are well-suited to examine the electoral connection between voters and candidates and to 'systematically investigate the contextual effect of the local power configuration on governance.'

While surveyers are searching for patterns and adding breadth to our knowledge, others are investigating events in a single location.[6] In this volume, 'attention to local particularities' is represented by Zongze Hu's ethnography of a Hebei village (chapter 7). Hu's participant observation uncovers what elections mean to villagers and leaders in one community, and illustrates how factional cleavages and lineage identities can rise to the surface when balloting and governance occur. Such studies, often conducted by anthropologists or sociologists, promise more consideration of the lived experience of elections and signal a new interest in biography, local micro-histories, and cultural practices. In a field still dominated by political scientists, they help us understand why, institutional reforms aside, some voters continue to believe that elections are not a viable way 'to choose popular and competent cadres.' Accounts that focus on grass-roots participants are especially apropos now that a good amount of time has passed since elections were revived in the late 1970s. Voting has a history, and issues that turn on perceptions, like apathy, trust, support, and legitimation, should be examined in specific communities as well as generally.[7]

Hu's call to consider 'the views and voices of those most affected' can also be addressed by paying more attention to Election Day. After a strong start in the 1990s, election observation has fallen out of fashion. Early monitoring efforts, organized by the Carter Center and International Republican Institute, could be profitably updated by on-the-spot observers who examine, for example, the details of vote-counting, proxy voting, and the disappointment of voters, who after hours of waiting, often hear the words 'wuxiao' (no result), because the 50% threshold for a valid election has not been met.[8]

Other approaches also deserve more representation. A rich sociology of elections would illuminate the effects of voting on various social groups. Jude Howell (chapter 9 in this volume) and Baogang He have led the way on womens' under-representation on village committees,[9] but we also need studies that examine what minorities, migrant workers, and religious believers make of elections, and how their position in society is affected (or not) by them.

Finally, some approaches and methods remain almost entirely absent from the literature on grassroots elections. The first articles by economists and game theorists are just beginning to appear.[10] Historians, for their part, have been noticeably silent on the antecedents of today's elections and studies based on experiments, such as Guan and Green's on the effects of door-to-door canvassing on voter turnout,[11] have broken new ground but have yet to be emulated.

New topics

Research topics are also changing. Careful examination of election procedures (Tan, chapter 6) and a lively debate over whether richer or poorer villages hold better elections (Zweig and Chung, chapter 11; Hu, chapter 12; Shi, chapter 13) is giving way to a focus on the consequences of balloting. Consequences, in the contemporary way of thinking, are understood broadly, including effects on: the 'exercise of power' (O'Brien and Han, chapter 1);[12] relations between elected bodies and Party organizations (Guo and Bernstein, chapter 10; Tan and Xin, chapter 8); procedural aspects of post-election governance (Alpermann, chapter 5); corruption;[13] land allocation;[14] fiscal transfers;[15] regime legitimacy (Schubert, chapter 3; Kennedy, chapter 4); feelings of empowerment;[16] and the development of citizenship consciousness.[17] Several recent studies have also stressed that elections are just one means to enhance accountability, and perhaps not the most effective one.[18]

For most researchers, grassroots elections mean village elections: a vast majority of studies of Chinese elections focus on village committees. A series of experiments with electing township leaders has produced a small literature, represented by Dong Li-sheng's contribution to this volume (chapter 14).[19] Local people's congress (LPC) elections are also gaining a spot on the research agenda, as seen in He Junzhi's chapter on four types of independent candidates (chapter 15). More studies like He's are desirable insofar as LPC elections have drawn only sporadic attention since the early 1980s, even as research on other aspects of congresses, such as lawmaking and oversight, has taken off.[20]

With knowledge of grassroots elections mounting, the time has come for more comparison, both domestically and internationally. Within China, elections to urban self-governance institutions should be considered alongside their rural counterparts.[21] Consecutive, different types of elections also suggest a natural experiment that is too good to pass up. In some localities, elections to county people's congresses and village committees take place several weeks apart, have the same districting and sometimes the same candidates, yet are conducted with strikingly different procedures (in 2002 in Yunnan, for example, village committee elections were nearer to international standards on nominating procedures, primaries, and secret balloting than people's congress elections, and civil affairs staff were more attuned to the requirements of free and fair voting than people's congress staff).[22] There are also many locations where village elections were held for some years, but now, owing to administrative reclassification, balloting takes place under less democratic urban rules. Such disparities offer a direct opportunity to explore the effects of differing procedures on voter interest, political participation, and accountability.

Beyond China, a dialogue should also be pursued with those who study local elections in other authoritarian regimes, past and present.[23] There is much to be gained by viewing China's experiences with elections beside those of Vietnam, Cuba, Central Asia, and the Middle East. Historical cases in East Asia (most notably, Taiwan), and even in Western Europe and Latin America before the advent of democracy, also promise to reveal much about how culture, institutional legacies, and historical accidents affect the role that elections play in illiberal polities.

International comparison can also help dispel misunderstandings about democratization. A broad field of view reveals that 'authoritarian elections are neither rare nor . . . inevitably undermining to autocrats' and that China's Communist Party is hardly an outlier in using elections to 'hold onto power'. As the chapters in this book make clear, regime breakdown and democratization are possibilities for China, but the more pressing questions today center on the persistence of authoritarian rule. In Gandhi's and Lust-Okar's words: 'Although elections sometimes may foster democratization, it is no longer easy to assume that elections necessarily undermine authoritarian regimes; in fact, the opposite generally appears to be true'.[24] Taking China's grassroots elections for what they are, rather than what they might become, allows the authors in this collection to sidestep teleology and contribute to the discussion about the origins, dynamics, and consequences of political reform in authoritarian states.

Notes

1 James Mann, *The China Fantasy: How Our Leaders Explain Away Chinese Repression* (New York: Viking, 2007). On village elections as a 'panacea', see pp. 18-20.

2 For this term, see Andrew J. Nathan, 'Authoritarian resilience', *Journal of Democracy* 14(1), (January 2003), pp. 6-17.

3 Kevin J. O'Brien and Lianjiang Li, 'Accommodating "democracy" in a one-party state: introducing village elections in China', *China Quarterly* 162, (June 2000), pp. 488-89; Frank N. Pieke, 'Contours of an anthropology of the Chinese state: political structure, agency and economic development in rural China', *Journal of the Royal Anthropological Institute* 10(3), (2004), p. 521.

4 So, Mann is both right and wrong. He is correct that his 'third scenario' (persistent authoritarianism) is the most likely medium-term outcome. But he has not noticed that among China scholars this scenario is also the betting favourite. Even for those who study protest, and who might be expected to espouse his 'upheaval scenario,' this view has been edging from consensus to near unanimity, and perhaps should be revisited for just this reason. For tentative signs of such a questioning, see Andrew J. Nathan, 'Authoritarian impermanence', *Journal of Democracy* 20(3), (July 2009), pp. 37-40.

5 For a recent nationwide survey of village elections, see 'Sample survey data on the status of Chinese villager self-governance', The Carter Center, 27 July 2009, available at http://en.chinaelections.org/NewsInfo.asp?NewsID=20561 (accessed 8 August 2009).

6 For an example, see Xueguang Zhou, '"Can a falling leaf tell the coming of autumn?" Making sense of village elections in a township . . . and in China', in Jean C. Oi, Scott Rozelle, and Xueguang Zhou (eds.) *Growing Pains: Tensions and Opportunity in China's Transformation* (Washington D.C.: Brookings Institution Press, 2009).

7 On apathy, see Jie Chen and Yang Zhong, 'Mass political interest (or apathy) in urban China', *Communist and Post-Communist Studies* 32, (1999), pp. 281-303; and Tan and Xin in this volume (chapter 8). On trust, see Melanie Manion, 'Democracy, community, trust: the impact of elections in rural China', *Comparative Political Studies* 39(1), (April 2006), pp. 301-24. On support, see Jie Chen, 'Popular support for village self-government in China: intensity and sources', *Asian Survey* 45(6), (December 2005), pp. 865-85. Legitimation is one of the hottest topics in the study of grassroots politics. See Gunter Schubert and Chen Xuelian, 'Village elections in contemporary China: new spaces for generating regime legitimacy? Experiences from Lishu county', *China Perspectives* 3, (2007), pp. 12-27; Stig Thøgersen, 'Parasites or civilisers: the legitimacy of the Chinese Communist Party in rural areas', *China: An International Journal* 1(2), (September 2003), pp. 200-223; and the chapters by Schubert and Kennedy in this volume (Schubert in chapter 3; Kennedy in chapter 4).

8 On a 2002 election observation trip, see Kevin J. O'Brien, 'Improving election procedures: some modest proposals', unpublished paper, 23 April 2006, available at http://papers.ssrn.com/sol3/papers.cfm?abstract_id=1157092 (accessed 13 August 2009).

9 Baogang He, *Rural Democracy in China* (New York: Palgrave, 2007), chapter 8. For studies of female political participation, see Weiguo Zhang, 'Marketization, democratization, and women's participation in village elections in contemporary rural China: a study of a north China village', *Journal of Women, Politics and Policy* 28(2), (2006), pp. 1-28; M. Kent

Jennings, 'Gender and political participation in the Chinese countryside', *Journal of Politics* 60(4), (November 1998), pp. 954-73; James Tong, 'The gender gap in political culture and participation in China', *Communist and Post-Communist Studies* 36(2), (2003), pp. 131-50.

10 Loren Brandt and Matthew A. Turner, 'The usefulness of imperfect elections: the case of village elections in rural China', *Economics and Society* 19(3), (November 2007), pp. 453-80; Hiroki Takeuchi, 'A game theoretic analysis of China's village elections', paper prepared for the *Annual Conference of the Midwestern Political Science Association*, Chicago, 12-15 April 2007.

11 Mei Guan and Donald P. Green, 'Non-coercive mobilization in state-controlled elections; an experimental study in Beijing', *Comparative Political Studies* 39(10), (2006), pp. 1175-93. Turnout in local people's congress elections has been a popular topic for survey researchers, and has led to disagreement over how to interpret a person's decision not to vote. See Tianjian Shi, 'Voting and nonvoting in China: voting behavior in plebiscitary and limited-choice elections', *Journal of Politics* 61(4), (November 1999), pp. 1115-39; Jie Chen and Yang Zhong, 'Why do people vote in semicompetitive elections in China'? *Journal of Politics* 64(1), (February 2002), pp. 178-97. On turnout for village elections, see Yang Zhong and Jie Chen, 'To vote or not to vote: an analysis of peasants' participation in Chinese village elections', *Comparative Political Studies* 35(6), (August 2002), pp. 686-712.

12 See also Björn Alpermann, 'The post-election administration of Chinese villages', *China Journal* 46, (July 2001), pp. 45-67.

13 Richard Levy, 'Village elections, transparency, and anticorruption: Henan and Guangdong provinces', in Elizabeth J. Perry and Merle Goldman, eds., *Grassroots Political Reform in Contemporary China* (Cambridge, MA: Harvard University Press, 2007), pp. 20-47.

14 Janet C. Sturgeon, 'Quality control: resource access and local village elections in rural China', *Modern Asian Studies* 43(2), (2009), pp. 481-509; John James Kennedy, Scott Rozelle, and Shi Yaojiang, 'Elected leaders and collective land: farmers' evaluation of village leaders' performance in rural China', *Journal of Chinese Political Science* 9(1), (Spring 2004), pp. 1-22.

15 Shuna Wang and Yang Yao, 'Grassroots democracy and local governance: evidence from rural China', *World Development* 35(10), (2007), pp. 1635-49.

16 Lianjiang Li, 'The empowering effect of village elections in China', *Asian Survey* 43(4), (July/August 2003), pp. 648-62.

17 Kevin J. O'Brien, 'Villagers, elections, and citizenship in contemporary China', *Modern China* 27(4), (October 2001), pp. 407-35. Baogang He, *Rural Democracy in China*, chapter 3.

18 On the limited effect of democratic institutions on public goods provision, compared with temple and lineage groups, see Lily L. Tsai, *Accountability without Democracy: Solidary Groups and Public Goods Provision in Rural China* (New York: Cambridge University Press, 2007), chapter 7. On religious practices substituting for elections, see Stephan Feuchtwang, 'Peasants, democracy and anthropology: questions of local loyalty', *Critique of Anthropology* 23(1), (2003), pp. 93-120.

19 Lianjiang Li, 'The politics of introducing direct township elections in China', *China Quarterly* 171, (September 2002), pp. 704-23; Tony Saich and Xuedong Yang, 'Innovation in China's local governance: open recommendation and selection', *Pacific Affairs* 76(2), (Summer 2003), pp. 185-209; Baogang He, *Rural Democracy in China*, chapter 12; Lianjiang Li, 'Direct township elections', in Elizabeth J. Perry and Merle Goldman, eds., *Grassroots Political Reform in Contemporary China,* pp. 97-116; Stig Thøgersen Jorgen Elklit, and Dong Lisheng, 'Consultative elections of Chinese township leaders: the case of an experiment in Ya'an, Sichuan', *China Information* 22(1), (2008), pp. 67-89.

20 Young Nam Cho, *Local People's Congresses in China: Development and Transition* (New York: Cambridge University Press, 2009); Ming Xia, *The People's Congresses and Governance in China: Toward a Network Mode of Governance* (London: Routledge, 2008); Kevin J. O'Brien, 'Local people's congresses and governing China', *China Journal* 61, (January 2009), pp. 131-41. For early studies of LPC elections, see Brantly Womack, 'The 1980 county-level elections in China: experiment in democratic modernization', *Asian Survey* 22(3), (March 1982), pp. 261-77; J. Bruce Jacobs, 'Elections in China', *Australian Journal of Chinese Affairs* 25, (January 1991), pp. 171-99. For more recent treatments, see Melanie Manion, 'Chinese democratization in perspective: electorates and selectorates at the township level', *China*

Quarterly 163, (September 2000), pp. 764-82; An Chen, *Restructuring Political Power in China: Alliances and Opposition, 1978-1999* (Boulder, CO: Lynne Reinner, 1999), chapter 3.

21 For a pioneering effort, see Robert Benewick, Irene Tong, and Jude Howell, 'Self-governance and community: a preliminary comparison between villagers' committees and urban community councils', *China Information* 18(1), (2004), pp. 11-28.

22 O'Brien, 'Improving election procedures'.

23 For a review of this literature, see Jennifer Gandhi and Ellen Lust-Okar, 'Elections under authoritarianism', *Annual Review of Political Science* 12, (2009), pp. 403-22.

24 For the quoted text in this paragraph, see Gandhi and Lust-Okar, 'Elections under authoritarianism', pp. 404 and 417.

Path to Democracy? Assessing village elections in China

KEVIN J. O'BRIEN and RONGBIN HAN

Election procedures in rural China have improved greatly over the last 20 years and a good number of reasonably free and fair elections have been held. But changes in the 'exercise of power' have not kept up with changes in the 'access to power'. In many communities, township authorities, Party branches, and social forces (such as clans, religious groups, and underworld elements) continue to impede democratic rule. This suggests that a purely procedural definition of democracy is problematic and that democratization depends on the power configuration in which elected bodies are embedded. Putting grassroots democracy into place goes well beyond getting the procedures right, and 'high quality' democracy rests on much more than convening good village elections every three years.

The launch of village elections in China has passed its twentieth anniversary. Elections officially began with the enactment of the *Organic Law of Village Committees* (1987, amended 1998). This law promised 'self-governance' (*zizhi*) via self-management, self-education, and self-service, which were soon reconceived as democratic election, decision making, management, and supervision. Since then, 'grassroots democracy' has become a term freighted with controversy for those who study Chinese politics, and elections have attracted a great deal of attention both domestically and abroad.[1]

Judging by procedures alone, village elections have achieved much. Balloting has been carried out in every province, with Guangdong, Hainan, and Yunnan finally conducting their first elections in 1999, and Tibet its first in 2002. Turnout rates have

---

1. For review essays, see Gunter Schubert, 'Village elections in the PRC: a Trojan horse of democracy?', Project Discussion Paper No. 19, (2002), available at: http://www.uni-duisburg.de/Institute/OAWISS/neu/downloads/pdf/orange/discuss19.pdf (accessed 25 July 2007); Björn Alpermann, 'An assessment of research on village governance in China and suggestions for future applied research', prepared for the China–EU Training Programme of Village Governance, Beijing, (2003), available at: http://www.china.uni-koeln.de/papers/No%202003-1.pdf, (accessed 28 July 2007).

generally been high, in many locations reportedly over 90%.[2] Surveys and direct observation by international monitors also show that the conduct of elections (including nomination procedures, competitiveness, and secret balloting) has improved over time.[3]

By many indicators, the future of grassroots democracy in China is bright, much as Tianjian Shi foresaw some years ago.[4] When tracing the introduction of village elections, Shi highlighted the role of democratically committed midlevel officials in the Ministry of Civil Affairs who employed an incremental approach that focused on extent first and quality later. This explanation accords nicely with most theories of democratization and its diffusion, and their emphasis on the role of leaders and their decisions.[5]

Is rural China on the path to democracy that Shi and others have suggested?[6] How should we assess the prospects for grassroots democracy in China? Viewing the mountain of evidence now available in light of the literature on democratization, we re-examine the practice of self-governance and suggest that the working definition of democracy adopted by most observers, which underscores its procedural components, is incomplete. This definition, in a word, leads analysts to over emphasize form at the expense of content. Instead, we follow Sebastian Mazzuca[7] and suggest a distinction between two dimensions of democratization, namely access to power and exercise of power. The introduction of elections has indeed begun to change the way in which village authorities gain power, but this has not necessarily transformed the way they exercise that power. Reducing rural democracy to well-run

---

2. Tong Zhihui, 'Cunji Xuanju de Lishi Fazhan he Xueshu Yanjiu' ['Historical development and academic research on village elections'], in Liu Yawei, ed., *Wusheng de Geming: Cunmin Zhixuan de Lishi Xianshi he Weilai* [*Silent Revolution: The History, Reality and Future of Village Elections*] (Xi'an: Xibei Daxue Chubanshe, 2002), p. 18; He Xuefeng, 'Cunweihui Xuanju Zhuhuanjie de Diaocha yu Fenxi: Hunansheng Sishigexian Cunweihui Xuanju Xinxi Huifang Huodong Baogao' ['An investigation and analysis of procedures of village committee elections: a report on the data verification of the village committee election in 40 counties in Hunan Province'], available at: http://www.chinarural.org/news_show.aspx?cols=1812&ID=11780 (accessed 1 December 2006). On an 86% turnout rate in 120 villages in Heilongjiang and Anhui, see David Zweig and Chung Siu Fung, 'Elections, democratic values, economic development in rural China', *Journal of Contemporary China* 16(50), (February 2007), pp. 25–26. On 71% turnout in 12 Anhui villages, see Qingshan Tan and Xin Qiushui, 'Village election and governance: do villagers care?', *Journal of Contemporary China* 16(53), (November 2007), p. 585. For 48% turnout (excluding proxy votes) in 12 Jiangsu counties, see Yang Zhong and Jie Chen, 'To vote or not to vote: an analysis of peasants' participation in Chinese village elections', *Comparative Political Studies* 35(6), (August 2002), pp. 692–693.

3. See Qingshan Tan, 'Building institutional rules and procedures: village election in China', *Policy Sciences* 37(1), (March 2004), pp. 1–22; Baogang He, *Rural Democracy in China: The Role of Village Elections* (New York: Palgrave, 2007), pp. 24, 39; Sun Long and Tong Zhihui, 'The standardization of villager committee election procedures', available at: http://www.cartercenter.org/documents/1096.pdf (accessed 29 March 2007). 'Election observation report: Fujian Province village elections, People's Republic of China' (Washington, DC: International Republican Institute, 2003); Melanie Manion, 'How to assess village elections in China', *Journal of Contemporary China* 18(60), (June 2009).

4. Tianjian Shi, 'Village committee elections in China: institutionalist tactics for democracy', *World Politics* 51(3), (April 1999), pp. 385–412.

5. See Guillermo O'Donnell, Philippe Schmitter and Lawrence Whitehead, *Transitions from Authoritarian Rule: Tentative Conclusions about Uncertain Democracies* (Baltimore, MD: Johns Hopkins University Press, 1986), pp. ix–x, also ch. 3; Alfred Stepan, *Arguing Comparative Politics* (Oxford: Oxford University Press, 2001), chs 5 and 8.

6. See also Qingshan Tan, *Village Elections in China: Democratizing the Countryside* (Lewiston, NY: Edward Mellen, 2006); He, *Rural Democracy in China*; Jamie P. Horsley, 'Village elections: training ground for democracy', *China Business Review* 28(2), (March–April 2001), pp. 44–52.

7. Sebastian L. Mazzuca, 'Reconceptualizing democratization: access to power versus excercise of power', in Gerardo L. Munck, ed., *Regimes and Democracy in Latin America* (New York: Oxford University Press, 2007).

elections oversimplifies the complexity of the local power configuration and turns village governance into much less than it is.[8]

Conceptualizing democracy and democratization

Though many observers speak of democracy when they examine self-governance in China, few of them have stopped to define the term. One reason for this may be that they seek to avoid courting controversy, as democracy is at root an 'essentially contested concept'.[9] Still, some efforts have been made by political theorists to standardize usage. For instance, many have taken Robert Dahl's definition of polyarchy as the first, most straightforward characterization of democracy.[10] Following Dahl and Schumpeter, they adopt a 'procedural minimum' understanding of democracy, which 'presumes fully contested elections with full suffrage and the absence of massive fraud, combined with effective guarantees of civil liberties, including freedom of speech, assembly, and association'.[11] Some analysts also add that elected governments must have the power to govern.[12]

The advantages of such a definition are clear. Above all, it facilitates measurement. But on the other hand, understanding democracy in a purely procedural fashion is problematic because it neglects the content of democracy. It does not answer the question of what democratic politics is, and instead focuses on how we might get it. Though choosing leaders through certain methods is an essential element of democracy, impeccable procedures do not guarantee democratic governance. This point is especially important because democracy does not simply denote majority rule,[13] but instead is usually seen to be a congeries of institutions that guarantees rule of law, separation of powers, protection of minorities, and protection of civil liberties.

Analytically, there are also at least two drawbacks to the procedural definition. First, it impedes classification because it fails to capture diverse forms of democratic practice. Democratization waves have produced a striking variety of regimes, many of which share important attributes but differ from each other and from democracies in advanced industrial countries. The simple procedural minimum definition cannot

---

8. On the relationship of village elections to temple associations, the tax-for-fee reform, and anti-corruption efforts, see Lily L. Tsai, 'The struggle for village public goods provision: informal institutions of accountability in rural China', John James Kennedy, 'The implementation of village elections and tax-for-fee reform in rural northwest China', and Richard Levy, 'Village elections, transparency, and anticorruption: Henan and Guangdong Provinces', all in Elizabeth J. Perry and Merle Goldman, eds, *Grassroots Political Reform in Contemporary China* (Cambridge, MA: Harvard University Press, 2007). For a discussion of the grassroots 'public sphere' and the role village elections play in it, see Mao Dan and Ren Qiang, *Zhongguo Nongcun Gonggong Lingyu de Shengzhang: Zhengzhi Shehuixue Shiye li de Cunmin Zizhi zhu Wenti [The Growth of Public Sphere in Rural China: Village Self-Governance from the Perspective of Political Sociology]* (Beijing: Zhongguo Shehui Kexue Chubanshe, 2006).

9. David Collier, Fernando Daniel Hidalgo and Andra Olivia Maciuceanu, 'Essentially contested concepts: debates and applications', *Journal of Political Ideologies* 11(3), (October 2006).

10. Mazzuca, 'Reconceptualizing democratization'.

11. David Collier and Steven Levitsky, 'Democracy with adjectives: conceptual innovation in comparative research', *World Politics* 49(3), (April 1997), p. 434; also Aurel Croissant and Wolfgang Merkel, 'Introduction: democratization in the early twenty-first century', Wolfgang Merkel, 'Embedded and defective democracies', and Leonardo Morlino, 'What is a "good" democracy?', all in *Democratization* 11(5), (2004).

12. Collier and Levitsky, 'Democracy with adjectives'.

13. Nowadays, few would say that democracy can be reduced to majority rule. However, a procedural minimum definition can encourage such a view.

comfortably embrace all these possibilities.[14] Second, this definition encourages prioritizing easily observable dimensions of elections, and downplaying other important attributes of democracy which are not covered in a definition that, most notably, excludes what happens after the voting ends. Attaching so much importance to forms and procedures, especially elections, leads analysts to overlook the substance of democracy and to treat it solely as a way to access power while neglecting how that power is exercised.

Researchers have, of course, noticed the first drawback and a number of techniques have been adopted to address it. For instance, David Collier and Steven Levitsky, among others, have developed a tool called 'diminished subtypes' to distinguish different types of democracy while avoiding concept-stretching.[15] The second drawback—emphasizing readily-measurable election procedures—has received less attention, and this is one reason why the first two generations of democratization studies, which focus on transition and consolidation, have had difficulty explaining the 'low quality' of new democratic regimes beset with corruption, cronyism, and weak accountability.[16]

Democracy, in our way of thinking, not only sets the rules for social forces to compete for political power; it also prescribes how power will be exerted to regulate those forces. Altering the way in which leaders are selected alone does not result in democratic rule, even with the presence of civil liberties. The mode in which political actors behave must also be democratized. And during the whole process, the citizenry must take up new responsibilities and play their role as well. Only with active participation can effective checks and balances be established that ensure the democratic operation of political power.[17]

Consider China's *Organic Law of Village Committees* (1998). The Law promised four democracies: election, decision making, management, and supervision. Whereas grassroots elections alter access to power, the latter three elements change the way power is exercised. However, of the four, access to power has attracted the bulk of the attention. Most studies have centered on the introduction of elections, how elections have been conducted, how the quality of elections can be enhanced, and voting behavior of villagers.[18] Of course, this research has taught us much, but might it be

---

14. Collier and Levitsky, 'Democracy with adjectives'.

15. *Ibid.* For other research on 'democracy with adjectives', see Croissant and Merkel, 'Introduction'; Merkel, 'Embedded and defective democracies'; and Morlino, 'What is a "good" democracy?'.

16. Mazzuca, 'Reconceptualizing democratization', p. 1. We depart from Mazzuca, however, and follow 'third generation' theorists, by treating improvements in the 'quality of democracy' as an element of democratization.

17. For similar 'third generation' understandings of democratization, see Larry Diamond and Leonardo Morlino, eds, *Assessing the Quality of Democracy* (Baltimore, MD: Johns Hopkins University Press, 2005); and Guillermo O'Donnell, Jorge Vargas Cullell and Osvaldo M. Iazzetta, eds, *The Quality of Democracy: Theory and Applications* (Notre Dame, IN: University of Notre Dame Press, 2004).

18. On the introduction of elections, see Schubert, 'Village elections in the PRC'; Shi, 'Village committee elections in China'; Daniel Kelliher, 'The Chinese debate over village self-government', *China Journal* 37, (January 1997); Kevin J. O'Brien and Lianjiang Li, 'Accommodating "democracy" in a one-party state: introducing village elections in China', *China Quarterly* 162, (June 2000). On voting behavior, see Zhong and Chen, 'To vote or not to vote'; Baogang He, 'A survey study of voting behavior and political participation in Zhejiang', *Japanese Journal of Political Science* 7(3), (2006). Attempts have begun to explore the three other components of village self-governance. In his report to the EU–China Training Programme on Village Governance, Björn Alpermann suggested that more attention be paid to post-election administration, decision-making, and control: Alpermann, 'An assessment of research on village governance in China'. On the effects of elections, more generally, see Guo Zhenglin and Thomas Bernstein, 'The impact of elections on the village

useful to assess grassroots political reform in China from a different perspective? In the next two sections, we evaluate the configuration of power in rural China using an approach that always keeps in mind the difference between accessing power and exercising power.

Accessing power in Chinese villages

Election implementation in rural China has improved both in terms of coverage and procedures. According to the Ministry of Civil Affairs, balloting is now held every three years in over 600,000 villages in all 31 provinces, with nearly 600 million voters taking part.[19] Since the revised *Organic Law* came into force in 1998, election procedures have also been spelled out by authorities at lower levels. By the mid 2000s, nearly every province had issued electoral regulations that matched, or went beyond, the national law, and detailed implementation guidelines had also been formulated by many prefectures, counties, and townships.[20]

Electoral procedures, touching on issues as varied as setting up steering committees and limiting proxy voting, have been clarified both on paper and in practice. During the first decade after the provisional *Organic Law* was passed, the absence of regulations concerning 'election steering committees' (*xuanju lingdao xiaozu*) drew much criticism.[21] Since 1998, both the *Organic Law* and most provincial regulations have come to include stipulations about how new, more circumscribed committees are to be organized and what functions they are to perform.[22] Of perhaps greatest importance, election committee members in the majority of villages are now selected by village assemblies, village groups, or village representative assemblies.[23] This should make them more independent and

Footnote 18 continued

structure of power: the relations between village committees and village Party branches', *Journal of Contemporary China* 13(39), (May 2004); Björn Alpermann, 'The post-election administration of Chinese villages', *China Journal* 46, (July 2001); John James Kennedy, 'The face of "grassroots democracy" in rural China: real versus cosmetic elections', *Asian Survey* 42(3), (May/June 2002); Lianjiang Li, 'The empowering effect of village elections in China', *Asian Survey* 43(4), (July/August 2003); Loren Brandt and Matthew A. Turner, 'The usefulness of corruptible elections', *Economics and Society* 19(3), (November 2007); Melanie Manion, 'Democracy, community, trust: the impact of elections in rural China', *Comparative Political Studies* 39(3), (April 2006).

19. 'Zuohao Minzheng Gongzuo, Qieshi Weihu Renmin Hefa Quanyi: Fang Minzhengbu Buzhang Li Xueju' ['Improve civil affairs work and earnestly defend people's legal rights: interview with the Minister of Civil Affairs Li Xueju'], *Renquan* [*Human Rights*] no. 5, (2004), p. 6.

20. Björn Alpermann, 'Provincial legislation on village elections', *Zeitschrift für Chinesisches Recht* no. 1, (2007); also Yuan Dayi, 'Cunmin Zizhi de Xianzai' ['The current situation of village self-governance'], paper prepared for EU–China Training Programme on Village Governance Conference, Beijing, 5–7 April 2006, available at: http://www.chinaelections.org/NewsInfo.asp?NewsID=92565 (accessed 2 August 2007).

21. See Jorgen Elklit, 'The Chinese village committee electoral system', *China Information* 11(4), (1997), pp. 4–5; Kevin J. O'Brien, 'Villagers, elections, and citizenship in contemporary China', *Modern China* 27(4), (October 2001), p. 420.

22. Alpermann, 'Provincial legislation on village elections'.

23. For data on election committees in 116 villages in six provinces, see Xu Zhigang, Liu Mingxing and Tao Ran, 'Cunzhuang Xuanju Zuiyou Guize de Fei Yizhixing' ['Incongruence in optimal rules for village elections'], *Zhongguo Nongcun Guancha* [*China Rural Survey*] no. 6, (2006), pp. 62–71. In the 2002 elections, village assemblies, village groups, or village representative assemblies selected election committee members in 98% of Shaanxi's villages. See 'Table of 2002 village elections in Shaanxi', available at: http://www.chinarural.org/news_show.aspx?cols=1810&ID=35295 (accessed 5 August 2007).

responsive, even though committees in most locations continue to be presided over by village Party secretaries or sitting committee directors.[24]

Voter registration helps ensure voting rights and the validity of elections. Though both the *Organic Law* and provincial legislation remain murky about precisely who can vote, stipulations that require publication of a voters' list 20 days before an election offer an opportunity to raise objections, and in some cases have led to lawsuits by those who felt they were excluded illegally.[25] In the 2002 Shaanxi elections, for example, voter lists were disputed in 7% of the province's villages, and although only 23% of villages published their list a full 20 days prior to the election, most villages issued theirs well before election day, as sometimes had occurred in the past.[26]

Candidate nomination has received much attention because it is crucial to an election's competitiveness and fairness. Control over the nominating process has been gradually loosened over the last two decades. In particular, selection through 'sea-elections' (*haixuan*), which entitles every voter to nominate primary candidates, has now spread to 26 provinces. Other forms of open nomination, such as joint or self-nomination, are also permitted in seven provinces.[27] At least four counties in Zhejiang, Jiangsu, Jiangxi and rural Chongqing went to new lengths in 2004 and 2005 and held direct elections without primaries or any prior selection of formal candidates.[28]

---

24. In Shaanxi's 2002 elections, for example, 79% of election committees were chaired by the Party secretary and 7% were chaired by the village committee director. See 'Table of 2002 village elections in Shaanxi'. Similar rates were found in other provinces: 87% and 6% in Fujian's 2003 elections, 91% and 7% in Chongqing's 2004 elections. See 'Table of 2003 village elections in Fujian', available at: http://www.chinarural.org/news_show. aspx?cols=1810&ID=35282 (accessed 11 August 2007); 'Table of 2004 village elections in Chongqing', available at: http://www.chinarural.org/news_show.aspx?cols=1811&ID=35745 (accessed 11 August 2007). On election committees in Jiangsu that are 'usually' led by village Party secretaries, see Zhong and Chen, 'To vote or not to vote', p. 696. In some places, local leaders continue to impede election committees. For examples from Shaanxi and Jiangxi, see Mu Ge, 'Xuanweihui he Cunweihui de Jiaoliang' ['The struggle between an election committee and the village committee'], available at: http://www.96990.cn/Blog/3/11206.shtml (accessed 6 August 2007); Xiao Tangbiao and Qiu Xinyou, 'Cunweihui Xuanju Zhong de Xuanju Weiyuanhui' ['Election committees in village elections'], *Qiushi* [*Seeking Truth*] no. 2, (2002), pp. 60–62.

25. For disputes that resulted in lawsuits, see 'Wu Shaohui Bufu Xuanmin Zige Chuli Jueding An' ['The case of Wu Shaohui disagreeing with a voter eligibility decision'], *Zhonghua Renmin Gongheguo Zuigao Renmin Fayuan Gongbao* [*Bulletin of People's Supreme Court, PRC*] no. 6, (2003), p. 29; Zhang Xinguo and Chen Junxian, 'Nongjiafei Jiafei le Xuanjuquan' ['Losing voter eligibility owing to marriage to a non-rural resident'], *Jiangsu Nongcun Jingji* [*Jiangsu Rural Economy*] no. 10, (2002), p. 34; 'Chen Chencai Xuanmin Zige An' ['The case of Chen Chencai's voter eligibility'], available at: http://www.gdcourts.gov.cn/alxc/ms/t20031225_2684.htm (accessed 4 August 2007).

26. 'Table of 2002 village elections in Shaanxi'.

27. Alpermann, 'Provincial legislation on village elections', p. 5. On opening the candidate selection process, see Kennedy, 'The implementation of village elections', pp. 63–64.

28. Ma Fuyun, 'Cunweihui Zhijie Xuanju de Moshi Yanjiu' ['Research on the election system of village committees'], *Zhongguo Nongcun Guancha* [*China Rural Survey*] no. 4, (2006), pp. 65–72; 'Zhejiang Jinhua Wu Houxuanren Xuanju Jiang Quanmian Tuiguang' ['Elections in Jinhua, Zhejiang without pre-selected candidates will be popularized'], *Lingdao Juece Xinxi* [*Information on Leadership Policy*] no. 15, (April 2005), p. 22; Xiao Mei, 'Tongzhou: Cunweihui Xuanju Jiang Changshi Wu Houxuanren Yicixing Zhijie Toupiao Xuanju' ['Tongzhou: one time ballot without pre-selected candidates will be tried in village committee elections'], available at: http://www.tz.gov.cn/tzdz/showinfo/showInfo.aspx?InfoID=2edb6a04-178d-4553-95ad-5aeb18f0f8f8 (accessed 6 August 2007); Huang Hui and Li Qing, 'Jiangxi Xuanchu Shoupi Zijian Haixuan Cunguan' ['The first village officials by self-nominated sea election are elected in Jiangxi'], *Fazhi Ribao* [*Legal Daily*], (31 October 2005). In the 28 provinces in which it is allowed, write-in candidates have on occasion been elected. Pan Jia'en and Jiang Yunxiang, 'Yuecun Beihou de Gushi' ['Inside story of Yue village'], *Zhongguo Gaige Nongcun Ban* [*China Reform Rural Edition*] no. 3, (2003), pp. 39–41.

Number of candidates is another indicator of competitiveness. When village elections were first introduced, non-competitive elections (*deng'e xuanju*) were common.[29] Today, multi-candidate elections have become the rule. Most provincial regulations prescribe that there be two candidates for village committee director and vice-director, and that the number of candidates for ordinary committee members should outnumber the positions available by at least one. Though this permits minimal competition for ordinary committee spots, 'sea-elections' and self-nomination can increase the number of primary and final candidates greatly.[30] In one southern village where only two formal candidates for director were put up, 25 additional individuals were nominated by villagers, and two of them made it to the list of final candidates. In the same election, villagers proposed 38 nominees for vice director and 66 for the four other seats on the village committee.[31]

Once nominees are set, campaigning, ballot secrecy, and the use of roving ballot boxes and proxy-voting are all important factors that affect whether villagers can express their preferences on election day. Elklit's early study found that campaigning amounted to little more than informal discussion among villagers because many local regulations failed to mention campaigning.[32] This has changed. Despite continuing anxiety about candidates 'pulling votes' (*lapiao*), candidates in most places are now given opportunities to deliver speeches or engage in other forms of campaigning. According to a 2000 survey conducted in 77 counties across Fujian, 90% of respondents said that candidates addressed either a village assembly or village representative assembly, and 27% reported that other campaign activities, including home visits and introductions by supporters, took place.[33] A similar survey in 40 Hunan counties showed that over 80% of voters reported that candidates spoke to village assemblies, village representative assemblies, or voters, either on election day or before.[34]

Enhanced ballot secrecy and security is also evident. Secret balloting was not a common practice when elections were first introduced, but this is no longer the case. In Fujian, a national pacesetter, none of the 1989 elections employed a secret

---

29. Elklit, 'The Chinese village committee electoral system'; O'Brien, 'Villagers, elections, and citizenship in contemporary China'; Ma Wenquan, 'Guanyu Cunmin Zizhi de Shijian yu Sikao' ['Practice and reflection on village self-governance'], available at: http://www.chinaelections.org/NewsInfo.asp?NewsID=23806 (accessed 6 August 2007).

30. Final candidates are usually chosen according to the number of nominating votes received, by a second round of voting, or by the village representative assembly or election committee. Xu Zhigang *et al.*, 'Cunzhuang Xuanju Zuiyou Guize de Fei Yizhixing', p. 68.

31. Dai Lichao, 'Gaopingcun Xuanju Guancha' ['Observation of Gaoping village election'], in Lianjiang Li, Guo Zhenglin and Xiao Tangbiao, eds, *Cunweihui Xuanju Guancha* [*Observation of Village Elections*] (Tianjin: Tianjin Renmin Chubanshe, 2001), pp. 44–112.

32. Elklit, 'The Chinese village committee electoral system', p. 9.

33. Song Yuehong, 'Fujiansheng 2000 Niandu Cunweihui Xuanju Tongji yu Huifang Diaocha Shuju Bijiao' ['Comparison of statistics and data verification of 2000 village elections in Fujian Province'], available at: http://www.chinarural.org/news_show.aspx?cols=1812&ID=11774 (accessed 6 August 2007).

34. He Xuefeng, 'Cunweihui Xuanju Zhuhuanjie de Diaocha yu Fenxi'. Campaign speeches have been encouraged by some local officials to combat unlawful campaign activities, such as attracting votes via coercion or buying votes with cash, gifts, or banquets. The logic is that institutionalizing campaigning will make elections less dependent on personal resources and also offer candidates regular channels to present themselves. Zhang Rongmin, 'Qiantan Guifan he Zhili Cunweihui Xuanju zhong de Jingzheng Xingwei' ['A preliminary discussion of regulating and managing campaign activities in village elections'], paper prepared for EU–China Training Programme on Village Governance Conference, Beijing, 5–7 April 2006, available at: http://www.chinaelections.com/NewsInfo.asp?NewsID=91176 (accessed 6 August 2007).

ballot, but by 1997 95% did.[35] The use of voting booths has been written into the *Organic Law* and efforts have been made to implement ballot secrecy nationwide, though with less than complete success.[36] A national survey conducted by the Ministry of Civil Affairs in 2005 found that 49% of villages made secret voting cubicles available.[37] Since many villagers are not accustomed to filling out votes in private or feel pressure from fellow voters not to do so, some localities have started to make use of a secret voting space mandatory. In Shaanxi's 2002 elections, for example, 96% of villages made such a space available and 5% made it compulsory.[38]

Two more aspects of voting, namely the use of proxies and 'roving ballot boxes' (*liudong piaoxiang*) deserve mention. As outside observers have long complained, these practices may have been designed to make elections more inclusive, but they also threaten ballot secrecy and are open to abuse.[39] Though neither practice has been banned nationwide, local regulations have limited both. For instance, in 2000 Fujian eliminated proxy-voting and introduced absentee balloting.[40] More recently, Chongqing and Gansu also banned proxy-voting.[41] In the 28 provinces that still permit it, restrictions are now in place: all have limited the number of votes proxies can cast, five provinces require written authorizations, and 15 require prior consent by the village election committee.[42] And there is evidence that implementation has followed the law. Whereas in Fujian 15% of villages allowed proxy voting before 1998, now only 3% do. In Jilin and Hunan, far less than 1% of villages prohibited proxy voting before 1998; now, 18% and 8%, respectively, do.[43]

Like proxy-voting, controls over roving ballot boxes are becoming stricter. Roving boxes are no longer an option in seven provinces including Hebei, Jilin, Jiangsu, Shanxi, Sichuan, and rural Shanghai and Chongqing. In Anhui and Hunan, voters using boxes must be registered with the election committee and a list of their names published. In Guangdong, consent from township authorities must be obtained before deploying roving boxes.[44] Reform here is evident even in provinces, such

---

35. The Carter Center, 'Report of the Fifth Mission on Chinese village elections', (20 June–3 July 1998), p. 4.

36. Alpermann, 'Provincial legislation on village elections', p. 6. One source claimed that over 90% of villages in 11 provinces used secret ballot booths. Shi Weimin, 'Zhongguo Cunmin Zizhi Zouxiang Weilai' ['China village self-governance in the future'], paper prepared for EU–China Training Programme on Village Governance Conference, Beijing, 5–7 April 2006, available at: http://www.chinaelections.org/NewsInfo.asp?NewsID=92552 (accessed 6 August 2007). See also Fan Yu, 'Cunweihui Xuanju Zhidu de Yanjin ji Tedian' ['Evolution and characteristics of the village committee electoral system'], *Zhongguo Nongcun Guancha [China Rural Survey]* no. 1, (2006), p. 63.

37. He, *Rural Democracy in China*, p. 33.

38. 'Table of 2002 village elections in Shaanxi'.

39. O'Brien, 'Villagers, elections, and citizenship in contemporary China', pp. 421–422; The Carter Center, 'The Carter Center delegation to observe village elections in China', (4–16 March 1997), p. 15; The Carter Center, 'Carter Center delegation report: village elections in China and agreement on cooperation with the Ministry of Civil Affairs, People's Republic of China', (2–15 March 1998), pp. 11–12; International Republican Institute, 'Election observation report: Sichuan, People's Republic of China', (November 1998), p. 11.

40. The Carter Center, 'Observation of village elections in Fujian and the conference to revise the national procedures on villager committee elections', (1–7 August 2000), p. 22.

41. Alpermann, 'Provincial legislation on village elections', p. 8.

42. *Ibid.*

43. Tan, *Village Elections in China*, pp. 234–250.

44. Yu Weiliang, ed., *Cunmin Weiyuanhui Xuanju Guicheng Jiaopian Shuoming [Overhead Transparencies on Village Elections: A Handbook]*, EU–China Training Programme on Village Governance, (2003), p. 58; Alpermann, 'Provincial legislation on village elections', p. 8.

as Jiangxi, which have villages that often sprawl over many square kilometers. In a survey of 40 Jiangxi communities following the 1999 elections, 40% of elections relied entirely on roving boxes, 53% used roving boxes in combination with other methods, and only 8% did not use them.[45] Province-wide statistics had changed significantly by 2002, with 29% of villages not employing roving boxes, and those only using them falling to less than 10%.[46]

Village elections in China remain far from perfect. Many procedural failings identified by Chinese and international observers, including the Ministry of Civil Affairs, the Carter Center, the International Republican Institute, and the European Union, have not been fully addressed. New problems are also emerging, such as vote-buying, literacy tests for candidates, interference in recall efforts, and 'hoodlum elections', where local toughs secure votes (or influence ballot-counting) through threats and intimidation.[47] Still, electoral procedures have improved greatly in the last two decades and a good number of competitive and reasonably fair elections have been held. Access to power, in other words, has expanded. But have similar changes in the exercise of power occurred?

Exercising power in Chinese villages

Observers have rightly noted that village elections exert some influence over political life in the Chinese countryside. Lianjiang Li, among others, has found that balloting has an empowering effect: free and fair elections can produce more responsive leaders and make them more impartial when enforcing state policies; it also provides an opportunity to dislodge cadres whom villagers like least.[48] John Kennedy and his coauthors, based on a 2000–2001 survey of 34 villages, likewise discovered that freely elected leaders were more accountable to villagers and that their land

45. Xiao Tangbiao, Qiu Xinyou, Tang Xiaoteng *et al.*, *Duowei Shijiao zhong de Cunmin Zhixuan* [*Direct Village Elections from Multiple Perspectives*] (Beijing: Zhongguo Shehuikexue Chubanshe, 2001), p. 27.

46. Out of 19,320 villages, 91% had election assemblies, 60% set up voting stations, 92% provided secret ballot booths and 71% used roving boxes. 'Table of 2002 village elections in Jiangxi', available at: http://www.chinarural.org/news_show.aspx?cols=1810&ID=35270 (accessed 9 August 2007).

47. He, *Rural Democracy in China*, pp. 59, 150, 214. On screening candidates and circumscribed rights of recall, see Alpermann, 'Provincial legislation on village elections', pp. 4–5, 10. For more on problematic recall efforts, see Xin Wang and Du Ke, 'Bamian Nan, Nan Zai Hechu?' ['Difficult to recall: where the difficulties lie?'], *Zhongguo Gaige Nongcun Ban* [*China Reform Rural Edition*] no. 10, (2004), pp. 26–27; Li Shan, 'Minxuan Cunguan: Feifa Bamian Shifei Duo' ['Elected village officials: illegally recalling them causes many problems'], *Jiangsu Nongcun Jingji* [*Jiangsu Rural Economy*] no. 1, (2003), pp. 42–43; 'Cunmin Bamian Buliao Cunzhuren: Wenti Chuzai Nali?' ['Villages cannot recall village committee chairs: where are the problems?'], *Lingdao Juece Xinxi* [*Information on Leadership Policy*] no. 13, (April 2007), p. 22. On a 'hoodlum election' in Shaanxi, see Kennedy, 'The face of "grassroots democracy" in rural China', p. 479. The Ministry of Civil Affairs has acknowledged many of these problems. See Guan Xiaofeng, 'Progress and problems mark elections', available at: http://www.chinadaily.com.cn/china/2007-07/10/content_6142535.htm (accessed 20 December 2007); also Kevin J. O'Brien, 'Improving election procedures: some modest proposals', unpublished paper, (23 April 2006), available at: http://papers.ssrn.com/sol3/papers.cfm?abstract_id=1157092; Qingshan Tan, 'Building democratic infrastructure: village electoral institutions', *Journal of Contemporary China* 18(60), (June 2009). On vote-buying suggesting that votes have value and interference by townships may be declining, see John James Kennedy, 'Legitimacy with Chinese characteristics: "two increases, one reduction"', *Journal of Contemporary China* 18(60), (June 2009).

48. Li, 'The empowering effect of village elections in China'; also Lianjiang Li and Kevin J. O'Brien, 'The struggle over village elections', in Merle Goldman and Roderick MacFarquhar, eds, *The Paradox of China's Post-Mao Reform* (Cambridge, MA: Harvard University Press, 1999), pp. 140–143; and Lianjiang Li, 'Elections and popular resistance in rural China', *China Information* 15(2), (2001), pp. 10–18.

management decisions reflected popular preferences for fair reallocation.[49] Along similar lines, Brandt and Turner have demonstrated that even corruptible elections can help curtail rent-seeking by local leaders,[50] while Baogang He has concluded that elections often lead village committee directors to place voters' interests over those of townships and Party branches.[51]

Grassroots balloting has also had a perceptible effect on villagers' attitudes and citizenship consciousness.[52] Kevin O'Brien has argued that elections are not only efforts to draw rural people into the local polity, but they are also an avenue through which citizenship practices may emerge before full citizenship is recognized.[53] Lianjiang Li has shown that free and fair elections enhance feelings of political efficacy and can help implant the idea that political power derives from the consent of the people.[54] And in a recent study of a long-time 'demonstration' (*shifan*) area, Gunter Schubert and Chen Xuelian suggest that elections can boost regime legitimacy, owing to a 'rational trust' that villagers come to have in their leaders, in which elections assure voters that this trust will be honored.[55] Melanie Manion, based on two surveys and other data collected between 1990 and 1996 from 57 villages in Hebei, Hunan, Anhui, and Tianjin, has also found that there is a positive correlation between electoral quality and villagers' beliefs that leaders are trustworthy.[56]

The impact of village elections cannot be denied. Elections, however, have not done away with several constraints that continue to impede democratic rule. Members of village committees may win their position through the ballot box, but once they gain office they still must take into account (and often compete with) township governments, village Party branches, and social forces, such as clans, religious organizations, and criminal gangs. In an ongoing struggle for power and legitimacy, tensions often arise between village committees and officials at the lowest rung of the state hierarchy, Party organs that remain the locus of power in a village, and societal groupings that possess their own sources of authority.[57] In many

---

49. John James Kennedy, Scott Rozelle and Yaojiang Shi, 'Elected leaders and collective land: farmers' evaluation of village leaders' performance in rural China', *Journal of Chinese Political Science* 9(1), (Spring 2004).

50. Brandt and Turner, 'The usefulness of corruptible elections'. On elections, both competitive and non-competitive, increasing the share of public expenditure in a village's budget, see Shuna Wang and Yang Yao, 'Grassroots democracy and local governance: evidence from rural China', *World Development* 35(10), (October 2007).

51. He, *Rural Democracy in China*, pp. 109–111.

52. Kennedy, 'The face of "grassroots democracy" in rural China'; Jie Chen, 'Popular support for village self-government in China: intensity and sources', *Asian Survey* 45(6), (November/December 2005); Manion, 'Democracy, community, trust'; Kennedy, 'Legitimacy with Chinese characteristics'.

53. O'Brien, 'Villagers, elections, and citizenship in contemporary China'. See also, Susanne Brandstädter and Gunter Schubert, 'Democratic thought and practice in rural China', *Democratization* 12(5), (December 2005), pp. 810–813; He, *Rural Democracy in China*, p. 50. On, however, villages with well-run elections in which civic consciousness has not noticeably increased, see Lily Tsai, *Accountability without Democracy: Solidarity Groups and Public Goods Provision in Rural China* (New York: Cambridge University Press, 2007), pp. 198, 223–226.

54. Li, 'The empowering effect of village elections in China'.

55. Gunter Schubert and Chen Xuelian, 'Village elections in contemporary China: new spaces for generating regime legitimacy? Experiences from Lishu County', *China Perspectives*, no. 3 (2007), pp. 12–27.

56. Manion, 'Democracy, community, trust'.

57. See Mao Dan and Ren Qiang, *Zhongguo Nongcun Gonggong Lingyu de Shengzhang*, pp. 53–68. Thomas P. Bernstein ['Village democracy and its limits', *ASIEN* 99, (April 2006), p. 30] writes: 'even when village elections work well, the power of elected village committees is limited because they necessarily function within an authoritarian political environment that is not structured to respond to the demands of constituents'. On data that suggest that village committees 'are still in the long shadow of township governments and village Party secretaries', see Tan and Xin, 'Village election and governance', p. 596; also Wang and Yao, 'Grassroots democracy and local governance', pp. 1635–1636.

communities, village committees have failed to achieve their potential, and in some they control few resources and are close to insignificant.[58]

Townships and village committees

Township governments, representing the formal state apparatus, are especially heavily implicated in efforts by village cadres to exercise power.[59] Björn Alpermann was among the first to note that 'the Chinese Party-state has been using self-government as another way to control rural politics'.[60] Indeed, the *Organic Law* (Arts. 4, 6) states that village committee members not only manage village affairs; they also fulfill tasks assigned by higher levels. Although the Law (Art. 4) stipulates that townships only 'guide' (*zhidao*) rather than 'lead' (*lingdao*) village committees, in practice, committees are often treated as line-organs of a township in high-priority policy areas.[61] Clashes, in these circumstances, become nearly inevitable when committee members dare to resist unpopular assignments, such as collecting levies, implementing costly 'target-hitting' (*dabiao*) programs, or completing other delegated tasks.[62] More often than not, when townships and village committees disagree, it is the village cadres who come out on the losing side.

Consider assessing levies, a recurring source of conflict between townships and villages in the 1990s.[63] This thankless task put elected cadres in a difficult position, insofar as they had to choose between fulfilling orders from above and keeping financial burdens down for fellow villagers. This dilemma, combined with perennially low compensation, made office-holding in some villages so unattractive that some cadres refused to complete their terms. In one study of 29 Hubei villages, He Xuefeng and Wang Ximing learned that committee directors in seven villages, frustrated by difficulties surrounding revenue collection, resigned within one year of their election in 1999.[64]

---

58. In a suburban village outside Tianjin that O'Brien visited in 1999, it was clear that the Muslim elders who managed the mosque dominated community decision making. Much younger village committee members appeared to be little more than their errand boys.

59. For a summary of reasons why local governments interfere in village affairs, see Alpermann, 'An assessment of research on village governance in China'; also, Bernstein, 'Village democracy and its limits', p. 33. On ways, however, that townships support free and fair elections, see He, *Rural Democracy in China*, pp. 142–146.

60. Alpermann, 'The post-election administration of Chinese villages', p. 47.

61. *Ibid.*, p. 46; also Xu Wang, *Mutual Empowerment of State and Peasantry: Village Self-Government in Rural China* (New York: Nova Science, 2003), p. 67. Björn Alpermann, 'Institutionalizing village governance in China', *Journal of Contemporary China* 18(60), (June 2009).

62. See Mao Dan and Ren Qiang, *Zhongguo Nongcun Gonggong Lingyu de Shengzhang*, p. 52. For a collection of such cases, see Xu Yong and Xiang Jiquan, eds, *Cunmin Zizhi Jincheng zhong de Xiangcun Guanxi* [*Township and Village Relations in the Process of Village Self-Governance*] (Wuhan: Huazhong Shifan Daxue Chubanshe, 2003). For case studies and statistical analysis of weak village committees, and a conclusion that 'even in villages with extremely good implementation of democratic reforms, citizens do not necessarily have a great deal of leverage over officials, accurate information about their activities, or a particularly strong sense of public duty', see Tsai, Accountability without Democracy, ch. 7, quoted text on p. 190.

63. Xu Liming, Zhang Linsheng and Wang Zhiheng, *Nongcun Shuifei Gaige Chuyi* [*Opinions on Rural Tax-for-Fee Reform*] (Beijing: Zhongguo Nongye Kexue Jishu Chubanshe, 2002), p. 158; also Xu Yong, 'Cunmin Zizhi, Zhengfu Renwu ji Shuifei Gaige' ['Village self-governance, government tasks and tax-for-fee reform'], *Zhongguo Nongcun Jingji* [*Chinese Rural Economy*] no. 11, (2001).

64. He Xuefeng and Wang Ximing, 'Cunzu de Guimo yu Ganbu' ['Scale of village groups and their cadres'], in Xu Yong and Xiang Jiquan, eds, *Cunmin Zizhi Jincheng zhong de Xiangcun Guanxi*, p. 502.

Unpopular target-hitting programs are another source of discord. Overly ambitious development schemes, image-building efforts, and fancifully high targets are often imposed on village committees.[65] Though the tax-for-fee reform and abolition of the agricultural tax simplified revenue collection, it did not free committee members from other duties assigned from above. Evidence from many locations suggests that to maintain and strengthen control over villages, some townships are turning 'soft targets' (*ruan zhibiao*) into 'hard tasks' (*ying renwu*) that cannot be downplayed or ignored. In Henan, for example, in the face of strong community opposition, villages have been saddled with target-hitting projects, such as building 40 methane-generating pits or 200 *mu* of vegetable sheds.[66] In another Henan county, higher-ups ordered that at least one collective enterprise be set up in every village within a year. Over 100 paper mills were built, all of which went bankrupt, causing enormous losses, a chorus of popular complaint, and lasting environmental damage.[67]

Unpopular tasks may also be foisted on villages by townships that encounter unexpected problems. For example, in order to develop the local economy, higher-ups sometimes compel villages to supply raw materials to or buy products from local enterprises. One committee director in Jiangxi explained how he felt 'pressure from both sides' (*liangtou shouqi*): township authorities assigned him a high procurement quota to prop up a bamboo ware plant that was desperately short of cash, but villagers were unwilling to sell their bamboo unless they received timely and sufficient payment. The director felt trapped and could not satisfy both the township and voters who had elected him.[68]

Townships often treat elected committees as if they were subordinates, and village leaders may find themselves squeezed, like the meat in an overstuffed sandwich, or as the Jiangxi director quoted above put it: 'like a rat caught in the bellows' (*laoshu jin le fengxiang*). Sometimes, it does not even take much pressure to coax committee members to 'voluntarily be responsible to higher levels' (*zijue duishang fuze*).[69] Fiscal realities and features of the cadre management system make it difficult to refuse jobs imposed by townships, whatever the views of voters.

To fulfill many of their responsibilities, such as providing public goods, committees often must rely on townships for help. The tax-for-fee reform deepened a

---

65. Cho Soo-sung, 'On the relationship between Chinese township/town governments and villager committees', Zhang Guangxiu, 'A study of the relationship between villager self-government and basic-level government', and Cheng Tongshun, 'The relationship between the township/town government and the village in the context of villager self-government in China', papers all prepared for the *International Symposium on Villager Self-Government and the Development of Rural Society in China*, sponsored by the Carter Center and the Ministry of Civil Affairs, Beijing, 2–5 September 2001.

66. Liu Tao, 'Shuifei Gaige hou de Zhibiaohua: Chongxin Jiedu Xiang, Cun, Zu, Min Guanxi' ['Target-setting after tax-for-fee reform: rethinking relations among townships, villages, small groups, and villagers'], available at: http://www.snzg.cn/article/show.php?itemid-6758/page-1.html (accessed 2 October 2007).

67. For this incident and county pressures placed on townships, which are then transmitted to villages, see Kevin J. O'Brien and Lianjiang Li, 'Selective policy implementation in rural China', *Comparative Politics* 31(2), (January 1999), p. 176.

68. Lan Yuanjun, 'Liangtou Shouqi hou Mo Chulai de Luzi' ['A way out of pressure from both sides'], *Xiangzhen Luntan* [*Township Forum*] no. 11, (2001), p. 14.

69. Mao Dan and Ren Qiang, *Zhongguo Nongcun Gonggong Lingyu de Shengzhang*, p. 53.

fiscal crisis in many villages (and townships), as local leaders lost the ability to raise funds they had previously depended upon. Constructing and repairing roads, maintaining irrigation systems, and supporting the elderly and disabled, all have become more difficult, especially in agricultural areas and communities where other social institutions cannot pick up the slack.[70] In order to obtain needed resources, village cadres tend to be cooperative when townships assign them even highly unpopular tasks.

Personnel management regulations have also created incentives that spur cadres to respond to demands received from above. The 'cadre responsibility system' (*ganbu guanli zerenzhi*) links bonuses and punishment to higher level assessments of performance. In many locations, the salary and bonuses of village committee members are determined by township authorities, and levels are set in accord with how well important assignments are carried out.[71] Some localities, in the wake of the tax-for-fee reform, have gone so far as to list village cadres on the township or county level payroll. This further empowers townships, and makes committee members more pliable in the face of demands from above.[72]

Finally, some committees do not control their own budgets. Entrusting village accounts to township management has become a common means to strengthen supervision of rural finances. This has created opportunities for townships to appropriate village funds and may leave elected bodies with virtually nothing to manage.[73] Although this need not enhance compliance, it does diminish the role of committee members, and makes how democratically they were elected somewhat beside the point.

Party branches and village committees

Village-level Party organizations are another obstacle to grassroots democratization. Though the *Organic Law* (Art. 3) states that Party branches should 'support villagers in developing self-governance and exercising their democratic rights', it also insists

70. See Tsai, *Accountability without Democracy*, ch. 7; also, Yuan Song, 'Gonggongpin Gongji Zhikun: Fucun Diaocha Lianzai (9)' ['Difficulties in public goods provision: ninth in a series of reports from the investigation of Fu village'], available at: http://www.snzg.cn/article/show.php?itemid-7233/page-1.html (accessed 2 October 2007).

71. One counter-trend, which should make elected cadres more accountable to voters, is that 'villagers' evaluations' (*minzhu pingchou*) are now sometimes consulted when township authorities decide on a village cadres' salary. But even in these cases, baseline salary is usually set by the township according to its own criteria. Cheng Sinian, 'Rang Cunmin Gei Cunguan Ping Gongzi de Banfa Hao' ['It is a good method to let villagers grade village cadres' salary'], *Nongcun Fazhan Luncong* [*Rural Development Forum*] no. 10, (2000), p. 45. Tian Yuanxin, Qu Xuan and Li Dao, 'Cunmin Gei Cun Ganbu Ding Baochou' ['Villagers assess how much village cadres should earn'], *Xiangzhen Luntan* [*Township Forum*] no. 3, (2005), p. 13; also Alpermann, 'The post-election administration of Chinese villages', p. 68.

72. This is not a nationwide practice, though it has been implemented widely. For details, see Ning Zekui, Liu Hailiang, Wang Zhengbing and Chai Haofang, 'Cunganbu Xiang Hechu Qu' ['Where village cadres are heading'], *Zhongguo Nongcun Guancha* [*China Rural Survey*] no. 1, (2005), p. 60; also Zhong and Chen, 'To vote or not to vote', p. 698.

73. Fubing Su and Dali Yang, 'Elections, governance, and accountability in rural China', *Asian Perspective* 29(4), (2005). On township supervision of village finances in five provinces, see Alpermann, 'Institutionalizing village governance in China'.

that branches are a village's 'leadership core' (*lingdao hexin*). This means that Party leaders play a dominant role in most locations, with the Party secretary usually considered the village 'number one' (*yi ba shou*), and the committee director the village 'number two' (*er ba shou*).[74]

Fieldwork and surveys of grassroots cadres have confirmed the pre-eminence of Party secretaries. In 1999, Liang Kaijin and He Xuefeng estimated that 80% of secretaries nationwide were their village's top power holder, whereas an in-depth study of eight communities in 2002–2003 concluded that Party secretaries had the final word in seven of them.[75] Baogang He likewise found that dominance of elected committees 'only takes place in a limited number of cases'.[76] In a survey of 111 committee directors in four Zhejiang prefectures, 15% of He's respondents said they had more power than the village Party secretary, while 71% reported that the secretary had more power.[77]

Given the Party branch's status as 'leadership core', it is often unclear what a village committee should take charge of: in what areas must the branch follow the committee's lead? The *Organic Law* and implementing regulations that we have seen fail to specify a clear division of responsibilities between the two bodies. This often leads to clashes over, for instance, collective resources, as committees and branches struggle to secure final say over enterprises, economic cooperatives, and land.[78] When elected cadres lose these skirmishes, as they often do, some have become so frustrated that they have withdrawn from political life. In 2001, *People's Daily* reported that 57 committee members from four townships in Qixia Prefecture, Shandong, resigned in protest against Party branches that monopolized village politics. They charged that a full year after being elected, branches still refused to give them access to the account books and the official seal that

---

74. Song Yuehong, 'Cunmin Zizhi Zhong de Liangwei Guanxi' ['Relations between village Party branches and village committees in village self-governance'], *Zhongguo Gaige Nongcun Ban* [*China Reform Rural Edition*] no. 7, (2002), p. 47; Yang Jirong, 'Lun Nongcun Jiceng Dangnei Minzhu yu Cunmin Zizhi de Xianjie yu Hudong' ['On grassroots democracy within the Party and its connection and interaction with village self-governance'], *Lilun yu Gaige* [*Theory and Reform*] no. 6, (2003), pp. 33–36; Chu Zhi, 'Cunzhishu Zenyang Danghao Yibashou' ['How can village Party secretaries perform well as number one'], *Dangyuan Ganbu Zhiyou* [*Party Members' and Cadres' Friend*] no. 9, (2002), pp. 12–13; also Zhong and Chen, 'To vote or not to vote', p. 697; Schubert and Chen, 'Village elections in contemporary China', p. 19; He, *Rural Democracy in China*, p. 114. On the growing power of village committees, but their continuing secondary status, see Tan and Xin, 'Village election and governance', pp. 588–593; also Wang, *Mutual Empowerment of State and Peasantry*, pp. 143–147.

75. Liang Kaijin and He Xuefeng, *Cunji Zuzhi Zhidu Anpai yu Chuangzhi* [*Institutional Arrangements and Innovations in Village-Level Organizations*] (Beijing: Hongqi Chubanshe, 1999), p. 118; Dong Jiang'ai, 'Cunji Xuanju zhong Xingcheng de Liangwei Guanxi Duili ji Chulu' ['Outbreak of rivalry between Party branches and village committees in village elections and its solution'], *Huazhong Shifan Daxue Xuebao, Sheke Ban* [*Journal of Huazhong Normal University, Social Sciences Edition*] 44(1), (January 2005), p. 56.

76. Baogang He, 'The theory and practice of Chinese grassroots governance: five models', *Japanese Journal of Political Science* 4(2), (2003), pp. 308–310.

77. He, *Rural Democracy in China*, pp. 112–113. On the relative power of Party secretaries and committee directors hinging on control over income-producing enterprises and land, see Jean C. Oi and Scott Rozelle, 'Elections and power: the locus of decision-making in Chinese villages', *China Quarterly* 162, (June 2000), pp. 513–539.

78. See Pan Jiawei and Zhou Xianri, *Cunmin Zizhi yu Xingzhengquan de Chongtu* [*Conflicts between Village Self-Governance and Administrative Power*] (Beijing: Zhongguo Renmin Daxue Chubanshe, 2004), pp. 145–146; also Xu Zhiyong, 'Xuanju Zhihou: Lijicun Cunmin Zizhi Diaocha' ['Post-election: investigation of village self-governance in Liji'], *Zhongguo Gaige Nongcun Ban* [*China Reform: Rural Edition*] no. 2, (2003), pp. 10–14; Bernstein, 'Village democracy and its limits', p. 36; Zhang Jingping, 'Jingxuan Cunguan de Jiaoliang' ['Struggle in the village election'], *Nanfeng Chuang* [*Southern Exposure*] no. 9, (May 2005), pp. 30–35.

symbolizes public power.[79] Such incidents are not rare. Guo Zhenglin found that in the two years after Guangdong introduced elections in 1998, over 800 committee members resigned, most often because they had been frozen out of decision making by Party branches.[80]

Even fairly powerful village committees are vulnerable to Party influence, through personnel overlap. Surveys have shown that a large number of committee members, and directors in particular, belong to the Communist Party. For instance, following Jiangsu's balloting in 2006, almost 90% (15,649 out of 17,411) of committee directors were Party members.[81] Figures for earlier rounds of voting in rural Shanghai (2002), Fujian (2003), and Shaanxi (2002) were 89%, 66%, and 66%, respectively.[82] Party penetration is important because, unlike elected cadres, whose legitimacy is based on popular votes, Party members who sit on village committees derive some of their authority from being agents of the Party-state.[83] This raises an obvious question: even when Party members have won a spot on a village committee in a free and fair election, will they stand with villagers when Party superiors instruct them to do otherwise?

Since the turn of the century, Party penetration of committees has taken a new, more institutionalized form, which, according to Sylvia Chan, strengthens over-representation of Party members and is a sign of the Party's intention 'to re-concentrate its power in rural areas'.[84] In July 2002, the Central Committee and State Council jointly issued a circular that endorsed 'concurrent office-holding by village chiefs and Party secretaries' (*yijiantiao*) and 'merging the Party branch and the village committee' (*liangwei heyi*).[85] This policy sometimes takes the form of village committees being elected first, and some of their members being placed on Party branches later (*xianzheng houdang*); at other times, it means the Party secretary and other Party branch members are encouraged to run in village committee elections at the first opportunity (*xiandang houzheng*). As a sure-fire way to reduce the size of the village payroll and mitigate tension between branches and committees, this

---

79. Cui Shixin, 'Cunguan Weihe Yao Cizhi' ['Why village heads want to resign'], *Renmin Ribao* [*People's Daily*], (21 March 2001); also Xu Zhiyong, 'Xuanju Zhihou'. For regulations concerning control of the village seal, see He, *Rural Democracy in China*, p. 112.

80. Guo Zhenglin, 'Cunmin Xuanju hou de Nongcun Dangzheng Eryuan Quanli Jiegou' ['The bicameral power structure of the rural Party apparatus and its administration in the wake of villagers' elections'], paper prepared for the *International Symposium on Villagers' Self-Government and the Development of Rural Society in China*, sponsored by the Carter Center and the Ministry of Civil Affairs, Beijing, 2–5 September 2001, p. 253.

81. 'Summarizing table of seventh round village elections in Jiangsu Province', available at: http://www.chinarural.org/news_show.aspx?cols=1810&ID=35289 (accessed 12 December 2006).

82. Percentages are calculated from the following tables: 'Table of 2002 village elections in Shaanxi'; 'Table of 2002 village elections in Shanghai', available at: http://www.chinarural.org/news_show.aspx?cols=1810&ID=35331; 'Table of 2003 village elections in Fujian'; all accessed 12 December 2006. For similar statistics on earlier elections in a number of provinces, see Pastor and Tan, 'The meaning of China's village elections', p. 140. For data, mostly from the 1990s, that show an increasing number on non-communists on village committees, see He, *Rural Democracy in China*, pp. 107–108.

83. Guo and Bernstein, 'The impact of elections on the village structure of power'.

84. Sylvia Chan, 'Villagers' representative assemblies: towards democracy or centralism?', *China: An International Journal* 1(2), (2003), p. 192. Baogang He, ('The theory and practice of Chinese grassroots governance', p. 309) also speaks of 'a deliberate attempt to strengthen the Party branch'.

85. 'Zhonggong Zhongyang Bangongting Guowuyuan Bangongting Guanyu Jinyibu Zuohao Cunmin Weiyuanhui Huanjie Xuanju Gongzuo de Tongzhi' ['Circular by General Offices of Party Central Committee and State Council on further improving the work of next round village committee elections), (14 July 2002), available at: http://www.gov.cn/gongbao/content/2002/content_61679.htm (accessed 1 December 2007); also Bernstein, 'Village democracy and its limits', p. 37; Guo and Bernstein, 'The impact of elections on the village structure of power', pp. 272, 275; He, *Rural Democracy in China*, p. 119.

initiative has been implemented widely.[86] In Shandong, authorities even prescribed that the overlap rate of the two top positions should exceed 80% and that of the full branch and village committee should reach 70%.[87] Having to face voters could make Party branch members more accountable,[88] but influence often flows the other way.[89] Overlapping membership, along with joint or consecutive meetings of the two organizations, can blur whether concurrent office-holders are responsible to their constituents or their Party masters.[90] Some Chinese researchers have even begun to wonder whether overlapping membership might lead to a return of unfettered rule by Party branches, especially Party secretaries, thus making village elections close to meaningless.[91]

Social forces and village committees

In addition to Party branches and townships, lineage groups, religious organizations, and criminal elements play a role in some villages. These social forces may gain access to public power through elections, or have other means to become involved with decision making and policy implementation. Although informal institutions may enhance accountability and promote public goods provision,[92] they also operate according to their own customs, norms, and rules, many of which have little to do with democracy.

---

86. For Shandong, see *Dazhong Ribao [The Masses Daily]*, (25 September 2004); for Henan, see http://news.sohu.com/20050715/n226325095.shtml; for Hunan, see http://www.chinanews.com.cn/news/2004year/2004-06-01/26/443107.shtml; for Anhui, see http://www.chinanews.com.cn/news/2004/2004-11-07/26/503213.shtml; for Hainan, see http://www.chinanews.com.cn/news/2004year/2004-07-23/26/463605.shtml; for Guangdong, see http://www.southcn.com/news/gdnews/gdtodayimportant/200501250071.htm; for Shanxi, see http://cpc.people.com.cn/GB/64093/64100/5946051.html (all accessed 30 November 2007).

87. Wang Kequn, 'Nongyeshui Quxiao hou Xiangzhen Guanli Tizhi Yudao de Wenti' ['Problems encountered in the township management system after abolishing the agricultural tax'], *Zhongguo Fazhan Guancha [China Development Observation]* no. 5, (2005), pp. 38–40. Guangdong also advocates 70% overlap of branches and committees. See Richard Levy, 'The village self-government movement', *China Information* 17(1), (2003), p. 34.

88. Dang Guoying, 'Liangwei Heyi Shige Hao Banfa' ['Concurrent holding of offices is a good solution'], *Zhongguo Gaige (Nongcun Ban) [China Reform (Rural Edition)]* no. 2, (2004), p. 28.

89. Party members remain subject to Party discipline, and they may also be more accommodating to township leaders. Lu Fuxing, 'Yijiantiao de Shixiao yu Lilun zhi Chayi' ['Gaps between real effects and theoretical implications of concurrent office-holding'], *Hunan Gong'an Gaodeng Zhuanke Xuexiao Xuebao [Journal of Hunan Public Security College]* 16(5), (October 2004), p. 17. Some researchers (Lianjiang Li, personal communication, November 2007) argue that what really matters is not who serves as both the secretary and director, but how one gets the two positions.

90. Zhang Yuanhong, 'Liangwei Heyi Qineng Tuiguang' ['Concurrent office-holding should not be promoted'], *Zhongguo Gaige [China Reform]* no. 8, (2001), pp. 56–57; Chang Zizhong, 'Cunliangwei Yijiantiao Wenti Baicun Tiaocha' ['One-hundred-village survey on concurrent office-holding in village committees and party branches'], *Xiangzhen Luntan [Township Forum]* no. 7, (2007), pp. 9–10; Qin Junbo, 'Cunzhishu Jianren Cunzhuren Ying Huanxing' ['Concurrent-holding of Party secretary and village head positions should be deferred'], *Xiangzhen Luntan [Township Forum]* no. 3, (2002), p. 12.

91. Chang Zizhong, 'Cunliangwei Yijiantiao Wenti Baicun Tiaocha'; Qin Junbo, 'Cunzhishu Jianren Cunzhuren Ying Huanxing'. Some authors argue that concurrent office-holding will help resolve personal conflicts between party secretaries and village committee directors, but cannot remedy organizational conflicts or reduce disputes over authority. Xu Zengyang and Ren Baoyu, 'Yijiantiao Zhenneng Jiejue Liangwei Chongtu Ma: Cunzhibu yu Cunweihui Chongtu de Sanzhong Leixing ji Jiejue Silu' ['Will concurrent office-holding resolve conflicts between the two organizations? Three types of conflict between village committees and Party branches and one possible resolution'], *Zhongguo Nongcun Guancha [China Rural Survey]* no. 1, (2002), pp. 69–74.

92. Lily L. Tsai, 'Solidarity groups, informal accountability, and local public goods provision in rural China', *American Political Science Review* 101(2), (May 2007); Lily L. Tsai, 'Cadres, temple and lineage institutions, and governance in rural China', *China Journal* no. 48, (July 2002).

Clans (*zongzu*), in particular, have experienced a resurgence in the reform era, and in some locations 'are once again sources of power and authority'.[93] While kinship ties need not always have a baleful effect on democratic rule, strong lineage attachments can become a mechanism through which individual rights and minority protections are infringed.[94] Majority rule sometimes produces dominance of one clan, or disruptive, ongoing struggle between several clans, which leads to fierce conflict and makes governance nearly impossible. For example, the Li lineage in one Hunan community used elections to usurp the power of a village committee and transformed grassroots government into an armed tool of clan power.[95] In another 'extreme case' focusing on disputed land adjustments in Shaanxi, open elections heightened clan tensions, turned a Party secretary against a committee director, and brought governance almost to a standstill.[96] Much more research is needed to learn how and when lineage ties affect village committees and the quality of democracy.

Religious organizations can also be obstacles to grassroots democratization when they compete with village committees for resources or leadership in community affairs. In one Shaanxi village, shortly after a committee and a Catholic church joined forces to build a primary school, wrangling over control of the school broke out. Instead of seeking a compromise, the church leaders publicized the conflict and mobilized their followers to challenge the elected cadres, resulting in a deep division in the village.[97]

Local strongmen and gangsters pose a far more direct threat to democracy. Stories of 'evil forces' (*hei'e shili*) undermining rural governance are increasingly common. Though some observers argue that imperfect election procedures make villages vulnerable to takeover by bullies and thugs,[98] others note that in some places representatives of 'black society' have obtained power by soliciting support from fellow lineage members, intimidating villagers, and promising decisive action.[99] Even when they fail to subvert a village committee, underworld forces can exert an

---

93. Bernstein, 'Village democracy and its limits', p. 38. In Lishu County, Jilin, like much of the Northeast, clans are not important power-brokers. See Schubert and Chen, 'Village elections in contemporary China', p. 20.

94. Xu Yong, *Zhongguo Nongcun Cunmin Zizhi* [*Village Self-Government in Rural China*] (Wuhan: Huazhong Shifan Daxue Chubanshe, 1997), pp. 354–366.

95. Yu Jianrong, 'Yao Jingti Zongzu Shili dui Nongcun Jiceng Zhengquan de Yingxiang' ['Be alert to clan influences on rural grassroots government'], *Jiangsu Shehui Kexue* [*Jiangsu Social Sciences*] no. 4, (2004), pp. 7–8.

96. Kennedy, 'The face of "grassroots democracy" in rural China', pp. 480–481. For evidence, however, that elections can also produce balanced village committees and mitigate lineage conflict, see Kennedy, 'The implementation of village elections', pp. 67–68. On declining clan influence overall, but continuing relevance especially in poorer, agricultural, and single surname dominant villages, see He, *Rural Democracy in China*, pp. 177–194.

97. Villagers claimed that this confrontation was even more intense than those that occurred during the Cultural Revolution. Miao Yuexia, 'Xiangcun Minjian Zongjiao yu Cunmin Zizhi: Yixiang Shehui Ziben Yanjiu' ['Rural religion and village self-governance: research on social capital'], *Zhejiang Shehui Kexue* [*Zhejiang Social Sciences*] no. 6, (November 2006), pp. 99–104. In some locations, temples and churches provide an alternative form of public accountability. Tsai, *Accountability without Democracy*.

98. He Xuefeng, 'Dangqian Cunmin Zizhi Yanjiu Zhong Xuyao Chengqing de Ruogan Wenti' ['Some problems in current studies of villagers' self-government'], *Zhongguo Nongcun Guancha* [*China Rural Survey*] no. 2, (2002), pp. 66–67.

99. Yu Jianrong, 'Jingti Hei'e Shili Dui Nongcun Jiceng Zhengquan de Qinru' ['Be alert to the invasion of evil forces into rural grassroots government'], *Juece Zixun* [*Policy Making Consultation*] no. 8, (2003), pp. 34–35; Sun Chunlong, 'Ruci Cunmin Zizhi' ['What village self-governance is like'], *Xin Xibu* [*New West*] no. 9, (2004), pp. 8–11.

influence by challenging, marginalizing or sidelining elected leaders.[100] Some gangs have gone so far as to set up 'private police stations' (*minban paichusuo*) and 'underground courts' (*dixia fating*) to handle disputes over land, debt, and other conflicts.[101]

The township, the Party branch, and an array of social forces constitute the local power configuration in which village committees are embedded. We have underscored the independent effect of each of these factors, but they can also work together to impede democratic governance. Strong clan ties combined with a powerful criminal sector can contribute to conflicts between a Party branch and a village committee;[102] Party cadres, after losing a village committee election, may turn to township allies or the underworld to maintain their position as top person in the village.[103] Improved electoral procedures have enhanced access to power, but elected cadres cannot escape the broader political and social context in which they operate.

Conclusion

In a country like China, grassroots democratization is a multi-faceted process that involves much more than holding a good election every three years. Two decades after the *Organic Law* first came into force, election procedures have improved significantly, both on paper and on the ground. Meaningful changes touching on steering committees, voter registration, candidate nomination, campaigning, secret balloting, and proxy-voting have taken hold and begun to expand access to power. Yet the quality of democracy in much of the countryside remains stubbornly low, mainly because village committees, once an election is over, are situated in a socio-political environment that has changed surprisingly little.

Village committees are surrounded on all sides. First, the state, represented by township authorities, has many opportunities to influence grassroots governance. Elected cadres are expected to complete tasks assigned by higher levels, much as their appointed predecessors were. Unwelcome duties, such as collecting levies or meeting unreasonable targets, regularly force committee members to choose between fealty to the township and responsiveness to fellow villagers. Financial reliance on townships and the role that higher levels play in cadre assessment inclines even the most democratically minded committee members to side with township superiors. Village committee members, in the end, are still subordinates—the place where state meets society—as much as they are the voice of voters who elected them.

---

100. Liu Lixin, Pao Jinxuan and Zhang Lingzhi, 'Hei'e Shili Ranzhi Nongcun Jiceng Zhengquan Toushi' ['Investigation of evil forces encroaching on rural grassroots governance'], *Sanyue Feng* [*March Wind*] no. 4, (2004), pp. 7–9.

101. Xu Liming, 'Cunmin Zizhi de Shehui Kunjing' ['Social predicament of village self-governance'], *Zhonggong Zhengzhou Shiwei Dangxiao Xuebao* [*Journal of the Party School of Zhengzhou Municipal Committee*] no. 3, (2005), p. 52.

102. Wang Jinhong, 'Liangwei Maodun: Jingyan Fenxi yu Lilun Piping' ['Conflict between Party branches and village committees: empirical analysis and theoretical critique'], *Huazhong Shifan Daxue Xuebao, Sheke Ban* [*Journal of Huazhong Normal University, Social Sciences Edition*] 44(5), (September 2005), pp. 18–24.

103. For an example, see 'Nongcun Queshao Shenme?' ['What is lacking in rural areas?'], available at: http://www.lwjx.com.cn/bbs/dv_rss.asp?s=xhtml&boardid=6&id=3210&page=15 (accessed 15 December 2007).

Second, village Party branches have no small say in decision making and policy implementation. In most communities, Party branches remain the dominant force and village committees play a distinctly secondary role. The Party branch's status as 'leadership core' is often evident in control over collective resources, such as land, economic cooperatives and enterprises, and also in overlapping membership on village committees. Despite efforts by many committee directors to assert their independence and exploit the legitimacy that elections confer, recent reforms that encourage concurrent office-holding may dilute the 'electoral connection'[104] by blurring whether committee members are responsible to their constituents or their Party superiors.[105]

Finally, informal institutions, including lineage groups, religious organizations, and criminal gangs, can interfere with democratic governance. Clans, churches or temples, and Mafia-like groups, can be alternative sources of authority and competitors for control over community affairs. In some villages, this has resulted in serious splits that bring governance to a halt. In others, elected cadres have been pushed aside, or turned into figureheads. In still others, sectarian interests have deeply penetrated village committees, sometimes leading to a trampling of minority rights.

Village elections alone are clearly not enough to ensure democratic governance. To understand democratization in rural China, we need ask not only how procedures are introduced and improved, but also how the village committees interact with other actors in the local power configuration. Though improving elections is a critical aspect of democratization, good procedures alone cannot guarantee high quality democratic rule. Long-time students of democratization have recognized this, too, with Larry Diamond and Leonardo Morlino, for example, arguing that a fully democratic regime not only satisfies popular expectations regarding 'procedural quality', but also allows citizens to enjoy 'quality of content' and 'quality of results'.[106]

This suggests some limits of this study and an agenda for the future. Examining constraints that impede democratization is not the same as assessing post-election governance, or how power is exercised in villages. In other words, obstacles notwithstanding, increased responsiveness is appearing in some places. For every analyst who concludes 'except in a few localities, elections have little positive impact on preventing rural authorities from abusing power',[107] another finds that elections have empowered villagers or enhanced accountability.[108] Beyond specifying the obstacles to democratization, we need more studies that explain how, when, and where elections have changed the relationship between cadres and voters.

---

104. The term was first made popular by David Mayhew and was brought to the China field by Melanie Manion. See David R. Mayhew, *Congress: The Electoral Connection* (New Haven: Yale University Press, 1974); Melanie Manion, 'The electoral connection in the Chinese countryside', *American Political Science Review* 90(4), (December 1996).

105. As we discuss above, it is also possible that these reforms will help democratize Party branches. For experiments with subjecting Party branch members to a village-wide vote of confidence, see Lianjiang Li, 'The two-ballot system in Shanxi Province: subjecting village Party secretaries to a popular vote', *China Journal* 42, (July 1999).

106. Larry Diamond and Leonardo Morlino, 'The quality of democracy: an overview', *Journal of Democracy* 15(4), (1994), p. 22.

107. Zhang Jing, *Jiceng Zhengquan: Xiangcun Zhidu Zhu Wenti* [*Problems of Rural Level Governance in China*] (Hangzhou: Zhejiang Renmin Chubanshe, 2000), p. 208.

108. For examples, see the sources listed in footnotes 48–56.

At the same, we also need more research on whether elections deter power holders from seeking personal gain above all else. The issue in some villages is not committee members who are pushed around by townships, Party branches, and social forces, but elected cadres who free themselves of all constraints and act only for themselves. Where does this occur? Why, in some places, are the constraints that we have emphasized and the ones that elections create both ineffective in preventing self-serving behavior? Are limited changes in governance after several rounds of elections a cause of increasing voter apathy,[109] as villagers conclude that whomever is in office will be corrupt and abusive, because 'all crows under heaven are equally black'[110] or 'it makes no sense to replace a full tiger with a hungry wolf?'[111]

As Norbert Bobbio reminds us, democracy is subversive in a highly radical sense because it subverts the traditional and natural notion that power flows downward.[112] Without denying the achievements of the last two decades, we have suggested that the process of putting democracy in place goes well beyond 'getting the procedures right', especially in an authoritarian setting where democracy is not the only game in town. Much as a one-day trip to observe an election reveals something, but not everything, about what the next three years will bring, changes in access to power can be trumped by a non-democratic environment that encircles an election victor.[113] Governance, even in a single village, has many components and expanded access to power conditions, but does not determine how power is exercised. 'High quality democracy' in rural China, let alone the whole nation, rests on much more than good village elections.

---

109. Wei Xinghe and Guo Yunhua, 'Zhengzhi Lengmo: Nongmin dui Cunweihui Xuanju de Yizhong Xingwei' ['Political apathy: one kind of villagers' attitude towards village committee elections'], *Qiushi* [*Seeking Facts*] no. 10, (2003), pp. 60–62; Wang Xiaojun, 'Zhixuan Lilian Zhihou de Cunweihui Xuanju Yanjiu: Yi Jiangxisheng T Xian 20 ge Cun Weili' ['Study of elections in 20 Jiangxi villages in T County which have experienced direct elections'], *Yunnan Xingzheng Xueyuan Yuanbao* [*Journal of Yunnan Public Administration College*] no. 1, (2007), pp. 82–85. But compare, Tan and Xin, 'Village election and governance', p. 597.

110. See Xie Meili, 'Wanshan Cunweihui Xuanju Zhidu, Cujin Xinnongcun Hexie Fazhan' ['Improve village committee electoral institutions and promote harmonious development of new rural areas'], *Zhongguo Xingzheng Guanli* [*Chinese Public Administration*] no. 11, (2006), p. 57; also see Kevin J. O'Brien and Lianjiang Li, *Rightful Resistance in Rural China* (New York: Cambridge University Press, 2006), p. 125.

111. For this remark, see Lianjiang Li and Kevin J. O'Brien, 'Villagers and popular resistance in contemporary China', *Modern China* 22(1), (January 1996), p. 34. For similar sayings involving famished wolves or tigers, see Xu Yong, 'Qianghua Minzhu Jiandu, Cujin Zhili Zhuanxing' ['Strengthen democratic supervision and promote governance transition'], *Xiangzhen Luntan* [*Township Forum*] no. 4, (2001), p. 10; He Xuefeng, 'Guanyu Cunzhuang Quanli Kuozhanxing de Taolun' ['Discussion on the expansion of village power structure'], *Yunnan Shehui Kexue* [*Yunnan Social Sciences*] no. 6, (2000), p. 39.

112. Norberto Bobbio, *Which Socialism? Marxism, Socialism, and Democracy* (Minneapolis: University of Minnesota Press, 1987), p. 74.

113. On placing elections in a comprehensive framework that goes beyond the village and also considers cadre behavior, villager awareness, and cultural context, see Gunter Schubert, 'Studying "democratic" governance in contemporary China: looking at the village is not enough', *Journal of Contemporary China* 18(60), (June 2009).

How to Assess Village Elections in China

MELANIE MANION

In assessing Chinese village elections we must sort and discriminate as we consult the 'mountain of evidence' that has accumulated over the past two decades. We can find anecdotal evidence to support practically any claim about village democratization, but from such stories we can learn nothing about the status, trends, or patterns of village democratization. This article evaluates what we can learn and have learned about grassroots democratization in the Chinese countryside from nationally and locally representative sample survey data.

The twentieth (and tenth) anniversaries of the provisional (and revised) *Organic Law on Village Committees* are an appropriate time for reflection on changes in the Chinese countryside and how we have met the challenges of studying them. The sweeping review of the literature by O'Brien and Han is an excellent point of departure for this reflection.[1] Moreover, as I argue below, their proposed new direction for scholarship on village democratization is timely.

A mountain of evidence

As O'Brien and Han point out, there is indeed 'a mountain of evidence' to turn to in assessing village elections in China. In consulting this evidence, however, we must sort and discriminate. Simply put, some evidence is better suited to answer some questions than others; some evidence illuminates little or not at all, regardless of the questions we put to it. What can we learn and what have we learned about Chinese village democratization from the cumulative evidence of the past two decades?

Consider anecdotal evidence. The village democratization experience has unfolded on an enormous scale and has reflected the huge variation that is mainland China. As a simple consequence of the country's scale and variation, we can find anecdotal evidence to support practically any claim about village democratization in one or

---

1. Kevin J. O'Brien and Rongbin Han, 'Path to democracy? Assessing village elections in China', *Journal of Contemporary China* 18(60), (June 2009).

across several of over 600,000 villages (or, indeed, in one or across several of nearly 3,000 counties). Colorful accounts are plentiful in the Chinese mass media (and in field observations). The impressions charm or alarm—but from such stories we can learn nothing about the status, trends, or patterns of village democratization.

Fortunately, we need not rely on anecdotes. Over the past two decades, scholars have conducted a good number of rigorous systematic studies of village democratization. These include well-designed case studies and probability sample surveys—some nationally representative, others locally representative. Below, I evaluate what we can learn and have learned from the two sorts of survey data.

More than two decades after passage of the provisional version of the *Organic Law on Village Committees* in 1987 and a decade after passage of the amended version in 1998, what is the overall status of village democratization? Mindful of the issues of scale and variation noted above, we can only confidently look to data from nationally representative sample surveys for an accurate descriptive snapshot. There are few reliable, nationally representative sample surveys that include enough of the relevant population and enough relevant items to inform such a picture. So far as I know, the most recent such study is a 2005 survey conducted by Tsai and colleagues.[2] From this survey, we learn that anonymous ballots, public vote counts, and multiple candidates for the post of village committee head are all now practically universal in village elections.[3] Other features of high-quality electoral procedure are less common. Roving ballot boxes supplement fixed polling stations in more than a third of the villages, and proxy voting is regulated in only a third. Authorities above the village level intervene in candidate nomination in nearly a third of the villages, and their approval is required for the final slate of candidates in two-thirds.

This picture of village democratization, which is mainly informative about procedure, reflects significant but modest achievements. More interesting perhaps is the picture of how electoral procedure has progressed over the years, especially after 1998. Procedural features mandated by the revised *Organic Law on Village Committees* are the norm in village elections after 2000. In addition to the three features noted above, these include direct election of village leaders rather than indirect election through village representative assemblies or other agencies. Where the law is silent or imprecise, however, township authorities often exercise their prerogative to influence the process, typically before the election.

Tsai also demonstrates that published univariate estimates from locally representative sample surveys diverge wildly from one another and, where comparison is possible, from the national picture. Exactly how wildly they diverge varies, of course, and scholars presenting such descriptive point estimates from local probability samples mostly eschew claims of broader generalizability—but the more

---

2. Lily L. Tsai, 'Governing one million rural communities after two decades: are China's village elections improving?', paper prepared for the *Conference on Growing Pains: Tensions and Opportunity in China's Transformation*, Stanford University, 2–3 November 2007. In addition, Tianjian Shi, working with the Social Survey Research Center at People's University in Beijing, conducted nationally representative sample surveys in 1990–1991 and 1993–1994. The latter is the basis for his estimate that 54% of villages had held contested elections by 1994 and his finding of curvilinear relationships between local economic development and implementation of electoral contestation. See Tianjian Shi, 'Economic development and village elections in rural China', *Journal of Contemporary China* 8(22), (November 1999), pp. 425–442.

3. Implementation ranges from 95 to 99%.

important lesson is that the relationship of such estimates to the status of village democratization overall is essentially unknowable without such a comparative exercise.

Although locally representative sample surveys are ill-suited to provide an accurate univariate descriptive picture of village democratization overall, they are well-suited to take advantage of temporal and cross-sectional variation in democratization across the Chinese countryside to inform about patterns and trends.[4] Many studies fall into this category, many of them cited and their findings summarized in the essay by O'Brien and Han. Without repeating here the findings they review, it is worth emphasizing that there is a sizeable body of scholarship focusing on the consequences for governance of variation in electoral procedure.[5] Indeed, some of this scholarship explicitly considers the constraints on governance presented by township authorities, village communist party branches, and social forces.

Scholarship based on locally representative sample surveys provides good evidence that village elections have significantly impacted political life in the Chinese countryside, not least of all by their effect on the relationship between ordinary villagers and grassroots leaders. For this reason, in the grand configuration of Leninist authoritarian political organization in mainland China, village elections strike me as a truly important pocket of institutional change. It would be naïve to expect elections alone to deliver high-quality democratic governance, in the Chinese countryside or elsewhere. O'Brien and Han paint a fairly pessimistic picture of governance in rural China—but in fact we have no way to assess, with the evidence available, the overall quality of governance. Of course, this is part of the problem that they properly bemoan. It will, however, be a serious challenge to arrive at an accurate picture of village governance overall. Certainly, neither well-designed case studies nor locally representative sample surveys will serve the purpose.

Theory, questions, timing

Research on Chinese village democratization has focused significantly on electoral procedure, usually without simplistically equating high-quality village elections with democracy *per se*. Is the focus misplaced? As I argue below, the focus of scholarship on access to power seems essentially sound. All the same, the strong caution issued by O'Brien and Han about the failure of most scholarship to take into proper account the 'local power configuration' in which village committees exercise power (or not) is timely. The modest progress in village electoral democracy has produced an environment that supports the research agenda they advocate.

How to assess village elections in China? The focus on procedure makes good sense, especially through the 1990s. In much research, it becomes (explicitly or

---

4. Moreover, so long as data are from a good-sized probabilistically selected representative sample in the locality, the statistical inferences about trends and patterns can often be reliably generalized beyond the sample. See Melanie Manion, 'Survey research in the study of contemporary China: learning from local samples', *China Quarterly* no. 139, (September 1994), pp. 741–765.

5. See also the discussion in Bjorn Alpermann, 'Institutionalizing village governance in China', *Journal of Contemporary China* 18(60), (June 2009).

implicitly) an inquiry into the effect of institutional change presumed to create incentives for ordinary Chinese and grassroots leaders to act (and expect others to act) differently than before. Theoretically, then, the focus posits that procedure is prior to governance. Put another way, it presumes procedure is an important bundle of variables that affects governance outcomes.[6] That is, the focus on electoral procedure presumes a link between access to power and exercise of power. Electoral procedure is surely not the only important bundle of independent variables in the picture—but it is the one that most obviously changed.

The extent to which changes in access to power have in fact affected exercise of power is not a simple theoretical presumption but an empirical question, demanding serious empirical testing. We think we know something about how electoral incentives work strategically to improve accountability of leaders to their constituencies, but the link between procedure and governance is also contextually grounded. Most of what we know about this link comes from research in advanced industrial democracies and other contexts very different from the Chinese countryside. Despite the different contexts, however, a good number of reliable scholarly studies attest to various pieces of the theorized link between access to power and exercise of power in Chinese villages. For example, features such as electoral contestation and citizen attentiveness are positively correlated with various measures of responsiveness of elected leaders to villagers, producing an 'electoral connection'—although there is nothing particularly Chinese about these mechanisms.[7]

At the same time, a confluence of events has probably overtaken the rationale for a focus on electoral procedure. First, as summarized in the previous section, there is now significant standardization along key, legally mandated dimensions in the procedural bundle studied over the past two decades. Second, central and local authorities have adapted to this procedural progress in a variety of ways. For example, O'Brien and Han point to a 2002 Central Committee and State Council circular that endorses what is effectively a merger of village communist party branches and village committees; Tsai's survey demonstrates that township authorities widely influence village elections to the extent permitted by law. Third, although we know less about how social forces such as lineage groups, religious organizations, and (especially) criminal elements affect village governance, we do know that lineage groups and religious organizations have become more assertive generally in the more tolerant political environment of the past two decades. In this sense, the social groups act as newly active players operating in the new environment of procedural progress, if not actively responding to it.

These events produce an imperative and offer an opportunity to push forward with a new wave of scholarship on village democratization, one that systematically investigates the contextual effect of the local power configuration on governance. The imperative is given by the changes in local context that we know (and others that

---

6. In studies of Chinese village elections, specific variables usually include (at least) candidate nomination, electoral contestation, and voting processes.

7. See, for example, M. Kent Jennings, 'Local problem agendas in the Chinese countryside as viewed by cadres and villagers', *Acta Politica* 38(4), (December 2003), pp. 313–332; and Melanie Manion, 'The electoral connection in the Chinese countryside', *American Political Science Review* 90(4), (December 1996), pp. 736–748.

we can only now suspect): responses of authorities and new assertiveness of social groups in the environment of popularly elected village committees. The opportunity also has to do with this environment. Even if we only want to investigate the effect of, say, township authorities on governance, we still must control for variation in electoral procedure so long as responses by township authorities are not isomorphic with procedural features. That is, the theoretical logic of an electoral connection has not disappeared. The empirical challenge of investigating the impact of the local power configuration has become more manageable in recent years, however, because village elections have settled into a relatively small number of procedural configurations. In short, what we know about procedural progress overall better allows us to take up the research challenge that new events demand of us.

Studying 'Democratic' Governance in Contemporary China: looking at the village is not enough

GUNTER SCHUBERT

Though it is important that future research on village elections focuses more systematically on the post-election period than on ongoing electoral institutionalization, it is not enough to look at the village level alone if one wants to assess the quality of village governance. What we need is a more comprehensive framework that includes an analysis of election procedures, cadre behaviour, villager awareness, and the larger cultural context, which would connect the village, township and county levels and shift attention toward legitimacy rather than 'democracy'.

Village elections were welcomed enthusiastically by many Western scholars, insomuch as they promised to test the hypothesis of 'creeping democratization' in reform-era China. Some observers hoped, if not expected, that they (and scattered experiments with township elections) might signal a bottom-up democratization of the political system. More recently, however, research on village elections has faded somewhat, for good reasons: the 'democratic promise' has not been kept. Popular political mobilization has not forced the regime to extend direct balloting to upper levels; nor has the centre shown a willingness to promote township elections as the next step in a drive to build 'socialist democracy' system-wide.

This loss of momentum offers us an opportunity to assess what we have learned so far, and to consider the consequences of village elections for the broader political system—its potential for reform, its resilience, its stability and legitimacy. At the same time, it is an opportune moment to reflect on blind spots that have developed in research on grassroots politics: spots that, if addressed, might reinvigorate scholarly interest in rural democracy and improve our understanding of the relationship between village elections and local governance.

In their fine overview of the village elections literature, O'Brien and Han convincingly argue that research on the quality of grassroots democracy has been largely neglected due to disproportionate focus on the procedural aspects of balloting.[1] Proceduralism, they explain, highlights observable practices (i.e. access to power), but ignores how power is exercised *after* elections are held, and how that affects the quality of village democracy. O'Brien and Han, citing a number of studies, do acknowledge that village elections have, at least in some localities, made policies and leaders more acceptable to voters, enhanced trust in local cadres, increased popular political awareness, and even nurtured a sense of citizenship. Elections have, they show, also become increasingly institutionalized, 'yet the quality of democracy in much of the countryside remains stubbornly low', mainly because village committees remain situated in a socio-political environment 'that has changed surprisingly little'.

O'Brien and Han then underscore several constraints that clearly 'impede democratic rule' and point to the need for closer examination of township interference in village elections, competition with party branches, as well as the influence of informal groups (clans, religious organizations, criminal gangs).[2] More specifically, O'Brien and Han argue that 'beyond specifying the obstacles to democratization, we need more studies that explain how, when, and where elections have changed the relationship between cadres and voters'; 'more research on whether elections deter power holders from seeking personal gain above all else'; and more examinations of why voter apathy and cynicism are growing.

On the whole, O'Brien and Han are right though I believe that the literature has produced a good deal more knowledge on the constraints they underscore than the authors recognize. Moreover, the distinction between procedural and contextual dimensions of elections is not as clear-cut as O'Brien and Han suggest, though some scholars do indeed focus on the procedural and institutional aspects of elections while downplaying the wider context within which they take place.[3] We should certainly do as O'Brien and Han advocate and gather ever more and comprehensive data to make sense of contemporary rural China's complicated reality. We definitely need more qualitative research stretching out over longer intervals, because brief research trips of several days or weeks are hardly enough to assess township intercession, party branch authority, or the role of informal groups in local governance. And, it must be added, we need more quantitative and 'mixed methods' research, not least because representative samples and sending ever more Chinese students into the field to conduct standardized interviews with (paid) villagers will not tell us everything we need to know. Studying village elections, in short, poses

---

1. Kevin J. O'Brien and Rongbin Han, 'Path to democracy? Assessing village elections in China', *Journal of Contemporary China* 18(60), (June 2009).

2. This point is also highlighted by Melanie Manion, 'How to assess village elections in China', *Journal of Contemporary China* 18(60), (June 2009).

3. A good example is the work of Qingshan Tan, e.g. *Village Elections in China. Democratizing the Countryside* (Lewiston *et al.*, The Edwin Mellen Press, 2006). In his contribution to the debate on O'Brien and Han's paper in this journal, Tan underlines that 'the top priority for rural governance is to build a democratic infrastructure, starting with electoral institutionalization'. Björn Alpermann has recently focused on electoral implementation at the provincial level and argues in his article in this issue that 'the exercise of authority has a procedural dimension itself' which must be closely watched. In that sense, both authors do, to some extent, disagree with O'Brien and Han's distinction between proceduralism and context. See Qingshan Tan, 'Building democratic infrastructure: village electoral institutions', *Journal of Contemporary China* 18(60), (June 2009). However, proceduralism can also be applied to post-election village governance. See Björn Alpermann, 'Institutionalizing village governance in China', *Journal of Contemporary China* 18(60), (June 2009).

substantial methodological challenges to China scholars. And these challenges are not made easier by the fact that China scholars have recently been confronted with the suspicion that most of the data they take out of China are unreliable or distorted.[4]

However, there are even more basic questions to confront before we enter the next phase of research on village elections. First, what are our guiding hypotheses? Consideration of this is conspicuously absent in O'Brien and Han's article, as they focus on the relationship between procedural democracy (as the independent variable) and intervening factors that enhance or impede 'high quality democracy in rural China' (as the dependent variable). They essentially restrict themselves to the question: what brings about good (democratic) governance, and what causes bad governance in China's villages? But why do we want to know this? To put it bluntly: why should we continue studying village 'democracy', or the exercise of power in China's villages, if we are already convinced that nothing 'big' is emerging in terms of a trend toward more democratization of the whole system? How relevant is the village level in the context of 'democratic governance' in contemporary China? O'Brien and Han should address these questions directly and begin by commenting on the overall direction research should take. Given what we already know, their argument for more research at the village level is otherwise not sufficiently compelling. The following intentionally contradictory statements might provide a starting point and some guiding hypotheses:

- The exercise of power in the post-election period has not changed substantially over the last 20 years. Though village elections have become increasingly institutionalized and have positively affected both cadre behaviour and the development of villager citizenship, they have not produced democratic village governance. Local power-holders have adapted well to the new institutional environment and have consolidated their political dominance while making few compromises. Villagers may feel empowered by village elections, but they have not gained genuine power.
- Village elections have not only become increasingly institutionalized over the last 20 years, they have also enhanced cadre accountability, increased citizenship consciousness and transformed cadre–villager relations so that village governance in the post-election period has become more democratic as well.
- Village elections have not only empowered villagers and enhanced cadre accountability, they have also contributed positively to political stability and regime legitimacy of the local state.
- Village elections enhance political awareness of villagers and increase their willingness to engage in resistance against local cadres, causing instability and a decline in the legitimacy of the local state.

Secondly, O'Brien and Han should provide a more detailed explanation of their benchmark for 'democratic governance'. They emphasize that 'the mode in which political actors behave' must be democratized, that 'the citizenry must take up new

---

4. See, for example, the provocative essay by Carsten Holz, 'Have China scholars all been bought?', *Far Eastern Economic Review*, (April 2007), pp. 36–40.

responsibilities and play their role as well', and that true grassroots democracy requires 'quality of content' and 'quality of results'. This is fairly abstract, but given their concerns, they likely mean that political actors (i.e. local cadres) must accept that elections make them accountable and that they must honour their constituents' preferences by promoting good and fair policies that benefit the majority—no matter what the township, the party branch or any other vested interest in the village says. Cadres must accept that villagers have the right to hold cadres responsible over the post-election period, and township and party authorities must refrain from interfering in the election process and post-election governance. This all accords with Western thinking on democracy, but may be somewhat beside the point when it comes to rural China. Though the concept of democracy should not be stretched by excessive attention to the specifics of a given community, democracy in China's villages might be founded on cultural characteristics that a Western political science perspective is ill-suited to recognize. For instance, are informal groups like clans or temple associations always detrimental to village democracy, or can they help institutionalize it, despite possible conflicts with Western understandings of 'one man, one vote'? Does township or party branch intervention always mean interference with village democracy, or could it reflect a broad consensus on collective decision-making and a longing for harmonious relations between different actors jointly responsible for the well-being of a village?[5] A questioning of established Western categories, reminiscent of that typically done by anthropologists, would enrich our understanding of local governance in rural China and prevent us from being trapped by our own theoretical assumptions. Without subscribing to unalloyed cultural relativism, a more interdisciplinary and culturally 'empathetic' approach to village democracy may be helpful for those of us trained as political scientists.

In sum, if we want to reinvigorate village election studies, what we need is some new hypotheses and a better (more endogenous) understanding of the meaning of 'democratic governance' in the Chinese countryside. A new approach should be based on a comprehensive analysis of *procedures, cadre behaviour, villager awareness (political thinking)*, and *cultural context*. The tricky aspect of this agenda is, of course, its operationalization. What, for instance, is the analytical point of reference for investigating cadre behaviour and villager awareness in the post-election period? One option is an empirical approach that starts with *specific policies* promoted by the village authorities or higher levels, and then asks: how are these policies formulated? Do they take villagers' interests seriously? Are feedback mechanisms in place when they are formulated and implemented? How do the villagers think of and respond to them? Alternatively, we can investigate the quality of certain *non-electoral institutions*—'supportive institutions' or 'accountability agencies' that 'supplement the electoral mechanism and control politicians' in the

---

5. See, for example, Tong Zhihui, *Xuanju shijian yu cunzhuang zhengzhi [Election Incidents and Village Politics]* (Beijing: Zhongguo Shehui kexue, 2004); Lili Tsai, 'Cadres, temple and lineage institutions, and governance in rural China', *China Journal* 48, (2002), pp. 1–27; Stephan Feuchtwang, 'Peasants, democracy and anthropology', *Critique of Anthropology* 23(1), (2003), pp. 93–120; Susanne Brandtstädter and Gunter Schubert, 'Democratic thought and practice in rural China', *Democratization* 12(5), (2005), pp. 801–819.

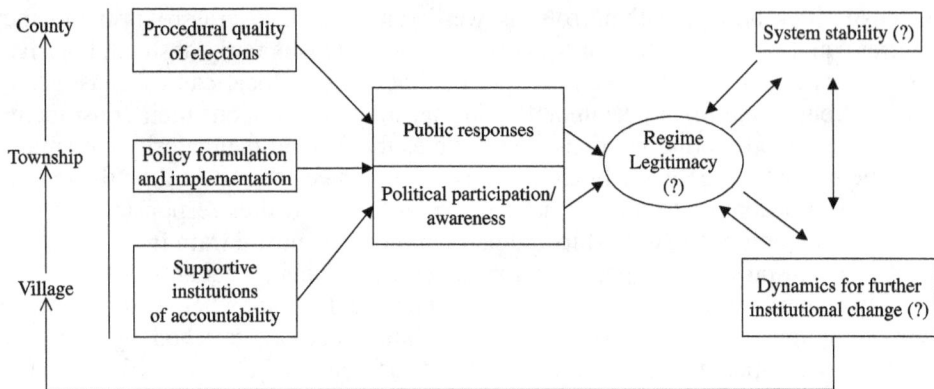

Figure 1. A legitimacy-based model to studying (democratic) governance in China's local state.
© Gunter Schubert.

words of Su Fubing and Yang Dali.[6] How much autonomy do these institutions enjoy? To what extent are they able to sanction corrupt or incompetent cadres? How well are they received by villagers?

Such an approach could be combined with a focus on the legitimacy of local governance rather than its democratic quality. This would mean studying the relationship between (engineered or evolutionary) institutional change and political legitimacy, the latter measured as support of villagers for (1) their cadres or (2) policy performance of institutions related to pre-defined goals (i.e. functional legitimacy).[7] When studying rural China, legitimacy is a concept much less prone to 'external framing' than 'democratic quality'. This agenda would entail both more micro-political and macro-quantitative studies on the nexus between electoral procedures and institutionalization, policy formulation and implementation, institutional design of 'accountability agencies', and public response/participation in a given locality. Such research could help create a realistic picture of the legitimacy that village governance generates (or does not), and how this impacts rural stability and the dynamics of institutional change.

One question remains: what do we know when we have identified varying degrees of political legitimacy in village China? How relevant is the village level to understand what is transpiring in the local state? Here I would argue that the new research agenda just outlined (see also Figure 1) should not be limited to villages, but should integrate townships and counties. Future research should move toward a comprehensive framework that connects these three levels and focuses equally on procedures, policies and 'accountability institutions'. Such research would encourage

---

6. Su Fubing and Yang Dali, 'Elections, governance, and accountability in rural China', *Asian Perspective* 29(4), (2005), pp. 125–157. The authors point, for instance, to the significance of tax-for-fee reforms, innovative rules to enforce the transparency of village finance (*cunwu gongkai*), the installation of Village Representative Assemblies and new modes of increased public participation in the selection of village party secretaries.

7. Gunter Schubert, 'One-party rule and the question of legitimacy in contemporary China: preliminary thoughts of setting up a new research agenda', *Journal of Contemporary China* 17(54), (February 2008), pp. 191–204. See also John James Kennedy, 'Legitimacy with Chinese characteristics: "two increases, one reduction"', *Journal of Contemporary China* 18(60), (June 2009).

new hypothesizing on system adaptability and regime legitimacy by building on findings derived from studies of the local state.

Further study of village elections only makes sense if it is put into a broader perspective of understanding local governance reform. Needless to say, this would require more collaboration between China scholars who work on the village, township and county levels. It would also entail more integrated research agendas that aim to make field data more comparable. This is difficult, but doable. In and of itself, after 15 years of stimulating and fruitful research, the village level has ceased to be of particular interest for political scientists—at least for those of us who are far more excited about studying the link between local governance (reform) and the evolution of China's political system.

Legitimacy with Chinese Characteristics: 'two increases, one reduction'

JOHN JAMES KENNEDY

Over the last 20 years, an increasing number of villagers have experienced free and fair elections, and this has contributed to the legitimacy of local democratic practices as well as the authoritarian regime. Yet, these improvements in election procedures can only occur when township officials are removed from the village leader selection process. As a result, the increase in regime legitimacy is closely tied to reduction in the authority of mid-level officials to directly select subordinates. This process, where it has occurred, has generated a bottom-up institutionalization of democratic practices, and suggests that researchers should not dismiss the importance of election procedures too quickly.

Kevin O'Brien and Rongbin Han provide the clearest assessment of the *Organic Law of Villager Committees* and village election literature to date.[1] They conclude that election quality has improved steadily over the last 20 years, but that most research conducted so far overemphasizes procedural aspects of democracy. They propose a new focus that highlights the post-election relationship between local leaders and villagers. This implies a closer examination of political outcomes, including how cadres exercise power, and also the effects of elections on regime legitimacy and support for local institutions.

Village elections reflect both a top-down and bottom-up process of legitimation. One bottom-up result of two decades of elections has been the institutionalization of democratic practices.[2] Operating in what Gunter Schubert has called a 'zone of legitimacy', village elections, when fully implemented, can be the building blocks for institutional legitimacy in China.[3] The irony is that village elections can legitimize local democratic practices as well as the authoritarian regime.

---

1. Kevin J. O'Brien and Rongbin Han, 'Path to democracy? Assessing village elections in China', *Journal of Contemporary China* 18(60), (June 2009).

2. This is similar to Melanie Manion's 'pocket of institutional change' within a single party system. See Melanie Manion, 'How to assess village elections in China', *Journal of Contemporary China* 18(60), (June 2009).

3. Gunther Schubert, 'One-party rule and the question of legitimacy in contemporary China: preliminary thoughts on setting up a new research agenda', *Journal of Contemporary China* 17(54), (February 2008), pp. 191–204; also see Gunther Schubert, 'Studying "democratic" governance in contemporary China: looking at the village is not enough', *Journal of Contemporary China* 18(60), (June 2009).

Recognizing these potential legitimation effects may require identifying zones of legitimacy where top-down political reforms have been carried out and bottom-up institutionalization can be observed. Given the gradual unfolding of local democratic reforms, both domestic and foreign researchers should not dismiss the import of village elections too quickly. Rather we might begin by looking for the evolution of legitimate representative institutions that are responsive to citizen demands and emphasize institutions over individual cadre qualities.

Direct grassroots elections in an authoritarian regime can have three outcomes that indicate steps toward greater legitimacy for both local institutions and the regime. One is an increase in citizen support for local electoral institutions. This means villagers may be dissatisfied with election results, but still embrace a fair election process. Second is a reduction in the authority of mid-level officials to choose subordinates. Fair elections should remove township officials from the village leader selection process. Third is an increased connection with the regime. Many villagers view local elections as a central government attempt to offer citizens the right to monitor and sanction local cadres. This links a local zone of legitimacy to regime support. A paradox for central leaders is that generating regime legitimacy this way is tied to reducing the authority of mid-level officials. As a whole, this process suggests two increases in support and one reduction in authority.

Increase in institutional support

Village elections at times generate greater support for institutional procedures than for individual cadres. Although elections can make leaders more accountable to their constituents, villagers may still not be satisfied with a given leader's performance. Legitimacy for local institutions, in other words, sometimes rests on villagers making a distinction between support for an elected cadre and the procedures which put him or her in office.

In his report to the 16th Party Congress, Jiang Zemin reiterated the view that the country should be run by combining rule of law with rule of virtue.[4] The CCP claims moral authority and stresses the importance of virtuous leaders. At the village level, attention to both law and virtue means that villagers should elect high-quality cadres. Jean Oi suggests that one possible outcome of the *Organic Law* is more efficient policy implementation as well as greater support for elected leaders.[5] Villagers may be more willing to accept unpopular policies, such as family planning and revenue collection, if these are administered by someone they selected rather than a person appointed from above. This suggests that villagers are more likely to support elected (rather than appointed) leaders.

Yet, according to a number of studies, there is almost universal dissatisfaction with elected village cadres. Surveys conducted by Tony Saich, Lianjiang Li and myself, asked rural respondents to rank their level of satisfaction with national, provincial,

---

4. 'Jiang Zemin delivers report to the 16th CPC National Congress', available at: http://www.chinese-embassy. no/eng/dtxw/t110238.htm (accessed 2 April 2008).
5. Jean C. Oi, 'Economic development, stability and democratic village self-governance', in Maurice Brosseau *et al.*, eds, *China Review 1996* (Hong Kong: The Chinese University Press, 1996), pp. 125–144.

county, township, and village leadership.[6] Township officials and elected village cadres received the lowest satisfaction and support scores in all three studies. This suggests that the *Organic Law*, even when fully implemented, has done little to improve villagers' view of local cadres. However, dissatisfaction with elected leaders can, contrary to what one might think, be interpreted as positive for legitimation. This is because villagers tend to have considerable faith in the laws and procedures that surround elections. Jie Chen's 2000 survey of 84 villagers in Jiangsu, for example, found significant diffuse support for elections coupled with low evaluation of the performance of elected leaders.[7] Despite widespread dissatisfaction with elected cadres, Ethan Michelson's 2002 survey of 36 villages in six provinces demonstrated that when local leaders make fair decisions concerning disputes, villagers are satisfied with the process, if not always the outcome.[8] In my own 2004 survey of 18 villages in Shaanxi, villagers generally disapproved of elected leaders, but in villages with free and fair elections, rural people still exhibited strong support for the electoral process. This is similar to citizen attitudes found in industrialized democracies where the approval ratings of elected officials are unstable and typically low, but confidence in the process by which leaders are chosen is high.

Reduction in mid-level authority

Although many studies have demonstrated continued township resistance to the *Organic Law*, there is also evidence of decreasing township interference in the election process. Moreover, fair elections can also improve the working relationship between elected leaders and township officials.

O'Brien and Han show that township officials continue to resist the *Organic Law* and often try to manipulate the election process and maintain control over elected leaders. This can produce clashes between township officials and elected leaders in which village cadres usually come out on the losing side. When this occurs, it certainly reduces the legitimacy of the election process and a cadre's ability to represent his or her constituents.

However, a number of studies also find minimal township involvement in the election process beyond basic preparation.[9] In these villages, local autonomy tends to be strong and elected leaders have a good working relationship with township officials. Although elected leaders have a dual responsibility to the township and villagers, they can best serve their constituents when they work well with the township government. Thus, manipulation is not needed when popularly elected cadres also do a good job carrying out orders from above.

---

6. Lianjiang Li, 'Political trust in rural China', *Modern China* 30(2), (April 2004), pp. 228–258; Tony Saich, 'Citizens' perceptions of governance in rural and urban China', *Journal of Chinese Political Science* 12(1), (Spring 2007), pp. 1–28.

7. Jie Chen, 'Popular support for village self-government in China', *Asian Survey* 45(6), (November/December 2005), pp. 865–885.

8. Ethan Michelson, 'Justice from above or justice from below? Popular strategies for resolving grievances in rural China', *China Quarterly* 193, (March 2008), pp. 43–64.

9. Jamie P. Horsley, 'Village elections: training ground for democracy', *The China Business Review*, (March–April 2001); Xu Wang, *Mutual Empowerment of State and Peasantry: Village Self-Government in Rural China* (New York: Nova Science Publishers, 2003), pp. 119–124; Baogang He, *Rural Democracy in China: The Role of Village Elections* (New York, NY: Palgrave, 2007).

Vote buying, oddly enough, may also be an indicator of township non-interference in elections. When township officials manipulate elections, candidates must curry favor with them in order to get elected. In this situation, election outcomes are decided by officials, and votes are not worth a penny. However, when elections are free from official interference voters determine the outcome, and the value of a vote increases. Thus, in some villages, ambitious, better-off candidates have turned to buying votes. Although vote-buying presents a new set of challenges, it is a problem that exists only because of reduced township interference and a fairer election process.

An essential feature of free and fair elections is uncertain outcomes.[10] Township officials manipulate elections in order to decrease this uncertainty, but this can also erode the legitimacy of local government. Therefore the legitimation of local governance is closely tied to reduction in the authority of mid-level officials to hand-pick their subordinates.

Increased connection with the regime

Although township officials are responsible for many election details, such as scheduling and voter registration, the national leadership has been the main force behind successful implementation. This leaves townships to take the blame for poor-quality elections, and in many cases, this is well deserved. Lianjiang Li has demonstrated that villagers can further distinguish between central leaders' intent and capacity to enforce the *Organic Law*.[11] Therefore, some villagers view the *Organic Law* as a worthy, if not always successful, attempt to protect them from abusive local cadres and to extend political rights. Moreover, when some people use the law to confront cadre misdeeds or when villagers participate in fair elections, the experience can increase their connection with the central government.[12]

Although the *Organic Law* was largely a top-down initiative, regime legitimacy originates below. Villagers now increasingly exercise the rights spelled out in the *Organic Law*, such as recalling an elected leader or demanding open accounting of public investment.[13] Even if the majority of villagers do not know the letter of the law and have never confronted a village committee member, they can still observe how others in the community use these laws. Villagers also see how elections can reduce corrupt behavior and increase accountability of village committee members. Even lower quality elections can provide incentives for leaders to be more responsive to their constituents.[14] These observations and experiences at the village level enhance the legitimacy of the central government.

---

10. Adam Przeworski, *Democracy and the Market: Political and Economic Reforms in Eastern Europe and Latin America* (New York: Cambridge University Press, 1991), p. 14.

11. Lianjiang Li, 'Political trust in rural China', p. 238.

12. Kevin J. O'Brien, 'Villagers, elections, and citizenship in contemporary China', *Modern China* 27(4), (October 2001), pp. 407–435.

13. Björn Alpermann shows that a number of provincial level implementation regulations for the 1998 *Organic Law* focus on public accounting and transparency in village financial matters. See Björn Alpermann, 'Institutionalizing village governance in China', *Journal of Contemporary China* 18(60), (June 2009).

14. Loren Brandt and Matthew A. Turner, 'The usefulness of imperfect elections: the case of village elections in rural China', *Economic and Politics* 19(3), (November 2007), pp. 453–479.

Observation and participation locally are not the only factors that increase regime legitimacy; citizens also connect village democratic experiences with national policies and laws that they hear about through the mass media. For example, 'building a new socialist countryside' has been publicized in every form of media from television and newspapers to rural billboards and roadside walls. This policy involves many aspects of rural life, but it stresses the importance of democratic elections and decision-making. When villagers participate in fair elections they can make a direct connection between national propaganda and village experience. This can legitimize local elections as well as the authoritarian regime.

Conclusion

Although uneven implementation persists, O'Brien and Han show that election quality has been improving over the last two decades with no imminent signs of reversal. Indeed, it is widely agreed that democratic practices have become more widespread and institutionalized. This means that villagers are not just demanding their rights; they are supporting democratic institutions and are involved in democratic practices, such as voting or resolving local disputes through elected village committees. This has resulted in a bottom-up institutionalization of democratic practices.

This suggests that two increases and one reduction is generating legitimacy for the authoritarian regime and local democratic practices *before* the establishment of national democratic institutions. Legitimizing political institutions from the bottom up, however, can put pressure on the central leadership to expand political reform. Indeed, the authoritarian leadership has created a situation where political legitimacy is tied to more electoral reforms. Of course, central leaders can always choose to slow down reforms and even end local democratization efforts, but this will eat away at regime legitimacy. In order to prevent this, top leaders may choose policies and laws that unintentionally erode their monopoly on political power. That is, they may accept losing some power in order to stay in power. This is not what was originally planned. However, unintended consequences and reforms that take on a momentum of their own may lead to 'democratization with Chinese characteristics' or in more general terms 'front-end' democratization within a single party system.

Institutionalizing Village Governance in China

BJÖRN ALPERMANN

Most studies of political reforms in rural China have concentrated on village elections, pointing out important effects of this democratic mechanism. However, while significant in broadening the 'access to power', even well conducted village elections fall short of altering the 'exercise of power', which has received far less research attention. Therefore, this article focuses on the procedural dimension of post-election village governance. It argues that there has been considerable formal institutionalization regarding the three democratic rights of decision-making, management and supervision in village affairs. This analysis is based on close scrutiny of provincial-level legislation on village governance, which constitutes a crucial, though largely untapped, source of information on village self-administration. In conclusion, the article suggests that progress in institutionalization has improved opportunities for villagers to manage their own affairs and control elected village officials, while at the same time strengthening the role played by Communist Party branches in village governance.

Two decades after the trial version of the *Organic Law on Village Committees* (*cunmin weiyuanhui zuzhifa*) came into force and one decade after the revised and final version of this law was enacted by the National People's Congress, the time is ripe to assess the progress made in village governance. In their assessment of grassroots elections, O'Brien and Han present us with a careful analysis of developments and limitations of village-level political reform.[1] Their argument can be summarized as such: differentiating between 'access to power' and 'exercise of power' the authors posit that most scholarly efforts at understanding changes in rural basic-level governance focus on the first, namely the analysis of village committee (VC) elections, while the second issue has largely been sidelined. They trace this imbalance in research interests to the minimalist and procedural understanding of democracy which is nowadays employed by many political scientists.

O'Brien and Han further argue that institutionalization of village elections has made great strides over the last two decades, but that this progress has not been matched by similar advances in post-election administration. In short, access to

---

1. Kevin J. O'Brien and Rongbin Han, 'Path to democracy? Assessing village elections in China', *Journal of Contemporary China* 18(60), (June 2009).

power has been considerably broadened but the actual exercise of power has yet to undergo complementary transformation. Even where they are democratically elected, village committees are still surrounded by state, party and social actors which vie for power in villages (i.e. township governments, village Party branches and their secretaries as well as clans and even criminal elements). Therefore, we need to look beyond electoral or 'procedural quality' and toward 'quality of content' and 'quality of results' if we are to advance our understanding of democratization in rural China.[2]

This is an insightful analysis which helps rebalance and reframe village governance research. However, the distinction between 'procedural quality' of elections and actual exercise of power should probably not be taken too far. This is because the exercise of authority has a procedural dimension itself: one which has not received sufficient attention in the literature so far. Therefore, this article picks up where O'Brien and Han left off by examining procedural rules for post-election village administration. The rationale for this is that instead of juxtaposing formal election rules and village governance, we have to examine formal institutions and actual practice in both elections and post-election administration. The *Organic Law* in its revised 1998 version refers to the 'four democratic rights' of villagers: elections, decision-making, management and supervision. In fact, there has been continuous institutionalization and innovation not only regarding elections, but also in the other three rights which together constitute the framework of village governance today. In short, the argument advanced here is that there has been extensive formal institutionalization in the field of post-election village governance which is evident by looking at codification at the provincial level.

Provincial regulations on village governance

My focus below will be on provincial regulations pertaining to post-election village self-administration, rather than application of these rules and procedures. Scrutiny of provincial-level legal documents, however limited, is a crucial step in the analysis of village governance. Scholars are sometimes tempted to look at national-level documents only and then contrast them with grassroots practice. In one rare piece focusing on non-electoral institutions, Su and Yang correctly point out that 'dynamic interactions between central intervention and local innovations will determine the evolutionary path of rural governance'.[3] However, usually lower-level agents do not receive national policies directly. Instead instructions are handed down step-by-step and some leeway exists at each level to adjust the policy or shift emphasis from one part of the message to another. Thus, we have to take provincial-level input into account as well.[4]

As Table 1 demonstrates, provincial governments have been busy drafting legal documents on village governance. Except for two cases (Qinghai and Tibet), all have

---

2. Somewhat in contrast to this proposition, others argue for a focus on further improving the quality of elections; see Qingshan Tan, 'Building institutional rules and procedures: village elections in China', *Policy Science* 37, (March 2004), pp. 1–22.

3. Fubing Su and Dali Yang, 'Elections, governance, and accountability in rural China', *Asian Perspective* 29(4), (2005), p. 138.

4. The same is of course also true for village election regulations; see Björn Alpermann, 'Provincial legislation on village elections', *Zeitschrift für Chinesisches Recht* 1, (2007), pp. 1–26; Qingshan Tan, 'Building democratic infrastructure: village electoral institutions', *Journal of Contemporary China* 18(60), (June 2009).

Table 1. Provincial legislation on village self-administration

Provincial-level unit	Implementation regulations (IR, *shishi banfa*): date of promulgation	Additional regulations: content, date of promulgation
Anhui	27 January 1999	Financial management (*Anhui sheng cun nei xingban jiti gongyi shiye chouzi choulao tiaoli*) (1 January 2003)
Beijing	3 August 2001	VRA (*Beijing shi cunmin daibiao huiyi guize*) (2003)
Chongqing	27 March 2002	
Fujian	28 July 2000, rev. 19 November 2005	
Gansu	26 May 2000	Publication of village affairs (*Gansu sheng cunwu gongkai tiaoli*) (1 January 2004)
Guangdong	27 November 1998, rev. 30 May 2002	Publication of village affairs (*Guangdong sheng cunwu gongkai tiaoli*) (6 June 2001)
Guangxi	1 December 2001	
Guizhou	28 November 1999	
Hainan	11 January 2001	Publication of village affairs (*Hainan sheng cunwu gongkai banfa*) (16 May 2005)
Hebei	24 September 1999	Democratic management (*Hebei sheng cunji minzhu guanli tiaoli*) (25 December 1998); Publication of village affairs (*Hebei sheng cunwu gongkai tiaoli*) (27 May 1999, rev. 15 November 2006)
Heilongjiang	10 August 2001	
Henan	29 September 2001	
Hubei	30 March 2001	Publication of village affairs (*Hubei sheng cunwu gongkai shishi banfa*) (19 March 2002)
Hunan	28 November 1999	
Jiangsu	29 June 2001	
Jiangxi	30 June 1999	
Jilin	1 March 2004	
Liaoning	30 March 2000	Democratic management and publication of village affairs (*Liaoning sheng nongcun shixing minzhu guanli he cunwu gongkai banfa*) (24 September 1998)
Nei Menggu (Inner Mongolia)	7 April 2000	
Ningxia	17 November 2000	Publication of village affairs (*Ningxia huizu zizhiqu cunwu gongkai banfa*) (12 April 1999, rev. 13 November 2006)
Qinghai	~	Villager consultation (trial) (*Qinghai sheng cun (xu) min yishi guize*) (2007?)
Shaanxi	8 September 1999	Publication of village affairs, democratic management (*Shaanxi sheng cunwu gongkai minzhu guanli banfa*) (10 December 2006)
Shandong	22 December 2000	Publication of village affairs (*Shandong sheng cunwu gongkai tiaoli*) (12 April 2006)
Shanghai	22 September 2000	
Shanxi	26 September 1999	Village assembly/VRA consultation (*Shanxi sheng cunmin huiyi, cunmin daibiao huiyi yishi guize*) (2007?)
Sichuan	21 July 2001	
Tianjin	12 September 2001	

Provincial-level unit	Implementation regu-lations (IR, *shishi banfa*): date of promulgation	Additional regulations: content, date of promulgation
Xinjiang	28 September 2001	Publication of village affairs (*Xinjiang weiwuerzu zizhiqu cunwu gongkai banfa*) (14 October 2004)
Xizang (Tibet)	~	
Yunnan	28 December 1999	
Zhejiang	22 October 1999	

Note: Only revisions after the promulgation of the final *Organic Law* in November 1998 are given. On election regulations see Björn Alpermann, 'Provincial legislation on village elections', *Zeitschrift für Chinesisches Recht* no. 1, (2007), pp. 1–26.
Sources: http://www.chinarural.org; http://law_lib.com and http://www.jlcy.gov.cn/zwgk/z2-zy/gk-0706.doc (last accessed 16 May 2008).

issued Implementation Regulations (IR) for the revised *Organic Law* and about half have promulgated rules and regulations on other aspects of village governance.[5] The focus below will be on IR because they provide the most detail on authority relations between different organs. But other regulations will also be discussed, particularly those relating to financial oversight and democratic management. As will become clear, there are important differences in the way village governance is codified in different provinces. Due to limitations of space the discussion here will only address three major areas: authority relations between the village committee and other institutional actors, village representative assemblies, and financial management and transparency of village affairs.

Authority relations

CCP branch

O'Brien and Han observe that the Chinese Communist Party (CCP) branch is the most formidable competitor for power for elected village committees. While the 1987 trial version did not even mention the CCP, the 1998 *Organic Law* clearly establishes the Party branch as the 'leadership core' among village-level organizations. Nevertheless, the Party is also required to guarantee that villagers engage in self-administration and enjoy their democratic rights. This dialectic between Party control and citizens' rights is characteristic of China's so-called 'socialist democracy'. But it leaves ample room for interpretation and, as empirical research has shown, the concern that the Party will dominate village organizations is well-founded.[6]

Eighteen out of 29 of the provinces simply replicate the clause contained in the national law in their respective IR; four fail to mention the CCP at all. Thus, Gansu, Hainan, Inner Mongolia and Yunnan revert to the practice of the trial version of not

5. To simplify matters only regulations (*tiaoli*), measures (*banfa*), and rules (*guize*) are taken into account here whereas mere opinions (*yijian*) or circulars (*tongzhi*) are left out. All official provincial documents other than IR are simply referred to as additional regulations. For exact names and sources see Table 1. A synopsis of all provincial IR is available from the author upon request.
6. Jean C. Oi and Scott Rozelle, 'Elections and power: the locus of decision-making in Chinese villages', *China Quarterly* 162, (June 2000), pp. 513–539.

including the Party in legal documents issued by the state while retaining CCP leadership via the Party's internal rules. Other provinces chose to explicitly subject the elected village committee under Party branch 'leadership' (*lingdao*), leaving no uncertainty about who is to call the shots in village governance. These are Guangdong, Shandong, Xinjiang, Hebei and Tianjin. The latter two even fail to include the clause on the CCP guaranteeing self-administration which makes their formulation appear even more unbalanced. As O'Brien and Han point out, although generally more detailed than the national law, none of the IR specify a clear division of responsibilities and authority between elected VCs and CCP branches. However, we will see that some of the provincial regulations on democratic management and publication of village affairs contain more specific rules on the role of the Party.

Township government

A second problematic authority relationship concerns relations between village committees and township governments.[7] Here the *Organic Law* is equally equivocal: it stipulates that township governments are to support and 'guide' (*zhidao*) VCs and to refrain from interfering in legally defined self-administration affairs. Still, VCs are obliged to assist township governments, which is often taken to mean that they are to implement state and Party policies delegated to them. This clause is repeated in 22 IR but many also include additional stipulations regarding the township–village committee nexus. For instance, 14 provinces require township administrations (or in some cases county governments) to conduct training for the elected VC members. This is crucial because elected village officials may not be familiar with relevant policies and procedures especially concerning financial management. However, training by higher-levels may also provide an opportunity to co-opt or unduly influence village committee members. A more direct form of control is mandated in five provinces where townships are requested to conduct oversight of village finances.[8] As Su and Yang highlight, village finances very often are in dire need of supervision. However, township administrations are not the ideal actor in this regard because villagers may perceive them as colluding with village officials to their own disadvantage.[9] Probably to dispel such concerns, Beijing is the only province that explicitly prohibits townships from seizing or handling village collective property.

Another interesting difference between provincial IR concerns tasks delegated by townships to village committees. Seven provinces explicitly allow such delegation, but five of these also stipulate that legal responsibility remains with the township government. Only in Gansu is responsibility transferred explicitly to the VC.[10] This is of significance in contentious domains such as land policy.[11] Conversion of

---

7. For instance township administrations still quite regularly interfere with village elections especially during candidate nomination; see Melanie Manion, 'How to assess village elections in China', *Journal of Contemporary China* 18(60), (June 2009).

8. These are Gansu, Henan, Hubei, Jiangsu and Xinjiang.

9. Su and Yang, 'Elections, governance, and accountability in rural China', pp. 143–146.

10. In Jilin no mention is made of legal responsibility. The other five are Fujian, Hunan, Jiangsu, Shanghai and Tianjin.

11. Also see Jin Taijun and Shi Congmei, *Xiangcun Guanxi Yu Cunmin Zizhi* [*Township–Village Relations and Villagers' Autonomy*] (Guangzhou: Guangdong Remin Chubanshe, 2002), p. 249.

agricultural land for industrial use or infrastructure projects has become one of the most controversial issues in rural China in recent years. It is vital that townships do not shirk accountability for expropriation simply by delegating these to VCs. Why Gansu bucks the trend and assigns responsibility to village committees, however, remains a mystery.

Village small groups

A third authority relation, usually not considered overly important, concerns village small groups. During decollectivization people's communes were replaced by township governments, production brigades by administrative villages, and production teams by 'village small groups' (VSG, *cunmin xiaozu*). Often these groups were formed on the basis of settlement structures, e.g. when one administrative village was subdivided into several natural villages, and quite commonly VSGs retained crucial administrative functions. For instance, in many villages agricultural land was not distributed evenly among all households but only among households of each VSG. This means that the team/small-group in fact is the owner of collective property rights over land, not the village/VC. Of course this is an area of enormous regional variation and generalizations are hard to make, but this makes it all the more worthwhile to look at IR and examine what role they assign to VSGs and whether they see them as a second level of self-administration or simply an appendage of the village.

All 29 provincial IR provide for the establishment of village small groups, mostly as an optional decision made by villagers themselves. Only in Hunan and Jilin is it implied that VSGs are mandatory, whereas in Guizhou and Sichuan their establishment requires township approval. Regarding VSG relations with other self-administration organizations, most provinces come down on the side of subordination of VSGs: 14 clearly establish leadership relations between the VC and the VSG. In Heilongjiang and Shandong VSGs are to carry out decisions by VCs but also those of the village assembly or village representative assembly (VRA). However, in Sichuan VSGs are only directed to execute village assembly and VRA decisions, while village committees are not mentioned in this context; and in Jilin VSGs are to hold assemblies of members to decide on their own affairs. This would imply a more indirect guidance relation between VSG and VC. In fact, this is what four other provinces stipulate. In Hebei, Shanghai, Shanxi and Tianjin VSGs are to 'assist the VC in its work' (*xiezhu cunmin weiyuanhui kaizhan gongzuo*)—the same expression used with regard to township–VC relations. Therefore, these six provinces can be said to give the small-group level more autonomy from the VC and to establish a second tier of self-administration.

However, it has to be added that most IR do not devote much space to this lower rung of administration. In terms of institutions, it mainly consists of one 'VSG head' (*cunmin xiaozuzhang*). This position is filled by election or selection from small-group members, a process which most often does not seem to be very formal [hence, the ambiguous expression 'selection' (*tuixuan*) instead of 'election' (*xuanju*) in most IR].[12]

---

12. Only six provinces use the term *xuanju* (Guangdong, Hainan, Henan, Jilin, Shaanxi, Shanxi), but in Shanxi this election may take place by ballot or simple show of hands. In Fujian and Sichuan both election and selection may be applied.

Wherever this is included in IR, their term or office is in synch with VC elections, but 14 IR do not contain such a stipulation. It is noteworthy that ten provinces provide that the system of publication of village affairs either is or may be extended to the VSG level.[13] This acknowledges their role in management of collective property and policy implementation, but compared with the Party branch or township government, VSGs are unlikely to rival VCs in power. Some authors are less sanguine about the institution we turn to next.

Village representative assemblies

VRAs came into existence over the 1990s as a local innovation that quickly received a positive response by Chinese and Western observers as a means to enhance village governance.[14] They appeared to close an institutional gap between village assemblies which are only held annually and the need to oversee day-to-day management of village affairs. They also were seen as an institution that would increase villagers' participation in crucial decisions. Hence, village representative assemblies were said to contribute to the realization of three of the four 'democratic rights', namely democratic management, decision-making and supervision. Accordingly, the revised 1998 *Organic Law* included VRAs as an organization to which village assemblies may delegate their decision-making and control rights. More recent research, however, has thrown serious doubt on the effectiveness of VRAs and their democratic credentials. Chan in particular criticized VRAs for being subservient to VCs and Party branches, thus giving rise to oligarchic authority structures within villages, instead of enhancing democratic participation.[15]

Checks and limitations on VRA authority

The concern that VRAs substitute for villagers' assemblies and usurp their participation rights should be taken seriously. The *Organic Law* is indeed quite sketchy about VRAs and only provides that they may be established in villages with large populations or spread-out settlement patterns where village assemblies often fail to meet the quorum requirement of over half the voters participating. Provincial IR mostly repeat this provision, but several also set up more detailed criteria concerning population size thus limiting the number of villages eligible for a VRA.[16]

Fifteen provinces simply repeat that VRAs can only be assigned certain tasks by village assemblies, but quite a few take additional precautions against VRAs becoming too dominant. Thus, Anhui, Chongqing and Beijing all require that the delegation of tasks to VRAs must be explicit. Otherwise, VRA members may only

---

13. Six include this provision in their IR: Chongqing, Hubei, Hunan, Shaanxi, Sichuan and Yunnan. Four other provinces do so in their additional village governance regulations: Gansu, Guangdong, Hainan and Xinjiang.

14. Susan V. Lawrence, 'Village representative assemblies: democracy, Chinese style', *Australian Journal of Chinese Affairs* 32, (July 1994), pp. 61–68.

15. Sylvia Chan, 'Villagers' representative assemblies: towards democracy or centralism?', *China: An International Journal* 1(2), (September 2003), pp. 179–199. Also see Björn Alpermann, *Der Staat im Dorf: Dörfliche Selbstverwaltung in China* [*The State in the Village: Village Self-administration in China*] (Hamburg: Institute of Asian Affairs, 2001), ch. 4.

16. Varying thresholds are applied in Guangdong, Jiangxi, Liaoning, Shanghai and Shanxi.

deliberate over but not pass decisions. In Hainan delegation even has to take written form. Nine provinces specify that VRA decisions must not contravene those of the village assembly.[17] Furthermore, most provinces reserve crucial privileges for the village assembly. In 16 provinces enacting village compacts or self-administration charters is under the sole purview of the village assembly and in 19 it possesses the exclusive right to recall VC members and hold by-elections. A few provinces also restrict decision-making on village development plans and the like to the village assembly.[18] As after-the-fact control, 24 provinces grant the village assembly the right to alter or nullify decisions taken by the VRA.[19] Also a third of provinces give those who voted for VRA representatives—but no other individual or organization—the right to recall and replace them.[20] And the same share of provinces demands that topics be publicized in advance of VRA meetings and members use this time to consult fellow villagers.[21] Thus, there seems to be some acknowledgement by provincial legislators that VRAs need to be controlled and restricted to prevent them from disenfranchising the rest of the village population. These are exactly the elements of direct democracy which Chan posits as necessary for the VRA system to work.[22]

Ex officio membership and the CCP

Having said that, there remain some controversial issues in the composition and conduct of VRAs. One is ex officio membership. The VRA is usually convened by the village committee which therefore also takes part in its deliberations. Nine provinces grant VC members voting rights in the VRA,[23] though in Shanghai they may only participate in a non-voting capacity, while in Inner Mongolia and Shaanxi they are expressly excluded from serving as delegates. Seven provinces automatically include VSG heads as VRA members, further blurring the line between officials and those who oversee their conduct.[24] Some other provinces incorporate delegates to People's Congresses and/or People's Political Consultative Conferences residing in the village into VRAs, sometimes in a non-voting capacity, but most often as full members.[25]

Even more problematic is the role played by the CCP branch. While only the IR of Shanghai and Tianjin automatically grant CCP branch members the right to participate in VRA meetings, Hebei's regulations on 'democratic management' also

---

17. These are Guangdong, Guangxi, Hebei, Heilongjiang, Henan, Hunan, Liaoning, Shanghai and Zhejiang.

18. This leaves seven provinces which do not limit delegation of tasks to the VRA in their IR: Beijing, Gansu, Jiangxi, Inner Mongolia, Shaanxi, Shandong and Xinjiang. However, Beijing does exclude VC elections and votes of recall as well as enacting village charters from delegation in its more detailed VRA rules.

19. All provincial IR except those from Beijing, Guizhou, Heilongjiang, Shanghai and Shanxi provide this right; but again, Beijing includes such a rule in its later VRA regulations.

20. Anhui, Beijing, Fujian, Hainan, Jiangsu, Inner Mongolia, Ningxia, Shanghai, Shanxi, Sichuan.

21. Beijing, Gansu, Guangxi, Hubei, Hunan, Jiangsu, Jiangxi, Jilin, Shanghai, Shanxi, Tianjin.

22. Chan, 'Villagers' representative assemblies', p. 197.

23. VC members are included in Guangdong, Henan, Hunan, Jiangsu, Jiangxi, Liaoning, Ningxia, Sichuan and Tianjin.

24. VSG heads are included in Hunan, Jiangsu, Jiangxi, Liaoning, Inner Mongolia, Sichuan and Tianjin. They *may* be included in Yunnan, but only in a non-voting capacity.

25. Gansu, Guangdong, Henan, Jiangxi and Ningxia include People's Congress members with voting rights, in Tianjin they *may* be included. In Hainan and Yunnan they may participate in a non-voting capacity.

require an 'appropriate share of CCP members' among VRA delegates. More worrisome still are additional regulations issued by Beijing, Hebei, Liaoning and Ningxia because these establish CCP branch control over the VRA agenda—a practice which probably is far more widespread because it is also included in a document on village governance issued by the Party and State Council in 2004.[26] According to these rules the village Party organization first collects proposals of topics to be discussed. Proposals may be made by the Party branch, the VC, the village collective economic organization or by joint motion of one tenth of villagers or one fifth of VRA members. The Party branch then holds a joint meeting with the village committee to discuss these topics and develop concrete opinions and suggestions. Lastly, the VC convenes the village assembly or VRA to decide on these proposals. The dominant role of the Party in the process is evident. For these reasons alone Chan's claim that most VRAs are subservient to village cadres seems plausible.

Among the many local innovations in village governance one is noteworthy in this respect, the 'Qingxian model', named after Qing county in Hebei. In this setup the village party secretary has to run in an election for the position of VRA chair and resign as secretary if unsuccessful. Also the VRA is made into a permanent decision-making body. Closer scrutiny of village affairs and more participation in important decisions should thus be possible. Nevertheless, it is hard to see this innovation as a launching pad for increased democratization.[27] If we keep in mind that in Hebei VRAs should comprise 'an adequate share of CCP members' and their agenda is controlled by the Party branch, this model instead appears to strengthen the CCP vis-à-vis the village committee via additional control of a Party-dominated assembly. In this respect it is more reminiscent of the Chinese People's Congress system than of Western-style democracy. To place this innovation in context, it is useful to recall that CCP secretaries often concurrently serve as chairpersons of People's Congresses without the congresses becoming hotbeds of democratization.[28]

Relations with VCs

Further support for Chan's claim that VRAs are becoming subservient to village cadres is provided by the fact that several provinces request that VRAs assist VCs in carrying out tasks. Apart from five provinces that do so in their IR, Beijing and

---

26. Zhonggong Zhongyang Bangongshi, Guowuyuan Bangongting [CCP Central Committee Office and State Council Office], *Guanyu Jianquan He Wanshan Cunwu Gongkai He Minzhu Guanli de Yijian* [*Opinions on Promoting and Perfecting Village Affairs Publications and Democratic Management*], (22 June 2004), available at: http://news.xinhuanet.com/zhengfu/2004-07/12/content_1591421_1.htm (accessed 16 May 2008).

27. According to Su and Yang, 'Elections, governance, and accountability in rural China', p. 154, '[a]mong these new innovations, the "Qingxian model" is closest to Western-style democracy, where parties are only vehicles to power', but they hasten to add that the CCP is unlikely to give up its political dominance any time soon.

28. Currently, at the provincial level 23 out of 31 party secretaries also serve as People's Congress chairs; see 'China data supplement—May 2008', *China aktuell*, pp. 30–36, available at: http://www.giga-hamburg.de/dl/download.php?d=/content/ias/archiv/cds/cds_0805.pdf (accessed 16 May 2008). Also see Young Nam Cho, 'From "rubber stamps" to "iron stamps": the emergence of Chinese local People's Congresses as supervisory powerhouses', *China Quarterly* 171, (September 2002), pp. 724–740. On, however, benefits for legislative development that arise from party secretaries leading local People's Congresses, see Kevin J. O'Brien, 'Chinese People's Congresses and legislative embeddedness: understanding early organizational development', *Comparative Political Studies* 27(1), (April 1994), pp. 80–107.

Qinghai include such a clause in separate regulations on village governance.[29] A dual role of representing constituent interests while also helping control the same constituency and making sure it complies with policy is in line with Chinese political thinking. The same reasoning of building 'bridges' between officialdom and the masses is often applied to societal organizations.[30] However, it is equally clear that such an approach may easily lead to a reversal of roles with VRAs ending up as instruments of control in the hands of village cadres instead of villagers.

Nevertheless, six provinces grant the village assembly or VRA significant rights in relation to the VC. For instance, five provinces provide that the VC cannot independently decide on the composition of its own subcommittees on such matters as mediation or public security. Instead subcommittee members are to be proposed by the VC and approved by the village assembly or VRA, the latter being the more likely scenario.[31] In Hubei, VRA representatives may participate in VC meetings in a non-voting capacity. And in Jilin ten VRA delegates may, through a joint motion, force an audit of village accounts on the VC. However indirect, all these stipulations may afford VRAs some measure of control vis-à-vis village committees and help make them more independent.

Qualifications

A final point of criticism is that some provinces establish criteria for becoming a VRA delegate that infringe upon the right of every villager to run for office. The same question has also stirred debate regarding VC elections.[32] Eight provinces list numerous qualifications for VRA delegates in their IR. Additionally, Beijing, Hebei and Qinghai adopted similar provisions in their rules on VRAs and democratic management. Apart from favoring elites who are educated and possess a 'competence for political consultation' (*you yishi nengli*), these qualifications beg the question of who controls their enforcement.[33]

Quorum and decision-making rules

On a more positive note, all provinces establish clear quorum and decision-making rules for VRAs which had been missing in the national legislation. On the other hand, these rules evince a bewildering degree of variation: in three provinces more than half of VRA members are sufficient to establish a quorum, while decisions are passed with simple majority of *all* those eligible to cast a vote.[34] In 21 provinces two-thirds of VRA members are required to establish a quorum, but decisions are passed with

---

29. The five are Heilongjiang, Hubei, Jiangsu, Liaoning and Xinjiang.

30. Jonathan Unger, '"Bridges": private business, the Chinese government and the rise of new associations', *China Quarterly* 147, (September 1996), pp. 795–819.

31. In Chongqing, Guangdong, Guangxi, Ningxia and Yunnan the VRA is directly mentioned in this context, while in Hunan this privilege is listed under the village assembly, but may be delegated to the VRA.

32. Richard Levy, 'The village self-government movement: elections, democracy, the Party, and anticorruption—developments in Guangdong', *China Information* 27(1), (2003), p. 30; Alpermann, 'Provincial legislation on village elections', pp. 4–5.

33. Chan, 'Villagers' representative assemblies', p. 189.

34. This is the case in Hainan, Liaoning and Yunnan.

either a simple majority of those present, two-thirds of those present or (most commonly) more than 50% of all those eligible to vote.[35] Three provinces do not establish a quorum rule, but require that all decisions need a simple (in Jiangxi and Ningxia) or even a two-thirds majority of *all* VRA members (in Hebei). To create even more confusion, a quorum is set at three-quarters of representatives in Shandong, while decisions are passed with a simple majority of all members. And for certain decisions—those on contributing money or labor to collective projects—Anhui requests four-fifths of VRA members be present and two-thirds of all representatives vote in favor. In brief, these examples demonstrate that formal institutionalization has progressed in recent years as more specific rules have been passed. However, provincial legislators apparently pay little attention to standardization across provinces.

Financial management and transparency

A final area of institutionalization is financial management and transparency, both of which pertain to villagers' right to 'democratic supervision'. The 1998 *Organic Law* mandated that certain village affairs need to be publicized at least twice a year. The focus of this 'village publication system' (*cunwu gongkai zhidu*) is financial matters, although other sensitive issues such as birth planning and land distribution are included, too. This emphasis has been reiterated in the 2004 national-level document cited above which also spelled out procedures more clearly. This circular mandated a higher frequency of publication, namely quarterly for regular notification and even monthly for financial data in villages with considerable collective property. In this it followed the lead of 13 provincial IR which had already stipulated that all or at least financial items be publicized every three months. The center also adopted another local innovation, namely specialized control groups consisting of villagers to supervise either financial accounts or all publicized items (called *licai xiaozu* or *cunwu gongkai jiandu xiaozu*). These control groups were already mandatory in 16 provinces and optional in another six before the 2004 circular was issued.[36] While publication aims to enhance transparency and thus raise trust in the probity of village leaders, control groups serve the purpose of checking the veracity of published items and especially financial aspects of village governance.

Members of control groups are either selected by the village assembly or the VRA and may also be recalled. Village committee members or their spouses and close relatives are generally excluded from serving, although only Ningxia and Shandong exclude CCP branch members as well. Several provinces grant villagers' control groups explicit rights and privileges to help them conduct oversight. For instance, in Shandong, Shanghai and Guangxi group members may participate as observers in VC meetings concerning financial matters. In Guangxi, Ningxia and Shaanxi the group may veto 'unreasonable' (*bu heli*) expenses which then have to be covered by the

---

35. The first is the case in Guangxi, Guizhou, Hubei, Hunan, Jiangsu and Xinjiang; the second in Inner Mongolia, Tianjin and Shaanxi (the latter according to its additional regulations). The third applies to Anhui, Beijing, Chongqing, Fujian, Gansu, Guangdong, Jilin, Heilongjiang, Henan, Shanghai, Shanxi, Sichuan and Zhejiang.

36. This takes IR as well as additional provincial regulations into account. That means there were only ten provinces without any regulations on establishing villagers' control groups.

person responsible; and a number of provinces specifically grant control groups the right to inspect not only accounts but also original receipts to verify each transaction. Significantly, these rights have also been adopted in the center's 2004 circular. Thus, at least according to formal procedures, villagers' control groups possess substantial leverage over village cadres. That said, the center also spelled out more clearly the process of publication and assigned a crucial role to the CCP branch. The village committee is to issue a publication plan which is inspected by the control group. The group may make additions or corrections which are in turn discussed by the Party branch and VC in a joint meeting resulting in a final plan to be executed by the VC. Again, the dominant role of the CCP in village governance is evident in these detailed provisions.

Finally, it is unclear to what extent villagers' control groups can actually exercise supervision and some available evidence points to low levels of villagers' trust in the accuracy of transparency-related publications.[37] Based on fieldwork in Henan and Guangdong, Levy concluded that the effects of different village-level systems on combating corruption have so far been limited. Nevertheless, he also highlighted increasing institutionalization not only of elections but also of other parts of the grassroots self-government agenda.[38]

Conclusion

Village elections have attracted the bulk of international attention devoted to political reforms in rural China. As an experiment with more democratic forms of governance in a one-party state, self-governance is significant in its own right and remains a worthy subject of scholarly inquiry. As several studies have shown, these elections have had an important impact on villagers' political efficacy and trust and have broadened 'access to power'.[39] However, their significance for the everyday lives of China's villagers remains limited without complementary reforms in other aspects of governance. As O'Brien and Han argued in their assessment, the 'exercise of power' in Chinese villages has not yet received appropriate research attention, although—as this article has demonstrated—there is significant institutional reconfiguration underway with regard to what is called 'democratic decision-making, management and supervision'. To contribute to the analysis of evolving governance mechanisms this study mainly confined itself to examining provincial-level legislation in an effort to show that institutionalization in this procedural dimension of the exercise of power has been substantial. Local experiments with new institutions have been taken up in implementation regulations and additional rules and measures promulgated at the provincial level before being adopted in national policy documents. In this way,

---

37. Su and Yang, 'Elections, governance, and accountability in rural China', p. 149; David Zweig and Chung Siu Fung, 'Elections, democratic values, and economic development in rural China', *Journal of Contemporary China* 16(50), (February 2007), p. 42.

38. Richard Levy, 'Village elections, transparency, and anticorruption', in Elizabeth J. Perry and Merle Goldman, eds, *Grassroots Political Reform in Contemporary China* (Cambridge, MA: Harvard University Press, 2007), pp. 44–47.

39. Lianjiang Li, 'The empowering effect of village elections in China', *Asian Survey* 43(4), (July/August 2003), pp. 648–662; Melanie Manion, 'Democracy, community, trust: the impact of elections in rural China', *Comparative Political Studies* 39(3), (April 2006), pp. 301–324; John James Kennedy, 'Legitimacy with Chinese characteristics: "two increases, one reduction"', *Journal of Contemporary China* 18(60), (June 2009).

provincial legislation has played a significant role in linking micro- and macro-levels in policy-making.

Western studies of village elections have shown a penchant for micro-level, empirical analysis with only the occasional study directed at either the macro- or meso-levels.[40] Without downplaying the work done so far, this article contends that valuable insights can be gained by looking at middle-range developments. This study has done so through the lens of provincial legislation, which until recently would have been exceedingly hard to come by. Today, these sources are available to researchers worldwide over the Internet and they should be used more systematically. This wealth of data, however, can only be analyzed employing a division of labor. In this sense, the current study points to some possible directions for future research.

Of course, new post-election procedures are far from perfect—be it in their institutional design or their application—and much more empirical research is needed to examine their effects on village governance. For instance, do different quorum and decision-making rules for VRAs affect participation in decision-making? Can villagers' control groups exercise real checks on cadre malfeasance? And what are the effects that these post-election instruments of self-government have on villagers' trust or efficacy? One particularly problematic area for study remains, unsurprisingly, the role of the CCP. Some governance institutions discussed above appear to strengthen the Party branch vis-à-vis other village actors. If so, this is certainly *not* an unintended side-effect, but the very idea behind these governance reforms. In the end, a perennial question remains: can there be meaningful democratization under the current one-party system? This question will continue to be debated for some time. In my view, while recognizing the democratic potential inherent in village self-government, we need to acknowledge that Party dominance is not just an unfortunate flaw in the current system of village governance. It is what this system is built to maintain.

---

40. This is to say that the unit of analysis is usually either the village or the individual. For an exception focusing on the macro-level see Kevin J. O'Brien and Lianjiang Li, 'Accommodating "democracy" in a one-party state: introducing village elections in China', *China Quarterly* 162, (June 2000), pp. 465–489; on the meso-level see Tianjian Shi, 'Village committee elections in China: institutionalist tactics for democracy', *World Politics* 51(3), (April 1999), pp. 384–412. Interestingly, in this issue Manion is arguing for more 'reliable, nationally representative sample surveys', while Schubert claims that '[w]e definitely need more qualitative research stretching out over longer intervals' and proposes to concentrate on the local state (village, township and county). See Manion, 'How to assess village elections in China', and Gunter Schubert, 'Studying "democratic" governance in contemporary China: looking at the village is not enough', *Journal of Contemporary China* 18(60), (June 2009).

Building Democratic Infrastructure: village electoral institutions

Village elections are presently at a crossroad: processes and rules still must be improved and further delays will only undermine the credibility of village elections. This paper adopts a historical perspective and an institutional approach to argue that reform of village electoral institutions is still a top priority in rural political development. It argues for the creation of a national electoral commission tasked with implementing, supervising, and adjudicating village elections. It then discusses the rationale for initiating candidate-initiated and candidate-centered elections and proposes altering campaigning as well as the 'two majority' rule. Last but not least, I advocate the synchronization of election dates. A fixed election date, at the provincial level if not nationally, would enhance the importance of elections, attract more media coverage, and foster civic culture.

Kevin O'Brien and Rongbin Han's article offers a meticulous survey of the literature on village elections and rural grassroots self-government.[1] After reviewing improvements and remaining problems, the authors raise two important points: village elections in many locations have yet to democratize basic-level governance; and village democracy amounts to much more than the conduct of free and fair elections every three years.

While not disagreeing with their overall assessment, this paper adopts a historical perspective and an institutional approach to argue that reform of village electoral institutions is still a top priority in rural political development.[2] Historically, rural China, of course, lacked a democratic tradition. Even though governance in the countryside was largely autonomous, local politics was dominated by elites and was shaped by the gentry, clans, and kinship. Most clan and kinship organizations were hierarchical and undemocratic. Mao's communization of rural production and governance indeed diminished rural autonomy and broke the traditional elite's hold

---

1. Kevin J. O'Brien and Rongbin Han, 'Path to democracy? Assessing village elections in China', *Journal of Contemporary China* 18(60), (June 2009).

2. An earlier version of this article was presented at the international conference on *Villagers' Self-Government and the Building of a New Socialist Countryside: Celebrating the 20th Anniversary of the PRC Organic Law of Village Committees*, Huazhong Normal University, Wuhan, China, 16–17 June 2007.

on power, but at the same time it imposed top-down Party control. Commune members were nominally masters of their own destiny but political participation was largely mobilized and passive. After decommunization, the state withdrew from village governance thereby creating a power vacuum in the countryside. At that point, some villagers decided to elect their own leaders. When those first elections began, villagers knew nothing about electoral rules and procedures. Since then, democratic rules and principles have been introduced and improvements have gradually brought village elections near to international standards. Self-governance has come a long way since the initial experiments commenced some 20 years ago.

Elections of village committees (VC), seen against China's long tradition of rural elitism and authoritarianism, is only the beginning of a long democratic transition at the grassroots. During this transition, the top priority for rural governance is building a democratic infrastructure, starting with electoral institutionalization.[3]

Village elections are presently at a crossroad: processes and rules still must be improved and further delays will only undermine the credibility of the entire reform effort. Many scholars, officials, and election practitioners in China believe that rural self-government has graduated from the electoral stage and should move on to a focus on democratic management, supervision, and decision making.[4] While this paper does not argue against this notion, better elections remain the crux of spreading democratic culture, and further democratization requires, above all, the institutionalization of electoral rules, procedures, and implementation.

This paper argues for the creation of a national electoral commission tasked with implementing, supervising, and adjudicating village elections. It then discusses the rationale for initiating candidate-initiated and candidate-centered elections and proposes altering campaigning as well as the 'two majority' rule. Last but not least, I advocate the synchronization of election dates. A fixed election date, at the provincial level if not nationally, would enhance the importance of elections, attract more media coverage, and foster civic culture.

Creating election commissions

Current electoral institutions, consisting mainly of central and local laws and regulations, do not say much about enforcement and adjudication. Civil service officials at the Ministry of Civil Affairs (MoCA) have been left responsible for election implementation and provincial and local civil affairs officials are responsible for conducting elections.

Despite their efforts to promote village democracy, putting the MoCA and its local bureaus at the center of the electoral process is problematic. First, the MoCA's dual

---

3. This priority does not preclude the importance of traditional social networks such as clans in contributing to rural political development during this long transition. See Gunter Schubert, 'Studying "democratic" governance in contemporary China: looking at the village is not enough', *Journal of Contemporary China* 18(60), (June 2009).

4. On formal institutionalization of democratic decision-making, management and supervision in village affairs, see Björn Alpermann, 'Institutionalizing village governance in China', *Journal of Contemporary China* 18(60), (June 2009).

role as implementer and adjudicator makes it difficult to avoid conflicts of interest. The MoCA helps formulate election laws and regulations, supervises nationwide implementation of rural balloting, and is empowered to interpret the law and handle election complaints. It is thus in the bureaucratic interests of the MoCA to retain its grip over elections and minimize bad publicity concerning election disputes. At the same time, MoCA officials depend on county and township governments to conduct balloting, meaning it must maintain a close working relationship with local officials.[5] When villagers have complaints about the fairness or manipulation and appeal directly to the MoCA for adjudication, the MoCA usually chooses to stay on the sidelines and reroutes complaints back to local civil affairs offices or local governments. The MoCA's hands-off approach and unwillingness to offend local officials suggests a need for an independent electoral commission capable of adjudicating electoral disputes.[6]

Bureaucratic interests have also led to a hodgepodge of electoral rules and processes, making it difficult to establish uniform implementation practices. Village elections have attracted national and worldwide attention and have given civil affairs officials a highly-visible platform for career advancement. Among civil affairs officials at various levels, some are truly enthusiastic about self-governance, some are more opportunistically motivated.[7] Regardless, they have generally supported election initiatives and innovations. In the process, many different rules and procedures have come into being. Because the national *Organic Law* is silent on most election details, many of these rules are inconsistent and do not conform to international election standards.

A separate and independent election commission is also needed simply because the MoCA is under-staffed and unable to oversee implementation of self-governance throughout the country. At the central level, the Division of Basic-Level Governance and Community Construction has only six staff members and two division heads. At lower levels, provincial departments and local bureaus of civil affairs seldom have more than two full time staff members working on village self-governance. Village elections are only a small component of local civil affairs work, and tasks such as 'building a new socialist countryside' or disaster relief sometimes crowd it out.

For all these reasons, it would be wise to create an independent national electoral commission and provincial electoral commissions. Despite the early successes of a ministry-centered approach, the MoCA should now use its influence to propose legislation establishing these commissions. Bureaucratic agencies are of course loathe to give up power, but existing arrangements run the risk of compromising the integrity of village elections. Reform along these lines would greatly reduce the involvement of townships in village elections, and make voters less dependent on government guidance and initiative.

---

5. For a detailed account of the MoCA's relationship with local officials, see Qingshan Tan, *Village Elections in China: Democratizing the Countryside* (New York: The Edwin Mellen Press, 2006), ch. 4.

6. One explanation for the role played by officials in the Ministry of Civil Affairs is that they employed an incremental approach that focused on implementation first and quality later. See Tianjian Shi, 'Village committee elections in China: institutionalist tactics for democracy', *World Politics* 51(3), (April 1999), pp. 385–412.

7. For an insightful study of MoCA officials' motives, career paths, and networking, see Long Yonxing, *Making Democracy Work: The Crafting and Manipulation of Chinese Village Democracy by Political Elites*, unpublished Ph.D. dissertation, National University of Singapore, 2004.

Allowing candidate-initiated nomination

In recent years, *haixuan* nomination has become commonplace. *Haixuan* was developed in Lishu, Liaoning as a method to nominate candidates without restrictions. A new 'one-time' version of *haixuan* permits the original nomination process to determine the election outcome, if the top nominee receives a majority of nomination votes and more than half of eligible voters have participated.[8] Only when the nomination process produces no top nominees who pass this so-called 'two majority test' will a formal election be held. This method has been gaining popularity recently, especially in Jiangsu, Zhejiang, Chongqing, and Guizhou, because technically it does not violate the two majority requirement, it is cost-effective, and it cuts the number of times villagers must come together to vote. Some officials also argue that it stimulates voter interest and sense of responsibility, reduces corruption associated with the nomination process, and makes it more difficult for township officials or village elites to manipulate elections.[9]

This 'short-cut', however, creates several problems in practice. First, many *haixuan* voters vote without knowing whether their preferred nominee is willing to serve. Voters thus run the risk of selecting someone who may not agree to hold office. This has happened in the past.[10] Second, if *haixuan* nomination proceeds without formal candidates, voters must depend on their prior knowledge of potential candidates. Third, in one-time *haixuan* elections, voters do not have an opportunity to hear from candidates after they are chosen, since there is no time for campaigning.

Some provincial regulations have addressed these issues. For example, Chongqing requires that villagers who want to run for VC positions register their candidacy with the village election committee (VEC). VECs then publicize candidate names in the order of the number of strokes of their last name five days prior to balloting. Candidates then have a chance to declare their desire for a specific VC position in a speech at meetings organized by the VEC. Villagers finally vote for self-declared candidates. If no candidates win a majority, the exercise becomes a primary in which the top vote-getters automatically become candidates in the formal election.

One-time *haixuan* can reduce multiple rounds of voting, thus saving time and money without sacrificing democratic principles and quality. However, to do this, it must meet two conditions: those who intend to serve must declare their candidacy and they have to campaign. The current arrangements for campaigning only provide voters limited access to candidates. Both candidates and voters would benefit from the formulation of detailed campaign rules which establish channels to interact. Vigorous campaigning would also enable voters to focus on candidates' qualifications and ideas and reduce the likelihood that villagers cast 'blind' votes.

Without formal candidates and campaigning, voters also sometimes elect VC members who do not get along with each other, which can render a VC ineffective. In Anhui, an experiment has been conducted to address this problem. It allows VC chair

---

8. Wang Zhenyao *et al.*, eds, *Zhongguo Cunmin Zizhi Qianyan* [*The Frontier of Chinese Village Self-Governance*] (Beijing: Zhongguo shehui chubanshe, 2000), pp. 90–97.

9. Lin Pingshun, 'Haixuan is an institutional innovation', *People's Daily*, (23 June 2004). See also, 'Villagers haixuan chiefs', available at: http://www.chinainnovations.org/showNews.html?id=3d5389ae85d711dcbc4d11ffd792b910.

10. Author's observation in Dongfeng County, Jilin, 13 March 1998.

candidates to select other VC members. An earlier version of this method was known as the 'combined election system of village committees' (*jingxuan zugezhi*).[11] The creator of this model, Xin Qiushui, who is a long-time researcher and practitioner of rural politics, believes that this model could remedy the shortcomings of *haixuan* nomination and lessen the influence of township officials and village clans, and produce a unified committee whose members support and are responsible to the VC chair.[12] Villagers would also be better able to hold the village committee accountable for its decisions. Compared to the traditional *haixuan* process, Xin's method would likely reduce infighting among VC members, because they would no longer be elected on their own merits and by different groupings in a village. Xin's experiment has received strong support from the Anhui provincial government, including former Party Secretary Lu Rongjing.[13]

Xin's experiment, however, has so far been confined to Anhui, partly because the MoCA and provincial civil affairs officials have not whole-heartedly supported it. They view Xin's model as violating the *Organic Law*, insofar as the law stipulates that every VC member be elected, not appointed. Owing to Xin's reputation and support he has received from some central and provincial leaders, MoCA officials have not opposed his experiment, but they have discouraged its spread. Xin later modified his model to accommodate the *Organic Law* by requiring that VC chair candidates nominate their own slate of VC candidates; the whole slate would then be subject to election. This revised model was used to conduct elections in Yuexi County in 1995 and Laian County in 1998.[14] More recently, Xin's model has gained momentum from a proposal at the National People's Political Consultative Conference advising the central government to adopt the model.[15] Although the proposal was sent back to Anhui, Xin's experiment was extended to the whole province for the 2005 village elections.

A candidate-centered election process has significant advantages. In an electoral system without party competition, voters can only choose individual candidates. Xin's model enables a VC chair nominee to present a slate of candidates who share similar views and who get along. This may also encourage VC chair candidates to better take into account the competence, clan background, and popularity of other nominees they put forward and run with. Lastly, a candidate-initiated process precludes the possibility of electing someone who does not want to serve and increases the likelihood that those who are running for office will put their heart into getting elected.

---

11. For a detailed description of the model, see Xin Qiushui, '"Jingxuan zugezhi" de shijian yu lilun—Cunweihui minzhu xuanju moshi de zhongda chuangxin' ['"The practice and theory" of a combined election system of village committees—an innovative model of democratic election of village committees'], *Xueshujie* [*Academics in China*] 5, (2001), pp. 45–54.

12. Author's interview with Xin Qiushui, Hefei, Anhui, 11 August 2003.

13. Zhang Chunsheng, *Wenhua fuping yu cunmin zizhi* [*Cultural Alleviation of Poverty and Village Self-Government*], a document titled 'A Combined Election System of Village Committees', internal publication, Hefei, Anhui, 15 January 2001, p. 13.

14. Bai Gang and Zhao Shouxing, *Xuanju Yu Zhili* [*Election and Governing*] (Beijing: Zhongguo shehuikexue chubanshe, 2001), pp. 170–172.

15. Former Anhui Party Secretary Lu Rongjing coauthored the proposal. See, Zeng Jianhua, '"Combined election system of village committees" is better than haixuan', (26 March 2005), available at: http://www.chinaelections.org/NewsInfo.asp?NewsID=10459.

Establishing candidate-centered campaigning

With a few exceptions, candidate-centered campaigning is uncommon in rural China. In national and provincial regulations, rules regarding campaigns are markedly few and vague. Neither the 1998 *Organic Law* or provincial election regulations provide detailed guidance. Many local implementation guidelines only allow the introduction of candidates by village election committees; some go further and permit candidates to make a speech to voters on election day.

In practice, posters or election speeches are the most common forms of campaigning. Comparatively few candidates campaign actively. Most candidates simply rely on village election committees to publicize their personal information.[16] Others make a brief speech at a rally on election day. The latter seems to be popular in villages where mass voting is held: candidates typically read a prepared statement outlining their background, experience, and what they will do to fix village problems. Occasionally, candidates answer questions, but few solicit probing questions.[17]

One difficulty with most election speeches is that they give voters little or no time to mull over a candidate's worthiness. In smaller villages where villagers know all their neighbors, they may not need much information to assess candidates, but in larger villages and in villages where elections are highly competitive, campaigns would make a difference in helping voters make up their minds.

In recent years, informal campaigns sometimes include visits to voter homes, banquets, clan networking, and even vote-buying.[18] Some of these developments can be attributed to the lack of rules on campaign funding. In the absence of guidelines, better-off candidates are spending more of their own money campaigning.

MoCA officials remain skeptical about Western-style campaigns, and regard them to be destabilizing and disruptive.[19] They tend to see self-initiated campaigns as challenges to officially guided elections and a source of controversies and disputes harmful to social stability. Officials also fear that campaigns could inspire enthusiasm for Western-style democracy and lead to overly rapid democratization. In 2001, the MoCA published a handbook that explained that 'village election campaigns have a fundamental difference from partisan campaigns of western countries'.[20] In fact, officials from the MoCA carefully avoided the word 'campaign', instead using the phrase 'village governance speech' (*zhicun yanshuo*) or 'publicity' (*xuanchuan*). Most provincial regulations that set out campaign rules adopt the same phrases; very few mention 'campaigning'.[21]

---

16. In this case, candidate information, often a simple biography, was either posted or broadcast on radio and closed-circuit television a few days before the election.

17. For a description of a candidate's election speech, see, Thomas L. Friedman, *The Lexus and the Olive Tree* (New York: Farrar Straus Giroux, 1999), pp. 60–61.

18. For a list of emerging election issues, see O'Brien and Han, 'Path to democracy?', footnote 47.

19. In my interviews, local officials often equated campaign with *luan* (chaos); some referred to campaigning as a 'political show'.

20. Minzhengbu jiceng zhengquan he shequ jianshesi [Ministry of Civil Affairs, Department of Basic-Level Government and Community Construction], *Zhonghua renmin gongheguo cunmin weiyuanhui xuanju guicheng* [*Handbook of Villagers' Committee Election of People's Republic of China*] (Beijing: Zhongguo shehui chubanshe, 2001), p. 74.

21. Excepting the Anhui election method, which specifically allows candidates to campaign provided they apply and accept the supervision of village election committees. Minzhengbu jiceng zhengquan he shequ jianshesi nongcunchu [Ministry of Civil Affairs, Rural Division of Department of Basic-Level Government and Community

Campaign rules are an important precondition of free and fair elections. Detailed and transparent standards can reduce bribery, vote-buying, and gift-giving, all of which are widespread in today's China.[22] Better campaign rules could also provide guidance for enforcing standards throughout the country. For instance, detailed campaign rules could specify the types of vehicles allowed, the volume of loud speakers, television access, debate procedures, rules for campaign funding and financing, street rallies, and campaign organization. But more importantly, campaign rules could promote orderly but competitive elections that draw voters' interest and participation.[23]

Current electoral institutions limit candidate-centered elections and campaigns in several ways. The *Organic Law* puts village election committees in charge of elections and only permits individual candidates to compete. This in essence discourages organized campaigning, whether by candidates or organizations. Beyond the *Organic Law*, township governments and election committees have the authority to define the scope of 'organized campaigns'. In Anhui, owing to Xin Qiushui's influence and support from the province, local officials have experimented with candidate-centered campaigns. Even there, however, candidates had to persuade the VEC to allow self-nomination. Upon becoming candidates, they also had to overcome the obstacle of campaigning for a full slate of VC candidates. If VECs nationwide adopted a more tolerant approach to candidate-initiated campaigns, candidates would run more informative and competitive campaigns. If VECs continue to impose restrictive campaign rules, then there is not much candidates can do to get their message out.[24]

Candidate-centered campaigns would also require new rules concerning competition and campaign financing. Rules are needed to provide candidates with a legal basis for running campaigns and usage of media, types of public rallies, public displays, transportation, loudspeakers, and so on. The current election rules do not cover campaign financing, because candidate-centered competitive campaigns are not common and traditional campaigns (e.g. door-to-door visits) do not involve large expenses. Currently, county, township, and villages all contribute to election funds, but not campaign financing. Given fiscal realities in poorer counties and townships, some villages do not have enough money to run elections, let alone provide for campaign financing. Progress in this regard will probably require that provincial governments set aside election funds and entrust provincial election commissions to ensure that each village election has similar support.

Footnote 21 continued

Construction], *Gesheng, zizhiqu, zhixiashi cunweihui xuanju banfa huibian* [*Compilation of Village Committee Election Methods of Provinces, Autonomous Regions, and National Cities*] (Beijing: An internal publication, 2002), p. 59.

22. Baogang He and Youxing Lang, *Xunzhao Minzhu Yu Quanwei De Pingheng: Zhejiang Cunmin Xuanju Jingyan Yanjiu* [*Seeking a Balance between Democracy and Authoritarianism: A Study of Villagers' Election Experience in Zhejiang*] (Wuhan: Huazhong shifan daxue chubanshe, 2002), pp. 270–278.

23. See Qingshan Tan, 'Building a village electoral institution: issues and policy recommendation', paper presented at the international conference on *Village Self-government in China: Past, Present and Future*, Ministry of Civil Affairs and European Union, Beijing, China, 5–7 April 2006, pp. 413–414.

24. For two well-publicized campaigns, see *Zhongguo Qingnian Bao* [*Youth Daily*], (15 January 2003 and 15 August 2001).

Changing the two majority rule to a plurality rule

Although the 1987 *Organic Law* did not mention the decision rule for a valid election, MoCA officials established a majority rule in their national guidelines and presented it as an 'insurmountable criteria of election'.[25] Their thinking was that this would encourage voter turnout and provide a democratic mandate for the winner. The 1998 *Organic Law* changed the criteria again and introduced a new two majority rule. In Article 14, it stipulated that an election is valid if more than 50% of registered voters vote *and* candidates are considered elected only when they win more than 50% of votes cast. This requirement is an improvement from the previous one of 50% plus one of the eligible votes of the entire village. However, it still results in a considerable number of run-offs in villages where votes are close and write-in candidates are popular.[26] It also causes problems in villages where election organization is weak and low turnout rates are common. Election officials then must struggle to mobilize additional voters to avoid a run-off election or to participate in it.

Lawmakers originally backed the two majority requirement because they argued that the legitimacy of an election derived from majority participation and that elections must reflect the will of most villagers. In proposing the legislation, MoCA officials and legislators took it as a matter of principle and set up the requirement without considering its feasibility. In reality, the two majority requirement is impractical as officials and voters find it difficult in many places to generate the two majorities. In order to produce a valid election, electoral officials often then resort to other means to boost turnout.

Local election officials often manipulate voter registration to meet the first majority requirement. In villages where a large number of villagers have left to become migrant workers, village electoral officials often de-register those who are not present. This practice often results in disfranchising eligible voters. A related issue arises in villages where there are many non-resident workers; election officials sometimes try to register non-residents, even though they are ineligible to vote. Their argument is that they are part of village life and have a stake in who leads the village. The real motive, however, is typically to get non-residents to vote in order to meet the first majority requirement. To legalize this practice, some provinces in recent years have devised rules that allow non-residents to vote if they meet a time test.[27]

Local election officials also promote the use of proxies and roving ballot boxes to boost turnout. Provincial regulations permit proxy voting, but generally restrict it to no more than two or three proxy votes per family. Election officials do not always enforce these restrictions because they often need proxy votes to meet the second majority requirement. Even in village election implementation standouts, such as

---

25. Li Xueju, *Zhongguo chengxiang jiceng zhengquan jianshe gongzuo yanjiu* [*Research on the Construction of Basic-Level Governance in Urban and Rural China*] (Beijing: Zhongguo shehui chubanshe, 1994), p. 90.

26. Voters can write in candidates. In some villages I observed, voters split their votes among several write-in and formal candidates. At the end of the day, no candidate could win a clear majority of votes. As a member of a Carter Center Delegation, I observed village elections in Fujian, Hebei, Hunan, Jilin, and Liaoning in 1997 and 1998. Last-minute write-in candidacies spoiled some elections as leading candidates fell just short of the 50% needed to win.

27. See, He Xiaohong, 'Cunmin zizhi yu nongmingong de zhengzhi canyu' ['Village self-government and political participation of rural migrant workers'], paper presented at the international conference on *Villagers' Self-Government and the Building of a New Socialist Countryside: Celebrating the 20th Anniversary of the PRC Organic Law of Village Committees.*

Jilin and Hunan provinces, voting via proxies or roving ballot boxes have accounted for more than 10 and 27% of the total votes cast, respectively. In other provinces, the percentage is often even higher.[28]

The two majority requirement has enhanced villagers' dependence on election officials and provided opportunities for electoral manipulation. To address these issues, a plurality rule could be adopted. It would help preserve the integrity of elections, simplify election procedures, and be cost-effective. Village officials would not have to connive to artificially boost turnout, and could instead focus on ensuring that elections were procedurally sound and truly reflected the will of the voters. The savings in time and resources would be large with fewer run-offs.[29] This would have many benefits in locations where as many as six separate elections are needed to meet the two majority requirement.[30]

Synchronizing election dates within a province

Another procedural issue is the lack of synchronized election dates. Most provincial election guidelines do not set election dates, leaving local authorities to do so. Provincial governments usually issue circulars that instruct local election officials to hold elections within a certain period, ranging from one month to one year. It is up to the county or township government to set specific dates for each election.[31] In some cases, village election committees select election dates.[32] In many provinces, each round of elections lasts for up to a full year.[33] Long election seasons produce election fatigue and place burdens on understaffed civil affairs bureaus.[34]

The rationale for a long election season is that balloting should take into account farmers' seasonal demands.[35] Still, it is feasible to have a single election date within a province. Seasonal patterns do not vary much within a province. The real reason for official reluctance to set a fixed election date is that provincial civil affairs officials must rely on local governments to conduct elections. For local officials, a single election date means that they will not be able to supervise elections village by village, thus endangering their control over the process.

Election dates could be synchronized around seasonal breaks, such as Spring Festival, when farming duties are light and family members return home. Beyond a

---

28. Author's interview with civil affairs officials in Inner Mongolia and Henan, August 2003 and July 2004. See also, Tan, *Village Elections in China*, ch. 6.

29. In my interviews, the majority of the interviewees agreed and expressed a desire for a plurality system.

30. Author's interview with civil affairs officials in Inner Mogolia and Henan, August 2003 and July 2004.

31. For a selection of provincial, county, and township election rules and methods see Mingzhengbu Jicengzhengquan Jianshesi, *Zhonghua renmin gongheguo cunming weiyuanhui xuanju gongzuo fanli* [*People's Republic of China Village Committee Election Implementation Cases*] (Beijing: Zhongguo Shehui Chubanshe, 1996).

32. Research Group on the System of Rural Villagers' Self-Government in China and China Research Society of Basic-Level Governance, *Study on the Election of Villagers' Committees in Rural China: Research Report on Villagers Self-Government 1993* (Beijing: Zhongguo Shehui Chubanshe, 1994).

33. This was the case in several provinces, including Fujian, Hunan, Hebei, and Jilin, where I observed village elections.

34. In our observation of Fujian elections in March 1997, we asked about the possibility of obtaining more election results and were told that elections had just started and the province's elections would not be completed until the end of the year.

35. I raised the election date issue with MoCA and local officials, but was told that it was impossible to have synchronized election dates since they would unduly impose burdens on farmers.

province, synchronization would be problematic, unless the *Organic Law* was revised and an inter-provincial election body was created to standardize election rules and supervise elections, but this could be resolved if a national election commission was established. At a minimum, provinces with a similar climate and similar farming schedules could all have elections on the same day.

Synchronization of election dates within provinces or even within a region is both desirable and cost-effective.[36] Synchronization would enable election officials to organize effective and uniform civic education and election training, but more importantly, a fixed election date every three years would enhance democratic culture in the countryside. Synchronized election dates would help foster civic consciousness and promote political participation and feelings of empowerment.[37] A province-wide election date would also enable the media to concentrate on elections and play a bigger role in publicizing a major provincial event.[38]

A fixed date is cost-effective because it would save time and manpower.[39] Synchronization would reduce costs associated with provincial mobilization and education and would also make it more efficient for election officials to conduct oversight. This experiment could be jumpstarted by selecting a few provinces to hold elections on the third or fourth day of Spring Festival. After evaluating the results, synchronization could be institutionalized in provincial election laws.

Conclusion

Improving election rules and procedures is an important part of institutional building; it regulates the behavior of involved parties, lowers transaction costs, and enhances institutional credibility. Village elections have been taking place for two decades now and rules and norms continue to evolve. While considerable progress is obvious, some rules and procedures are outdated (or have unfortunate unforeseen consequences) and should be revised.

Further improvement is crucial. An independent electoral commission would enhance electoral professionalism and scale back the role of the Ministry of Civil Affairs in conducting elections. The impartiality and expertise of such a commission would help minimize fraud and enhance electoral credibility. Rule improvements surrounding candidate-initiated campaigning and election synchronization would require amendments to the *Organic Law* or a new national election law. A new village election law embracing the proposed rules would help institutionalize village elections further and develop China's democratic infrastructure.

---

36. Qingshan Tan, 'Building institutional rules and procedures: village elections in China', *Policy Sciences* 37(2), (2004), pp. 1–22.

37. Scholars have argued that regular and voluntary elections provide a good avenue for the development of citizenship practices. See, Kevin J. O'Brien, 'Villagers, elections, and citizenship in contemporary China', *Modern China* 27(4), (2001), pp. 407–435.

38. The decision by Dong Feng County in Jilin to synchronize village elections struck us as an excellent way to conduct a countywide civic education campaign using television and radio advertising during a concentrated period. The Carter Center Report, 1998.

39. One of the recommendations made in the 1998 Carter Center report was to synchronize election dates at the country level to improve opportunities for civil education and reduce the cost.

Power to the People? Villagers' self-rule in a North China village from the locals' point of view

ZONGZE HU

This article examines ethnographically the implementation of the Organic Law *and practice of 'villagers' self-rule' in a North China village from 2003 to 2004. Based on in-depth interviews and participant observation, it recounts the election of a villagers' committee and the functioning of a 'democratic supervisory small group'. It shows that critical disparities exist between what Chinese policymakers and many scholars argue for on the one hand (for instance, enhancing cadre accountability, empowering ordinary villagers, and promoting grassroots democracy), and how most villagers view the actual practices on the other. It concludes that the locals' negative views are not idiosyncratic, the vision of 'rule by the people' remains difficult to take root, and that local metaphors are resourcefully used to make sense of newly-introduced practices.*

Market-oriented reforms have brought remarkable changes to China's rural areas since the late 1970s. The post-Mao reforms and grassroots political reforms in particular are characterized as 'complex' and 'incremental'. At an early stage, striking economic growth was accompanied by radical changes in local power arrangements and in everyday interactions between cadres and ordinary villagers. In many places, cadre–mass relations deteriorated; party-state apparatus was paralyzed; and political stability was under serious threat. Largely to cope with such a crisis in rural authority and state legitimacy, Chinese officials began to promote the 'villagers' self-rule' (*cunmin zizhi*) countrywide. The 'villagers' committee' (*cunmin weiyuanhui*) that originated as a grassroots institutional innovation was made the key component of *The Organic Law of Villagers' Committee of the People's Republic of China* (promulgated in November 1998, a trial version in 1987).[1]

The *Organic Law* sets out to enforce villagers' self-rule in all rural areas. It stipulates that the villagers' committee is a self-ruling grassroots mass organization by which villagers manage their own affairs, and educate and serve themselves. The *Law* formulates a clear objective of promoting grassroots democracy in rural China, and emphasizes 'democratic elections' (*minzhu xuanju*) and 'democratic supervision' (*minzhu jiandu*) of the villagers' committee, besides 'democratic decision-making' and 'democratic management' (Articles 1 and 2). Crucial to the policymakers' agenda, and at least theoretically, the *Organic Law* provides an institutional framework to enhance cadre accountability as well as empower ordinary villagers to make their own decisions, thereby improving village leadership and grassroots governance.[2] Villagers are entitled to directly choose among themselves those who are impartial, honest and upright, and public-spirited to be chairman, vice-chairman, and members of their villagers' committee in free, fair, and periodic elections. Those elected are expected to help protect villagers' lawful rights, boost local economy, and improve the public good. In addition to the villagers' assembly and the villagers' representative assembly, the 'open management of village affairs' (*cunwu gongkai*) is recommended as a way to restrain the daily behavior of village cadres and render them accountable to their constituents. How has the *Law* been implemented at the grassroots level and affected specific communities afterwards? What are the differences between this official agenda and local participants' actual views of the implementation?

A growing body of literature has examined the emergence and incremental development of villagers' self-rule, with a clear focus on direct elections of the villagers' committee. With a few exceptions, the researchers all to a certain degree suggest that effective enforcement of the *Organic Law*, and especially direct elections of the villagers' committee, are the key to making incumbent cadres more responsive to

---

1. On the evolvement and enforcement of the *Organic Law*, see Zhongguo jiceng zhengquan jianshe yanjiuhui, eds, *Zhongguo nongcun cunmin weiyuanhui huanjie xuanju zhidu* [*Study on the Election of Villagers' Committees in Rural China*] (Beijing: Zhongguo shehui chubanshe, 1994). For the examination of its formulation and complex implementation process in English literature, see for example: Kevin J. O'Brien, 'Implementing political reform in China's villages', *Australian Journal of Chinese Affairs* 32, (July 1994), pp. 33–59; John Dearlove, 'Village politics', in Robert Benewick and Paul Wingrove, eds, *China in the 1990s* (Vancouver: UBC Press, 1995), pp. 120–131; Daniel Kelliher, 'The Chinese debate over village self-government', *The China Journal* 37, (January 1997), pp. 63–86; Jorgen Elklit, 'The Chinese village committee electoral system', *China Information* 11(4), (1997), pp. 1–13; Xu Wang, 'Mutual empowerment of state and peasantry: grassroots democracy in rural China', *World Development* 25(9), (September 1997), pp. 1431–1442; Zhenyao Wang, 'Village committees: the basis for China's democratization', in Edward B. Vermeer, Frank N. Pike and Woei Lien Chong, eds, *Cooperative and Collective in China's Rural Development: Between State and Private Interests* (Armonk, NY: M.E. Sharpe, 1998), pp. 239–252; Jude Howell, 'Prospects for village self-governance in China', *The Journal of Peasant Studies* 25(3), (April 1998), pp. 86–111; Lianjiang Li and Kevin J. O'Brien, 'The struggle over village elections', in Merle Goldman and Roderick MacFarquhar, eds, *The Paradox of China's Post-Mao Reforms* (Cambridge: Harvard University Press, 1999), pp. 129–144; Tianjian Shi, 'Village committee elections in China: institutionalist tactics for democracy', *World Politics* 51(3), (April 1999), pp. 385–412; and Kevin J. O'Brien and Lianjiang Li, 'Accommodating "democracy" in a one-party state: introducing village elections in China', *The China Quarterly* 162, (June 2000), pp. 465–489.

2. For the agenda and efforts of Chinese officials, particularly those at the mid-level of the official hierarchy and those serving in the Civil Affairs bureaus, see for example: O'Brien, 'Implementing political reform in China's villages'; Kelliher, 'The Chinese debate over village self-government'; Howell, 'Prospects for village self-governance in China'; Tianjian Shi, 'Village committee elections in China'; and Suzanne Ogden, *Inklings of Democracy in China* (Cambridge, MA: Harvard University Press, 2002), pp. 183–220.

ordinary villagers' demands and ousting those who are corrupt, incompetent, and unpopular. Using regional or national data, they posit a positive correlation between the quality (i.e. the degree of openness, fairness, and competitiveness) of village elections and the performances of cadres. The improvement of village elections and villagers' self-rule in general is depicted as an important way to change the structure in rural governance. Along these lines, some positively hold that democratization is under way in the Chinese countryside, despite many obstacles. As villagers' civic and democratic consciousness rises, the entire political system will slowly change toward democracy from the bottom up.[3] For instance, Xu states that villagers' self-rule is an 'experimental form of democracy' with Chinese characteristics.[4] Unger argues that 'democracy is creeping into previously taboo areas', as village elections expand.[5] Levy points out that the new discourse and mechanisms of village self-rule include progress toward 'popular democracy', with the potential to undermine the existing power structure.[6] Howell anticipates that villagers' enthusiastic support of direct elections will create a more representative system and participatory culture.[7] O'Brien maintains, when Chinese villagers recast the official discourse of democratic elections to challenge improper practices, they have direct elections as an opportunity to claim their citizenship.[8] Wang even predicts that the Chinese form of self-rule reveals a peaceful and orderly democratic transition, a different pathway to democracy from that as presented in Western mainstream democratic theory.[9]

On the whole, scholars have presented an overall picture of, and useful data on, village elections and villagers' self-rule in rural China. They have generally used, however, an institutional approach to detect cross-regional features and patterns. What remains to be done is ethnographic case studies of how the *Organic Law* and villagers' self-rule have been carried out in a specific village community. Given the immense sociocultural differences among various regions in rural China, it is crucial to highlight local particularities and provide concrete examples of real people at the mundane level. More importantly, scholars have seldom thoroughly examined what

---

3. In addition to the aforementioned articles, see for example: Xu Yong, *Zhongguo nongcun cunmin zizhi* [*Villagers' Self-Rule in Rural China*] (Wu Han: Huazhong shifan daxue chubanshe, 1997); Zhang Hou'an, Xu Yong, Xiang Jiquan *et al.*, *Zhongguo nongcun cunji zhili* [*Village Governance in Rural China*] (Wu Han: Huazhong shifan daxue chubanshe, 2000); Jin Taijun and Shi Congmei, *Xiangcun guanxi yu cunmin zizhi* [*Village Relations and Villagers' Self-Rule*] (Guangzhou: Guandong renmin chubanshe, 2002), pp. 162–193; Melanie Manion, 'The electoral connection in the Chinese countryside', *American Political Science Review* 90(4), (December 1996), pp. 736–748; Amy B. Epstein, 'Villager elections in China: experimenting with democracy', in US Congress, Joint Economic Committee, *China's Economic Future: Challenges to US Policy* (Washington, DC: Government Printing Office, 1996); Robert A. Pastor and Qingshan Tan, 'The meaning of China's village elections', *The China Quarterly* 162, (June 2000), pp. 490–512; Baogang He, 'Village elections, village power structure, and rural governance in Zhejiang', *American Asian Review* 20(3), (Fall 2002), pp. 55–89; Baogang He, 'Are village elections competitive? The case of Zhejiang', in Joseph Cheng, ed., *China's Challenges in the Twenty-first Century* (Hong Kong: City University of Hong Kong Press, 2003), pp. 71–92.

4. Xu Yong, *Zhongguo nongcun cunmin zizhi*.

5. Jonathan Unger, *The Transformation of Rural China* (Armonk, NY: M.E. Sharpe, 2002), p. 221.

6. Richard Levy, 'The village self-government movement: elections, democracy, the party, and anticorruption—developments in Guangdong', *China Information* 17(1), (2003), pp. 28–65.

7. Howell, 'Prospects for village self-governance in China'.

8. Kevin J. O'Brien, 'Villagers, elections, and citizenship', in Merle Goldman and Elizabeth Perry, eds, *Changing Meanings of Citizenship in Modern China* (Cambridge, MA: Harvard University Press, 2003), pp. 212–231.

9. Xu Wang, 'Mutual empowerment of state and peasantry'.

villagers' self-rule and village elections really mean to grassroots participants themselves.[10] We have yet to present the locals' own views of villagers' self-rule, particularly their interpretations of the election and supervision of a villagers' committee; and such views are of critical importance to our theoretical reasoning.[11] To what extent do residents in a village community regard the villagers' committee as a mass organization and a way to empower ordinary people? Do they feel 'democratic election' and 'democratic supervision' is the key to holding cadres accountable and a crucial step toward grassroots democratization? To address these issues thoroughly, the researcher needs to conduct intensive field research, build significant trust with the locals, and gain a deep understanding of local histories and cultural practices.

This article has grown out of such an ethnographic project. Based on long-term field studies and in-depth interviews, it recounts the election process of a villagers' committee in August–October 2003, and the functioning of a 'democratic supervisory small group' (*minzhu jiandu xiaozu*) until August 2004 in Ten Mile Inn, a North China village.[12] By presenting the locals' views on these practices, it reveals that a gap exists between the expectations and interpretations of Chinese policymakers and many scholars on the one hand, and the ways in which ordinary villagers understand their actual practices on the other. The 2003 direct election was pretty free and fair, at least quite competitive; but for many participants, it is not an effective way to choose popular and competent cadres. It does not restrain cadre behavior or increase accountability, as structural accounts of institutional change nearly always imply. The democratic supervisory small group is intended to improve cadre accountability, a key step in building grassroots democratic institutions; but many locals discount it. The villagers' committee is actually perceived as a village-level government by which officials rule the ordinary people, instead of a mass organization by which villagers manage their own affairs, as the *Law* stipulates.

The article is divided into four sections. The first section introduces the village community; the following two sections detail the process and impacts of 'democratic election' and that of 'democratic supervision', respectively. The concluding section addresses the implication of villagers' self-rule.

Field research in Ten Mile Inn

The village of Ten Mile Inn is located at the eastern foothills of the Taihang Mountains, about 375 miles southwest of Beijing, and falls under the jurisdiction of Dongshi Township, Wu'an County, Hebei Province. The village has 2,115 people, 602 households, and 13 village small groups. Although many youths manage to find employment in non-agricultural fields, there is no collectively owned enterprise.

The village has traditionally been a multi-lineage community, and today has 20 surnames for local household heads. The Wangs were the earliest settlers; this lineage

---

10. A few exceptions are: Ogden's *Inklings of Democracy in China* (pp. 211–216); and John J. Kennedy, 'The face of "grassroots democracy" in rural China: real versus cosmetic elections', *Asian Survey* 42(3), (May/June 2002), pp. 456–482.

11. Due to its scope, in this article I have left out the issue of 'democratic decision-making' and 'democratic management'.

12. I am indebted to the villagers, who offered honest answers in my numerous interviews. For their protection, I have left out all their real names. The name of the township has also been changed to ensure anonymity.

is the biggest, comprising about 50% of the village population. Those surnamed Fu have two different ancestors, and comprise about 20% of the households. Another big lineage, Li, has about 100 households. The Zhang lineage has about 30 households. Each of the remaining surnames has only several households.

From the beginning of its settlement until the early 1960s, a large field divided the village into two *de facto* hamlets, the Upper Fort and the Lower Street. Largely based on territorial cults, the Lower Street, despite geographically an entity, was socially and politically further divided into the North Area and the South Area. Since their first settlement in 1526, the Wangs have lived close together in the South Area, while the majority of Lis have resided in the Upper Fort. One Fu lineage has settled in the Upper Fort; members of another Fu have mostly resided in the North Area. Despite the Chinese party-state's intermittent attempts to discourage popular rituals, members of the same lineage or lineage branch have held weddings, funerals, and Chinese New Year festivities together. Meanwhile, the keen competition among residents of the three different neighborhoods in performances at regular temple festivals and annual Chinese Lantern festivities has contributed to their strong localistic identities. The Upper Fort residents in particular have shown strong solidarity, and once attempted to break from the Lower Street residents to build their own village.

From the early 1990s, as many residents moved into new houses built on newly assigned lands, the field dividing the Upper Fort and Lower Street disappeared. Despite such mixed residency, villagers still strongly identify with their own lineage, lineage branch, and neighborhood, and conform to their past habits, whenever there is an important ritual or competition among lineages, lineage branches, or neighborhoods. As we shall see, this long-acting crosscutting identity will greatly influence village elections.

From 1947 to 1948, Isabel and David Crook studied land reform in the village.[13] To examine changes in the local power structure, I conducted intermittent sociological studies there from 1997 to 1999, when I lived in the village office building and closely observed the daily operations of the fourth villagers' committee. I revisited the village in the summers of 2000 and 2001. In June 2000, I had a chance to observe the election of the fifth villagers' committee, and talked to a range of participants. I conducted my dissertation fieldwork there from August 2002 until August 2003, shortly before the election of the sixth villagers' committee. In the summer of 2004, I returned to the village mainly to examine the 2003 election. I conducted in-depth interviews with all villagers who had competed to become candidates for the villagers' committee, and talked to adults of different ages, social standing, education levels, occupations, political factions, and positions in lineages. I paid close attention to the arguments and counter-arguments of two 'factions', one led by Fu Shuanjin from the North Area and another by Fu Qingguo from the Upper Fort. I also observed the founding and operation of the democratic supervisory small group. This article is based on that period of research, but it also benefits greatly from the previous field trips. Trust and intimacy, born of long-term field research, are

---

13. Isabel Crook and David Crook, *Revolution in a Chinese Village: Ten Mile Inn* (London: Routledge & Kegan Paul, 1959); and Isabel Crook and David Crook, *Ten Mile Inn: Mass Movement in a Chinese Village* (New York: Pantheon Books, 1979).

crucial in examining local factions and collecting the locals' frank remarks on village politics.

Village election in 2003: practices and participants' comments

On 9 August 1984, the first villagers' committee was established in Ten Mile Inn to replace the previous brigade committee. The residents elected its chairman, vice-chairman, and members. But the election was only for show, as were the ensuing three elections that generated the second, third, and fourth villagers' committees in March 1989, January 1994, and July 1997. In each election, the village party branch committee chose the candidates and submitted the list to the township government for approval. The list had more candidates than the actual positions of the committee, but except for those sure to serve on the committee, all the rest were either very old or sick, and unlikely to receive any vote. Even if these people, along with some villagers who were not listed, did receive a few votes, the election results would not be different. Every time, the working personnel urged voters to elect only those whom the party branch committee wanted. More than half of the final ballots were collected from roving boxes, and were actually filled out by the working personnel. There was not much difference for the villagers' representative assembly. It had been established since 1994, but it was also the party branch committee that appointed the members.

One month after the promulgation of the *Organic Law* in 1998, the Rural Work Department of the Hebei Provincial Party Committee released its *Regulations on Village-Level Democratic Management*. The *Regulations* underscore the need to build an institutional system for grassroots democratic management, and highlight the role of 'democratic election' and 'democratic supervision' of the villagers' committee. Meanwhile, the Provincial Civil Affairs Bureau pushed Wu'an county officials to hold more open and direct elections. The county officials conducted some experiments in 1999, and began to enforce direct elections for all villages in 2000. In June, therefore, Ten Mile Inn residents elected their villagers' committee through direct election for the first time. The 2003 election to be detailed followed the basic procedures of the 2000 election, although there were some differences, which I will discuss shortly.

In May 1999, the village party secretary who had served in the position for more than a decade was ousted, after several villagers, including the village chairman, filed reports to higher authorities on his embezzlement of village funds. The chairman and another deputy party secretary, Fu Shuanjin, fought for the vacancy, and Shuanjin finally won. Once in the new position, Shuanjin ousted the chairman, the vice-chairman, and two members of the fourth villagers' committee. To build up his own power, he appointed Wang Ping deputy party secretary and Zhang Shun village accountant, and chose Fu Qingguo to be manager of the village's electrical facilities. These three men had never been involved in village politics, yet the appointments were backed by the township's cement factory director and finance committee chairman. These two officials, who are brother-in-laws and relatives of the three new cadres, planned to pull strings from behind the scenes. With their secret support and

Shuanjin's maneuver, all three were successfully elected to the fifth villagers' committee in 2000. Qingguo, to his own great surprise, became village chairman.

Upon their dismissal, however, the fourth village chairman and several others lodged a series of reports on Shuanjin's mishandling of a village factory and his violation of family planning policies. Shuanjin was soon removed from his party secretary post in July 2000, just two weeks after the village election. The deputy secretary Ping became secretary. Ping, the accountant, and the newly elected chairman Qingguo took over the village leadership; they were called the 'Clique of Three' (*san ren xiao jituan*) because of their close collaboration. Thanks to Ping's arrangements, the other two joined the Chinese Communist Party without the mandatory period of probation. After the 2000 election, the aforementioned cement factory director made his 16-year-old nephew village treasurer, who soon collaborated closely with the Clique of Three. While the two township officials had the final say on many village issues, the Clique stopped listening to their original promoter Shuanjin. Shuanjin was annoyed at such disrespect, and plotted to regain the village leadership. This was the backdrop to the 2003 election that was characterized by keen competition between the two factions, one headed by defender Qingguo and the other by challenger Shuanjin. The electoral process could be divided into four main stages.

Stage one: electing the villagers' representative assembly

As before, in late June 2000, the party branch committee and the fifth villagers' committee chose the candidates of villagers' representatives for all 13 villager small groups. The cadres then convened a meeting for each group and asked participants to vote symbolically by a show of hands. Most villagers showed up just for the one *yuan* allowance, but this was to change in the 2003 election thanks to the *Procedures on Villagers' Committee Elections in Hebei Province*, which became effective on 1 November 2002. Wu'an county officials were forced to adopt more democratic procedures in all major stages of village elections, including that of formation of the villagers' representative assembly.

Against this backdrop, 42 representative seats were divided among 13 villager small groups according to their sizes. On the rainy morning of 28 August 2003, the party secretary Ping announced the decision over the village loudspeaker, and encouraged villagers to elect their representatives. Village cadres were divided into teams and sent to hold elections in each small group. Every household was asked to send a delegate to a designated place to write on a ballot the names of the villagers whom s/he wanted to be representatives for her/his small group. Voters could nominate anyone who was over 18 and stayed in the village most of the year, and those receiving the highest votes became representatives. It was at this stage that the secret contest between the two factions started to surface.

As the Clique of Three, under pressure from township officials, had to let villagers elect their representatives by secret ballot, Shuanjin heard that the upcoming villagers' election committee would be elected by these representatives for the first time as well. A close ally of the Clique organized the election in the first small group, and urged voters to re-elect the three representatives picked by the Clique before. Further annoying several voters, he counted the ballots at a secret place, and two more ballots appeared than the actual number of voters. Hoping to gain control over the villagers' election committee, Shuanjin, the challenger of the Clique, urged his supporters to file complaints with the township government. Township officials agreed to hold another election, but never followed through. Meanwhile, in the ninth group to which the party secretary Ping belonged, the organizer wanted to use a roving ballot box but was dissuaded by a Shuanjin supporter. The election had to be held twice since one more ballot appeared than the actual number of voters in the first round. In the end, Ping was not elected as a representative of his group, while Shuanjin successfully won a seat in his group.

Stage two: formation and operation of the villagers' election committee

The morning after the 42 representatives were elected, they were convened to elect, by secret ballot, a villagers' election committee that was to have a chairman, a vice-chairman, and seven members. Each one could nominate up to nine villagers, and those receiving the highest votes would serve on the committee. Two township officials oversaw the election, while emphasizing that Ping should be elected chairman. During the voting, the Clique tried an abortive trick. When the representatives arrived at the meeting place one after another, the Clique recorded their names and distributed to each of them a piece of paper. After they began to write their candidates' names on the paper, a Shuanjin supporter suddenly noticed that the number '21' was on the back of his ballot. He checked with a representative nearby and found that that person's ballot was marked number '24'. He immediately called for suspension of the voting, causing a commotion among the representatives. Apparently, it was a trick to match voters with their ballots. Shuanjin and several other representatives forced the Clique to re-distribute new pieces of paper for voting. Finally, the vice-chairman of the fourth villagers' committee received the highest votes and became chairman of the first elected villagers' election committee. Ping's votes only ranked third, and he could only be made vice-chairman.

The election committee took full charge of the election until the formation of the sixth villagers' committee. The fifth villagers' committee had no right to intervene, although its chairman Qingguo succeeded in joining the election committee. A majority of villagers creatively used the metaphor of *liku fang* and *dangjia de* to poke fun at the election committee and its chairman. In the area, a *liku fang* (lit. chamber of gifts and goods) is founded upon a person's death and disbanded right after the burial. It comprises the person's (his or her husband) close lineage members, and is led by the *dangjia de* (head of the person's lineage branch/lineage). The *liku fang* officiates the entire funeral, while the deceased's family members, including the mourning sons and daughters, must follow all its directions. In full command of the ritual, yet only temporarily, *liku fang* is a perfect metaphor for the election committee.

After its formation, members of the committee received training on election procedures. Then, they began to prepare a full list of eligible voters. The preliminary list came from the villagers' residence records, but to make sure that the list was accurate and up to date, they posted it on village walls for public scrutiny. They made and numbered five ballot boxes. They selected some villagers' representatives as vote readers, vote recorders, and vote supervisors for the 'primary election' (*chuxuan*), and publicized it by hanging such posters as 'seriously carrying out the election of villagers' committee' all over the village. They also distributed voters' identification cards to each household and informed them of the election date.

Stage three: nominating candidates for the villagers' committee

As the preparation was underway, those planning to become candidates for the villagers' committee were busy campaigning, largely in secret. About 20 villagers (all male), including all incumbent cadres, participated in the competition. Each told me that the other participants paid several home visits, door to door, to almost all local residents, but denied that he had done the same. They all claimed that they spoke only to close lineage members, friends, and relatives, the so-called *ziji ren*. Ordinary villagers, however, insisted that all participants had campaigned by paying home visits, yet no one had ever mentioned what he would do if elected. Campaigners usually visited a villager's house in the early morning or at night to avoid attention. A typical scenario went like this. The campaigner would hesitate at first, trying to cotton up to the host for a while, and then say: 'You know, the election of the villagers' committee is coming, and I want to serve on it. I haven't planned to visit your house. But all other people are running around. So I thought I should also come by to ask you to vote for me on the election day'! Older campaigners would add, 'You see, I am old and unable to get other jobs. So please do me a favor and vote for me so that I can make a living by serving on the villagers' committee'. The host would answer, 'Don't worry! I'll definitely give you a vote'!

At the beginning, I was puzzled about why participants felt ashamed to admit their campaign efforts. I soon learned that local people all have negative feelings about such secret efforts, and there is no positive term for campaigning. Their general impression about this period is that it was 'bustling with activity' (*nao honghong*) and 'teeming with chaos' (*luan*). They regard the campaign efforts as 'running for votes' (*paopiao/lapiao*), 'playing little tricks' (*gao xiao dongzuo*), 'doing underground work' (*gao dixia gongzuo*), or 'running about and ganging up' (*gao chuanlian*), all used in a derogatory sense. They also use the metaphor of 'paying New Year visits' (*bainian*) to deprecate the campaigners. The campaigners' home visits in the early morning, door to door, closely resemble the ways in which local inferiors (those of younger age and generation) must prostrate themselves to their superiors at every Chinese New Year.

As the primary approached, competition between the two factions (the Clique and its allies versus Shuanjin and his supporters) intensified. Drawing upon terms that had been popular during the Cultural Revolution, villagers called the first faction 'power-holders' (*dangquan pai*) because its key members were cadres in office. The latter was named 'rebels' (*zaofan pai*) since they planned to overthrow the Clique and regain power. Shuanjin succeeded in persuading several incumbent cadres and the election committee chairman, all his former opponents in 2000, to join his faction.

On 15 September, a date set by township officials, everything was ready for the nomination of candidates for the sixth villagers' committee. Around 8 am, more than

20 township officials arrived at the village office building where the election committee members were waiting. Soon afterwards, over the village loudspeaker, the chairman urged voters to go to their designated polling stations with their voter IDs. Voters from the first to third village small groups should gather at the grain supply center; those from the fourth to sixth at the village theater, the central polling station; those from the seventh and eighth at the primary school; those from the ninth, tenth, and thirteenth at the veterinary center; and those from the eleventh and twelfth should gather in the Upper Fort. The election committee members, the working personnel, and township officials were also divided into five groups. The committee members would officiate at the stations, while the officials would supervise the election process.

When organizers were preparing at the stations, voters started to arrive in twos and threes. The mass voting started around 9 am, after more than half of the voters had shown up at each station. The election took the form of 'sea election' (*haixuan*) and secret ballot. The committee members first read aloud some document that states the importance of village elections for grassroots democracy and details the electoral process laid out in the *Hebei Procedures on Villagers' Committee Elections*. Each voter was to receive a blank ballot bearing the Township Election Committee's stamp, and might nominate up to nine villagers who were over 18. The nine nominees receiving the highest number of votes would become candidates for the seven-member villagers' committee. Since some voters were illiterate, any literate person was allowed to help fill out up to two ballots as long as the illiterate were present. After explaining the election procedures, the committee members asked the voters to choose vote reader, vote recorder, and vote supervisor by a show of hands. Ballot boxes were opened so that voters could see that no one had cast a vote yet. The committee members then called out the voters' names according to the final voter registration list. One family after another, voters presented their voter IDs, received blank ballots, and filled them out at the polling booths, i.e. three separate desks at each station. Basically, a family voted together at one desk, and it was hard for them to see what others were writing at the other two. After the ballot was dropped into a box nearby, each voter was given one *yuan* as allowance. Some returned home immediately, while others stayed and waited for the results. The working personnel counted the ballots on the spot, and compared the number to that of blank ballots distributed earlier. At each station, the ballots collected were fewer than those distributed, so the election was valid. Then, the vote reader read aloud the nominees' names; the recorder recorded and counted them on a board; the supervisor stood nearby, making sure that the names on the ballots match those on the board. They had to have a group consultation before voiding any ballot. The voters staying behind stared at the board intently, and burst into laughter whenever a child or bedridden villager was nominated. After counting the votes, the working personnel all gathered at the central station for a final tally. The election committee chairman then announced the results over the village loudspeaker. The names of the first nine nominees and the numbers of votes they received were also posted on village walls.

Besides Qingguo, who received the most votes, the other six members of the fifth villagers' committee all became candidates for the new committee. Shuanjin, head of the faction of 'rebels', received the fourth highest number of votes. His close ally, the election committee chairman, ranked tenth and did not become a candidate because his name had been invalidated on more than 50 ballots. At each polling station, the organizers were supposed to remind voters to specify the sex and village small group of their nominee on the ballots, if the nominee had the same name as another villager. The chairman was in charge of the central station, but he did not bring up the issue to the voters who were from his own neighborhood, the South Area, and most likely to nominate him. Many voters, therefore, did not specify his group number. Another villager happened to have the same official name as his, although the man was mainly known by a different nickname. In the end, more than 40 ballots were voided at that single station. Amazed at this result, the chairman's supporters demanded that he be added as an extra candidate. Despite a letter signed by more than 100 voters, township officials turned down the request and simply told them to nominate him again in the formal election if they still wanted to.

Stage four: electing the villagers' committee

Some campaigners tried to remain neutral before the primary. Soon after it, all nine candidates clearly sided either with the 'power-holders' or the 'rebels'. The competition between the two reached its peak before the formal election on 1 October. That morning, voters again gathered at the five polling stations to cast ballots. The election followed the basic procedures of the primary, and the one key difference was the ballots. This time, the candidates' names appeared on each ballot in a sequence based on the number of votes each had received in the primary. Three blank rows were shown below the names. In the first row, a voter was expected to draw a circle below the name of the candidate whom s/he wanted to be the chairman. In the second row, s/he would draw a circle below the man whom s/he chose as vice-chairman. In the third row, s/he would draw up to five circles, one below each man whom s/he wanted to be a committee member. Voters were not allowed to choose the same person twice. If a candidate lost the race for chairman or vice-chairman, those votes would be added to any that he received for the membership position. A voter could also nominate any villager over 18 whose name did not appear on the ballot.

The result was beyond the candidates' expectations. To be elected as a committee member, one must receive more than half of the valid votes. In fact, only the leaders of the two factions received more than the requisite 488.5 votes. Qingguo was re-elected village chairman and Shuanjin became the vice-chairman. None of the other seven candidates received enough votes to become a committee member. Shunguo, a key member of the Clique, happened to get 488 votes. Those supporting his faction were distressed by his exclusion by only half a vote, yet members of Shuanjin's faction gloated at his misfortune. Surprisingly, 286 voters re-nominated the election committee chairman, this time with his village group number clearly identified.

Article 19 of the *Hebei Procedures on Villagers' Committee Elections* stipulates that before the formal election, a candidate *may* (my emphasis) inform voters of his/her plans if elected, and answer their questions. The township government did not allow these optional campaign speeches, although several villagers requested them. Article 29 requires that another election must be held if fewer than three people are elected and cannot form a villagers' committee, but the township party secretary did not authorize such an election. To make matters worse, township officials dissuaded Shuanjin from serving as vice-chairman only five days after the election, since he could not get along with Chairman Qingguo and Party Secretary Ping.[14] Villagers made fun of the election by teasing Qingguo as the 'leader of an "illegal" villagers' committee of which he was the only member' (*guanggan siling*).

Local interpretations: advantages and disadvantages of direct village elections

The locals' views on village elections have largely been shaped by the grassroots practices mentioned above, rather than from theoretical reasoning. They draw a clear distinction between formalistic elections before 2000, known as 'recommendatory elections' (*tuixuan*), and the 2000 and 2003 'direct elections' (*zhixuan*).

As discussed above, the Chinese party-state has been promoting direct village elections to enhance cadre accountability and improve grassroots democracy. The 2003 Ten Mile Inn election was indeed quite free and fair. It was a 'sea election', with two more candidates than the number of committee positions in the formal election. Secret balloting was used to some extent. But how do local participants view such an election? Do they see it as a way to improve village leadership? What are their opinions on its relationship to democracy? In my interviews, I found that a great majority of villagers, especially those of poor education, tended to emphasize the negative aspects, and were reluctant to admit any positive side even when I questioned them closely. Many were quite indifferent to village elections, but before I discuss the majority view, I will first address the more positive minority opinion.

Some knowledgeable residents suggested that direct elections are beneficial to the village, at least theoretically, because their purpose is to choose cadres of 'great ability and moral integrity' (*decai jianbei*) and to remove the mediocre, incompetent, and corrupt. One reason defender Qingguo defeated his opponent Shuanjin, they insisted, was his virtue. It is widely admitted that Shuanjin was more capable than Qingguo. Shuanjin was dedicated to his work, and had rich experience from his many years of involvement in village politics. That he successfully persuaded several of his former opponents in 2000, including the election committee chairman, to join his faction showed his abilities in political maneuver; but he made arbitrary decisions and acted willfully on his own. As his nickname 'little dog' implied, he was deemed a rascal. He would have arrogated all power to himself and no one could have overseen him, had he been elected the chairman. By contrast, Qingguo is an honest and gentle person in word and deed. He admitted openly that he lacked the talent and political experience to bring substantial change to the village. In his first term, he made no major contribution to the public good, but he cleaned the street garbage by himself, instead of spending village funds on hiring people. Many who voted for him were 'choosing the best cornstalk to make a rifle barrel', in other

---

14. After over two years of maneuver behind the scenes, Shuanjin was successfully elected as chairman of the seventh villagers' committee and regained the village party secretary post in 2006. Although Jingguo, Shuanjin's opponent, managed to become vice-chairman, he was the only person from the Clique to serve as part of the village leadership. Being unable to get along with the previous 'rebels', now 'power-holders', Jingguo left the position. Shuanjin's complete control over the village leadership concluded the battle between the two factions.

words, making the best out of a rather limited pool. Another metaphor they used to describe their choice was that they would accept the draught animal as long as it did not kick and bite.

Some educated locals argued that village cadres would make more efforts, even unsuccessful ones, to improve the public good and try to 'do practical things' (*ban shishi*) for the residents, if they were directly elected. The desire to be re-elected would make cadres feel more psychological pressure and a sense of responsibility. Villagers could see firsthand that the members of the fifth villagers' committee did not behave as arrogantly and bureaucratically as previous ones, but tried to be friendly in daily interactions. The cadres confirmed such observations. They, and Qingguo in particular, pointed out that they had tried to bring prosperity to local residents, paid more attention to ordinary folks, and had once attempted to defend their fellow villagers' lawful interests against orders from the township government. As they put it, 'We do not feel guilty because we haven't treated the voters unfairly'. Direct elections clearly raised their consciousness of serving the people, thereby enhancing cadre accountability to some extent.

Those who felt that they had some power in influencing the election results also suggested that they enjoyed some democratic rights. A young man exclaimed, 'It is marvelous that we're promoting democracy'! Some who enjoyed discussing village politics indicated that direct election was a way for them to learn about democracy, although to fully enforce it in rural China would require a long process. They said, 'Once getting started, it can never turn back, but only move forward'! Each round of election would teach them how to conduct freer and fairer ones. Therefore, we might argue that in the eyes of some villagers, direct election represented an early stage of democratization. In the long run, they would develop a higher level of democratic consciousness and a keener sense of managing village affairs by themselves.

Although this subset of relatively educated villagers noticed the importance of direct election for cadre accountability and grassroots democracy, a great majority argued that it was useless and meaningless, if not harmful, to the village. For them, its key feature was 'chaos and disorder' (*luan huiliao*). Direct election could not select competent or noble-minded cadres, or what they called 'shepherds', nor could it prevent incumbent cadres from misconduct or hold unpopular and corrupt ones accountable. Some emphasized its various disadvantages for the village, and preferred instead the pre-2000 indirect, rigged elections. In the past, they argued, the village party committee chose candidates for a villagers' committee only after careful consideration. Some youths full of vitality and originality were usually included in the committee, which was an efficient way to cultivate new young cadres. Like the supporters of direct election, these opponents had their reasons.

At first, these critics doubted the motivations of those campaigners. For them, the campaigners never planned to work for the public good, but only competed for their own interest and strived to pocket village funds. Whoever joined the committee, and especially became the chairman, he would get rich. The residents would never benefit. The keener the competition, the more the candidates had to gain from elected positions. One reason Shuanjin failed in his contest with Qingguo in 2003, they suggested, was the fight over potential gains among members of his faction.

Villagers sarcastically described the candidates' efforts to get elected as 'scrambling for *laopen*'. *Laopen* is a small clay pot that holds the ashes of paper money burned at every local funeral. It is smashed by the deceased's eldest son, biological or adopted, upon the coffin's removal out of the house for burial, a symbolic action showing the son's entitlement to the deceased's properties. When a person dies without a son, members of his (or her husband's) lineage will fight over the *laopen*. In their home visits, some old campaigners admitted that they ran for the committee member position in order to get an 'easy yet lucrative job' (*qiaohuo*). After he was first elected chairman in 2000, Qingguo said in public, 'I feel as if I just found a decent job'! Once Shuanjin was removed from his party secretary post and succeeded by Ping, some villagers joked, 'A hungry wolf showed up right after the rapacious dog is slaughtered'! It is better, they argued, not to have a direct election since more such elections only produce many more greedy cadres, and each new generation is worse than the previous one. To use their metaphor, 'A yellow weasel gives birth to whelps, with the younger generation being worse than the older'. Moreover, they argued, some campaigners plan to make their fortune in only one term and do not intend to run in future elections. As a result, even if a person of great ability and moral integrity can be chosen through direct election, s/he will in the end go along with the others in their evil deeds.

Such pessimistic attitudes toward direct elections are also based on the widely held belief that local election practices prevent the selection of a person of great ability and moral integrity. First, to get elected, one has to 'gang up with others to form a faction' (*labang jiepai*). This was clearly illustrated by the struggle between the 'power-holders' and the 'rebels'. In fact, all the villagers' representatives were also divided into two camps. For this reason, many believed, each direct election creates new conflicts and enemies, and consolidates the old, among villagers. The more elections there are, the stronger factionalism will grow. Noting that members of three factions fought each other with knives in a nearby village, several residents worried whether a similar situation would take place in Ten Mile Inn's future elections. Second, one needs to belong to a big lineage in order to be elected. No matter how incompetent a candidate is, I was assured, close members of his lineage would vote for him, at least for committee membership.[15] With votes from kinsmen highly valued as 'lineage votes' (*jiazu piao*), only people from the Wang, Fu, Li, and Zhang lineages have a chance to win. Third, 'localism' is of great importance in elections. The constant rivalry among the three neighborhoods, the Upper Fort, the South Area, and the North Area, motivates residents to choose candidates only from their own area. Upper Fort residents are particularly known as 'being of one mind' (*xinqi*). The only major contribution Qingguo made to the village was that he spent village funds in building a water pool for the Fort residents in early 2003. A resident of the Fort himself, he received 172 valid votes from the 197 voters on 1 October 2003. Another nine votes were voided only because voters mistakenly wrote his name twice on their ballots. During the election, some shouted: 'No one should become a traitor. We

---

15. For the effect of kinship on village elections, see: Ogden, *Inklings of Democracy in China*, p. 205; Baogang He, 'Kinship, village elections and structural conditions in Zhejiang', in Gungwu Wang and Yongnian Zheng, eds, *Damage Control: The Chinese Communist Party in the Jiang Zemin Era* (Times Center, Singapore: Eastern University Press, 2003), pp. 142–172; Zhang Hou'an *et al.*, *Zhongguo nongcun cunji zhili*, pp. 800–848.

should only elect candidates from our Upper Fort'. Residents of the South Area are also famous for their solidarity. Those fighting for the election committee chairman's candidacy were mostly from that area, and nominated him again in the formal election. Fourth, it is extremely difficult, if not impossible, for a person who has never been involved in village politics to compete with incumbent cadres. The incumbents gain public attention in their daily interactions with ordinary villagers. They win over some future voters by offering small favors with village funds. If they can also have support from the village party secretary, it will be more likely for them to be re-elected. After the first wave of direct village elections, the county officials noticed that some newly elected chairmen fought with party secretaries over the village leadership. To tackle this situation, they started to enforce a system called 'yizhi sanhua' (lit. one mechanism and three gradual changes) in May 2000 (revised in 2002).[16] The central purpose was to reiterate that the village party branch is the 'leadership core', the party secretary is 'commander in chief' and 'in full charge' of village affairs, and that the party branch and its secretary should lead the villagers' committee and its chairman. This measure has given party secretaries more power in manipulating villagers' committee elections. Last but not least, a man who has affinities in the village is more likely to be elected. Qingguo's re-election was partly because his wife and mother, and their respective lineages, are from the Lower Street.

At first, I puzzled over why these folks regarded it as impossible to select upright and competent cadres via direct elections. I had simply assumed that everyone wanted to choose the best leaders, and that such cadres would surely be elected if there were any, but I soon learned that the two men who were widely seen as exceptionally competent had no interest in joining the committee. Voters themselves were also responsible for the problems. A preliminary survey found that only about 10% of voters really cared about the public good, and were committed to choosing cadres who were capable and dedicated. About 25% of voters were indifferent to village elections. The opportunistic attitude was also popular. Some voted for those who visited their house most often; others simply chose incumbents; still others voted only to get the one yuan allowance. To use their idiom, 'Wang Yansan (a villager in the 1940s) would enlist, no matter who came to recruit soldiers, the Nationalists or the Communists'. While these voters were like 'grass on top of a wall, bending with the wind', about 60% of villagers were unswerving supporters of particular candidates. But these 'diehards' (sidang) were either the candidates' family and close lineage members, their friends and relatives, or those expecting some future favors. A few voters also poked fun at the election by nominating children or bedridden people.

---

16. One mechanism is 'villagers' self-rule under the leadership of the party branch committee', which includes the 'leadership core', 'institutional constraints', 'educational management', and 'evaluation'. The three gradual changes are 'standardization in the work of the party branch committee', 'villagers' self-rule according to law', and 'regularized democratic supervision'. This system has gained national attention. For media reports, see for example: He Wei, 'Bian "liang zhang pi" wei "yi tiao xin", Wu'an shi tansuo "yizhi sanhua" xin jizhi' ['Changing "two faces" into "one heart", experimenting new mechanism of yizhi sanhua in Wu'an'], People's Daily, (13 May 2001), p. 3; and Wu Weizheng, 'Hangshi dang zai nongcun de zhizheng jichu' ['Consolidating the basis of party rule in rural areas'], People's Daily, (11 October 2002), p. 1. During the seventh villagers' committee election in April 2006, it became widely popular all over Hebei Province that one person holds both the secretary and the chairman positions, a practice that locals joked about as one horse with two saddles.

Formation and operation of the democratic supervisory small group

Both the *Organic Law* and the *Hebei Regulations on Village-Level Democratic Management* state that 'democratic election' of the villagers' committee is only the first step in promoting villagers' self-rule and building a democratic system. 'Democratic supervision' of the committee is said to be another key objective. Then, how have the regulations on 'democratic supervision' been carried out in Ten Mile Inn, and how do local residents view such practices?

Drawing upon the guidelines on 'open management of village affairs' stated in the *Law*, the *Hebei Regulations* lay out such procedures for democratic supervision of the villagers' committee as 'administering village affairs openly', 'managing financial affairs democratically', 'evaluating village cadres democratically', 'setting time for democratic discussion', and 'auditing village finances regularly'. In Wu'an, the *yizhi sanhua* system mentioned above further specifies the rules on 'regularizing democratic supervision'. The purpose is clearly to restrain the daily behavior of village cadres, forcing them to govern their community according to law and in a more democratic way as well as holding those who are greedy and corrupt accountable. The *Hebei Regulations* and the Wu'an rules have been posted on the walls of the village office building since 1997 and 2000, respectively. Supervisory organizations were also established, but acted only perfunctorily, due to a lack of close attention and supervision from higher authorities. For instance, by regulation, the 'democratic supervisory small group' has the right to oversee all village financial activities.[17] All income and expenditure receipts must be reviewed, verified, and approved by the group periodically. Without the group's stamp and/or the leader's signature, receipts cannot be put into the village account books. The group is also authorized to veto any unreasonable expense. Such a group had been founded in Ten Mile Inn as early as 1998, but its leader was appointed by the top village cadres, and he never bothered to check any receipt before stamping it. From June 2000 to early 2004, village accountant Shunguo even kept the official stamp himself and could use it anytime. Then, on 4 July 2004, this situation changed as, for the first time, the villagers' representatives elected a supervisory group. While direct elections of the villagers' committee were enforced from above, the creation of this new group was mainly pushed from below, especially by a retiree surnamed Wang. Again, this development cannot be understood without attention to the factional conflicts mentioned above.

Shortly after the 2003 villagers' committee election, the 'power-holders' and the 'rebels' began a competition for the party branch committee election. Ping won his re-election as party secretary in his contest with Shuanjin in late October, but three members of the 'rebels', all Shuanjin's opponents in 2000 yet siding with him from early 2003, did not get into the committee, and hence started to lodge reports against Ping and the Clique. They turned to a retiree, Mr Wang, for help. Wang had assisted several groups of villagers in filing complaints to higher authorities, leading to the removal of both Shuanjin and his predecessor from their posts of party secretary. That Wang excelled in this regard resulted from his thorough knowledge of state policies.

---

17. In the region, the group is often a combination of the 'democratic financial management small group' (*minzhu licai xiaozu*) and the 'village affairs supervision small group' (*cunwu jiandu xiaozu*).

He has been persistent and dauntless, even in the face of harsh intimidation from local officials. Despite his previous involvement in ousting Shuanjin, Wang became a strong supporter of Shuanjin's faction in the elections, partly because of his personal grudge against the Clique. In their petitions, he and the three 'rebels' drew on the fact that Ping had allowed the other two members of the Clique to join the Communist Party without any probation. They also suspected that the Clique had spent village funds in buying votes during the party branch committee election. As the petitioning intensified, one Clique member Shunguo beat up one of the plaintiffs, and had to pay the victim 23,000 *yuan* in order to avoid a lawsuit that could have landed him in jail. In March 2004, local officials were finally forced to annul the two cadres' party membership and dismissed Ping from his secretary post, after the complaints reached the Hebei Provincial Governor. But the Clique had its supporters too, who succeeded in boycotting two rounds of party committee elections shortly afterwards. Under this stalemate, the township party secretary appointed a man from a nearby village as Ten Mile Inn's party secretary. Since he took the job in 2002, the township party secretary had been deeply concerned about Wang's complaints. He purposely chose this outsider in the hope that, as Wang's old classmate, the man could dissuade Wang from filing further reports and causing 'instability' under his governance. But Wang was determined, to use his own words, 'to overthrow the existing village regime, which was based on nepotism, and create a new one that will select cadres in a fair, transparent, and impartial way'. The first step, in his view, was to re-establish a supervisory small group by direct election.

Therefore, upon Wang's request, on the sunny morning of 4 July, the newly appointed party secretary convened the villagers' representatives to elect a new supervisory small group by secret ballot. Some 33 of the 42 representatives finally showed up, only after he constantly urged them to do so over the village loudspeaker. Each representative was asked to nominate up to five adult villagers, excluding the incumbent cadres and their close kinsmen. The five who receive the highest number of votes would become members of the new supervisory group. All members elected turned out to be villagers' representatives, and three of them were 'rebels'. The plaintiff who had been beaten was elected the group leader. It was widely believed that he was chosen because of his previous feud with the attacker, the accountant Shunguo. The next day, Shunguo was asked to hand the group's stamp to him.

Soon after its formation, the supervisory small group was authorized to review all the village expenditures for the first half of 2004, but as before, with the village party secretary's encouragement, the group leader scanned the receipts perfunctorily in three hours and affixed a stamp of approval all by himself. Later on, he confided to me that he had already received 23,000 *yuan* in compensation from the village accountant, which was beyond his expectation, and he no longer wanted to create new conflict with the Clique. Knowing the situation, however, Mr Wang called for a re-examination of the accounts by all group members, this time adding all the village incomes. At first, the party secretary rejected this demand and reported the case to the township party secretary, in the hope that he could handle the issue, but on 13 July, Wang urged the township secretary to study the *Advice on Improving 'Making Village Affairs Public' and Democratic Management*, one day after its publication in the *People's Daily*, and threatened to lodge complaints if he did not follow the document. The General Offices of the Communist Party's Central Committee had issued the *Advice* on 22 June to ensure ordinary villagers' right to 'know about', 'participate in', 'make decisions on', and 'conduct supervision of village affairs'.

After two weeks of negotiation behind closed doors, all group members started the new review on 27 July. The next evening, in a tense atmosphere, Qingguo and Shunguo, two members of the Clique, were forced to account for some unreasonable expenses, including telephone bills, entertainment fees, and a disguised form of vote buying. Five receipts were singled out for further explanation. One was for 20,600 *yuan* in the name of 'agricultural taxes', which had not been in the account book but appeared during the new review. Shunguo did not show up at the next night's meeting. When the village party secretary urged him to attend, he resigned as village accountant. When I left Ten Mile Inn on 15 August, some villagers were suspecting that Shunguo had used the money as payment to the group leader, whom he had beaten up. Since he had kept the group seal, he could have stamped the receipt and later added it to the account book without expecting any re-examination. Meanwhile, Wang tried to help one member of the supervisory group, a 'rebel' who had long planned to work as a village cadre, to become the new village accountant. These two were also pushing for an audit of all the village account books since 2000, in the hope of further ousting Qingguo, the incumbent village chairman and the last member of the Clique.[18]

As we have seen, the supervisory small group has actually figured centrally in restraining cadre behavior and enhancing cadre accountability. Qingguo conceded that the reimbursement of his phone bills should have restrictions. He was much embarrassed by the issue of vote buying. In the period of re-examination of the account books, all villagers I spoke to agreed that Qingguo had become a new person, humble and discreet. They said that he was much more arrogant early that year when the party secretary post was vacant and he firmly controlled the village leadership. Shunguo, his close ally, was also forced out of the office. For this reason, one young man referred to the group as an 'anti-corruption bureau'. A handful of villagers expressed approval for the group's veto of unreasonable expenses, but I was surprised to find that many residents did not really care about the review. For them, the plaintiff had been elected the group leader because the voters wanted to '*cao* (fuck with [lit.] or play tricks on) him' and 'make him play the role of a running dog'. With his well-known cunning, the group leader himself tried to avoid direct confrontations with Qingguo and Shunguo. As the 'audit' (*chazhang*) proceeded, some people argued that the group was 'causing trouble by nit picking' (*zhao cha'er*) and the two factions were scrambling for power and gain. 'If the "rebel" becomes the new village accountant', I was told, 'he will be the same'! In fact, one elected member, who was neutral in the factional competitions, made numerous attempts to withdraw from the group. For him, along with some folks, entertainment fees were absolutely necessary for cadres to govern a village today.

Mr Wang has also played a crucial role in the founding and operation of the new group, and in enhancing cadre accountability. He was directly involved in the

---

18. Later on, the township party secretary put a stop to the audit, and the receipt of 20,600 *yuan* was left without explanation. As mentioned in Note 14, Qingguo lost his contest with Shuanjin in the 2006 village election, and Shuanjin regained his party secretary post by replacing the appointed outsider.

dismissal of three consecutive party secretaries, all for more or less financial misconduct. The township party secretary had to bow to his request, and paid him two secret visits. He pushed the group members to re-examine the village account books, although some did not want to execute such duties. He even tried to force his own nephew, Qingguo, out of office, an action totally against local moral codes. In our conversations, he claimed to adhere to justice, abhor corruption, and to offer legal assistance in helping others lodge reports. He said that he was trying to 'do practical things' for the village, but a great majority of villagers did not appreciate such efforts. Only a few acknowledged his contribution to the public good. One said: 'If there were several more people as upright, selfless, and dauntless as Old Wang in this village, cadres would not dare to embezzle. It would also be easier to promote democracy'. Most people, however, doubted Wang's real motivation for intervening in village politics, since he had reportedly started the battle against the cadres after one personal issue was mishandled. They suspected that Wang and those who filed complaints were using each other for their own ends. They criticized him for 'being disruptive' (*bu pinghe*) and 'purposely making trouble' (*zuoluan*) by ousting one party secretary after another. Otherwise, they reasoned, the residents would be better off under a stable leadership. Unfortunately, some argued, the township government appointed a man from a nearby village as Ten Mile Inn's party secretary. This was 'humiliating', because it showed that 'in this community, we [they] don't have a capable and upright person'. For them, 'corruption is inevitable today. Just let those cadres eat meat [i.e. engage in gross embezzlement] so that we can also drink some soup [i.e. gain some modest benefits]'! Some also pointed out that ousting village cadres from their current positions was not an effective way to hold them accountable. Indeed, both Shuanjin and Ping, the two consecutive party secretaries, later found a new and more decent job at the township government because of their close connections with the township party secretary. For all these reasons, very few villagers wanted to interact with Mr Wang; most changed the subject whenever I mentioned his name in conversation. One retired township official regarded him as the village's 'public hazard' (*gonghai*). Some hated him so much that they secretly cut his phone line three times, uprooted his crops, and once set his house on fire. That he has engaged in open sexual affairs with three women in the village only intensified such hatred. One neighbor called him a 'rascal' and his home 'evil lair'.

Conclusion: power to the people?

In this article, I have presented an ethnographic inquiry into the direct elections of villagers' committees and then the founding and operation of a supervisory small group in a North China village. Although I detailed the process of institutional building, my emphasis was on the locals' own interpretations of these grassroots political reforms. Contrary to the arguments presented in many village election studies and the expectations of Chinese policymakers, a majority of my informants did not regard direct election as an effective way to select competent and impartial cadres, or to hold unpopular and corrupt ones accountable. Along with other negative comments, they felt that direct election became a vessel for factional maneuver. 'Grassroots democratization' via free and fair elections did not seem to concern them either. Meanwhile, the supervisory small group, and particularly Mr Wang who pushed for its re-establishment and operation, actually restrained the behavior of local cadres. As the township party secretary had to give in to Wang's requests, several top village cadres were forced out of office. Thus, we may argue, Wang and the group have enhanced transparency and facilitated grassroots democracy, but many villagers did not appreciate such efforts. Like direct elections, the operation of the group was an integral part of the factional politics in the community. This case study, therefore, shows the importance of digging deeply through the level of actions and practices to the intimate level of the participants' own understandings. In other words, in assessing institutional building, we must pay close attention to the views and voices of those most affected.

Some may maintain that this is only an exceptional case, or that my informants' indifferent attitudes toward 'democratic election' and 'democratic supervision' will gradually change as the practices proceed. I contend, however, that the village is not as idiosyncratic as many would assume.[19] I also anticipate that 'democratization' has a long way to go, if not impossible to achieve, in the village, since strong lineage identities, contests among the three neighborhoods, and factionalism have figured centrally, and will continue to do so, in village-level politics. To follow Ogden's argument about a distinctive Chinese way of 'democracy', I hold that the notion of 'rule by the people' may remain difficult to take root, even if such democratic forms as free and fair village elections are well established.[20] A brief discussion on villagers' own understandings of 'villagers' self-rule' suffices to make the point.

The official regulations define 'villagers' self-rule' as the practices by which villagers manage their own affairs and directly exercise democratic rights, particularly via a villagers' committee. Despite the change from 'brigade committee' to 'villagers' committee' in the official discourse since the mid-1980s, Ten Mile Inn villagers, especially those over 40, still addressed themselves frequently as 'brigade members' (sheyuan), instead of 'villagers' (cunmin). Except for cadres, some highly educated residents, and those traveling extensively, most informants knew nothing about 'villagers' self-rule', the Organic Law, the Hebei Regulations, or the Wu'an yizhi sanhua system. They generally regarded the committee as a local branch of government, instead of a 'mass organization for self-management, self-education, and self-service'. Except for some cadres, a great majority regarded 'village cadres' as 'village officials' (cunguan), and considered it proper that they should be 'governed and administered'. Many posited that human beings were born essentially different and unequal, although they also touched on the fluid boundary between 'officials' (dangguan de) and 'ordinary people' (lao baixing). For instance, borrowing a metaphor from the imperial era, some described themselves as those doomed to 'carry the sedan chair' (taijiao de) as opposed to the officials who 'sit in the sedan chair' (zuojiao de). Some contended that 'purlins are purlins, while beams are beams' (ling jiushi ling, liang jiushi liang), meaning that different types of people can only fit into different social positions. Moreover, almost all informants, the village chairman Shunguo included, agreed that the village party secretary should

---

19. On the similar negative assessments of and indifference to direct elections, see for example: Ogden, *Inklings of Democracy in China*, pp. 211–215; and Kennedy, 'The face of "grassroots democracy" in rural China'.

20. Ogden, *Inklings of Democracy in China*.

make a final decision on all important village affairs. Like the *dangjia de* (heads) of local lineages, they firmly believed, only the secretary should *dangjia* for (i.e. take full charge of) the whole village community, even if the actual person may be incompetent in the position. My informants' view of the villagers' committee, their disposition towards authority, and their conception of village governance clearly call into question the argument that the committee is of utmost importance to practicing villagers' self-rule.

Some may contend that I underestimate the abilities of Chinese farmers to embrace new ideas and practices. On the contrary, in this article, I have highlighted the ways in which ordinary people have creatively employed metaphors to make sense of their lifeworlds. Drawing upon cognitive science, Lakoff and Johnson correctly emphasize that metaphor figures centrally in our conceptualization of the world.[21] They further argue, 'complex metaphors' stem from 'primary metaphors' that are essentially grounded in the human body. They also maintain that the metaphorical mapping from the 'source domain' (i.e. sensorimotor) to the 'target domain' (i.e. more abstract and emotional) is cross-cultural and part of the 'cognitive unconscious' for all human beings, although they touch on particularity in their American examples. The many metaphors discussed in this article, however, show that they are culturally and historically specific, not to mention that they are not always embodied. For instance, 'carrying the sedan chair' and 'sitting in the sedan chair' are drawn from Imperial China. 'Power-holders' and 'rebels' come from the tumultuous years of the Cultural Revolution. The *dangjia de* (head of a lineage branch/lineage) derives from lineage rituals, particularly funerals. 'Purlings' and 'beams' are used in house construction. The boundary between the so-called 'source domain' and 'target domain' is also never clear-cut. My informants' conceptualization of the election committee and its chairman as *liku fang* and *dangjia de* will surely influence their further understanding of the second set. Their experiences and memories from different contexts and historical periods have multiple layers that are constantly shaping and reconstituting each other. Further political reforms mean not only new experiences to learn, but also more to draw upon to understand the 'old'. More important, people have political agency in strategically making use of metaphors for their own purpose. In this case, while governmental officials emphasize 'power to the people', my informants poked fun at the election committee and the campaigns by highlighting the negative meanings of *liku fang* (lit. chamber of gifts and goods) and *bainian* (lit., paying New Year visits). While many took power inequality for granted, they simultaneously challenged it by selectively using other metaphors. For instance, one suggested that the relationship between 'ordinary people' and 'village officials' is like water and a boat: 'While the waters can bear the boat, they can also sink it'. To conclude, unraveling the participants' own (often ambivalent) views, particularly grasping their metaphors, is crucial for us to understand 'villagers' self-rule', and similar local political reforms at other times and in other sociocultural contexts.

---

21. George Lakoff and Mark Johnson, *Metaphors We Live by* (Chicago, IL: University of Chicago Press, 1980); George Lakoff and Mark Johnson, *Philosophy in the Flesh: The Embodied Mind and its Challenge to Western Thought* (New York: Basic Books, 1999); George Lakoff, *Women, Fire, and Dangerous Things: What Categories Reveal about the Mind* (Chicago, IL: University of Chicago Press, 1987); and George Lakoff, *Moral Politics: How Liberals and Conservatives Think*, 2nd edn (Chicago, IL: University of Chicago Press, 2002).

Village Election and Governance: do villagers care?

QINGSHAN TAN and XIN QIUSHUI

Village elections at the grassroots level have been regularly conducted for more than a decade in the context of the Chinese political system. Both negative and positive views have been expressed and written on village elections. How does one evaluate Chinese village elections? Free and fair elections require conformity to international election principles, rules, and procedures. This study develops a minimum procedural criterion to assess if village elections have followed internationally-accepted rules and procedures of free and fair elections. We also measure the meaningfulness of village elections by examining the effects of elections on village governance and villagers' life. We find that elections have been conducted in a manner consistent with proscribed rules and procedures and are generally free and fair, and there is a considerable convergence of views of villagers and cadres who see that elections are meaningful in producing positive changes in village governance and life. The data also confirm that elected villagers' committees are still in the long shadow of township governments and village Party branches.

Free and fair elections require conformity to international election principles, rules, and procedures. After ten years of implementation of the 1987 Organic Law on the Villagers' Committees (Experimental), with vast variations in election procedures and processes, China updated the experimental law in 1998. The new Organic Law on the Villagers' Committees incorporates some basic principles of free and fair elections and stipulates detailed election rules and procedures. It represents an attempt to standardize village elections and bring election rules and procedures up to international standards. It requires elections to be conducted in conformity to secret ballots, free nomination, multi-candidacy, primaries, one person one vote, open count, and on the spot announcement of election results. Various views and reports have been expressed and written on village elections conducted after the 1998 Organic Law, raising questions and offering answers to the nature, meaning, and impact of village elections. Are village elections for real? Do village elections conform to basic democratic election principles? Can village elections produce meaningful results that alter the traditional political structure and governance in rural China?

How does one evaluate Chinese village elections? Are they real and meaningful or just a show case? In trying to assess Chinese elections, Larry Diamond and Ramon Myers put forth three minimum universal criteria: elections have to be free, fair and meaningful.[1] They are free if legal barriers to entry for parties and candidates are low; freedom for candidates to campaign is assured; and voters encounter little or no coercion in casting their votes. Elections are fair if they are administered by neutral, competent, impartial, and credible organizations. Elections are meaningful if they confer real power to elected officials. How can these criteria be applied to village elections in China? China does not have a competitive multi-party system, and China does not have an independent electoral commission to administer elections. Does this mean that village elections are unfree, unfair, and meaningless?

In a different article, Robert Pastor and Qingshan Tan propose two other criteria to assess the meaning of village elections.[2] First, village elections should not be judged categorically but rather regarded in the context of China's history as lying on a democratic continuum. If an election helps improve rural governance and deepens democratic election rules, procedures and principles, then China is gradually moving ahead. Second, village elections can be assessed with two critical elements of the electoral process: namely choice and secret ballot. Taking into consideration China's conditions and incorporating these two criteria, we modify Diamond and Myers's criteria to a minimum, operational definition to assess if village elections are 'free', 'fair', and 'meaningful' in the Chinese context.

First, since China does not have multi-parties to compete in village elections, thus a critical remaining element is whether voters are free and have real choices in nominating candidates and voting for their choices by secret ballots. Second, village elections are administered by a village election committee often presided over by a village Party branch secretary. Therefore the key to a fair election is whether the electoral process is perceived by voters as impartial and electoral rules and procedures are administered free of violation, interference, and fraudulence by village election committees. Third, village parties and township governments (hereafter TG) used to exercise dominant control over village affairs before the introduction of village elections. How a villagers' committee (hereafter VC) handles or is perceived to handle village affairs and their relations with voters, Party branches and township government is critically important to the assessment of VCs' meaningful autonomy and real power conferred by the electorate. Lastly, VC elections are supposed to improve village governance. Analysis of election impact on village governance enables us to assess meaningful elections if they make any positive differences in rural life.

Using this minimum definition as our analytical framework, this empirical study seeks to address the following questions: Do villagers care about elections? What do they think of election processes and procedures? Have elections produced meaningful change in rural governance?

---

1. Larry Diamond and Ramon H. Myers, eds, *Elections and Democracy in Greater China* (New York: Oxford University Press, 2001).
2. Robert Pastor and Qingshan Tan, 'The meaning of China's village elections', *The China Quarterly* 162, (2000), pp. 490–512.

Review and research

Village elections, despite the problems of procedural incompleteness and implementation variations,[3] have been generally viewed positively by international and Chinese observers, scholars, and officials as an important political development in the Chinese countryside.[4] Elections give villagers a chance to choose their village leaders,[5] and they have considerably altered the political structure of village governance.[6] Elected villagers' committees and village representative assemblies (hereafter VRA) are the new forces of village autonomy permitted and encouraged by the Chinese government to strengthen village self-governance in the countryside.[7] Village elections as part of political development in the countryside were viewed and analyzed as a 'short march' to democracy or Chinese style of democracy.[8]

Today there are 681,277 villages throughout China.[9] Given the numbers of villages, the enormity of the election task can be appreciated.[10] Village elections, however, lack uniformity and consistency.[11] Debates within the top leadership, hesitant provincial officials, and reluctant local cadres all in one way or another contributed to the uneven development of village elections.[12] Studies have

---

3. Kevin J. O'Brien, 'Implementing political reform in China's villages', *The Australian Journal of Chinese Affairs* 32, (1994); Ann Thurston, *Muddling toward Democracy* (Washington, DC: US Institute for Peace, 1998); Pastor and Tan, 'The meaning of China's village elections'.

4. International Republican Institute, *Election Observation Report: Fujian, People's Republic of China* (1997); International Republican Institute, *People's Republic of China Election Observation Report* (1994); Lianjiang Li, Zhenlin Guo and Tangbiao Xiao, eds, *Cunweihui Xuanju Guancha* [*Observing Village Committee Elections*] (Tianjin: Tianjin renmin chubanshe, 2001); The Carter Center, *Carter Center Delegation Report: Village Elections in China and Agreement on Cooperation with the Ministry of Civil Affairs, People's Republic of China* (Atlanta: The Carter Center, 1998); The Carter Center, *The Carter Center Delegation to Observe Village Elections in China* (Atlanta: The Carter Center, 1997); Yong Xu and Yi Wu, eds, *Xiangtu Zhongguo De Minzhu Xuanju* [*Democratic Election in Rural China*] (Wuhan: Huazhong shifan daxue chubanshe, 2001).

5. Pastor and Tan, 'The meaning of China's village elections'.

6. Jude Howell, 'Prospects for village self-governance in China', *Journal of Peasant Studies* 25(3), (1998), pp. 88–111; Jonathan Unger, *The Transformation of Rural China* (Armonk, NY: M.E. Sharpe, 2002).

7. Daniel Kelliher, 'The Chinese debate over village self-government', *The China Journal* 37, (1997), pp. 67–75; Susan V. Lawrence, 'Village representative assemblies: democracy, Chinese style', *Australian Journal of Chinese Affairs* 32, (July 1994), pp. 61–88; Kevin J. O'Brien and Lianjiang Li, 'Accommodating "democracy" in a one-party state: introducing village elections in China', in Diamond and Myers, eds, *Elections and Democracy in Greater China*, pp. 101–125; Tianjian Shi, 'Village committee elections in China; institutionalist tactics for democracy', *World Politics* 51(3), (1999), pp. 385–412.

8. Baogang He and Youxing Lang, *Xunzhao Minzhu Yu Quanwei De Pingheng* [*Seeking Balance between Democracy and Authoritarianism*] (Wuhan: Huazhong shifan daxue chubanshe, 2002); Lawrence, 'Village representative assemblies'; Henry S. Rowen, 'The short march: China's road to democracy', *The National Interest* 45, (1996), pp. 61–70.

9. Ministry of Civil Affairs Department of Finance and Administration, *China Civil Affairs' Statistical Yearbook 2003* (Beijing: China Statistics Press, 2003), pp. 148–149.

10. This number is down from 1,019,000 villages in 1991. It shows an on-going merging of villages that began following the introduction of village elections in the late 1980s. See The Ministry of Civil Affairs, ed., *Zhongguo minzheng dongji nianjian* [*Statistics Yearbook of Chinese Civil Affairs*] (Beijing, 1992), p. 1716.

11. In his recent visit, former President Jimmy Carter spoke positively about village elections and called for improvement of election rules and procedures. See Josephine Ma, *South China Morning Post*, (9 September 2003). For a recent study on synchronization of village election, see Qingshan Tan, 'Building institutional rules and procedures: village election in China', *Policy Sciences* 37, (2004), pp. 1–22.

12. Bai Yihua, 'Cunweihui zuzhifa danshengji' ['The making of the Organic Law of Villager Committees'], *Zhonggong tangshi ziliao* [*Historical Reference of Chinese Communist Party*] 1, (2003), pp. 88–97; Tan, 'Building institutional rules and procedures', pp. 1–22.

investigated various practices and cases of village elections with respect to participation, election rules and procedures, impact on governance, the relationship of VCs with village Party branches and township governments.[13]

The existing literature offered various assessments based on election observations, government published data and case studies. They provided valuable insights into the processes in which village elections were conducted and they analyzed the dynamic interactions between villagers and village organizations such as VRAs and VCs and how elections impact upon rural governance. With few exceptions,[14] studies of village elections still need to broaden the scope of investigation incorporating more empirical data.

Based on the foregoing criteria, this article employs the survey data to assess village elections and their impact on rural governance from the perspective of villagers. Specifically, our research compares and analyzes the views of villagers and village cadres on election processes and their assessment on how elections affect village governance. Our research objective is to find out if there is significant convergence or divergence of views among villagers and between villagers and village cadres on election processes and governance.

This research is based on the survey and interviews we conducted in Anhui province. In China, Anhui is often considered as a pioneering province. Anhui is a typical agricultural province and is well-known for taking initiatives in agricultural reforms; it is the birthplace of the two key national agricultural reforms, the household contract reform in 1978 and the fee for tax reform in 1995. Anhui is the agricultural barometer of major central agricultural reform.[15]

We selected 12 villages from seven townships in five counties and distributed our survey questionnaire to the villagers and cadres chosen from the 12 villages.[16] We supplemented surveys with interviews with those villagers who for various reasons could not fill in the survey forms. All the interviews were conducted with the same questionnaire as in the survey. The first survey was conducted from May to June 2002. We subsequently carried out a follow-up survey in March and April 2003. Out of 1,550 survey forms, we collected 1,503 valid surveys of which 1,299 were from villagers and 204 from village cadres.

13. Sylvia Chan, 'Village self-government and civil society', in Joseph Cheng, ed., *China Review* 1998 (Hong Kong: The Chinese University Press, 1998), pp. 235–258; Amy B. Epstein, 'Village elections in China: experimenting with democracy', in Joint Economic Committee US Congress, ed., *China's Economic Future* (Washington, DC: Government Printing Office, 1996), pp. 403–422; Melanie F. Manion, 'The electoral connection in the Chinese countryside', *American Political Science Review* 90, (December 1996), pp. 235–258; Tan, 'Building institutional rules and procedures'.

14. Manion, 'The electoral connection in the Chinese countryside'; Jean C. Oi, 'Election and power: the locus of decision-making in Chinese villages', in Diamond and Myers, eds, *Elections and Democracy in Greater China*, pp. 149–175; Baogang He, 'Village elections, village power structure, and rural governance in Zhejiang', *The American Asian Review* xx(3), (Fall 2002), pp. 55–89.

15. Premier Zhu Rongji often remarked that 'I always come to Anhui to do field study whenever the central government is about to make an important decision on agriculture'. See, Chen Jiadi and Chun Tao, 'Zhongguo nongmin diaocha' ['Investigation of China's peasants'], *Dangdai* [*Contemporary*], (June 2003), p. 7.

16. It should be noted here that we used a simple random sample in the targeted population of the 12 villages, but at the county and township level, we conducted a judgmental sampling. We acknowledge that the lack of total random sample implies limitations on our findings.

Village elections: free and fair?

Participation is an important behavioral indicator to measure villagers' efficacy and interest in village elections.[17] Participation takes on a special meaning when the Chinese government encourages and emphasizes turnout rate in elections. This is because the government often uses mobilizational techniques to encourage villagers to come out and vote in order to raise villagers' awareness of elections.[18] For this reason, election officials often reported very high turnout rates (over 90%) in village elections.[19] Our survey seeks to investigate if turnout rate was as high as reported and what motivates villagers to vote. The data demonstrate a high rate of participation across the sample population, but not as high as suggested. The majority of voters vote because they have a chance to elect their own leader and impartiality is the most important criterion for the voters to choose the candidates.

Our survey shows that 71% of the respondents participated in the last round of elections. For those who voted, we break down the age group and find that voter turnout rate increases with age; younger villagers have a slightly lower rate of participation. Villagers with primary schooling and higher income (10,000–50,000 annually) have over 88% participation rate, while younger and better educated villagers vote the least, largely due to their work migration from villages to cities. Out of those who did not participate in the last election, 63% (238 out of 379) did not vote because they believed that the election was just a showcase since candidates were already predetermined. Some 21% (80) did not vote because of their busy work.

Of the villagers who voted, 95% indicate that they participate in the election because they can elect their own leaders. This response is rather uniform among the surveyed villagers. As for the criteria with which voters cast their ballots, there are similar answers across the sample population: 86% of the respondents use 'impartial governing' as the most important criteria for assessing candidates. Only 4% cast their votes looking for leaders to enrich their life. The survey result is counter-intuitive to the authors' own observation and studies linking elections to emerging, middle-income villages.[20] The explanation may lie in those surveyed villagers' persistent view of the double agent role of village officials.[21] Village cadres were viewed as primarily serving the township government because they were appointed by the township government in the past. Villagers may still hold the same view and want elected officials to be impartial in playing their double-agent role. At the same time,

---

17. Shi, 'Village committee elections in China'; Manion, 'The electoral connection in the Chinese countryside'; Kent M. Jennings, 'Political participation in the Chinese countryside', *American Political Science Review* 91(2), (1997), pp. 361–372.

18. Differences should be acknowledged between mobilizational elections in the pre-reform period and village elections. Any election can not be considered free and fair if election processes are not free of violation, prevarication or interference with rules and procedures. For this reason, production brigade elections that were conducted during the commune era were viewed with much skepticism and regarded as a mobilizational scheme for the Chinese Communist Party; see John Burns, *Political Participation in Rural China* (Berkeley: University of California Press, 1988).

19. Minzhengbu jicengzhengquan he shequ jianshesi, ed., *Quanguo cunweihui xuanju qingkuang fenxihui lunwen ji* [*Collection of Papers on the Analysis Conference of National Village Committee Election*] (Ningbo, Zhejiang, China: November 2002).

20. O'Brien, 'Implementing political reform in China's villages'; Epstein, 'Village elections in China'; He and Lang, *Xunzhao Minzhu Yu Quanwei De Pingheng*, pp. 152–178.

21. Xu and Wu, *Xiangtu Zhongguo De Minzhu Xuanju*, pp. 3–16.

as elected officials gain power and control over village resources, villagers expect them to manage and distribute resources impartially.

Candidate selection

Candidate selection is an important criterion for a free and fair election. The existing literature studied various aspects of candidate selection in village elections, including different rules and methods of primaries in candidate selection.[22] Our sample focuses on villagers' perception of and attitudes towards selection processes and influences. The data show a high percentage of voters who are involved in the candidate selection and nomination and view the selection process positively, but the data also reveal quite a number of voters who perceive township officials to be an influential factor in the nomination process.

About 72% of the respondents said that they participated in the selection and nomination process; 14% did not participate. While 52% of the voters do not agree that township government officials influence the selection of candidacy, 14% of the voters believe that candidates were already predetermined by township officials (Figure. 1). Some 17% think that village Party branches selected final candidates, and thus pre-fixed the election outcomes. Many villagers (34%) responded by saying that they were not sure whether township officials interfered in the candidate selection. This high percentage of ambiguity reflects a persistent suspicion of those villagers who could not believe that township officials would totally wash their hands clean in the nomination process.

Election processes and procedures

Election rules and procedures are written in the Organic Law and are operationalized in the Anhui provincial village election handbook. The handbook requires members of village election committees to be nominated by village small groups and elected by village assemblies or village representative assemblies.[23] Our surveys ask villagers to give their views on any possible violations of election processes, rules and procedures by village election committees. The surveys generally confirm the villagers' positive view on the election process, but also show that a quarter of those surveyed have no idea about the election process. Free nomination, private voting, polling stations, and open count were observed and practiced in the election process. The data identify some factors perceived by a few voters to have influenced elections such as clan influence and vote-buying practices. The data display a noticeable percentage of respondents who do not have any idea about the election process. This could be a function of both lack of interest in and information on candidates and candidates' campaigns.[24]

---

22. Pastor and Tan, 'The meaning of China's village elections'; Rong Hu, *Lixing Xuanze Yu Zhidu Shishi* [*Rational Choice and Institutional Implementation*] (Shanghai: Shanghai yuandong chubanshe, 2001).

23. Anhui minzhengting, *Anhui cunmin weiyuanhui xuanjugongzuo shouce* [*Election Work Handbook of Anhui Villager Committees*] (Hefei, Anhui: 2002), pp. 43–44.

24. According to the authors' own election observations, election campaigns generally take the form of a speech on Election Day by the two candidates for VC chief. So far, there is no national or local law regulating type of campaigns and campaign funding. In recent years, election campaigns have been quite heated in some places, involving candidates employing TV crews and a campaign truck. See Lu Liedong, *Campaign: The Real Meaning of Village Election*, (19 August 2003), available at: http://www.people.com.cn/GB/14576/28320/29243/29247/2025250.html

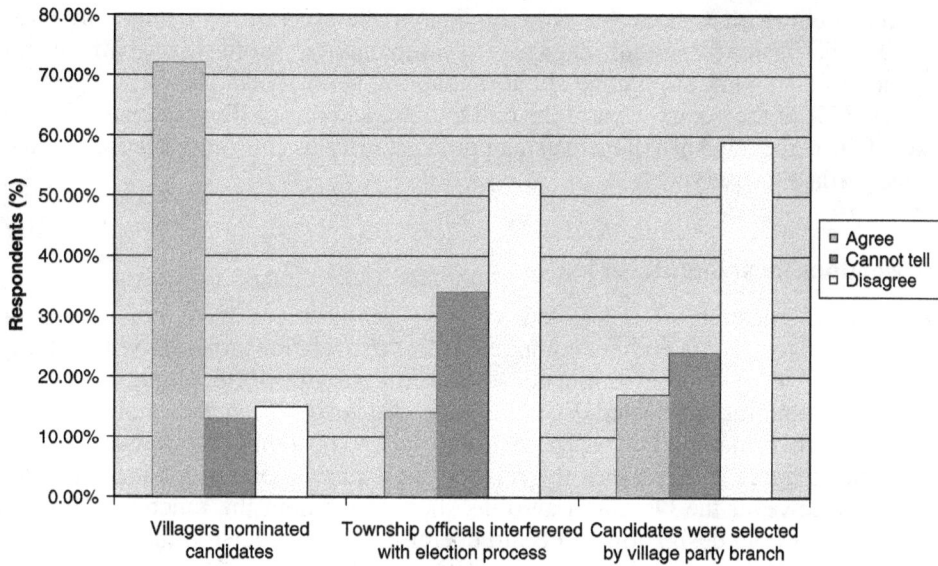

Figure 1. View on candidate selection.

Figure 2 displays the general view of the respondents on the election process. The majority express their trust in the integrity of the ballot, both in terms of ballot collecting and open count. Clan is found not to be a major factor in the election: 5% of villagers see that clan and kinship factors were responsible for the election outcome. Vote-buying does not appear to be a significant problem in the election: 7%

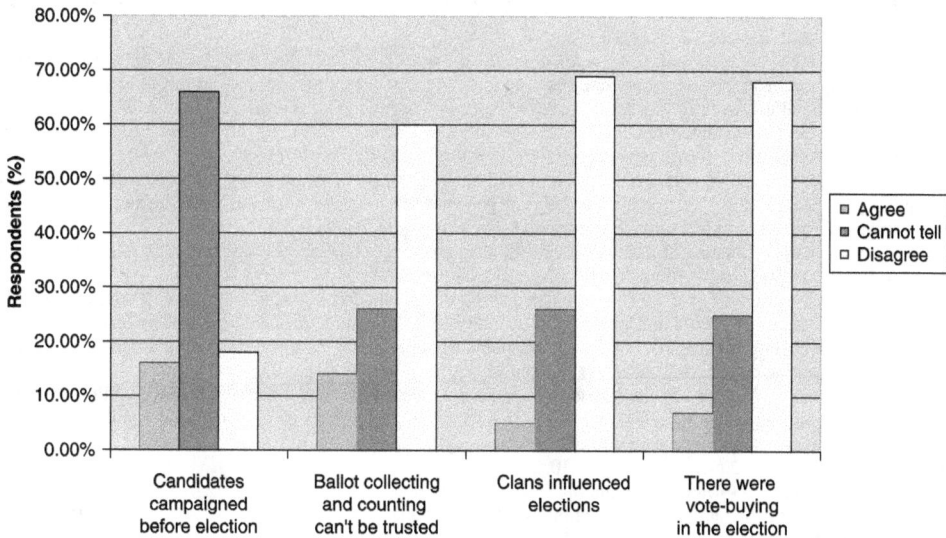

Figure 2. View on election process.

of voters believe that there was vote-buying in the election.[25] While a minority believes that candidates did engage in campaigning, more than half of the respondents do not know anything about candidates' campaigns.[26] In our samples, we find that 83% of the voters went to the poll to vote, and only 13% voted using roving boxes. This percentage of villagers using polling stations is considered above average in other villages observed.[27]

Are elections meaningful?

Elections are meaningful if elected villagers' committees have real power in managing village affairs and are autonomous in their relationship with village Party branches and township governments. According to the 1998 Organic Law on Villagers' Committees, elected VCs are supposed to be the autonomous body of village self-government. Township governments are no longer administratively in control of villagers' committees; the relationship becomes one of guidance (*zhidao guanxi*).[28] However the Organic Law falls short of defining the functions of VPBs and VCs other than designating VPBs to exercise 'core' leadership in the village.[29] Since then, tensions have risen between VCs and TGs and VPBs in many places where TGs and VPBs were reported to interfere and interrupt the works of VCs.[30] The tension reached the apex when 57 elected VC chiefs collectively resigned in Shangdong in 2001.[31] The rising tension itself is an indicator of the increasing governing power VCs have acquired since elections were introduced. In other places, VCs are gaining an upper hand over VPBs in village decision making. Township governments had to rely on elected governing bodies to carry out state and Party policy.[32]

Our survey asks whether villagers regard villagers' committees as an important governing body. We also survey villagers' views on the function of villagers' committees and their relationship with village Party branches and township

25. Vote-buying (huixuan) needs to be defined in China. Election officials often consider such practices as treats of meals, giving out cigarettes or petty money as vote-buying and see such practices as serious threats to elections. A recent study found that over 30% of those surveyed believe vote-buying is common and on the rise. See Baohang He, 'Are village elections competitive: the case of Zhejiang', in Joseph Y. S. Cheng, ed., *China's Challenges in the Twenty-First Century* (Hong Kong: University of Hong Kong Press, 2002), pp. 71–92.

26. This is not because of villagers' unawareness of campaigns, but because many candidates did not actively conduct any campaigns since an election campaign is generally discouraged in practice. For further discussion on campaigns, see Tan, 'Building institutional rules and procedures', pp. 8–14.

27. According to the authors' election observations, the percentage of villagers casting votes in roving boxes was much higher in Jiangxi, Tianjin, Yunnan, and Jilin. Authors' observations from 1998 to 2003.

28. One of the most controversial issues in the making of the election law was the township relationship with villager committees. Many central and local officials wanted township governments to have leadership relations with villager committees (lingdao guanxi). For the controversial debate, see, Bai, 'Cunweihui zuzhifa danshengji'; Tyrene White, 'Reforming the countryside', *Current History* 91, (September 1992), pp. 275–276.

29. Article 3 of the Organic Law designates village Party branches to exercise the core leadership function while supporting and ensuring villagers' self-governance. This vague language gives no clear definition on the function of village Party branches and village committees.

30. *People's Daily*, (12 October 2000), p. 10.

31. *People's Daily*, (21 March 2001), p. 4.

32. Guo, 'Cunmin xuanjuhou de dangzhibu: kunhuo, douzheng yu quanligeju' ['Party branch after village election: confusion, struggle, and power posture'], in Li *et al.*, eds, *Cunweihui Xuanju Guancha*, pp. 595–626; Howell, 'Prospects for village self-governance in China'.

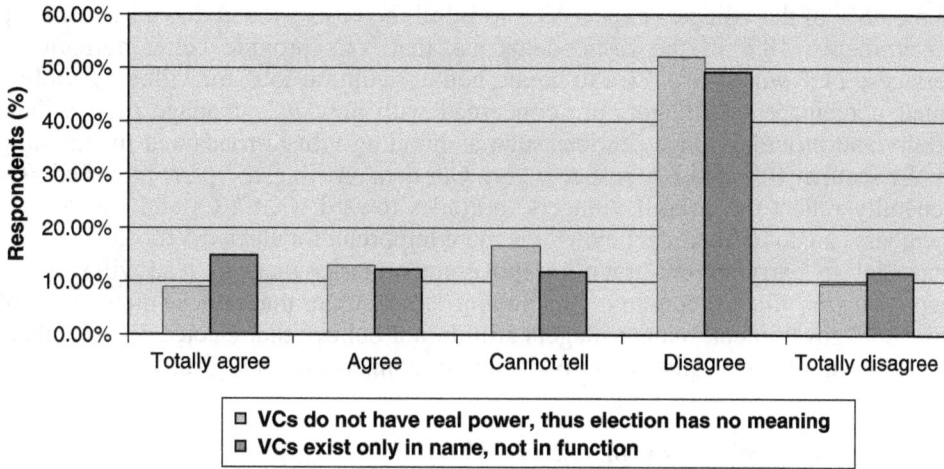

Figure 3. Views on village committee power.

governments. The data display mixed responses on the issues: the majority still think that VCs do have power and resources to govern, but at the same time they see the VC role as primarily serving the township government and VCs are still secondary to Party branches and township governments whose opinion and decisions often prevail over that of VCs.

VC power and functions

Figure 3 shows identical views on VC governing power and functions. Some 62% believe that VCs do have power in governing village affairs and that elections are significant. A similar majority disagree that VCs exist only in form, believing they do actually function; 27% see VCs as just 'flower vases' for the Party branch, while 22% are not clear about VCs' actual power.

We followed up villagers' views on VC functions with a question regarding what villagers expect VCs to perform and accomplish. Figure 4 summarizes the findings.

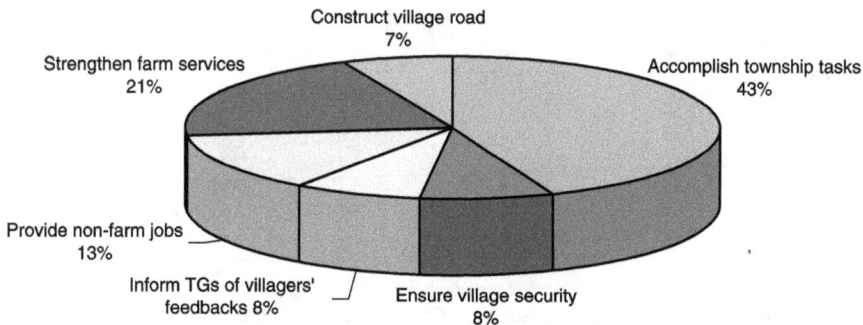

Figure 4. Functions of village committee.

Some 38% of the villagers expect VCs to fulfill the tasks handed down by township governments; 18% of the respondents ask that VCs provide better agricultural services; 11% would like VCs to create non-agricultural jobs for villagers. Only a small percentage of villagers are concerned with how VCs manage their village affairs and provide village services such as building village roads and maintaining public security (6% and 7%, respectively). Our data on villagers' perceptions of VCs generally reflect the overall villagers' attitudes toward what VCs and elected VC members can do for them, believing it is more important for elected VC officials to be impartial in carrying out township government tasks than to lead villagers in improving the village economy. This finding demonstrates that after so many years of rural self-government, many villagers still do not believe that elected VC members really serve villagers rather than township governments as their primary duties.

VC autonomy in relations with VPBs and TGs

Our survey solicits the view of villagers and cadres on VC autonomy in relations to VPBs and TGs. The data confirm that VCs are still the junior partner even if VCs command better respect from villagers over VPBs in the eyes of villagers. Figure 5 depicts and compares the views and perception of reality of villagers and that of cadres with respect to VC–VPB relations. There is a big gap in villagers' views of what the relationship should be and in villagers' perceptions of reality. Even though more than half of the respondents do believe that VCs are elected by villagers, thus village Party branches should respect VC decisions, only 30% of villagers see it as the

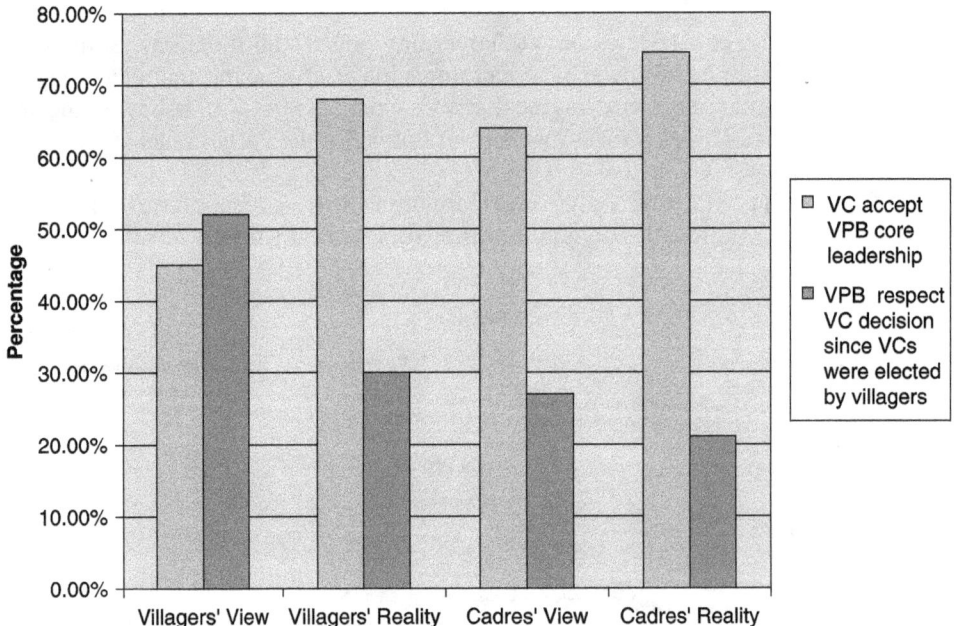

Figure 5. View and perception of reality on VC–VPB relations.

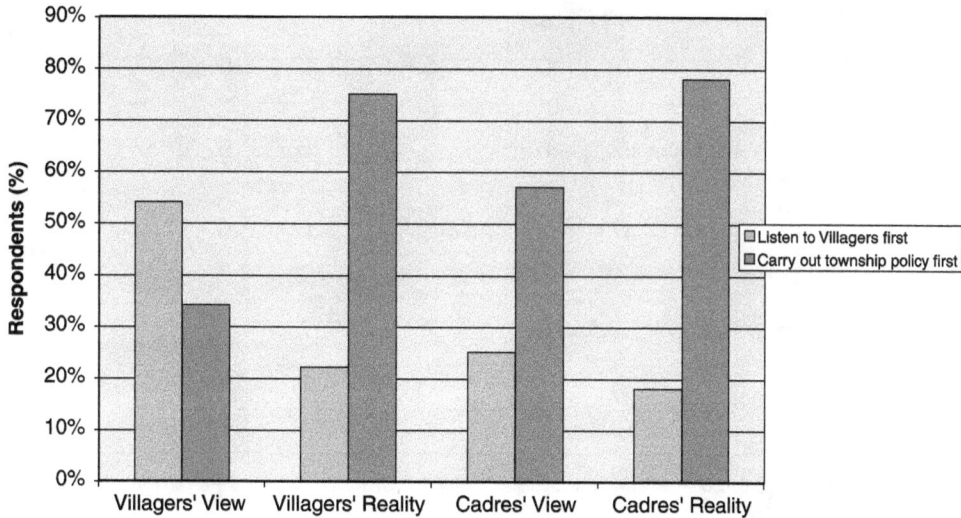

Figure 6. View and perception of reality on VC–township relations.

case in reality. When looking at cadres' perceptions, the reality is even dimmer. Only 21% of the cadres say that VPBs have any respect for VCs in reality.

There is a greater discrepancy in villagers' perceptions of what should be done and what has actually been done when it comes to governing priorities. Figure 6 shows township governments are still in a predominant position in ensuring villagers' committees to carry out government tasks. Despite the majority of voters in support of VCs taking care of village business first, VCs are perceived to give top priorities to government policies and tasks in their actual administration of village affairs. Again, differences exist between the views of cadres and those of villagers: a majority of cadres expressed their opinion that they should follow township government instructions. There is a high correlation between villager and cadre perceptions of VCs giving priorities to township tasks in reality.

In our survey, we try to find out whether socioeconomic and political factors affect villagers' perceptions of VC autonomy. The data show that higher income is positively associated with village support for village autonomy. The majority of the villagers with $5,000 or more annual income expressed their support for VCs to take care of village business and for VC decision making. We find that there are no significant variations in perceptions as far as age, education, and political affiliations are concerned. More than half of the villagers across the sociopolitical spectrum believe VCs should represent villagers and VC decisions should be respected by VPBs.

Impact of elections on village governance

Recent studies yield different conclusions on election impact on village power and governance. Some demonstrate that village elections have changed the locus of

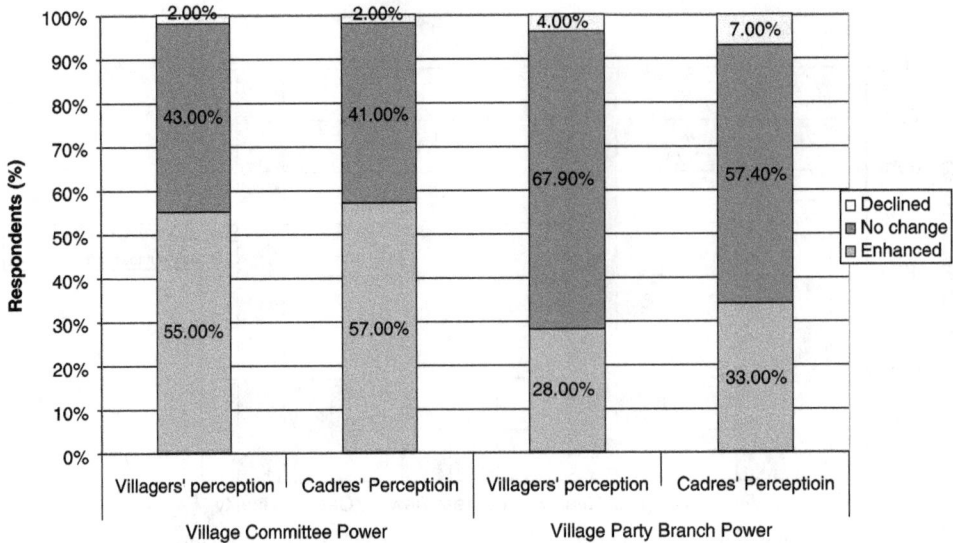

Figure 7. Perception distribution of village power.

village power,[33] reduced rural corruption and promoted stability.[34] Others conclude that village elections did not change the village power structure.[35] Our survey focuses on how villagers and cadres look at socio-economic and political changes as a result of village elections. We then compare the differences in views held by villagers and cadres, respectively.

Impact on VC and VPB power

The survey asks villagers and cadres about their views on the changes in VC and VPB power since the introduction of village elections. Figure 7 outlines the responses from villagers and cadres. Both villagers and cadres who believe that VC power has increased since the elections outnumbered those who believe the opposite. A large number of respondents respond by saying that they do not see such change. There is no significant difference in numbers of villagers and cadres who see an increase of VC power. In contrast, only a smaller number of villagers and cadres see that VPB power has increased. The majority of those surveyed believe that VPB power remains unchanged, while a few more cadres perceive that PPB power has actually declined.

How do we reconcile this impact data with the foregoing survey indicating the role of VCs being secondary to VPBs? We can view this power balance as tilting toward VCs as VC power increases. However, the impact data also show that the majority of villagers and cadres see no change in VPB power, much less in decline, which means

33. Oi, 'Election and power'.

34. Chen Zhemin, ed., *Cunmin Zizhi De Lilun Yu Shijian* [*Theory and Practice of Villager Autonomy*] (Tianjin: Tianjin renmin chubanshe, 2000), ch. 7.

35. He and Lang, *Xunzhao Minzhu Yu Quanwei De Pingheng*, pp. 63–90.

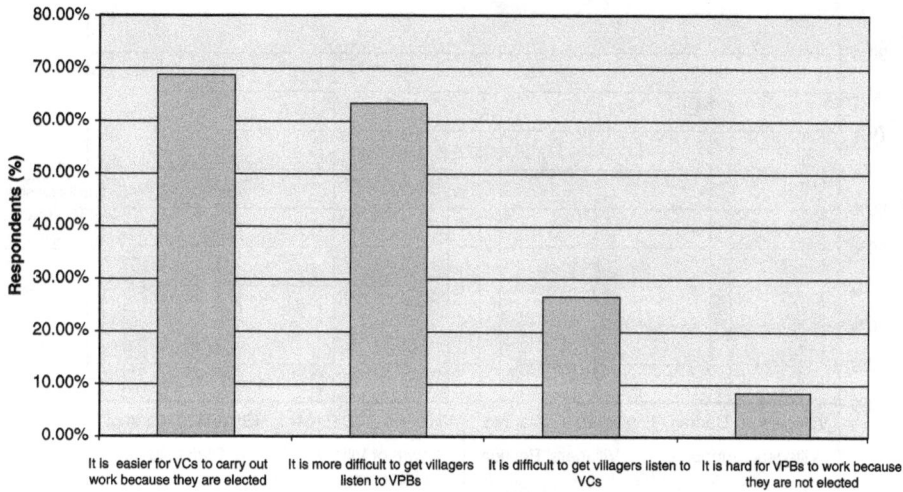

Figure 8. Election impact on VC and VPB work.

VPBs have been able to retain their hold on power. The change in VC power is not great enough to upset the VPB grip of power in three important aspects: control of villagers' committees' official seals, use of signature rights, and management of village enterprises.[36]

Nevertheless, growth in VC popularity is consistent and accounts for rising tensions between VCs and VPBs. We survey cadres' views on villager–VC and villager–VPB relations. Figure 8 indicates an improvement in relations between villagers and VCs, while showing problems in the relationship between villagers and village Party branches. The majority of cadres (69%) reply that VCs have better working relations with villagers and elections make it easy for them to do their job. Some 63% of the surveyed cadres find it more difficult for the Party branch to lead villagers due to diversity of opinion; 8% of the cadres point out that the Party's difficulty with villagers is due to the fact that Party secretaries are not elected, while 7% of the cadres believe that Party's difficulty is rooted in villagers' desire to monitor every move of the Party branch.

The rise of VCs and decline of VPBs in popularity are contributing to the increasing tension and have become a cause for concern for both local and central governments. The recent experiment to subject village Party secretaries to a 'two-ballot' election or to recruit elected village chiefs to be Party secretaries represents a government attempt to address the issue.[37] Though endorsed by the central government,[38] conferring the top two posts onto one elected official is a relatively

---

36. Chen, *Cunmin Zizhi De Lilun Yu Shijian*, pp. 232–233.

37. The two-ballot system refers to a process in which Party secretary candidates were selected by a slate of village Party branch members and village representatives. Once selected, candidates are subject to village opinion and eventually voted on by villager Party members. The method changes the past practice in which township authorities appointed village Party secretaries. See, Liu Ya, 'Cunmin zizhi yu dangzhibujianshe de neizai lianxi' ['The linkage of building Party branches and village autonomy'], in Zhang Mingliang, ed., *Cunmin Zizhi Luncong* [*On Village Autonomy*] (Zhongguo shehui chubanshe, Beijing, 2001), p. 398.

38. The CPC 14th document officially endorses and promotes the two-ballot practice. See *People's Daily*, (19 August 2002).

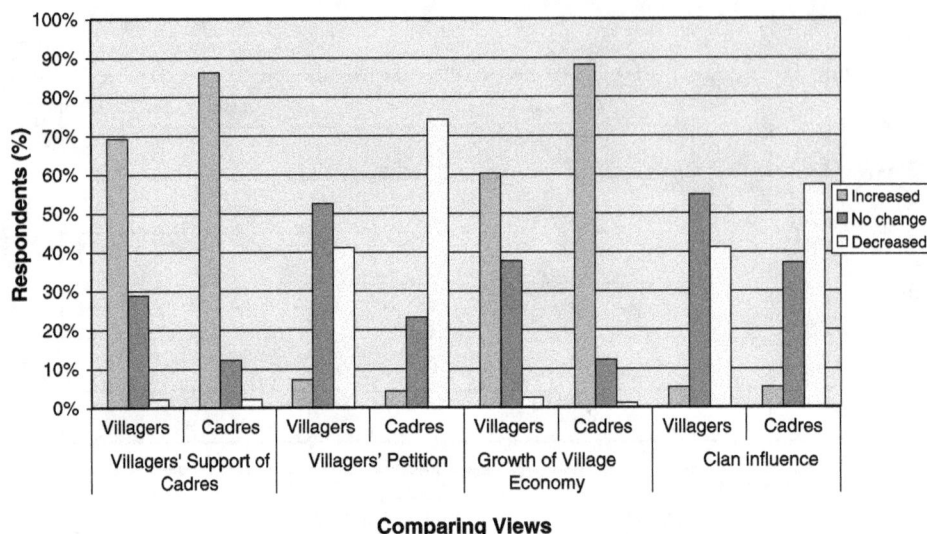

Figure 9. Election effects on village governance.

new practice.[39] The percentage of villages adopting this practice is still very small in villages throughout China, with the exceptions of Shangdong, Guangdong and Hainan, where over 60% of villages have adopted the practice.[40]

Impact on village governance

The survey covers four aspects of village governance and asks the villagers and cadres to give their assessment on election impact on these four areas. The data find that the majority of the respondents view elections as positively effecting village governance. Figure 9 summarizes the result of the data and compares villagers' answers with cadres'.

The first aspect is cadre–villager relations. Relations between cadres and villagers were quite tense before elections were introduced; many villagers did not trust cadres. In our survey, 69% of the respondents indicate that the tension has been greatly or somewhat greatly reduced or improved, and 29% of the villagers have seen no change in the meantime. Compared with villager's views, cadres' views on this issue are more optimistic: more cadres believe improvement has occurred while fewer see no change.

The second aspect is villagers' appeal. Due to the tension mentioned above, villagers often resorted to appeals to higher authorities in the past for the wrongdoings of village cadres. To some extent, elections have helped reduce such

39. Lianjiang Li, 'The two-ballot system in Shanxi Province: subjecting village party secretaries to a popular vote', *China Journal* 42, (July 1999), pp. 103–108; Bai Gang and Shouxing Zhao, *Xuanju Yu Zhili* [*Election and Governing*] (Beijing: Zhongguo shehuikexue chubanshe, 2001), ch. 4.

40. According to authors' visits and interviews, less than 20% of villages have adopted the practice in Neimenggu, Hunan, Yunnan, and less than 10% in Guangxi, Shanxi, and Anhui. See also Minzhengbu jicengzhengquan jianshesi, ed., *Quanguo cunweihui xuanju qingkuang fenxihui lunwen ji.*

appeals to higher authorities: 41% of the respondents affirm, with a range from greatly to somewhat greatly, the reduction in appeals, while more than half of the villagers believe that there has been no change. A large discrepancy is found between cadres' perceptions and villagers' views on this issue. The majority of the cadres (74%) see a reduction in villagers' appeal and far fewer cadres (23%) respond with no change. The differences in perception may not be justified by the actual numbers of appeal cases.[41] We speculate that many villagers were still not satisfied with the state of village affairs and many things need to be done before villagers actually change their perceptions.

The third aspect is village economy. In terms of how elections have improved village economy, many respondents hold quite positive views. The majority of the respondents point out that village economy has been at least somewhat improved and one-third respond by saying there has been no change. Again, we find a divergence in cadres' views from those of villagers. Close to 90% of the cadres view the improvement of village economy positively and only 12% of cadres indicate no such improvement.

The fourth aspect is clan influence. The survey shows a mixed view among village voters on clan influence in village affairs. The minority of the respondents see clan influence has actually declined, while the majority does not see any change in clan influence. However, the cadres respond to the survey with a confident tone. The majority believe that clan influence has been reduced and fewer see no change in clan power. About the same small percentage of the villager and cadres respondents report an increase in the clan's influence on village affairs. Overall, our survey finds that clan influence is sporadic and minimum; this finding is consistent with some ongoing research on clan influence in China.[42]

Impact on participation

To what extent do elections affect villagers' participation in village governance? The survey focuses villagers' and cadres' views of election effects on villagers' interest in elections, attention to village affairs, and general political awareness. The data demonstrate a clear pattern of increasing participation on the part of villagers. Figure 10 compares the views of villagers and cadres and shows a high degree of consensus on the three measurements of participation.

Of the villager respondents, 74% indicate that villagers have become more interested in village elections, compared to 84% of the cadre respondents who believe that villagers' interest in elections has increased. Also, 77% of the respondents see an increase in villagers' attention to village affairs and most cadres have the same view. About the same percentage of villagers point out an increase in villagers' political awareness, and the majority of the cadres (83%) agree that elections help to raise villagers' political consciousness.

41. Local township and village officials confirmed in interviews with the authors that appeal cases have dropped throughout the countryside. It could be the result of village self-governance or of other channels that are now available to address villagers' grievances.

42. Xiao Tangbiao, Lu Liedong and Luo Xinzuo, eds, *Zongzu, xiangcun quanli yu xuanju* [*Clan, Village Power and Election*] (Xian: Xibei daxue chubanshe, 2000), pp. 3–34.

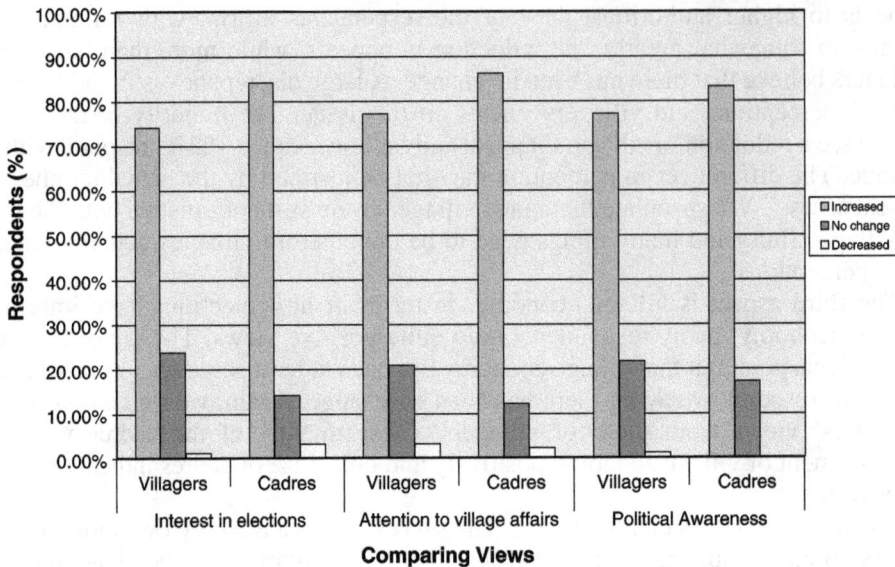

Figure 10. Impact on villager participation.

Conclusion

Village elections at the grassroots level have been regularly conducted for more than a decade in the context of the Chinese political system. The national Organic Law and local election rules and procedures have been promulgated and implemented. Lack of a competitive party system poses a challenge to assess village elections according to prevailing international standards and norms. This study develops a minimum procedural criterion to assess if village elections have followed internationally-accepted rules and procedures of free and fair elections. We also measure the meaningfulness of village elections by examining the effects of elections on village governance and villagers' life.

Based on surveys and interviews, we find that villagers agree that elections have been conducted in a manner consistent with proscribed rules and procedures and are generally free and fair. Village elections reveal little evidence on the possible violation of the two critical elements of elections, free nomination and secret ballot. However, the data show a good portion of villagers are still skeptical about or ignorant of the election process, which suggest that education, training, improvement in election rules and procedures, and implementation of rules and procedures should be an on-going process.

The research finds that village autonomy is hinged upon two influential factors: township governments and village Party branches. The data confirm that elected villagers' committees are still in the long shadow of township governments and village Party branches. This finding, in support of published reports and studies, suggests that village autonomy should be viewed in the context of the existing rural political structure. Villagers' committees as an autonomous organization need to be equipped with matching autonomous power to better serve villagers and other functions.

Notwithstanding VC limited autonomy, we also find that there is a considerable convergence of views of villagers and cadres who see that elections are meaningful in producing positive changes in village governance and life. Elections have generally raised villagers' political efficacy, improved villager–cadre relations, and increased the power of villagers' committees. This finding should not obscure the fact, however, that elections have not changed everyone's life and status quo in rural governance is still being perceived by many villagers.

Our findings are somewhat at odds with some perspectives in the existing literature that generally discount the importance of village elections and their impact on governance, since village elections are confined to grassroots governance and do not affect the real power of government. Our research shows that even if it has not been extended to township or county government, a village election is still meaningful and important from the perspective of village voters. Villagers do care about village elections and governance.

If our data reveal a pattern, and if villagers' committees continue to gain popularity among villagers and village Party branches try to hold on to power, we may be observing a trend of rising tensions between the two village organizations spreading throughout the countryside. There is no easy way to solve this problem, particularly in the light of a lack of formal rules defining the role and function of village Party branches. The central attempt to subject Party secretaries to the two-ballot election may reflect the Party desire to improve the Party image in the countryside, but to confer the two village top positions on one elected official may not resolve the tensions in the eyes of villagers and may even create new problems in village autonomy.[43] There is no mechanism to check an all-powerful village chief concurrently holding the two top village positions. Ultimately, caring villagers will have to ask the question: to whom is the elected village chief responsible: township government officials or electoral villagers?

43. Bai and Zhao, *Xuanju Yu Zhili*, pp. 296–299.

APPENDIX

Sampling

Our survey consists of two groups: villagers and village cadres. In the first village group, the sample is designed to be representative of the target village population at the village level in the selected counties in Anhui. We use a purposive sampling to include five counties taking into account different levels of economic development and geographical features. We include poor counties in the mountainous regions and middle-level counties in the plain region. Then we used a simple random sampling to select between one and three villages from each county as our secondary sampling units. The third stage of selection was village households for a simple random sampling. All of the villages surveyed had gone through a round of elections since 1988.

In the selection of households, we used household registrations obtained from villagers' committees as the database for constructing the sampling frame. We distributed the questionnaires to the selected households and followed up with interviews for those households that for various reasons did not fill out the questionnaire. It should be pointed out that we did not use the Kish table to select respondents within households. Because of village customs, most of the time we agreed to interview the head of the household who was usually a male villager. Thus male villagers were oversampled in our survey.

In the second group of village cadres, the 204 village cadres surveyed are a nonprobability sample; 14 are village Party branch secretaries, 19 are vice Party secretaries, 13 villagers' committee chairmen, 11 vice villagers' committee

Table 1. Villagers' sampling structure, $N(\%)$

Gender	Male	1,040	(80.1)
	Female	259	(19.9)
Age	Below 20	3	(0.2)
	20–29	138	(10.6)
	30–39	505	(38.9)
	40–49	345	(26.6)
	50–59	206	(15.9)
	Above 60	102	(7.9)
Education	Illiterate/semi-illiterate	130	(10.0)
	Elementary	475	(36.5)
	Middle School	540	(41.6)
	High School	146	(11.2)
	College	8	(0.6)
Political affiliation	CCP member	147	(11.3)
	Youth league member	121	(9.3)
	No political affiliation	1,029	(79.2)
	Other party member	1	(0.1)

chairmen, 26 villagers' committee members, 15 village party members, 78 village small group leaders, 12 village accountants, and16 other cadres.

The first survey was conducted from May to June 2002. We subsequently carried out a follow-up survey in March and April 2003. Out of 1,550 survey forms, we collected 1,503 valid surveys of which 1,299 were from villagers and 204 from village cadres. Table A1 displays the structure of the villager sample.

Women's Political Participation in China: in whose interests elections?

JUDE HOWELL

This article takes up the issue of women's political participation in village committees in China. Of interest is the decline in and continuing low level of women's political participation in village governance structures in the reform period, and particularly following the widespread introduction of competitive village elections since 1988. The dominant explanation given for women's numerical under-representation in village committees, and in politics more generally, focuses on women's lack of self-confidence, which inhibits them from standing as candidates, and on the enduring drag of 'feudal' attitudes, which construct women as inferior to men, and therefore not capable of leadership. These two factors combined have in turn a material effect, as son-preference advantages boys in access to basic schooling, who thus, particularly in poorer rural areas, end up with higher levels of education, and greater opportunities in waged employment. The common solution adopted by the All-China Women's Federation (ACWF), China's largest women's organisation, lies in a two-pronged attack: first in the ideological realm, targeting men and women's sexist attitudes and concomitantly promoting a discourse of equality, and second, in the material realm by raising women's skills. It is argued here that this dominant text on women's under-representation in village committees masks a more complex conjuncture of variables that shape women's position in local politics. Social practices, economic structures, institutional norms and procedures, and political culture all prey on, revitalise and reproduce gendered notions of the appropriate place of women and men in political life.

Introduction

The idea of competitive elections for political positions is a fundamental tenet of a democratic polity. Competitive elections provide the citizen not only with choice but also a means to hold leaders to account, the ultimate sanction being the ousting of unpopular, incompetent or corrupt leaders from public office. Democratic competition assumes an even playing-field, where differences of class, gender, wealth and ethnicity are bracketed. However in practice power differentials embedded in social and economic inequalities create barriers of entry to political participation. This is true not only in established liberal democracies such as the UK, USA, and Germany but also in liberalising socialist regimes such as China.

This article takes up the issue of women's political participation in village committees in China. Of interest is the decline in women's political participation in village governance structures in the reform period, and particularly following the widespread introduction of competitive village elections since 1988. The dominant explanation given for women's numerical under-representation in village committees, and in politics more generally, focuses on women's lack of self-confidence, which inhibits them from standing as candidates, and on the enduring drag of 'feudal' attitudes, which construct women as inferior to men, and therefore not capable of leadership. These two factors combined have in turn a material effect, as son-preference advantages boys in access to basic schooling, who thus, particularly in poorer rural areas, end up with higher levels of education, and greater opportunities in waged employment. The common solution adopted by the All-China Women's Federation (ACWF), China's largest women's organisation, lies in a two-pronged attack: first in the ideological realm, targeting men and women's sexist attitudes and concomitantly promoting a discourse of equality, and second, in the material realm by raising women's skills. It is argued here that this dominant text on women's under-representation in village committees masks a more complex conjuncture of variables that shape women's position in local politics. Social practices, economic structures, institutional norms and procedures, and political culture all prey on, revitalise and reproduce gendered notions of the appropriate place of women and men in political life.

This article begins by sketching the emergence of village elections in the reform period and the impact of these on female representation in rural politics. The next section focuses on the conjuncture of variables affecting rural women's participation in political office. In the final section we examine recent attempts to resist rural women's exclusion from the political domain and the challenges facing women in doing so. The article draws upon extensive fieldwork in three counties in Hunan province carried out in 2002 and 2003.

The representation of women in rural politics

The consolidation of Deng Xiaoping's power in 1978 paved the way for fundamental reforms in the rural economy. The decollectivisation of agriculture, the introduction of the household responsibility system and the opening up of agricultural markets changed not only the structure of rural economies but also social and political life. With the declining importance of ideology and Deng Xiaoping's endorsement to 'get rich quick', the incentives to engage in politics began to weaken. Rising economic wealth brought with it new avenues of power, success and status. However, with the breakdown of the former commune system of governance and the lack of an established alternative model, a plethora of governance arrangements mushroomed across China's rural areas. Though the new 1982 Constitution incorporated the idea of direct elections to village committees, and a year later village committees and township governments replaced the old structures of the People's Commune, there was still in practice no unified or regularised system of rural governance.[1] In some areas village governance structures had weakened or even collapsed as villagers concentrated their attentions on tending their private plots. For township authorities this created severe difficulties in raising taxes from villagers and in implementing Party directives such as family planning targets or grain procurement. In other areas there were serious problems of rural unrest as local authorities extracted excessive and unwarranted fees from farmers. Clan rivalry, corruption, extreme localism, rural unrest and a vacuum of leadership and authority pointed to a crisis of rural governance.

Aware of the growing diversity in governance structures across rural areas, the disjunctures between old political and new economic institutions, and the perceived threat to stability of rural riots and protests, senior leaders within the Party such as Peng Zhen, Deng Xiaoping and Hu Yaobang along with key advocates within the Ministry of Civil Affairs, the ministry responsible for administering village elections, began to actively promote the regularisation and standardisation of competitive village committee elections from the mid-1980s onwards. However controversy within the Party as well as resistance from township and county cadres concerned about the loss of power and control led to considerable delays in the introduction of relevant legislation and its initial experimental status.[2] The National People's Congress finally passed the experimental Organic Law on Villagers' Committees in November 1987, taking effect from June 1988. From this point onwards the idea of village committees began to take off. In November 1998 the law was further amended, and made permanent, thereby dampening any further fundamental disagreement with the new system of rural governance. By the turn of the millennium nearly all villages in China had held at least one round of elections for village committee positions, and in more pioneering provinces such as Fujian and Zhejiang

---

1. Jude Howell, 'Prospects for village self-government in China', *Journal of Peasant Studies* 25(3), (1998), pp. 90–91.

2. Those in favour of competitive elections argued that these provided a way of ousting corrupt and incompetent leaders and promoting younger, more educated and competent leaders, who enjoyed local support, into positions of power and authority. In this way the Party could not only achieve more effective governance at the village level but also rejuvenate and enhance its legitimacy at the grassroots. They also allowed villagers to be more involved in decisions affecting their villages, thus thwarting the tide of political apathy. A more legitimate and accountable leadership would in turn make it easier for the township authorities to extract resources and maintain social order. Those against competitive elections feared the upward spread of demands for elections, the election of leaders that the Party could not easily control, and unabated rural unrest. For further details about support and opposition to competitive village committee elections see Kelliher Daniel (1997) 'The Chinese debate over village self-government', *The China Journal* 37, January, pp. 63–90, Li and O'Brien (1999), O'Brien, Kevin (1994) 'Implementing political reform in China's villages', *The Australian Journal of Chinese Affairs* 32, July, pp. 33–59, O'Brien Kevin and Li Lianjiang (2000) 'Accommodating "democracy" in a one-party state: introducing village elections in China', China Quarterly 162, pp. 465–89, Jakobson (2004) 'Local governance: village and township direct elections', pp. 97–120 in Jude Howell (ed) *Governance in China*, Rowman and Littlefield Publishers Inc., lanham, Boulder, Shi Tianjian (1999) 'Village committe elections in China: institutionalist tactics for democracy', *World Politics* 51, 3, pp. 385–412, and Wang Zhenyao (1996) 'Village committees: the foundation of the Chinese democratisation (unpublished manuscript), pp. 1–12.

were well into their third or fourth round of elections. Moreover, some villages had begun to experiment with elections for leadership of the Party branch,[3] and some townships such as Buyun in Suining City, Sichuan province, had initiated the competitive election of leaders.[4] Though there is still considerable variation in election procedures and practices across China's 930,000 villages,[5] and though problems such as clanism, vote buying, the refusal of township authorities to accept elected leaders, continue, the practice of competitive elections for village committees has now been established and regularised. However, with power often lying in the hands of the unelected Party branches,[6] competitive village elections do not yet hail the coming of a democratic era in China, though they may serve as a vital stabilising factor in a process of rapid socio-economic change.[7]

The village elections in China have drawn considerable attention from researchers, journalists and politicians both within China and outside. Yet despite the substantial literature on this subject in Chinese and English, surprisingly little has been written about women's participation in village committees, village Party branches, village groups or village assemblies. This is not just because of the lack of gender disaggregated data on village committee members but also because the issue has not gained sufficient political attention for it to trigger investigation, study or analysis, let alone prompt the systematic collection of gender disaggregated data.[8] Although in many villages the Party branch continues to be the most authoritative and powerful political institution, the village committee nevertheless has several functions, which are significant in the everyday lives of both men and women. These include not only the implementation of Party directives from above relating to grain procurement, taxation and family planning, but also the development of the village economy, maintenance of social order, mediation of disputes, women's work, infrastructural development, and public health. As women take prime responsibility for childcare, domestic activities, care of the elderly, and increasingly in many rural areas of China, of agricultural labour, the decisions enacted in village committees, and the resources committed, bear directly upon the quality of women's lives.

Yet women are numerically under-represented on village committees, not least because in the context of competitive village elections, they are less likely than men to be nominated as candidates and even less likely to be voted for as members or chairs of village committees. According to Article 9 of the Organic Law on Villagers'

---

3. Li Lianjiang, 'The politics of introducing direct township elections in China', *China Quarterly* no. 171, (2002).

4. Li Lianjiang, 'The two ballot system in Shanxi Province: subjecting party secretaries to a popular vote', *The China Journal* no. 42, (1999); Linda Jakobson, 'Local governance: village and township direct elections', in J. Howell, ed., *Governance in China* (Lanham: Rowman and Littlefield, 2004), pp. 97–120.

5. According to the Carter Center China Village Elections project, village elections have occurred in some 700,000 villages, reaching 75% of the population. Available at: www.cartercenter.org/documents/nondatabase/chinavillagefactsheetpdf, accessed 17 December 2004.

6. Kevin O'Brien and Li Lianjiang, 'Accommodating "democracy" in a one-party state: introducing village elections in China', in Larry Diamond and Ramon H. Myers, eds, *Elections and Democracy in Greater China* (Oxford: Oxford University Press, 2001).

7. Jean Oi and Scott Rozelle, 'Elections and power: the locus of decision-making in Chinese villages', in Diamond and Myers, eds, *Elections and Democracy in Greater China*.

8. It is noteworthy that none of the selected EU/China research projects take up the issue of gender in village elections, even though the issue was raised in the original design mission documents (see: www.chinarural-org/euchiprog/research.html, accessed 5 December 2004).

Committees, the village committee should include 'an appropriate number of women' (*funu ying dang you shidang de ming'e*).[9] Available statistics suggest that only 1% of village committee chairs are women and 16% of village committee members are women.[10] Though there is some inter- and intra-regional variation, in general men outnumber women on village committees, with one woman on a committee being the norm. In some villages not a single woman has been elected to the village committee. In the 14 villages in one town we visited in Hunan province, there was not one female head of the village committee, and only one female village Party secretary. This town in turn fell under the administrative authority of a large city, which covered 771 villages. Amongst these villages, there were only five female village committee chairs, making up less than 1% of the total.

Though the lack of gender disaggregated data prevents an accurate tracking of women's participation over time, available evidence suggests that women's participation in village committees has declined over the last 30 years. Compared with the politically charged days of the Cultural Revolution, when women in urban and many rural areas were swept up in the tide of political activism, assuming leadership positions in campaigns and revolutionary organs, women's participation in rural political institutions in the reform period has diminished. The new revolutionary committees of that era opened up opportunities for women's political involvement, with women receiving training in political leadership. In Shanghai, for example, women accounted for 22% of the revolutionary committees in 1973[11] and in some areas women made up 50% of cadres at lower levels.[12]

This pattern of numerical under-representation of women in positions of authority and the decline of representation in the reform period are not peculiar to China's villages. At all levels of the political system, from the national level down to county and township, women are under-represented in leadership positions. Of the 24 members in the Politburo in 2004, only one is a woman, namely, Mme Wu Qi.[13] Of the 198 Central Committee members elected at the 16th Party Congress in 2002, only five were women, accounting for just 2.5%.[14] Women fare better in the National People's Congress (NPC), where they account, as of 2004, for just over one fifth of delegates. However, only two out of 15 vice-chairs and 21 out of 160 delegates on the NPC Standing Committee are women, making up just 13% in each case of the total. In over five decades of Communist Party rule, there has never been a single female General Party Secretary. At the county and township levels male domination of leadership positions prevails. To illustrate, in a county government in Hunan

---

9. It also requires there to be 'a member or members' from minority populations'. See Organic Law on Villagers' Committees in Jiangsu Sheng Min Zheng Ting, *Cunweihui xuanju gongzuo zhinan* [*Village Committee Elections Work Manual*] (Jiangsu Province Civil Affairs Bureau, 1995), p. 4.

10. Fan Yu, 'Cunweihui xuanju: nongcun funu fazhan de jiyu yu tiaozhan' ['Village committee elections: opportunities and challenges for rural women's development'], in China Women's Research Conference and UNIFEM, eds, *1995 Shijie Funu Dahui Wu Zhou Nian Yanjiuhui* [*1995 Beijing Plus Five Conference*] (Beijing, 2000), pp. 273–275.

11. Elisabeth Croll, *Feminism and Socialism in China* (London: Routledge and Kegan Paul, 1978), p. 327.

12. Joan Maloney, 'Women cadres and junior-level leadership in China', *Current Scene: Developments in the People's Republic of China* 8(3–4), (March–April 1975), pp. 17–18.

13. See www.china.org.cn, accessed October 2004.

14. Du Jie, 'Women's participation in politics in the transition to a market economy in China. Progress in high level politics since 1995', unpublished paper for UNRISD Contribution to *Beijing Plus Ten*, June 2004.

province, as of 2003, there were only two female town and township governors out of a total of 35, accounting for a mere 6%.[15] The decline in women's numerical representation in village committees is mirrored also at the national level. The last woman to serve in the Politburo Standing Committee was Jiang Qing, Mao's second wife, during the height of the Cultural Revolution.[16] The number of female delegates in the 10th NPC elected in 2003 fell by 1.5% compared to the previous congress. Female representation in the NPC peaked at the 4th Congress in 1975, with women accounting for 22.6% of delegates and 25% of NPC Standing Committee members, figures that have not been attained since.[17]

Apart from the numerical under-representation of women in village committees, another recurring pattern is that women are usually assigned portfolios associated with their reproductive and domestic responsibilities. Whilst men tend to be allotted tasks such as economic development or infrastructural construction, female committee members are given charge of women's work, family planning, or health. Village committees are thus sites through which gender relations are played out and reproduced, and where gendered private roles come to determine men's and women's public roles. The social construction of family planning as a matter for women and not men results in women always being assigned this responsibility at the expense of other tasks such as economic development which are not regarded as exclusive and essential to their sex. Indeed county and township committees responsible for organising village elections have encouraged villagers to put forward female candidates in the final voting round so as to ensure compliance with family planning targets set from above. Women thus gain their positions on the village committees not by virtue of their recognised general competence, but because of the necessity of having a woman to carry out family planning. Illustrative of this pattern is one village we visited in Ning Xiang County, Hunan province, where there had only ever been one woman on the village committee since elections were first held in 1987, and this woman was always the head of the women's committee, bearing responsibility for women's work, family planning and raising women's economic status. This gendered division of labour around public roles is mirrored also at the national level where senior female political leaders tend to be assigned portfolios relating to women and children. For example, after the Liberation of China, Long March veterans such as Cai Chang, Kang Keqing and Deng Ying Chao were given charge of portfolios concerned with women and children, rather than say defence, transport or trade.

The gendered nature of village committees is reflected not only in the differential assignment of tasks to men and women, but also in the way men and women are positioned in the hierarchy, thereby empowering men and women differently. Men head 99% of all village committees in China. That men occupy the highest positions of power and authority in village institutions, be these the village committee or the Party branch, reflects a similar weave at higher levels of the Party/state hierarchies. Where women are

---

15. Interview, April 2003.

16. In fact, at the 9th Party Congress in 1969 Ye Qun (wife of Lin Biao) and Jiang Qing (wife of Mao Zedong) were the first women ever to be elected to the Political Bureau. See Yuan Yi Ming, *Zhongguo Dangdai Funu Baike Zhishi Quanshu* (Beijing: Zhiming Ribao Publishing Company, 1997), p. 1472.

17. Ding Juan, 'Analysis on the track of Chinese women's participation in the government and public affairs', unpublished paper given at the *Sino–British Symposium on Women's Political Participation*, Beijing, October 2000.

found in politics, they are usually deputy provincial, county or township governors, deputy mayors, deputy premiers, and deputy village chairs. So whilst there are female vice-premiers to the NPC, there is no female chair. The first woman to become a provincial governor was Gu Xiulian in 1983 in Jiangsu province, and the first female provincial Party secretary was Wang Shaofen in 1985 in Jiangxi province. In the capital city of Hunan province, as of 2003, women accounted for one out of six mayors, that is 17%, one out of 13 Party committee members, 8%, 68 out of 400 provincial People's Congress delegates, 17%, and only one out of nine People's Congress Standing Committee members, 11%.[18] In one township under the capital city, there was not a single female member of the township leadership team and not a single female Party secretary. Of China's 6,000 mayors in all cities and counties, women account for only 500, that is less than 10% of the total, and most of these women are deputy mayors.

How can we then explain the numerical under-representation of women in village committees? Why is it that the introduction of choice has worked against women rather than being an opportunity for women to gain greater ground in the local political arena? Why do women on village committees get assigned portfolios deemed compatible with their reproductive and domestic functions? In the next section we explore the complexity of reasons underpinning women's low representation on village committees.

Explaining women's low representation in village committees

Gender researchers have put forward a combination of reasons explaining women's numerical under-representation in politics. These include not least gender socialisation, structural factors such as the gender division of labour in the economy and household, gender ideology, and political and institutional barriers.[19] Though all these variables contribute in varying degrees to women's under-representation in village committees in China, the introduction of village elections has brought to the surface the challenges of enduring negative attitudes towards women, the weakness of state intervention through ideological means to fundamentally alter gender stereotypes, the institutional barriers to women's greater participation in politics and the male political culture dominating politics at all levels. In this section we explore the complex intermeshing of these factors that results in keeping women out of positions of power and authority at village level.

Sexist attitudes towards women's participation in politics remain deeply entrenched in rural China, despite the over four decades of state gender ideology that proclaims the equality of men and women. Sayings such as 'nu zhu nei, nan zhu wai' ('women live inside, men outside') capture well the pervasive attitude that women's place is in the home, the public sphere belongs to men, and therefore that women's destiny is not in leadership. The political campaigns to bring women into waged employment in the 1950s, the ideological narratives of the Cultural Revolution period that sought to erase the notion of any differences between the male

---

18 Interview, Civil Affairs Bureau, provincial Organisation Bureau and provincial Women's Federation, April 2003

19 Joni Lovenduski and Vicki Randall, *Contemporary Feminist Politics. Women and Power in Britain* (Oxford: Oxford University Press, 1993); Vicki Randall, *Women and Politics* (London: Macmillan, 1987); Dorothy McBride Stetson and Amy G. Mazur, eds, *Comparative State Feminism* (London: Sage, 1995)

and female sex, and the appointment (rather than election) of women to positions of authority in village organisations aimed to undermine 'feudal' notions of women as inferior and less equal to men. However, the introduction of choice by village residents in the selection of leaders has opened up a sore wound, laying bare the enduring social beliefs about the appropriate roles in the economy and household of men and women, and the relative superiority of men over women.

These social beliefs are manifest in the way both government officials as well as rural residents, whether male or female, describe and explain the differences between men and women, and particularly the reluctance of villagers to nominate and vote for female candidates. Recurring notions are women's 'low quality', their passivity, their lack of competitiveness, and their disinterest in public matters as their lives, identities and consciousnesses gravitate around their families. Interviews with township and county female government officials, and female village leaders carried out in Hunan province in spring 2003 revealed how these beliefs and attitudes were internalised and surfaced both as factual statements and explanations. For example, the vice-President of a city Women's Federation in Hunan province pointed to women's 'low quality' (*funu suzhi di*) as a contributory factor to their low level of political participation. In her words, 'Women village cadres play a minor role. It is very difficult for women to become Party secretaries. They don't have enough ability. Their quality is lower than that of men's—that is their education level, their general knowledge'. Not only does women's own internalisation of these ideas hinder them from putting themselves forward for election, but the attitudes of male leaders, who occupy most positions of authority in the Party/government hierarchies, can also act as a barrier. The head of a county-level organisational bureau in Hunan province recounted that male leaders commonly made statements such as 'what can female cadres do?' (*nu ganbu neng gan shenme?*). His key point was that the attitude of the local Party secretary, whether at county, township or village level, to the promotion of women, could be central to whether women move into decision-making positions and also up the bureaucratic ladder.

The recurring refrain of women's supposed 'low quality' is problematic on two fronts. First, it focuses on the individual woman, and especially the rural woman, as the source of both the problem and its solution. Second, it masks the way in which other structural, institutional and political factors shape the engagement of men and women in local politics. To expand on the first point, the ACWF devotes considerable energy to raising the 'quality' of women through training programmes and dedicated campaigns. In the new market-oriented economy of the reform period the ACWF at all levels organises training programmes for rural women to acquire specialised skills such as growing fruit trees, pig-raising, and chicken-breeding. Its long-running 'Four Selfs Campaign' aims to raise 'women's self-respect, self-confidence, self-reliance and self-development'. Whilst son-preference has worked to favour educational opportunities for boys over girls in rural areas, particularly in poor and remote locations, leading to measurable differences in educational progress for boys and girls, the constant focus on girls and women as the site of correction detracts attention from addressing the underlying problem of son-preference, and deeply entrenched sexist beliefs, norms and practices. Ironically the constant thrust to improve women reproduces the notion that women always 'lack' certain qualities and skills compared to men.

This institutional focus on women has its roots in a state gender ideology that has operated with a unitary focus on 'women' rather than a gender analysis that takes the relations between men and women to be socially constructed. State-derived feminism in China, that is, the complex combination of official gender ideology, practical strategies and institutional arrangements used to advance women's status,[20] builds upon the work of Engels, Lenin, Marx and Mao on the 'woman's question', which links women's subjugation to historical and material forces. In the context of state socialism, collective ownership and planning of the economy, the material underpinnings of women's subjugation are therefore removed. The traces of women's subjugation that surface in the persistence of sexist attitudes belong thus to the realm of ideology. It is therefore in this realm that such attitudes are to be challenged. At the same time accepting that 'feudal thinking' remains and continues to influence the educational opportunities of women, the ACWF seeks to subvert this through campaigns aimed at enlightening women about their capabilities and enhancing women's skills through training. This dominant paradigm that is circulated through the primary agency of the ACWF shapes the way that women's under-representation in village elections is understood and the kind of remedies that are to be applied to the patient. This then brings us on to the second point, namely, that such analysis has the effect of masking the way institutional, structural and political factors also shape women's participation in politics and therefore impeding changes in these areas.

Male bias in nomination and selection processes, the importance of Party membership, the 'bamboo ceiling effect' of vague quotas, and institutional discrimination against women as reflected in differential salaries and pensions, and gendered differences in career trajectories are but some of the institutional factors that shape women's participation in politics. The impact of male bias arises out of male domination of key political institutions in the Party/government and at village level, and the procedures for nominating and selecting candidates. Key institutions related to the election processes are dominated by men and by Party members. The village election committees at township and county levels, which guide and supervise the village elections, the village Party branches, the village groups which often put forward candidates, the village assembly, and household heads, are all predominantly male. Given that women are under-represented in the Party and the significance of gendered social networks which glue together the male-dominated institutions, women face considerable institutional challenges from the very beginning of the election process. Furthermore, due to the variability in nomination and selection procedures across China's villages, there is considerable scope for gendered processes to intervene.[21] To illustrate, in some villages it is the heads of households, who are usually male, that nominate candidates initially. In other villages it might be the heads and representatives of village groups, who again are predominantly male, that make the initial nominations. In some villages when it comes to the second round of whittling down the number of

---

20. For a full analysis of state derived feminism and its implications for and effects on female political participation see Jude Howell, 'Women's political participation in China: struggling to hold up half the sky', *Parliamentary Affairs. A Journal of Comparative Politics* 55(1), (2002), pp. 43–56.

21. In an attempt to standardise practices and improve transparency, the CCP Central Committee and State Council issued in July 2004 the 'Views of the General Offices of the CCP Central Committee and State Council on strengthening and improving the systems of making village affairs public and exercising democratic management'. See *China People's Daily*, (13 July 2004), in *Summary of World Broadcasts*, (30 July 2004), p. 8.

candidates to two more than the number of vacant positions, the village election committee, village group heads and representatives, which again are mainly populated by men, decide on which candidates should go forward to the final round.

Unclear selection criteria also open up the space for gendered attitudes and beliefs to affect the nomination of candidates. When asked about the desirable attributes of village leaders, township officials and incumbent village leaders referred to vague notions such as 'willing to serve the masses', 'putting energy into work', 'should love doing things'. At county and township level election organising committees often stipulate the requirements for candidates, promoting thereby a particular profile of candidates. Typically a candidate should be young (between 18 and 45 years of age) so as to rejuvenate village bodies, educated (usually with at least lower secondary school education), competent (as proven by the economic success of their own household), and have good moral behaviour (as seen in the lack of a criminal record and compliance with the family planning policy).[22] These criteria potentially discriminate against women, whose life patterns are more noticeably interrupted by childcare responsibilities.

Aware that enduring social prejudices were hindering women's participation in politics, the central government inserted Article 9 into the temporary 1988 and then permanent 1998 Village Organic Law, whereby village committees were required to have 'an appropriate proportion' of women. In 1999 the Ministry of Civil Affairs circulated a document 'Suggestions for the Guarantee of a Proper Portion Among Members of Village Committees'. The vagueness of the clause in the Law renders its implementation difficult as there is no obligation on provincial, county or township governments to interpret this either as requiring all village committees to have female representation or to have more than one woman on such committees. Progressive local governments taking up this issue, such as Shandong and Hunan provinces, introduced local regulations in 2002, which specified that the law should be interpreted to mean 'at least one woman'.[23]

Though the 1988 and 1999 Village Organic Law, the 1999 Circular and the provincial regulations adopted in places such as Hunan and Shandong have increased the pressure on county and township governments and villages to put forward female candidates and to raise villagers' awareness of the issue, they have also had unintended consequences. First, in practice the vague quota has cast a bamboo ceiling on women's representation. So 'a certain proportion of women' as in the Law, or, as in the case of Hunan and Shandong provinces, 'at least one woman' become interpreted as a maximum of one. The rope to save women turns instead into a noose. Local government officials and village leaders become satisfied if one woman has been elected to a committee, and there the saga ends. In the three counties we visited in Hunan province most village committees had one female member, but few had more than one. To illustrate, in a township in Xiangxi prefecture in Hunan province, only one out of ten villages had more than one woman on the village committee. State intervention can make a difference, but

---

22. Ministry of Civil Affairs Research Group on Direct Village Elections System, *Zhongguo Nongcun Cunmin Weiyuanhui Huanbie Xuanju Zhidu* [*Study on the Election of Villagers' Committees in Rural China*] (Beijing: Chinese Society Publishing House, 1993).

23. See, for example, Document 16, issued by Hunan Province Civil Affairs Bureau and Women's Federation in 2001, *Guanyu zai cunminhui huanbie zhong baozheng cunweihui banzi zhong you shidang nuxing cengyuan de yijian* [*Suggestions on Protecting an Appropriate Number of Female Members on Village Committees in the Elections for Village Committees*].

that difference is in turn limited by social norms, attitudes and practices that underlie intervention processes, particularly in a context of decollectivisation and the availability of alternative channels of wealth and prosperity.

The second unintended consequence relates to the efforts of the Women's Federation and local Civil Affairs Bureau to promote female candidates for positions on the village committee. In Hunan, Hebei and Shandong provinces, for example, the local Women's Federations have sought to train and encourage the heads of village women's committees to stand for election. This in turn has led to experiments in competitive elections for the position of head of the women's committee, with the aim of making the committee more representative and legitimate. The outcome is that the one woman on the village committee tends also to be the head of the village women's committee. This not only limits the range of 'women's interests' represented but also again links women's political participation to their particular identity as a woman. Given that the head of the women's village committee often doubles as the family planning person, then the entry-points for women into politics continue to be shaped by women's reproductive roles. This in turn is exacerbated by the fact that villagers will be encouraged by the village election committee to select a woman candidate so that family planning targets can be achieved.[24] Together this reinforces the notion that women can only enter politics if they come as representatives of their gender, rather than say their class or ideology, and justifies the allocation of only gender-related portfolios to women. Thus the vagueness of well-intended legal measures to ensure the participation of women in village elections, coupled with pressure to select someone to take charge of family planning targets, combines to limit women's numerical representation to a lone one, thereby casting a bamboo ceiling above women.

Though Party membership is not a criterion for standing as a candidate for election to the village committee, the Party nevertheless is a significant channel, laden with symbolic and often material resources, for promoting particular candidates in election processes. Though there are successful candidates who are not Party members, they are strongly encouraged afterwards to join the Party. In this way village elections serve as a means both to rejuvenate and relegitimate the Party. Moreover, Party membership is usually essential for promotion up the hierarchies of the Party/state. Even though non-Party members can and do stand for village elections, the majority of village committee members belong to the Party. However women are significantly under-represented in the Chinese Communist Party (CCP). Indeed, women's participation in the CCP is even less than in other parties in China.[25]

---

24. In some villages we visited in Hunan province, the family planning person was tokenistically counted as on the village committee, even though they had not been selected as a candidate, because otherwise the committee would have no female members. This ambivalence became obvious when asking about the numbers of village committee members and their identities.

25. It is noteworthy that the percentage of female members of the Chinese Communist Party is the least of all political parties in China. According to Guo Li, 2001, 'A tentative analysis on disposition of gender proportion in the leading body at all levels' in *Supplement of 2001 'Collection of Women's Studies'*, published by Collection of Women's Studies, Beijing, cited in Du Jie, 2004, 'Women's participation in politics in the transition to a market economy in China: progress at high level politics since 1995', draft paper for UNRISD Contribution to 'Beijing Plus Ten' 2004) the Friendship Association of Taiwan Democratic League had the highest proportion of all women in political parties in China, with women accounting for 64% of total membership, whilst the Chinese Peasants and Workers Democratic Party came second, with 47%. Available figures put female membership of the Chinese Communist Party at around 15% as of 1998.

As indicated earlier, only five out of 198 members of the Central Committee of the Chinese Communist Party are women, a mere 2.5%, whilst only one out of 24 members of the Politbureau is a woman. In Changsha city, the capital of Hunan province, as of 2003, there was only one woman out of 13 members on the provincial Party committee. Similarly at township and county levels a similar pattern of under-representation prevails. For example in Ning Xiang County, Hunan province, as of 2003, there are only 5,850 female Party members out of a total of 58,625, accounting for just 10%. Similarly in the villages under a township in Liuyang City, Hunan province, only one out of 14 village Party secretaries is a woman. Aware of the under-representation of women in the Party, Liuyang City Party Committee issued a document in 2002 requiring that women made up 20% of Party representatives in the city and surrounding areas. However without any clear strategy for implementing this and for moving beyond a minimum of 20%, it will take some time before there is progress in this area. Given that women are under-represented in village Party branches, they lack a significant institutional channel for promoting them in village elections.

Even if women do get into positions of power and authority, they continue to face institutionalised forms of discrimination such as lower salaries, less favourable pension entitlements, and fewer opportunities for promotion. Women responsible for women's work in villages receive little or no remuneration for their efforts. In one village we visited in Feng Huang County, Hunan province, the head of the women's committee, who was also a village committee member, received less than all other village committee members, on the grounds that compared to the Party secretary, family planning person, village head accountant and secretary, she was not a 'main cadre' (*zhu ganbu*). Though family planning cadres are better paid than women committee heads in villages, they both receive less favourable treatment in relation to pensions. Key people in the village committee and Party branch, such as the village head, Party secretary and accountant, are entitled to a pension after 20 years of service. However, neither the family planning cadre nor the head of the women's committee are entitled to this benefit. The undervaluing of women's contribution is reflected also in their lower status. In March 2002 Hunan provincial government issued a circular that reaffirmed the 1989 policy requirement that grassroots women cadres should have the status of section-level cadres after eight years of work experience and three years of assessment. Nevertheless, this has still not been widely implemented, not only because of a failure to treat this with urgency but also because of an apparent lack of pressure from higher levels of the ACWF.

Finally, the gendered pattern of career trajectories also shapes the way women and men progress up Party/government ladders and participate in village political structures. First, as there are fewer women in leadership positions in villages, women tend to get assigned responsibility for women's work and/or family planning. Often women are on the village committee precisely because higher levels of government require the implementation of the family planning policy. Being locked in this way into women's work and/or family planning, women do not get opportunities to develop other skills and experience which are more highly valued and considered important for assuming top leadership positions. Second, at township and county levels women tend to be assigned to the local Women's Federation or given responsibility for family planning work. As the status of the Women's Federation is lower in the pecking order of government departments and mass organisations, women are held back in their careers, whilst young men advance directly up the civil service/Party ladders. Third, given the emphasis upon relative youth in promotion criteria, women are again disadvantaged as in their late twenties women are bearing and rearing children. When faced with work that requires extensive travel around villages and townships, women with young children struggle to manage both work and domestic demands, or decline these tasks, accepting that this will constrain their promotion. By the time their children mature into adulthood, women are in their mid-forties and approaching retirement. As women civil servants retire five years earlier than their male counterparts at the age of 55 rather than 60, they again miss out on promotion to more senior positions. At village level pressure from above to promote younger candidates again works against older women, who free of childcare responsibilities, could now take on the tasks of village committee membership.

Apart from these institutional constraints, women's participation is also shaped by various structural factors, such as the gendered division of domestic labour, marriage practices, lower educational opportunities for girl-children, women's positioning in the waged economy, and gendered boundaries of mobility. With the decollectivisation of agriculture and rural–urban migration, the farming of land has increasingly been left to women. As women take prime responsibility for domestic affairs, and increasingly take on agricultural work and side-line activity, they have even less time to participate in village governance processes. The gendered division of domestic life makes it easier for men to participate in village public affairs. As domestic work does not have neat boundaries of time, it can be difficult for women to participate in village election meetings that are held at lunch-time or in the evening, when children need attending to and food preparation is underway. The absence of child-care facilities during village assemblies or village elections again militates against women's participation. The centring of women's lives around the household in turn contributes to a perception amongst village leaders, many villagers and government officials that they are less concerned with the outside world, and therefore less capable of understanding public affairs.

As in many parts of China rural women move into the husband's household, not only do the parents invest less in their daughters' education and futures, but village leaders also do not devote much attention to the development of leadership skills amongst young girls and women, as they are destined to leave the village. In the new village women are seen as strangers. As a result women lack the social networks built up during childhood through school, family and friends that men can mobilise to rally support in elections. They have to start again to build up networks of friendship, trust and solidarity that men have cultivated through schooling, friends, work and family ties.[26] Women are thus disadvantaged when it comes to standing for election as they have less 'social capital' to draw upon, compared to men with several decades of

---

26. As David Wank points out in his discussion of *guanxi*, the strongest obligations in the *guanxi* system are produced by birth, and particularly direct kin on the father's side. The engendering of *guanxi* as well as women's relocation to their husband's village work thus together to disadvantage women in developing a similar stock of social capital to draw on in village elections. See David Wank, 'The institutional process of market clientelism: guanxi and private business in a south China city', *China Quarterly* no. 147, (September 1996), pp. 820–838.

accumulated networks of solidarity and support. As one female village committee chair in a county in Hunan province explained, it takes a long time for women marrying into a village to win the confidence of other village residents.

In addition to these structural factors, a male dominated political culture plays a key role in keeping women out of politics, be this at village, provincial or national levels. At stake here are political cultural practices such as heavy drinking, toasting and smoking, which function to nurture and consolidate bonds of male solidarity and are interpreted as indicators of leadership ability. These practices pose a problem for women leaders as smoking and drinking are in general seen as inappropriate for women and undermine their reputation. Women are thus placed in a no-win situation. If they participate in smoking and drinking, then they risk sullying their reputations; if they do not engage in drinking rituals, then they risk failing to build up their networks of influence and power. That political culture is a serious gender issue in politics was apparent from our interviews with women leaders at township, county and village levels. For example, a female township vice-Party secretary in Hunan province describes her experiences of working in a male-dominated work environment as follows:

> Women's status is not high. Higher levels require lower levels to have women cadres but, for myself, I am not pleased about being promoted because of the family burden ... and I don't like the work environment. ... At county, township levels, other cadres look down on women ... they think they are not convenient ... they discriminate against us. They feel it is not convenient because we don't drink. The environment, the culture of drinking ... we don't like this but sometimes you have to join in.[27]

In some villages in order to protect their reputations women village committee members will make explicit efforts to avoid any ambiguity in their interactions with men. For example, the head of one village committee in Hunan province related her strategy as follows: 'I avoid staying alone with men. I keep the conversation short. I take care of my actions. I don't go out on my own to discuss with a man'. The pervasiveness of a male-dominated political culture involving practices that have the potential to damage women's standing places an additional burden on women seeking to engage in political life.

Enduring sexist beliefs and norms, gendered divisions of labour in the economy and household, institutional policies and practices, and political culture and values all combine to varying degrees in villages to create barriers to women's greater numerical representation. Is there any room for optimism? As will be discussed in the next section, there are several reasons to hope that the future might be more optimistic.

Resisting women's subjugation in rural politics

Though the introduction of competitive village elections has led to a decline in female representation in village committees, this trend is also meeting with some resistance, both from within the ACWF and the relevant department of the Ministry of Civil Affairs and from rural women. Already in the mid-1980s academic

---

27. Interview, April 2003.

researchers and cadres within the ACWF began to draw attention to the declining numerical representation of women in Party/state structures at all levels and in both urban and rural areas.[28] Some Women's Federations had already begun in the late 1980s to introduce measures such as minimum quotas for women, stimulating in turn a debate about the pros and cons of quotas for women. In Heping District of Shenyang city the head of the Women's Federation even challenged the notion of quotas as ceilings and managed to raise the representation of women in the local People's Congress from the quota of 25% to 31.7%.[29]

As competitive village elections swept across China's villages in the 1990s, some cadres in national and local level Women's Federations began to meet and plan ways of countering the downward spiral of female representation. The Women's Federation of Qianxi County, Hebei province was one of the first to set up training sessions in 1999 for potential female village committee chairs and members.[30] Other provincial and city women's federations also began to introduce specialised training for rural women to enter political leadership positions in villages. These training sessions provided opportunities for women from a diversity of villages to share experiences, learn about the political system, and gain confidence.

Apart from training, some progressive Women's Federations such as in Shandong province and Hunan province have introduced local measures to promote women's participation. For example, in Hunan province a joint document was issued by Hunan provincial Women's Federation and the Rural Grassroots Section of the Ministry of Civil Affairs, which interpreted Article 9 of the national Village Committee Organic Law to mean that there should be at least one woman on a village committee. Some counties in Hunan have also issued their own directives echoing the substance of the provincial document. Local level officials involved in the village election committee are thus obliged, in theory at least, to ensure that every village has female representation. A similar initiative was taken in Shandong province, where the local Women's Federation and Civil Affairs Bureau jointly issued a document, requiring there to be at least one woman on the village committee. As a result the numbers of women on the committee increased after the next elections. As mentioned earlier, in some provinces such as Hunan, local officials have seized this opportunity to introduce competitive direct elections for the heads of women's committees and to then promote this woman as the candidate for a village committee position.

In a workshop organised by the Ministry of Civil Affairs in August 2004 in Beijing, academics, NPC delegates, female village committee heads and cadres from national and provincial Women's Federations came together to discuss ways of increasing female representation on village committees. Inspired by the reservation

---

28. Ma Lizhen and Ji Xiaocun, 'Report about a work conference on training women cadres for selection and promotion', *Zhongguo Funu*, (October 1990), pp. 11–13; Tamara Jacka, *Women's Work in Rural China. Change and Continuity in an Era of Reform* (Cambridge: Cambridge University Press, 1997), p. 88; Guo Donggui, 'Why do women cadres lose elections?', *Chinese Law and Government: Women and Politics in China* 26(6), (November–December 1993), pp. 7–18; Li Xiaojiang, *Eve's Transcending: a Theoretical Outline of Women's Studies in China* (Zhengzhou: Henan People's Press, 1988); Wang Qi, 'State–society relations and women's political participation', in Jackie West, Zhao Minghua, Chang Xiangqun and Cheng Yuan, eds, *Women of China. Economic and Social Transformation* (Basingstoke: Macmillan Press, 1999), pp. 19–44.

29. Gordon White, Jude Howell and Shang Xiaoyuan, *In Search of Civil Society. Market Reform and Social Change in Contemporary China* (Oxford: Clarendon Press, 1996), p. 88.

30. Interview, Director of Civil Affairs, Qianxi County, August 1999.

of one third of seats for women in India's village councils, a proposal was put forward at this meeting to amend the Villagers' Committee Organic Law so as to ensure a minimum quota of women.

All these initiatives suggest that progressive women within the ACWF and the rural grassroots division of the Ministry of Civil Affairs are resisting the numerical under-representation of women in village committees and using their organisational positions, social networks, and the legal framework to establish institutional barriers to discrimination. However laws, regulations and measures are only as good as their implementation. There the crux of the problem lies. For without pressure from above local level officials are not likely to pay much attention to such directives.

Though state-derived feminism perpetuates paradoxically the myth that women are less able than men through its singular focus on women as the subject of change, it is also the case that women's consciousnesses are fluid, variable and not wholly open to capture. Women do not readily accept that their 'quality is low' and do not internalise forever, or continually, stereotypic attitudes that position them as inferior to men. This became evident in interviews with village women leaders, who expressed not only confidence in their own self-worth, but also clarity about the extent of male prejudice in society. For example, one female village head in Hunan province described the discrimination she encountered but still maintained a sense of her own self-worth and the capabilities of women:

> On the whole men don't trust women and despise women. Some men are not very civilised and say women ... even if they improve their abilities, they still discriminate against women. If you haven't had the experience of being in contact with them, you can't believe they could despise you—many people see women as less capable as men. They need practice to show women can do as well as men. This is a difficulty in my work. Many women are capable. Also there are things men can't do. Men will say but 'you're not a man' ... I don't mind speaking. I'm not afraid of anything. ... Whatever men can do, I think I can do. I have self-confidence. First you have to believe in yourself.[31]

Finally outmigration over the last 20 years from poorer, agricultural areas to richer, industrialising coastal areas has reaped vast changes in the structure of village life. On the one hand male outmigration has often left women wholly responsible for less well rewarded agricultural labour. This has in turn opened up channels for women to enter village positions. However, some researchers and government officials then explain women's leap into leadership positions by the absence of any male competition. The underlying sexism in such interpretations leaves women in a no-win situation: if they become the head of a village committee, it is only because there are no male competitors; if there are male competitors, then the fact they do not succeed shows that they are less suited to leadership. On the other hand, there is also considerable female outmigration. Such women may stay for several years working in assembly-line factories in Guangdong or Fujian. Though their conditions of work are harsh, they also gain new skills and knowledge, fresh perspectives and wider horizons. No longer can the argument be made that 'women lack outside experience' and therefore are not suitable for village leadership. This generation of young

---

31. Interview, April 2003.

women, who may at some point return to their villages, provide some optimism that village politics could change in the future.

However, from the research we carried out, it is clear that it will still take time for attitudes to change as gendered social norms continue to be a constraint on women's participation. For example, in the run-up to the 1998 elections in a village in Xiangxi prefecture, Hunan province, eight out of 27 female candidates (30%) had worked outside compared to 12 out of 34 male candidates (35%), a slightly higher proportion but hardly sufficient to explain women's low representation in leadership positions. Similarly in Luo Yixi township, Guzhang County, Hunan province, women constitute about half of all migrant workers. Yet only one village head in the township is female and only two out of 17 Party secretaries are female. In any case, the lack of outside experience does not mean that women cannot learn the skills of leadership. The excuse of 'lack of outside experience' becomes in turn a way of denying women the opportunity to acquire appropriate skills and experience.

Conclusion

In this article we have proposed that political choice through the ballot paper is a gendered process with gendered outcomes. Without state intervention, enduring social norms and attitudes that are disadvantageous to women gaining political power and authority are likely to prevail. This has been reflected in the declining numerical participation of women in village politics. However, state intervention in China has in Communist Party tradition, as manifested through ACWF discourses and policies, targeted primarily the individual woman as the main focal point of change. In doing so it has paradoxically reproduced sexist litanies that portray women as always 'lacking' some quality or another. Moreover, because state intervention has not grappled with masculinity, not least due to the absence of any gender analysis, patriarchal and sexist attitudes to women have persisted and worked to keep political positions a male preserve.

The recent attempts to turn this around and make democratic elections work for women provide some glimmer of hope that the situation might ameliorate in the future. This will require not only the introduction of quotas and positive measures to promote women, but also greater scrutiny of the way recruitment and promotion procedures within the Party, village organs and government structures discriminate against women. It will also require fresh analysis of the structural constraints that face rural women such as the lack of child-care facilities, and the timing of elections and village meetings. Perhaps most challenging of all will be the need to examine the culture of politics, and in particular the exclusionary effects, both for women and men, of a political style that relies on heavy drinking, smoking and banqueting.

The Impact of Elections on the Village Structure of Power: the relations between the village committees and the Party branches

GUO ZHENGLIN with THOMAS P. BERNSTEIN

Village committee elections are one of the major innovations of the reform era. Electoral processes have elicited much scholarly and public attention. Less attention has been devoted to studying the impact of this innovation on the relations between the elected village committee chair persons and the appointed Party secretaries. This article shows that conflicts can arise between the two because the basis of their legitimacy and authority differs. A concrete instance of conflict is control over collective economic resources and financial decisions. The field research on which much of this article is based was done in southern Guangdong, where villages tend to be quite industrialized and wealthy. In these villages, control had hitherto been vested in the secretaries. Now, town leaders had to adjudicate jurisdictional disputes between village committees and the Party branches. Often they preferred to side with the latter, since secretaries were likely to be more responsive to their superiors than elected village chiefs. A solution to these conflicts that is now being widely adopted in rural China is to require that Party secretaries run for the post of village committee chair, thereby in effect merging the two institutions.

Introduction

Village elections have rightly aroused much attention among scholars within and without China. A substantial literature examines the electoral process—its fairness, openness, and competitiveness.[1] Increasing attention is also being devoted to the

---

1. For an excellent overview of research on these topics, see the special issue of *China Quarterly*, (162), 'Elections and democracy in Greater China', (June 2000).

longer-term impact of the elections on rural politics. Survey research by Li Lianjiang, for instance, shows that where elections are fair, elected leaders come under greater pressure from their constituents to act on behalf of their interests.[2] This article seeks to contribute to our understanding of the impact of elections by focusing on the relations between the elected village committees (VC) and the village Party branch (VPB), particularly those between the VC chairperson and the Party branch secretary. This is also an issue that is now receiving some attention in the literature.[3]

The introduction of direct elections of the village committees and of the establishment of the village assemblies or representative assemblies (VRA) implied the diversification or pluralization of formal political power in the villages. Power was now based on two different sources of authority. The VC chair was elected 'from below' (*zi xia erh shang*). His/her authority was based on the consent of the governed, the voting citizenry. The Party secretary's source of authority was his/her status as an agent of the Chinese Communist Party as a whole. He/she was chosen from above (*zi shang erh xia*) by the superior Party committee and his/her selection was ratified by the branch members who constituted only a small fraction of the adult population. Because a VC chair was elected by the entire population, he/she was likely to enjoy greater legitimacy among villagers and to enjoy their trust to a greater extent than the appointed VPB secretary. The major, underlying question is whether and to what extent the elections posed a challenge to the power and legitimacy of the CCP's primacy in rural areas and if so, what the regime could do about this.

Before the introduction of direct elections, the village Party secretary had been the undisputed boss of the village (*yibashou*). Now, power was supposed to be shared. To be sure, the 'Organic Law on the Organization of Villager Committees' (henceforth, Organic Law) specified that the Party should be the 'leadership core'.[4] It should exercise leadership 'over important matters' while the VC should take charge of specific issues. But so ambiguous a formula said little about concrete jurisdictional issues and the division of labor between the two leaders. Chinese scholars and officials devoted much attention to the question of how to distinguish the two roles but usually only reiterated the general principle of Party primacy.[5]

This analysis of the VC–VPB relationships is based on fieldwork by scholars from Guangzhou's Zhongshan University, chiefly Guo Zhenglin, supplemented by findings from Guo's research in Hunan and Jiangsu carried out between 1995 and 1998. The research was done in Southern Guangdong in the form of periodic investigations in villages in three Guangdong municipalities, Zhongshan, Xinhui and Nanhai, in the period from February to September 1999. In September 1999, Thomas Bernstein joined in the fieldwork. This included interviews with town and

2. Li Lianjiang, 'Elections and popular resistance in China', *China Information* XV(2), (2001), pp. 1–19.

3. See, for instance, John James Kennedy, 'The face of 'grassroots democracy' in rural China: real vs. cosmetic elections', *Asian Survey* XLII(3), (May/June 2002), pp. 456–482.

4. *Zhonghua Renmin Gongheguo Cunmin Weiyuanhui Zuzhi Fa* (Beijing: Falu Chubanshe, 1989).

5. See for instance, Xu Yong, 'Lun cunmin zizhi beijing xia dang zuzhi yu zizhi de xietiao' ['On coordinating party and self-governing organizations against the background of villager autonomy'], *Xuexi yu Luntan* (1), (1998), pp. 89–92.

village cadres, and villagers' representatives. Part of the research involved partici-pation in an investigation of 'villagers' self-government and rural transition' in February and March 1999 by departments of Zhongshan municipality, which covered 25 villages in 12 towns. From April to June, formal and informal interviews were conducted with cadres in the towns and villages of Pingzhou and Nanzhuang. In September, in Xinhui, with the help of the Xinhui city Youth League, research was done in three towns and three villages, which included six meetings with cadres from the towns and villages. Topics studied included village elections, the relationship between the VPBs and the VCs, and villagers' burdens.

The field research was done at a crucial period of time. Unlike other provinces Guangdong did not hold village elections until 1998–1999. Until then, there had been a system of rural administrative districts (*nongcun guanli qu*), whose cadres were appointed by the towns and who had no independent authority but were simply the agents of their superiors.[6] Beginning in 1998 and through the first half of 1999, rural reform in Guangdong aimed at replacing the administrative districts with elected VCs in order to implement villagers' self-government.[7] After the elections, the issue of allocation of authority in the villages arose and caused substantial conflict. How did this conflict work itself out? We begin by briefly examining Party leadership in the countryside, followed by case studies of conflict from several villages, an analysis of the role of the towns and higher authority in these conflicts, and an analysis of the emerging return to one-person leadership, albeit under new conditions.

The crisis in the rural Party

The social and economic changes that swept through rural China beginning with decollectivization had, as is well known, a deleterious impact on village Party branches. As of 2001, there were 1,357,000 rural grass roots branches with a membership of 29.5 million. From 1994 to 2000, 356,000 were rectified because they were 'weak, listless', paralyzed, or because they presided over backward or poverty-stricken villages. The goal was to revitalize them, raise their level of competence, recruit new, younger members, and, to instill in the branch members 'democratic' consciousness and methods. The Party secretaries and the branch members were to be educated to make village affairs public (*cunwu gongkai*) and to practice democratic politics, including village elections.[8]

Traditionally, as noted, village Party secretaries monopolized village-level power. They allocated tasks according to the principle that 'the Party secretary is

---

6. On the power relations between the administrative districts and town Party-governments, see Guo Zhenglin, 'Chinese Party and government relationship in transition: the reform of Guangdong rural power structure', paper delivered at the 5th Annual Conference of the David C. Lam Institute for East–West Studies at Hong Kong Baptist University and the Centre for East and Southeast Asian Studies at Lund University, Lund, Sweden, 18–20 October 1999.

7. On the process of the reform, see 'Shishi cunmin zizhi: Guangdong nongcun guanli tizhi de zhuanxing' ['Implementing villagers self-government: the transition of the Guangdong rural administration district system'], in Guo Zhenglin, *Zhongguo Cunzheng Zhidu* [*The Village Political System of China*] (Beijing: Zhongguo Wenlian Chubanshe, 1999), pp. 137–150.

8. *Xinhua*, (14 June 2001), in *FBIS* (614), (16 June 2001).

in command and mobilizes cadres into action' (*shuji guashuai, fenbing bakou*). The monopoly of power, it is important to note, extended to control over village collective economic resources, which in southern Guangdong, an area of highly developed TVEs, was of major significance. Under Guangdong's system of rural administrative districts, Party secretaries often were also the heads of the village economic committees (VEC). Party secretaries usually kept the financial accounts under wraps, a situation that elicited popular distrust and anger.[9]

In national perspective, the monopoly of power had both beneficial and harmful results. In some famous cases, such as Huaxi village in Jiangsu province and Nanjie and Liuzhuang villages in Henan, extraordinarily successful economic development took place under the leadership of powerful secretaries.[10] The resulting high standards of living led to villager contentment and social peace. Some Chinese observers believed that the key to economic development and social stability in the rural areas lay in finding capable and competent VPB secretaries.

But for every success story of effective, developmental leadership by a VPB secretary, a counter example can be cited of tyrannical rule and gross abuse of power. Some secretaries acted as local emperors (*tu huangdi*). Some were said to be more vicious than the worst of the landlords of old. One such tyrant acquired the name Huang Shiren, the notorious landlord in the ballet, 'White Haired Girl'. A famous case is that of Yu Zuomin of Daqiu village in Tianjin city, who led the village's extraordinary economic development, but who frequently defied higher authority and grossly abused his power, including complicity in murder, which eventually landed him in prison.[11] Another such case was that of the secretary of Fenghuo village in Shaanxi, who after the Great Leap Forward managed to become a deputy secretary of the municipal Party committee by means of bragging, cheating, and making use of clan relationships.[12] Of course, most secretaries fell between the two extremes. But the problem of abuse of power and the consequent chronic tensions between cadres and peasants was serious enough to prompt the regime to decide that major remedial measures were needed.

In Southern Guangdong, the rural Party was beset by several serious problems, of which two stood out. One was the deterioration of the Party's image in the eyes of the villagers as a result of corruption. Many farmers said that 'the red caps have the power to engage in corrupt behavior. The more corrupt they are, the more they praise the leadership of the Communist Party'. An official disclosed that in a Zhongshan city village, the inhabitants had submitted a collective petition to the Civil Affairs Bureau, complaining that their VPB had sold land for 100 million RMB, of which villagers only saw 900,000. The rest simply disappeared. The petitioners defiantly said: 'Why do the superiors like to put "red caps" on these blood-suckers? They've ruined land which was passed to us from generation to

---

9. Interviews, Guangzhou Civil Affairs Bureau, May 1999.

10. For a study about them and their villages, see Feng Zhi, *Zhongguo San Da Cun* [*Three Famous Chinese Villages*] (Wuhan: Huazhong shifan daxue chubanshe, 1998).

11. See Bruce Gilley, *Model Rebels: The Rise and Fall of China's Richest Village* (Berkeley: University of California Press, 2001).

12. See Lu Yaogang, *Daguo Guomin* [*Great Nation's Populace*] (Beijing: Zhongguo Dianying Chubanshe, 1998).

generation'.[13] Peasants deeply resented such leaders. If villagers were able to elect the VPB secretaries, they wouldn't hesitate to throw such 'exploiters' out. Corruption severely damaged the image of the Party and often resulted in villagers rejecting Party member candidates for the VCs.

The introduction of direct elections created a rival authority that confronted the village Party with the challenge of regaining its authority in the eyes of the people. Many peasants, whose political awareness had grown, felt that the VCs genuinely represented them and hence should be the repositories of their trust. How then could the VPB's authority as the core of the leadership be regained and maintained? This dilemma was behind experiments with subjecting prospective Party secretaries to a test of popular approval, of which the two-ballot system in Huoqu county, Shanxi, is the best know example. Under this system, villagers could recommend which of the Party members they preferred as branch secretary.[14] It differed from the system of concurrent office-holding, which obliged the Party secretary to establish his/her popularity by winning the VC election (cf. last section).

The second problem was lagging recruitment of young people. The rural Party organizations were aging everywhere. In one town in Southern Guangdong, more than half of the 800 Party members were over 60 years of age. Many elderly Party secretaries who had been in office since the Mao era were not qualified to cope with the tasks of modern management, especially of large TVEs. Without the recruitment of younger, capable managers, the Party was in danger of becoming increasingly irrelevant. Now that the VPB had a competitor in the form of the VC, if it was to continue to be a significant player in village affairs, it had to have the managerial capacities to do so.

An investigation report by a municipal Party committee pointed out that fewer and fewer of the talented emerging social and economic elites were applying to join the Party. Opportunities to make money reduced the incentive to join the Party. As one village cadre, a VC secretary, observed, 'Now what is most useful is a bank note (*chapiao*), not a Party card. Soon our VPB will become a "white haired branch" '.[15] Conversely, where there were fewer opportunities for individual advancement, joining remained an attractive option for young opportunists. 'I think I'll first join the Young Pioneers, then the Communist Youth League and finally the Communist Party. I will go to work in a Party committee after graduation. With power, things can easily be done, such as getting jobs for your children'; and, 'we all want to join the Party. This is because you can get promoted when you are a Party member. You can have power when you are promoted. And with power you can become rich. None of the Party members in our village are now poor'.[16]

Party branches were told to concentrate their energies on the recruitment and training of new members so as to rejuvenate and reinvigorate the membership. At

---

13. Interview with official of Guangdong's Civil Affairs Bureau, May 1999.
14. See Li Lianjiang, 'The two-ballot system of Shanxi: subjecting village party secretaries to a popular vote', *China Journal* (42), (July 1999), pp. 103–118.
15. Village survey of Zhongshui, Hunan, January 1996.
16. Stanley Rosen, 'The Chinese Communist Party and Chinese society: popular attitudes toward party membership and party image', *The Australian Journal of Chinese Affairs* (24), (July 1990), pp. 51–92.

the same time, subjecting the Party branches to implicit or explicit competition by the VCs would also, it was hoped, provide an incentive to them to raise their capabilities.

VC challenges to the Party branches after the elections

Initially, the elections caused a great deal of confusion and uncertainty over the delimitation of authority both among the Party secretaries who wore the 'red cap' and the VC chairmen who wore the 'yellow cap'. Bewildered Party secretaries asked their superiors what use it was to have elected chairpersons as long as there was the core leadership by the Party? By the same token, the village chairs were also perplexed: if the leadership of the Party must be adhered to, why bother with elections in the first place? For their part, the superior town officials worried whether the elected VCs would fully carry out the instructions of the towns in the same way as when cadres had been appointed.

Conflicts over VPB refusal to surrender power to the VC were common in Guangdong. One source was financial control. As an official of the Guangdong Civil Affairs Bureau put it 'the major complaint in the replacement of the administrative districts with village governments is that the original rural cadres refused to hand over control over financial and other affairs to the VCs'. In addition to economic power, the right of appointment of cadres also caused disputes. The following four cases, based on records of meetings with village Party secretaries and VC chairpersons convened by town Party committees, provide vivid illustrations of conflicts that arose when VCs sought to assert their new power.

1. Daling village, Huoju town, Zhongshan city

The VC's newly elected chairman, not a Party member, had been the manager of a factory under the village corporation (*gongsi*) and naturally had always obeyed the secretary's orders. Once elected to the new office, however, he sought to take charge of the finances of the village collective assets, as stipulated in the Organic Law, leaving the secretary only with the 'hammer and sickle'—his seal of office—but without economic power. Yet, the same law, as noted, stipulated that the VPB was the 'core' leadership which should decide 'important matters'. The Party secretary, a man in his fifties, was confused and indignant: was this not an attempt by people outside the Party to seize power? What the 'leadership core is supposed to mean is beyond my comprehension', he said, noting that 'there are seven or eight articles in the Law which prescribe the functions of VCs, and they are very concrete and specific', reinforcing his impression that his power had been drained of substance. If important decisions were to be confirmed by our Party branch, then what was the use of the Villagers' Representatives Assembly (VRA), he complained. He stubbornly insisted 'that since the Party's leadership is predominant everywhere, your VC cannot be exempted'. The VC director responded:

> I do not mean to oppose the leadership of the Party branch, which must be conducted in accordance with the Law. But it stipulates that the VC chairman is the legal

representative of the village economic collective and is supposed to take charge of village accounts, money and personnel. Furthermore, if there is any mistake with village affairs, the villagers will not accuse your VPB but the VC. How can it be possible that you wield the 'the big power' and I bear the responsibility?[17]

Complying with higher-level demands, the Party secretary handed over the account books and the seals, leaving him with little to do, while the VC chairman became an extremely busy man. He chaired the VC meeting at which tasks were allocated among the members. He worked out procedures for the VC, he posted data on village affairs, he settled villager disputes, received superior officials, and he devoted himself to planning the village's future development. The VC member in charge of economic affairs dealt with the management of the village enterprises, was responsible for enterprise safety and the supply of water and electricity, and supervised enterprise operation. The committee member in charge of security ran the village security team and coordinated activities with the town public security office. Another member was in charge of villagers family planning and assisted the town in the administration of migrant populations and their birth control.

Nominally, the Party secretary was still in control as the *yibashou*. He continued to chair meetings on issues which required joint action by both the secretary and VC chairman, such as comprehensive management of security and family planning. The 'responsibility' documents (*ziren shu*) on security and family planning also required both signatures, because the superiors wanted to make sure that both leaders were bound to them.

Without economic power, the secretary felt that these functions were useless. He was often absent, playing mahjong, and left other VPB members free to do as they wished. The superiors regarded this kind of branch as weak and paralyzed. In the two months after the village elections, from December 1998 to January 1999, around 10% of the VPBs in Zhongshan city were in the same situation as the Daling village branch. However, by March 1999, we were told that most of them had been 'readjusted' and had now reached the 'four standards' with regard to 'revolutionization', proper age distribution, educational attainments and professionalism. In these villages, the weakened conditions of the VPBs was apparently a temporary one.

2. *Zhangjia village, Zhongshan*

In Zhangjia village, Zhongshan, conflict also arose over control of economic assets. The village economic development company had assets of over 50 million RMB and a net annual income of over 5 million. Half of the 9,000 villagers were shareholders and only they were entitled to its welfare distribution. Under the district administration system, the Party secretary had concurrently served as the head of the board of directors, while the head of the administrative district was the general manager, but it was the secretary who held the decision-making power. The newly elected village chairman was in his thirties. He had studied economics in college as a self-financed student and then returned to the village. The Party

---

17. Interviews, Zhongshan, March 1999.

secretary had employed him as his assistant. In late 1998, he was nominated as one of the candidates for VC chair and elected by a wide margin, apparently because of his competence.

From then on his good personal relations with the Party secretary soured over the issue of control. As in the preceding case, if the Party secretary continued to be in control while the VC chairman held the overall responsibility, an intolerable situation would arise. But if the VC chair were to take over, he would in effect be openly seizing power from the veteran secretary, in the process deeply offending his old mentor. After giving the matter some thought, the VC chairman did officially claim his legal rights. The Party secretary thereupon cursed him, accusing him of 'pulling down the bridge after crossing the river', i.e. of ingratitude.

3. Shabian village, Zhongshan

In Shabian village, also in Zhongshan, the Party secretary was an old cadre first recruited during land reform. Having worked assiduously for the villagers for so many years and having contributed so much to the booming collective economy, he felt he deserved people's respect and saw no reason why villagers would oppose him. Nevertheless, a conflict arose over the question of auditing accounts, a crucial issue for villagers. The old secretary complained that the villagers did not show gratitude even though he had been an honest and incorruptible cadre. He said:

> There are always some troublemakers (*pingtan gaoshou*) in the village, who are not satisfied with whatever cadres do and constantly look for pretexts to find fault with them.[18] They like to file complaints with higher-level authorities even though they don't have evidence of wrongdoing and inflict great pain on the cadres. There are troublemakers among the villagers' representatives. In my village, the 18 elected 'clear-accounts representatives' viewed us as enemies. They arbitrarily demanded that the deputy Party secretary hand over the account books of the village economic committee. But he refused, pending my return from the town. Since they couldn't find the books, they broke the windows of the branch office and detained the deputy secretary, whom they told to confess as if he were a landlord under interrogation. The town police and I arrived with a video camera, but the villagers surrounded us and blocked the car for nine hours. Troublemakers make a storm out of a teacup. Does the law on village organization entitle them to take illegal actions and ignore Party leadership?

He then bitterly recounted how the elected representatives collected the account books and posted three guards to keep watch over them. Ten or so people spent days examining them. Their leader went so far as to duplicate data from them, which he posted and sent to the municipal anti-corruption bureau, accusing the village cadres of embezzlement. The municipal authorities responded that this method of checking the accounts was wrong. Villagers, however, invoked the 'Law on Village Organization', claiming that it was up to the VRA to decide whether or

---

18. '*Pingtan gaoshou*' is the equivalent of '*diaomin*', troublemakers. Cf. Li Lianjiang and Kevin O'Brien, 'Villages and popular resistance in contemporary China', *Modern China* XXII(1), (January 1996), pp. 30–47.

not to examine the accounts. The VRA indeed voted to continue examining the accounts. The Party secretary complained, 'I cannot understand who is the boss, the villagers or the superiors. If even the superior leaders can be disobeyed on issues such as the examination of the accounts, what will be next? Will the affairs of our Party branch also be decided by taking a vote?'[19]

4. Da'ao village, Huidong county

When corruption was not just suspected but real, conflict became even more acute. In Da'ao village all the cadres of the original administrative district lost the elections. Villagers called them a 'swarm of locusts', charging that the Party secretary who had replaced the old corrupt one in 1997, had learned nothing from his predecessor's fate, but was even more blatantly engaged in selling collectively owned land and embezzling collective funds. The havoc wreaked by these worthies was such that only some 20 mu of farmland remained of the original 200 mu. The ten million RMB which the village received for the land sales was wasted or embezzled, leaving the village without resources. The new VC had to borrow 2,000 yuan from the town government before it could even begin to check the books. Yet, the Party secretary, who resented his loss of the elections, adamantly refused to hand over the account books and other records despite repeated requests by the VC chairman and the urgings of town cadres. As he put it,

> Huang Tengzhu (the elected chairman) and his men are not Party members. They are poorly educated and their quality is low. Some have been subjected to reform through labor. They are unqualified as cadres and are not entitled to lay down the law to the Party branch or to govern the masses. They have not prepared the VC's plan. How can I transfer power to them?

Most likely, the Party secretary was afraid that his misdeeds would be exposed.

The power of appointments also became a source of friction. The Party branches had always controlled appointments of village cadres. Now, the VCs threatened to take this away from them as well. For example, after the elections in Jiangwei village of Huoju town, Zhongshan, the VC chairman fired the Youth League secretary and the head of the village militia without consulting the Party secretary, and he also prepared to remove some department managers of the village-owned company. His intent was to solidify the power of the VC. Moreover, the director felt that it was unreasonable for the village collective to pay the wages of the Youth League secretary. As for the militia head, if his subsidy was to be paid out of the village budget, the VC or VRA would have to decide how much it should be. Of course, the Party secretary could not tolerate this affront and he immediately petitioned the town Party secretary, who told the VC director to correct his mistakes at once. The VC director replied: 'This was a VRA decision which cannot be rescinded unless the VRA is reconvened'. It seems that the

---

19. Interviews, Zhongshan, March 1999.

traditional Party control over cadres was now to be replaced by elections and democratic decisions.

Another Party secretary, also full of indignation, complained that in his village, 'the VC suspended the subsidies for the Youth League secretary and the head of the militia, arguing that they should ask the Party secretary for their salary because the Party branch appointed them. But now, the chairperson controlled village finances so the Party branch had to ask the VC for money with which to pay them. Doesn't this leave us in an intolerably embarrassing situation?'

These cases are instructive in several ways. They show how elections brought to the surface latent villager resentment at boss rule, especially when corruption was involved. They demonstrate that elections are important in developed villages and not just in poorer ones, as several scholars have argued.[20] They illustrate the importance of personal relations, but they also show the salience of formal rules. Party secretaries were quick to take advantage of the provision on Party leadership in the Organic Law so as to enable them to retain power. By the same token, the Law was also invoked by VC chairpersons who insisted on their prerogatives. As one chairman commented in an interview: 'curb the CCP's power by using the CCP's law'.[21]

Refusal by Party secretaries to transfer power over village affairs after elections was a problem not only in rural Guangdong, where villager self-government had only recently been implemented, but also in villages in other parts of China which had years of experience with elections. It existed even in such national demonstration counties for village self-government as that of Zhao county in Hebei. According to an investigation carried out by a graduate student at Beijing University, the villages that he studied had some kind of village representative organization, but unless the Party secretary was open-minded, it would not be able to make decisions. In each of these villages financial power and administrative seals remained in the hands of the Party secretaries, except when a secretary's wife or relative acted on his behalf. No VC chairperson was able to take charge. Some villages were fortunate to have honest and upright Party secretaries, but most were stuck with secretaries who sought to enrich themselves, bully the timid, or abuse their power to the point of beating and handcuffing people. The researcher wondered how a demonstration county could be so lacking in the spirit of self-government.[22]

---

20. See Jean C. Oi, 'Economic development, stability and democratic village self-governance', in Maurice Brosseau et al., eds, China Review 1996 (Hong Kong: The Chinese University Press, 1996), pp. 125–144; and Tianjian Shi, 'Economic development and village elections in rural China', Journal of Contemporary China 8(22), (November 1999), pp. 425–442.
21. Interview, Nanhai, April 1999.
22. Research carried out in July 1997, by Yang Zili, reported on the website of Beimei Ziyou Luntan, (February 1999). On Zhao county, see also Susan V. Lawrence, 'Village representative assemblies, Chinese style', Australian Journal of Chinese Affairs (32), (July 1994), pp. 61–68; and see Yang Aimin, 'Hebei Zhao xian de di shixing cunmin daibiaohuiyi zhidu de sikao' ['Reflections on VRAs in Zhao xian of Hebei and other rural areas'], in Wang Zhongtian and Zhang Chengfu, eds, Xiangcun Zhengzhi-Zhongguo Cunmin Zizhi de Diaocha yu Sikao [Rural Politics: Investigations and Reflections on Villagers' Self-Government in China] (Nanchang: Jiangxi renmin chubanshe, 1999), pp. 265–275.

The role of town Party leaders

Town Party committees came under pressure to adjudicate between the VCs and the VPBs. They were not, however, impartial but tended to favor the Party secretaries, who, in their view, were more likely to be obedient. According to the Organic Law, the relations between the town (or township) governments and the VCs, which legally were mass organizations and formally part of the government, was one of 'guidance' (*zhidao*) rather than 'leadership' (*lingdao*), meaning that the VC could not simply be ordered around. Just as the Law left the relations between VPBs and the VCs in an ambiguous state, so it stipulated that VCs were expected to comply with and implement government policies and to abide by laws and regulations even as it defined the VCs as self-governing or autonomous (*zizhi*) mass organizations. During the debates over adoption of the Law, worries were expressed that the 'guidance' relationship would permit the VCs to defy higher-level directives and become bastions of independence (*tubaowei*).[23] It is not surprising that many township officials feared that free elections would make it difficult to control the VCs, especially if 'troublemakers' were elected.[24] Even if that did not happen, how to comply with the Law yet carry on normal business became a source of anxiety. In one town in Zhongshan city, for example, after the elections, the leaders worried that if they sent documents (*wenjian*) directly to the VCs for implementation, they would be creating a leadership relationship, thereby violating the Law. Although afraid to leave the VCs in ignorance of its documents, they did not send any to the VCs for over a month. Zhongshan city officials confirmed that other towns were acting in a similar way.

Such problems did not in principle exist in the relationship between the town Party committees and the VPBs, which, under the rules of democratic centralism, was one of direct subordination. It is therefore not surprising that township authorities, anxious to fulfill their duties, preferred to work through the VPBs than through the VCs even after the elections.[25] According to a report by Zhongshan municipality, 'Many towns' sent down documents requiring that after the abolition of the administrative districts, the Party secretaries should 'temporarily' assume the directorships of the village economic committees. In response, more than half of the VC chairs went to the towns and demanded their rights. Due to the prevalent dissatisfaction, the towns revoked these documents and re-appointed the village chairmen as VEC directors.

---

23. For analysis of these debates, see Kevin J. O'Brien and Lianjiang Li, 'Accommodating "democracy" in a one-party state: introducing village elections in China', *China Quarterly* (162), (June 2000), pp. 465–489.
24. See Tong Zhihui, 'Shaanxi sheng, Jinbian xian, Huangjiamao, Yingdiliang cun "xiangzheng cunzhi" guanxi de shizheng fenxi' ['Empirical analysis of the relations between the township administration and village governance in Huangjiamao and Yingdiliang villages of Jinbian county, Shaanxi province'] and, 'Minzhu de zaoyu jiqi fansi-Shaanxi sheng, Jinbian xian, Maotuan cun cunweihui xuanju shizheng fenxi' ['The confrontation of democracy and reflection on it: empirical analysis of VC elections in Maotuan village, Jinbian county, Shaanxi province'], both in Wang Zhongtian and Zhang Chengfu, eds, *Xiangcun Zhengzhi*, pp. 79–89, pp. 217–237. For a contrasting report on Zhao county, Hebei, see Sylvia Chan, 'Villager self-government and civil society', in Joseph Y. S. Cheng, ed., *China Review* (Hong Kong: The Chinese University Press, 1998), pp. 235–258.
25. Interview, Zhongshan, March 1999. Li Lianjiang also found that some township officials have begun to depend on appointed VPB secretaries to implement local policies. See Li Lianjiang, 'Elections and popular resistance in rural China'.

The villagers' democratic pressure resulted in this change. Similarly, in Fengtai village of Zhongshan city, immediately after the election, the VC expressly demanded that it assume control over the village economy. The Party secretary appealed to his superiors, who replied that he was to be the economic chief. No sooner had the decision reached the village than the VC convened a VRA and told the Party secretary to attend and to hand over economic power on the spot. Fearing that the villagers would organize a collective visit to the higher levels (*jiti shangfang*), which would make them look bad, the town leaders rescinded their order and power was transferred.[26]

After the elections, the towns thus depended more and more on the VPBs. Some town leaders were highly supportive when secretaries asked for instructions but cold-shouldered the village chairmen, one of whom said indignantly: 'The town shows so much preference for the Party members. Are we bred by step mothers?' One town stipulated that with regard to eight questions, only the signature of the Party secretary could validate village decisions. Over half of the VC chairpersons joined in sending up written objections, obliging the town to rescind its order. Another town even went so far as to prescribe that the VPB secretaries should receive full-time salaries while the VC chairmen should be paid according to the subsidy system of reimbursement for time worked. If enforced, this would have been an unreasonable and unlawful local policy (*tu zhengce*). It was promptly rejected by the VC chairpersons after consideration by the VRAs.

The result of these pro-VPB interventions deepened the conflict between the VPBs and the VCs. The town leaders hoped that the use of administrative power would keep the VCs under control, hence enabling them to continue to enforce 'local policies' that violated policies and laws and often were highly injurious to peasant interests and threatened to provoke resistance.[27]

The Zhongshan city Party committee responded by reassuring the village Party secretaries that they were the top leaders even while telling them that the elections were here to stay and that they had to adapt to the new situation. At a meeting convened by a town Party committee at which village secretaries complained that the VCs were challenging their 'magic weapon' (*fabao*) as the core of village leadership, a cadre from the city Party committee explained:

> The municipal Party committee leaders call for upholding Party leadership but also for promoting of villager self-government. You first-line cadres harbor doubts, so do the higher levels. However, it is clear that in Zhongshan, whatever happens, irrespective of village elections and villager self-government, you village secretaries will be the top leaders. Without Party leadership, there would be anarchy. The situation described by village secretaries indicates that there are already sprouts of anarchy. A Party secretary and his deputy in a village of Dayong town, stopped going to work for three months after the elections, so that the village lost the leadership core. I have also read in a report that some village Party secretaries said that village elections were useless and

---

26. Investigation report by Zhongshan city, 'Guanyu lishun nongcun guanli tongzhi de ruogan wenti de diaocha baogao' ['Investigation report on questions of facilitating rural management systems'], unpublished, (1999), p. 8.

27. On resistance, see Li Lianjiang and O'Brien, 'Villages and popular resistance in contemporary China'; also Kevin O'Brien and Li Lianjiang, 'The politics of lodging complaints in rural China', *China Quarterly* (143), (September 1995), pp. 756–783.

could be the first step towards the collapse of the CCP. Their wording may be exaggerated but it shows the great impact of the elections.

But we cannot stop the elections because there are side-effects. I think that you are grumbling too much. The press has described so many advantages of the elections; can you not perceive them at all? Do you feel so much pressure and fear of disaster, that the CCP will collapse? You should be firm in believing that this will never happen.[28]

A 30-year-old town Party secretary who concurrently served as the town's head of government, forcefully reinforced the views of the Zhongshan Party committee. He affirmed that the VC chairman was in fact the legal representative of the VEC, so secretaries should stop fighting over this point. The VCs could not function without any concrete power. As for the VPBs, he said,

the Party is the core of the leadership of village affairs. The problem is how you play your role as the core. Since the superiors attach importance to villagers' self-govern-ment, implementing this must be your main task as well (*zhongxin renwu*). What self-government led by the Party means, as I understand it, is that the Party shall lead and support the villagers in the elections according to law and to guarantee that the VCs implement the policies of the Party and obey state laws. Irrespective of whether VPB members are elected to the VCs, they must actively join in their work and seize the initiative in the village's important decision-making. And, the town has already specified your salaries about which you are concerned, and which requires that you, as the *yibashou*, are in principle one level above the VC chairmen.[29]

Thus the town leader asked the Party secretaries to take the concrete step of handing over economic power to the VC chairs but otherwise left the role divisions unclear.

One Zhongshan city official, instead of vigorously intervening to settle the jurisdictional disputes, essentially side-stepped the issue by suggesting that the VCs bring suit to claim their rights: 'Da'ao village has established a new VC, whose legal representative is Huang Tengzhu. If the former leaders refuse to hand over control over village affairs, the elected director can resort to legal channels by bringing a case before a court of law for the resolution'.[30] But a long-drawn out lawsuit was hardly a solution. Given the realities of Party secretaries' power, the VCs needed strong support from the authorities above the village, otherwise they were likely to continue to be in a subordinate position. Since the towns could not show unprincipled preference for either side, they talked to the VC directors about the importance of respecting the VPB leadership and to the secretaries about the necessity of establishing the system of VCs. This indefinite attitude did not do much to resolve the conflicts.

Was there a possibility that a cooperative system of 'dual power' could sustain itself? Our research yielded only a very few cases in which both VPBs and VCs were strong. One successful example came from a village in Nanhai city, where 'two good brothers (*yige dangjia*) described themselves as seeking to make money

28. Based on notes and a related investigation report, Zhongshan, March 1999.
29. *Ibid.*
30. Lin Weixiong and Liu Haibin, 'Da'ao cun wenti keyi tongguo falu tujing jiejue' ['The problems of Da'ao village can be resolved by legal means'], *Nanfang Nongcun Bao*, (11 April 2000).

separately but settling accounts together'. They jointly promoted the development of the village collective economy and jointly safeguarded the finances. Important issues such as road construction, the building of houses, the establishment of new factories, doing business, and handling the welfare distributions, were decided by the VRA after both committees drafted a joint resolution. The town leader praised this arrangement as adhering to the leadership of the Party while simultaneously implementing villager self-government.

In such a village, the Party secretary was not merely the nominal first man in control but also retained much traditional power, such as nominating village cadres, approving village regulations and responsibility contracts, and presiding over meetings, which were not taken over by the village chairperson, election notwithstanding. There was something of a tacit understanding that in exchange for retaining these powers the secretary gave up his status as the legal representative of the village collective economy.[31]

But such villages were few and far between. Sayings such as 'two donkeys cannot be tied to one tree', 'a village cannot have two Zhu Laozhongs', or, 'there cannot be two suns in the sky' attest to this point. Cooperation required good personal relations between the secretary and the chairperson, but also some kind of institutionalized mechanism for power sharing and cooperation. Without the latter, cooperation floundered when personal relations between the two leaders deteriorated. The rights and obligations of the VPB and VC had to be clearly determined, together with concrete rules of the game and rules for monitoring cadre performance. The following case shows that it was possible to arrive at such an institutionalized solution.

Wanfeng, Shenzhen, was a wealthy village with an annual income of over 30 million yuan, an indicator of the great importance to villagers of regulating the economic power of the cadres. A joint meeting of the VPB and VC drafted rules stipulating the responsibilities of the Party secretary, the village chair, the members of both VPB and VC, and the roles, rights and duties of various organizations. This draft was then submitted to the VRA for discussion. Every villager was entitled to be heard. Once adopted, everyone was obliged to abide by the rules and regulations.

Both secretary and chairperson were given equal authority over the approval of financial expenditures of up to 40,000 yuan at a time, while individually they could only approve expenditures that didn't exceed 1,000 yuan. Expenditures above these levels had to be examined and approved by the village financial chief inspector (*zongjian*), who was chosen by the VRA and therefore had independent authority. He was also not allowed to serve on either the VPB or the VC. This inspector had the right to request that the VC convene a general assembly or to do so directly, bypassing the VC. Thus, in Wancheng, the power of the purse and the administrative power were to some extent separated from the two committees. This restriction on the powers of the two committees was also conducive to the maintenance of a balance of power between VPB and VC.

---

31. Nanhai investigation, 1999.

While it was not clear whether there were special characteristics other than wealth that enabled Wancheng successfully to divide power, the fact that it was able to come up with institutional innovations highlighted one of the underlying defects in the building of rural democracy in China, namely the apparent absence of clearly specified rules that governed the respective roles of the VPBs and VCs and constrained the behavior of village cadres generally. Such rules were needed not only for intra-village power relations but even more important, in the relations between the village authorities and the towns/townships and counties. The underlying sources of these deficiencies is the regime's systemic unwillingness to recognize the legitimacy of conflicts of interest in Chinese politics and hence the reluctance to recognize that there is a real need for constitutional mechanisms to manage conflict.

The emergence of concurrent office holding

After the turn of the millennium, merger of the VPBs and the VCs seemed to be the answer of choice to the jurisdictional and power conflicts between the two. The main method for achieving this was to oblige the Party secretary to run for the office of VC chair, thereby establishing his/her acceptability to the villagers.

To begin with, in many provinces, the proportion of Party members in the VCs had long been very high. As of 1996, it was 71% in Liaoning province, 74.3% in Henan province, 81.5% in Hebei province, 77.8% in Beijing, 89.5% in Tianjing, and 91% in Shanghai. The percentage of Party secretaries who were elected to the VC chairmanship varied: it was 36% in Shanghai but only 12.1% in Qingdao, Shandong.[32] In Guangdong, however, as of 1999, 56% of village chairpersons served concurrently as Party secretary. In Xinhui city, over 80% of the two posts were held by one person and in Nanhai, 60%.[33]

In 1999, Liaocheng city, Shandong, adopted a rule requiring Party secretaries to run in the elections. The result was that 77% of the VPB secretaries, 4,933 in all, were elected chairpersons. Those secretaries who lost were replaced by the winner of the VC election. If the latter was not already a Party member, he would quickly be recruited and would eventually be appointed secretary if he maintained a good record. In Liaocheng, 613 secretaries were 'readjusted', thereby raising the concurrence rate to 86.7%. In one town, seven of 38 secretaries lost the VC elections and were replaced by the winners.[34] Concurrent office holding solved the problem of jurisdictional conflict, eliminated duplication as well as power struggles. It also lightened the burdens of the peasants. Excessive taxes and fees were a crucial source of conflict between the state and the peasantry. In large parts of the country, especially those that were agriculture-dependent and lacked access to TVE profits, public goods had to be funded by squeezing the peasants. Part of the locally raised

---

32. Wang Zhongtian and Zhang Chengfu, *Xiangcun Zhengzhi*, pp. 91 and 95. For discussion of concurrent office holding, see Daniel Kellher, 'The Chinese debate over village self-government', *The China Journal* (37), (January 1997), pp. 63–86.

33. *Yangcheng Wanbao*, (6 May 1999), p. 1; Xinhui investigation, 1999; Nanhai investigation, 1999.

34. *Nongmin Ribao,* (11 December 1999).

funds were required to pay village-level cadres. Merging the posts of Party secretary and VC chair represented a significant saving of direct benefit to villagers. In Liaocheng, 16,089 VC members also served in Party branches, resulting in a reduction in the village cadre force of 26,000 and a saving of 20 million yuan. Reportedly, cadre–mass relations improved significantly.[35]

Concurrent office holding ignored the old political reform goal of separating Party from government. It also in effect restored the role of the top leader in charge, the *yibashou*, now fortified by his/her dual positions, or at least a single group of key leaders. In his study of southern Hebei villages, Bjorg Alpermann found that as before, there was a dominant *lingdao banzi*, a leadership group, which was responsive to the townships rather than to its constituents. In this case, the townships continued to be able to manipulate the elections in most villages.[36] Thus, where elections were not free and fair, a fairly widespread situation in rural China, the potential for gross abuse of concentrated power remained.[37] In contrast, when elections were free and fair, the requirement that a Party secretary had to win the electoral competition for VC office probably did serve as an incentive for him/her to be more responsive to the interests of the constituents. How a Party secretary might respond when these interests ran counter to those of the superior town or township Party committee to whose discipline he/she was subject, is a question for further research.

Concurrent office holding represented official recognition that the CCP had to refurbish its legitimacy and authority in the villages by requiring that its village secretaries and often many or most branch members as well had to seek electoral approval.[38] Requiring the Party secretary to run for election for the VC in order to retain his/her post was something of a break with Leninist principles. It reflected the urgency of the task of improving the tense relations between Party and peasants. In historical perspective, this innovation had its counterpart in the practice of mass participation in the rectification of Party cadres during the Mao era, which also entailed mobilization of pressure from outside the Party, as exemplified by the 'Four Clean' campaign of 1964. As O'Brien and Li found, there is a 'campaign nostalgia' among villagers subjected to the oppression of unaccountable power-holders. Having to run for VC office can be viewed as a more institutionalized substitute for old-style campaigns.[39]

Our September 1999 investigation included the study of three villages in Xinhui city, whose Party secretaries were also VC directors.

---

35. *Ibid.* For an analysis of the tax burdens, see Thomas P. Bernstein and Xiaobo Lu, *Taxation without Representation in Contemporary Rural China* (New York: Cambridge University Press, 2003). Chapter 7 of this book examines the role of village committees in burden reduction.

36. Bjorg Alpermann, 'The post-election administration of Chinese villages', *The China Journal* (46), (July 2001), pp. 45–68.

37. For one such case, from Xinjiang, see *Xinhua*, (29 December 2001), *FBIS* (1229), (29 December 2001).

38. See Susan V. Lawrence, 'Village democracy: direct elections are becoming more open in the Chinese countryside, but will those reforms extend to higher levels of government?' *Far Eastern Economic Review*, (27 January 2000), p. 17.

39. See Kevin J. O'Brien and Lienjiang Li, 'Campaign nostalgia in the Chinese countryside', *Asian Survey* 39(3), (1999), pp. 375–394.

1. Sanyi village of Siqian town

In the village elections of the first half of 1999, villagers directly and openly nominated candidates and then elected the village director and six VC members. They chose the Party secretary, age 53, as chairperson. The six VC members were also members of the branch committee, thus achieving full concurrence.

The Siqian town secretary, who was present at the interview, added that the elections were free, since Siqian town practiced 'sea elections' (*haixuan*), in which VPBs and townships were not allowed to nominate candidates, leaving villagers free to do so on their own. Nine Party secretaries were chosen to be village chairmen in the town's 14 villages. They retained their posts as secretaries. In cases where the secretaries failed to be elected, the new chairmen were nominated to be Party secretaries. According to the town secretary, the elected chairpersons enjoyed the trust of the VPBs, the VCs, and of the villagers. The town leaders, he noted, had greater confidence in leaders whom villagers trusted. He added that if villagers elected a non-Party member as chairperson, their decision would be respected. If the chairperson qualified for Party membership, he/she would be recruited. He/she could then run in the next election three years hence. Victory would demonstrate the chair's high reputation among the masses. The town Party committee would then certainly recommend him/her to the branch members as the candidate for Party secretary. But such a situation had not thus far arisen.

2. Tianhu village of Luoken town

The Party secretary, named Chen, was only 26 years old and had joined the Party while in the military. Upon demobilization in 1994, the town appointed him as the cashier of the administrative district and in 1997 promoted him to be the vice director and concurrently Party branch committee member of the district. In May 1999, he was elected village chairperson and in July the town Party committee nominated him to serve as secretary, a choice of which the village Party members approved. The seven members of the Party branch were all elected to the VC, thereby establishing a pattern of across-the-board concurrent office holding.

Secretary Chen seemed to be a capable 'first man in charge', judging by his performance. He was empowered by the elections and not just by the superiors, because had he not been elected director, the town Party committee would not have nominated him as VPB secretary. Chen maintained excellent relations with the town. Taihu village was relatively poor. Its collective income in 1998 was only just under 80,000 yuan, whereas that of the entire town was 500 million. Because of this disparity, the town did not extract funds from the village. Villager financial burdens were less than 2% of per capita incomes, none of which went to the town. Moreover, the town leaders decided to help the village implement its blueprint for 'shaking off poverty and becoming rich'. In promoting this cause, Chen must have pleased the town leaders since he opposed the use of funds donated to the village by overseas relatives for the building of an ancestral hall, as village elders had proposed. Chen strongly opposed this idea on the grounds that the fund should be used to build a good primary school. An ancestral hall, no matter how good looking, would be used only a few times a year, whereas the school would be in constant use. A temple could be built in the future, after the educated children had achieved success. He added, 'the overseas relatives shared my view point which thus prevailed'.

3. Yangmei village of Sanjiang town

Yangmei village of Sanjiang town had 700 families and over 2,000 people, distributed among nine village small groups (cunmin xiaozu). Eighty percent were named Rong and the others, Nie, Yu and Chen. The Party secretary, age 56, admitted that his post had always been held by a Rong. He had been in office for nine years and was also a member of the Xinhui municipal people's congress. During his term of office, the villagers' life steadily improved with development. The income of the village now exceeded 3 million yuan and net per capita incomes totaled 4,500 yuan. For several years running, villagers did not have to hand over money or grain, since the village assumed this burden.

Secretary Rong's authority among villagers appeared to us to be rather paternalistic (fuqin ban de quanwei) but if so, he clearly enjoyed strong support. In the elections of May 1999, the villagers nominated more than 80 candidates for VC chairman but Party secretary Rong won by a huge margin. He told the visiting researchers:

> Village elections are of course something good in that they can elect a leader whom people think is fair. The ancient saying has it that there are no two suns in the sky. There can only be one head in one village, whether he is called VPB secretary or VC chairman. One person, one head. If there were two heads, he'd be a monster. Villagers elected me because they have confidence in me. According to the needs of the branch, I became secretary. So we have one head of the village rather than a two-headed monster. Should villagers elect another person chairman, I would definitely give up my office. Without a leader, a flock of birds would disperse. Without a core [leader], there would be dissension and villagers would form factions and they would fight among themselves.

In this case, Rong's position as the undisputed leader accepted by both villagers and townships was undoubtedly facilitated by the village's growing prosperity. In poorer, agriculture-dependent villages, he would have come under much greater pressure to balance the demands of the town against those of the villagers, particularly with respect to township claims on scarce village resources. In such circumstances, had he then sided with his constituents, the town leaders might well have rethought their willingness to agree to concurrent office holding.

In this secretary-chairman's case, one may ask, what political institution, in the final analysis, did he identify with, the VC or the VPB? It seems that none of the administrative posts, whether in the production brigade, the administrative district, or the VC, meant much to him. What seemed really to matter were the interests of the village, or more likely, given the dominance of his surname, his clan, which was the source of his paternalistic authority.[40] Village elections were simply a

---

40. For anthropological studies of authority in village societies, see Wang Mingming, 'Cunluo shiye zhong de jiazu, guojia yu shehui' ['Lineage, state and society on the perspective of village communities'], 'Minjian quanwei, shenghuoshi yu quntidongli' ['Civil authority, ethnography and group motive'], and Luo Hongguang, 'Quanli yu quanwei: Helongtan de fuhao tixi yu zhengzhi pinglun' ['Power and authority: symbolic system and everyday political appraisals in Helongtan village'], all in Wang Mingming and Stephan Feuchtwang, eds, Xiangtu Shehui de Zhixu, Gongzheng yu Quanwei [Order, Justice and Authority in Rural Society] (Beijing: Zhongguo zhengfa daxue chubanshe, 1997), pp. 20–122, 258–315, 333–384.

quantitative symbol of this authority. Informal, village-level authority was much more important for him than his formal posts, the authority of which was that of the political system as a whole. In all these cases, our interviewees regarded joint office holding as a success.

In July 2002, concurrent office holding emerged as the arrangement favored by the Central authorities. The Central Committee and State Council General Offices issued a 'Notice' on the new round of VC elections, now to be held in the light of Jiang Zemin's 'important thinking' on the 'Three Represents', which called for the CCP to represent the most advanced productive forces, advanced culture, and the basic interests of the masses. It recommended (*tichang*) the nomination and election of the leading group of VPBs to the Village Committees, as well as election of Party members to the post of villager small group chief (*cunmin xiaozu zhang*) and also to the VRA. Candidates for VPB secretary should first run in the VC elections. If they received popular recognition, they should then be nominated for the post of secretary. Failure to be elected VC chairperson meant that they should not be nominated for the secretarial post. The 'Notice' also recommended that in large villages with numerous Party members, those elected to the village Party committees be chosen as committee members via intra-party elections. Finally, outstanding non-Party VC members and villager small group heads should be recruited into the Party, 'thereby continuously injecting fresh forces into the rural grass-roots Party organizations'.[41]

The political implications of concurrent office holding are contradictory: on the one hand, in line with the 'Three Represents', the Communist Party is not willing to tolerate autonomous institutions but is determined to bring them under Party control. Those hoping that China will increasingly become pluralized even in its political institutions will be disappointed. On the other hand, Party secretaries cannot simply be appointed from above but must win popular support in regular elections. In principle, this is a step forward in terms of the goal of democratization and of holding officials accountable.

---

41. 'Zhonggong Zhongyang Bangongting-Guowuyuan Bangongting fachu tongzhi jinyibu zuo hao cunmin weiyuanhui huanjie xuanju gongzuo' ['The CC and State Council General Offices issue notice on further doing a good job in the next round of elections'], (14 July 2002). A translated version is by *Xinhua*, (18 August 2002), *FBIS* (818), (18 August 2002).

Elections, Democratic Values, and Economic Development in Rural China

DAVID ZWEIG and CHUNG SIU FUNG

This paper assesses several assumptions underlying the promotion of democracy and good governance in rural China. We draw on a 1999 survey of 120 villages in four counties, two in Anhui and two in Heilongjiang provinces (sample of 2,997 households, including villagers, cadres and entrepreneurs). First, we look at how institutionalized 'democratic procedures', such as secret ballots, multi-candidate elections, public nominations, and village contracts, are in these villages. Then we analyze villager views on economic development and democracy, finding that villagers want more democracy, even if the economy is doing well. Third, we assess their views on the election process; do they see elections as efficacious, fair, and competitive, or do they feel that the local power elite manipulate outcomes? Fourth, we found that the richest people are less supportive of democracy, with the most democratic being middle-income households. Finally, elections have increased local elite turnover, cadres understand this, and therefore, democracy does lead to good governance.

Introduction

Within a decade of the decollectivization of rural China (1978–1983) and the enormous economic boom generated by decollectivization, rural China fell on hard times.[1] Particularly after the urban reforms of 1984 and rapid urban economic growth in the mid- to late-1980s, rural China's economic conditions deteriorated. The price scissors between urban and rural goods, which had narrowed in 1978–1983, expanded significantly. As many as 20% of rural villages lacked real political authority. In the 1990s, local taxes and fees, imposed by cash-strapped rural cadres, created political hostility and social conflict that threatened the Communist Party's

---

1. On rapid rural industrialization, see Jean C. Oi, *Rural China Takes Off* (Berkeley: University of California Press, 1999). For a more general overview of rural reform, particularly in Jiangsu Province, see David Zweig, *Freeing China's Farmers: Restructuring Rural China in the Deng Era* (Armonk, NY: M. E. Sharpe, 1997).

grip on power in the countryside.[2] As a result, the number of rural protests increased almost four-fold between 1993 and 1999.[3]

In response to these challenges, China's leaders, egged on by younger reformers, have sought to introduce greater democracy and mechanisms of good governance into rural China.[4] These include village elections, village contracts, village assemblies and transparent financial management within the villages. These reforms, they hope, will increase villagers' willingness to invest in capital construction projects, such as new roads, under the assumption that if their own elected officials call on them to do so, they will.[5] Moreover, it is anticipated that more economic growth and democracy will promote political stability. Thus, their support for democracy remained highly instrumental and not an end in itself; so long as democracy strengthened state power and national economic growth, it would be supported.

Conceptual perspectives on democracy and economic development

This paper assesses several assumptions underlying the promotion of democracy and good governance in rural China.[6] A most common argument in the political science literature is that economic development leads to democratization. Quantitative and qualitative studies generally confirm this relationship.[7] For Huntington, 'few relationships between social, economic, and political phenomena are stronger than that between level of economic development and existence of democratic politics'.[8] And while Przeworski and Limongi tried to refute the argument that economic development leads to democracy,[9] Boix and Stokes reconfirm that assumption,[10] as did Londregan and Poole.[11] Nevertheless, the Latin American experience in the 1970s

---

2. For an excellent study of 'peasant burdens', see, Thomas P. Bernstein and Xiaobo Lu, *Taxation without Representation in Rural China: State Capacity, Peasant Resistance, and Democratization* (Cambridge University Press, 2003).

3. Data from the Fourth Research Institute of the Public Security Ministry show a jump in the number of protests from 9,709 in 1993 to 32,000 in 1999. Li Lianjiang in his seminar, 'Do Villagers Trust the Central Government', Hong Kong University of Science and Technology, 30 October 2002. By 2005, there were over 86,000 urban and rural protests.

4. Lianjiang Li and Kevin O'Brien, 'The struggle over village elections', in Merle Goldman and Roderick MacFarquhar, eds, *The Paradox of China's Post-Mao Reforms* (Cambridge, MA: Harvard University Press, 1999).

5. Wang Zhenyao, 'Village committees: the basis of China's democratization', in Eduard B. Vermeer, Frank N. Pieke and Woei Lien Chong, eds, *Cooperative and Collective in China's Rural Development* (Armonk, NY: M. E. Sharpe, 1998), pp. 239–256.

6. On China's democratic development see Suzanne Ogden, *Inklings of Democracy in China* (Cambridge, MA: Harvard University Press, 2002).

7. Kenneth A. Bollen, 'Issues in the comparative measurement of political democracy', *American Sociological Review* 45(2), (1980); Dietrich Rueschemeyer, Evelyne Huber Stephens and John D. Stephens, *Capitalist Development and Democracy* (Chicago: University of Chicago Press, 1992); and Larry Diamond, 'Economic development and democracy reconsidered', in Gary Marks and Larry Diamond, eds, *Re-examining Democracy* (Newbury Park: Sage, 1992).

8. Samuel Huntington, *The Third Wave: Democratization in the Late Twentieth Century* (Norman, OK: University of Oklahoma Press, 1991), p. 311.

9. Adam Przeworski and Fernando Limongi, 'Modernization: theories and facts', *World Politics* 49, (January 1997); and Adam Przeworski, Michael E. Alvarez, Jose Antonio Cheibub and Fernando Limongi, *Democracy and Development: Political Institutions and Well-Being in the World, 1950–1990* (London: Cambridge University Press, 2000).

10. Charles Boix and Susan C. Stokes, 'Endogenous democratisation', *World Politics* 55 (July 2003), pp. 517–549.

11. John B. Londregan and Keith T. Poole, 'Does high income promote democracy?', *World Politics* 49 (October 1996), pp. 1–30.

and 1980s suggests that, while middle levels of economic development are conducive to democratization, both poverty and higher levels of economic development could generate authoritarianism.[12]

In rural China, the relationship between economic development and democracy may also be curvilinear. In very poor communities, local governments cannot afford ballot boxes, and villagers may be too busy making ends meet to care about good democratic procedures.[13] At the other end of the economic spectrum, the most industrialized and collectivized villages have the financial wherewithal to resist democracy. Oi and Rozelle found that the competitive nature of elections decreased in the top decile of villages in terms of their levels of industrialization. However, in the other 90% of villages, they found no relationship between economic development and electoral politics.[14] In this vein, Guangdong Province was the last major province to introduce village elections. Perhaps middle-income regions, where numerous private businesses want less intrusive leaders and more transparent polities, are where we find the socio-economic roots of democratization and a positive relationship between economic development and democracy. Still, Hu's research in Fujian Province found greater participation and more competition in wealthier villages, which also did a better job of instituting various election laws.[15]

Our research questions[16]

In light of the above discussion, the key questions driving this study are as follows.

1. Is rural China democratic? Has the level of democracy increased, and have villagers become more aware of the opportunities democracy affords them? How institutionalized are 'democratic procedures', such as secret ballots, multi-candidate elections, public nominations, and village contracts?

2. Are villagers satisfied with economic development alone, or do they believe that democratic reforms are necessary even if there is good economic growth? Do they see elections as efficacious, fair, and competitive, or do they feel that the local power elite manipulates outcomes? Do more democratic nomination systems increase government legitimacy?

3. What is the relationship between economic development and democracy? Are richer areas, or richer people, more supportive of democracy? Are cadres in wealthier areas more or less supportive of democracy? How does the emerging

12. Guillermo A. O'Donnell, *Modernization and Bureaucratic-Authoritarianism: Studies in South American Politics* (Berkeley: University of California Press, 1979).

13. See Amy Epstein, 'Village elections in China: experiments with democracy', in Joint Economic Committee, Congress of the United States, ed., *China's Economic Future: Challenges to US Policy* (Armonk, NY: M. E. Sharpe, 1997), p. 418; and Tianjian Shi, 'Economic development and village elections in rural China', *Journal of Contemporary China* 8(22), (1999), pp. 425–442.

14. Jean C. Oi and Scott Rozelle, 'Elections and power: the locus of decision-making in Chinese villages', *The China Quarterly* no. 162, (June 2000), pp. 513–539.

15. Hu Rong, *Cunmin zizhi jiagou xia de cunmin weiyuanhui xuanju: Fujian sheng 1997 nian ge'an yanjiu* [*Village Elections within the Framework of Village Autonomy: Research on Case Studies from Fujian Province*], City University, unpublished Ph.D. thesis, 1999.

16. Most of the funding for this research came from the United States Institute of Peace, with further support coming in the form of a Direct Allocation Grant, Hong Kong University of Science and Technology, with funds coming from the Research Grants Council, Hong Kong.

rural middle class see democratic development? If the answers to these questions are positive, continued economic growth could transform rural politics.

4. Finally, have elections increased leadership turnover? How do local elites perceive electoral politics? Does the ballot box discipline cadres so that democratically elected cadres are less prone to misbehave—i.e. does democracy lead to good governance?

Methodological issues

With the cooperation of a research centre in China, we drafted two detailed surveys, one for villagers and another for cadres. Due to financial and political limitations, however, the survey was carried out in 1999 in two provinces, Heilongjiang and Anhui, with two counties selected in each province and 30 villages selected in each county for a total of 120 villages. In each village we selected 20 villagers at random, for a total of 2,400 villagers. We also pinpointed 237 individuals who ran their own businesses—approximately two in each village—whom we categorize as entrepreneurs and treat as the emerging middle class. Finally we interviewed 360 cadres, including from each village the party secretary, the current director of the Villager Committee, and one other cadre who did not hold either post. About 20% of informants were women.

Unfortunately, we could not collect time series data on the elections. Election data only reflected the village's most recent election. Thus we cannot talk about how elections or better governance over time changed popular political attitudes. Moreover, the elections in Heilongjiang Province all occurred in 1996–1997 (with only one in 1998), before China's National People's Congress passed a law announcing its preference for direct nomination by villagers. Fortuitously, in Anhui, all the villages held elections in 1999, with about half of them following the '*haixuan*' system, or other forms of direct nominations by villagers.[17] Thus, though we have no time series data, we can still try to assess whether better democratic procedures—in the form of more direct nominations—affected villagers' attitudes towards the government and political reforms. Still, we must recognize that we cannot show causality—it is possible that areas introduced more democratic forms of nominations because the people and/or local government supported greater democracy.

The context of the village study

All 120 villages were predominantly agricultural, with little variation in demographic or socio-economic characteristics of the two Anhui counties. Per capita income for the two counties as reported in *Anhui Provincial Yearbook, 2000* was RMB 2,182 (Anhui A) and RMB 2,201 (Anhui B), while the provincial average was RMB 1,900.[18] In Helongjiang, the per capita income in one county in 1999

---

17. According to the '*haixuan*' system, anyone possessing their democratic rights can run for office. Then, through a series of ballots, the number of candidates is cut until only two or three remain. These candidates compete for Village Director.

18. *See Anhui tongji nianjian, 2000* [*Anhui Statistical Yearbook*], p. 589, and *Zhongguo tongji nianjian, 2000* [*China Statistical Yearbook*], p. 332.

(Heilongjiang A) was RMB 2,637, but the second county, Heilongjiang B, was significantly poorer, with a per capita income of RM 1,227,[19] and significantly below the provincial average per capita income of RMB 2,165. In terms of per capita income as derived from the village records, the two Anhui counties and Heilongjiang B were relatively similar. Anhui A and B had a mean income of 1,983 and 1,827, respectively, while Heilongjiang B had a mean per capita income of 1,877. However, Heilongjiang A had a mean per capita income of 3,273.[20] This pattern also holds true for per capita income, measured by the number of household appliances. In the two Anhui counties, 79 and 84% of all households had three household appliances or less. In Heilongjiang B, 64% of villagers had three items or less, while in Heilongjiang A, the richest county, 58% of villagers reported having three household items or less.

Education levels also varied. The mean number of years of schooling of the Anhui counties was 5.1 and 5.7, while in Heilongjiang, the richer of the two counties had a mean score of 6.8, while the poorer county had a higher mean of 7.2. There was also greater inequality in the level of individual schooling in Anhui than in Heilongjiang, as measured by the standard deviation.

As outlined above, the political context of the survey varied between the two provinces as well. Both counties in Anhui held their elections in 1999, after the National People's Congress passed the new Organic Law, while most Heilongjiang elections came in 1996–1997. As a result, nominations in Anhui were far more democratic (Table 1).

The practice of democracy in rural China

How well established are democratic institutions in these communities? Indicators of the level of democracy include voting rates, secret ballots, multi-candidate elections, a village contract, whether the villagers felt that village leaders were publicly sharing financial records with them, and how many times elections had been held in the community (Table 1).

Almost 70% of villagers reported that their community had multi-candidate elections,[21] a much higher rate than that reported by numerous observers for the 1995–1997 period.[22] However, our survey occurred in summer 1999, after the spring 1999 reform of the Organic Law on Village Elections by the National People's Congress. Over 79% of villagers reported that their village used secret ballots. Similarly, 91.4% of our villagers reported satisfaction with the level of transparency of the village's financial reports, while 78% of villagers reported that their leaders had signed a contract with the villagers, both important steps in improving local governance. On the other hand, candidates made speeches before the election in only

19. *Heilongjiang tongji nianjian, 2000 [Heilongjiang Statistical Yearbook]*, p. 439.
20. Either the villages selected were not representative of the county overall, which we doubt, or reported income by the local governments is quite different from that reported by the statistical yearbooks.
21. In most villages, villagers gave mixed reports as to whether or not the election had been democratic. Some villagers, perhaps women or migrant workers, simply did not know what types of procedures had been used in the most recent elections. So any village where over 65% of the 20 informants said that there had been multi-candidate elections was considered as having undergone a multi-candidate electoral process.
22. O'Brien and Li cite estimates by the US State Department, Shi Tianjian's nationwide survey, and their own survey, with most estimates falling between 10 and 30%. See Kevin J. O'Brien and Lianjiang Li, 'Accommodating "democracy" in a one-party state: introducing village elections in China', *The China Quarterly* no. 162, (June 2000).

Table 1. Measures of democratic procedures, by province, 1996–1999

	Percentage of villagers reporting	
Procedures employed	Heilongjiang	Anhui
Voting rate	84	85
Villages with multi-candidate elections	66	74
Villages with more democratic nominations*	23	47
Secret ballot	80	79
Election speeches	26	19
Village contracts	88	68

Notes: * Please see footnote 24.
Source: Survey in rural China, Summer 1999.

22% of the cases. According to Pastor and Tan, since villagers know the candidates intimately before the election, there is little need for campaigning.[23] Still, if elections were really competitive, candidates should want to make speeches to differentiate themselves on important policies from their opponents.

We also had results on how candidates were nominated, and broke those responses into two categories: more democratic nomination (MDN) systems and less democratic nomination (LDN) systems. The MDN category included villages using the *haixuan* system—which the Ministry of Civil Affairs posits as the fairest nomination system—those whose villagers nominated candidates directly, self-nominations, nomination by a unified group of villagers, or nominations by representatives of the households. Nominations by organizations, such as the party committee, the election committee, the villager representatives assembly, nominations by 'powerful or privileged people in the village', and people 'who did not know' how the nomination occurred, all fell into the LDN category.[24]

In our overall sample, 43% of villagers reported that their village used more democratic nomination systems, but in Anhui Province, which held its elections in 1999, the share of MDN elections was significantly higher. In the paper, we compare the findings of these two cohorts, in part because we believe that MDN villages and villagers who live in MDN villages, represent a more democratic trend, and we wish to see how that trend affects attitudes and beliefs about local politics.[25]

Our villages' voting rates were rather high—86% of villagers reported voting in the villager committee elections—but this is the easiest medium through which

---

23. Robert A. Pastor and Qingshan Tan, 'The meaning of China's village elections', *The China Quarterly* no. 162, (June 2000), pp. 490–512.

24. Villagers in the same village had very different memories of how the election had transpired. So we used a 50% rule; if more than 50% of villagers reported nomination forms that fell into the more democratic category, we scored the village as MDN. In five villages, nine or ten villagers reported that their village had used '*haixuan*', but 10–11 people in the same village said that either they did not know, or that some local organization had nominated the candidates. Our view is that if 50% of villagers did not know what system was used then it was not a well functioning democratic system and therefore we scored it as a less democratic nomination system.

25. For an in-depth analysis of these two cohorts, see David Zweig and Chung Siu Fung, 'Do new institutions create new politics? The impact of "*haixuan*" or direct nominations for village elections on elite and villager attitudes', paper presented at the International Symposium: *Villager Self-government and Rural Social Development in China*, Ministry of Civil Affairs and the Carter Center, 2–5 September 2001, Beijing.

people can participate. Also, 21% of people had encouraged others to vote, 13% nominated candidates, while another 10% of villagers voluntarily participated in the meeting of the Villager Assembly or the Village Party Committee. Only 10% of villagers reported not participating in any form of political activity at all.

Elections as a source of support for the government

What were the villagers' attitudes towards elections? If they saw elections as fair and competitive, and felt that the CCP or other administrative forces were not too influential in determining electoral outcomes, the elections may become legitimate and help stabilize the political system. However, if they felt that local power holders could manipulate electoral outcomes, democracy would remain formalistic and yield few positive political outcomes.

For example, people may feel that party officials control the electoral outcome through manipulating candidate selection. So, we asked villagers—'what do you think of the CCP's level of influence over elections?' Surprisingly, only 10% saw the party's influence as 'very great'; 22% saw the CCP as having 'a certain level of influence'; 22% saw it as having 'not much influence'; while 21% saw it as having 'no influence'. Finally, 21% said that they 'did not know'. Even if we assume that those who selected 'did not know' were afraid to say that the CCP had too much influence, 43% did not feel that the CCP had very much influence.

Similarly, we asked people to respond to the statement: 'If a ministry or bureau wants to control the election, they need not control the voting but instead can control the selection of candidates'. The responses? 'Totally agree'—6.5%; 'relatively agree'—18%; 'don't agree much'—21%; 'totally disagree'—20%; 'don't know'—27%. Thus, 41% of respondents felt that outside forces do not control candidate selection or electoral outcomes. In Anhiu Province, villagers in MDN villages were even more likely to 'totally disagree' (25%) or 'disagree' (21%) than villagers in LDN villages, whose scores were 'totally disagree'—19% and 'don't agree much'—15% (total 34%) (MLA, $p = 0.01$).[26]

Overall, villagers believed that elections were becoming more competitive and fair relative to the previous election. In our survey, 15% of villagers saw the level of competitiveness as being 'very intense', 40% saw it as being 'relatively intense', while 22% saw no change. Only 7% saw the recent elections as 'not intense at all'. Similarly, 18% saw the most recent election as 'fairer', 41% saw it as 'a little fairer', and 21% saw no change. Only 7% saw the most recent election as 'a bit less fair' or 'far less fair' than previous ones.

These findings were particularly true in villages with more democratic institutions. Based on a multi-variate analysis, the best explanations for 'level of perceived fairness' was whether villages allowed voters two or more ballots—villages that allowed some voters two or more ballots were seen to be very unfair—and whether there were more candidates than positions. In Anhui, when we asked rural inhabitants to rank the level of fairness of the electoral process, 70% of villagers whose village used more democratic nomination systems selected 'fairer' or 'a bit fairer', while

---

26. MLA refers to the Mantel–Haenszel Test for Linear Association and is a good statistical test of linear relationships of Likert scales.

Table 2. Perceived level of fairness in MDN and LDN elections, Anhui Province, 1999

Perception of elections	MDN villages	LDN villages
Became fairer	18%	13%
Became a bit fairer	52%	39%
No change	10%	19%
Became a bit less fair	7%	6%
Became far less fair	3%	3%
Don't know/No response	10%	20%
Total	100%	100%

Notes: MLA, $p = 0.001$. When we calculate the MLA value, we put the 'Don't know/No response' between 'No change' and 'Became a bit less fair' category.
Source: Survey in rural China, Summer 1999.
Question: Was the most recent election fairer than the previous election?

only 52% of LDN villagers did so ($p < 0.001$). Therefore, villagers in villages with more democratic nomination systems, saw more fairness in the electoral process (see Table 2).

Similarly, villagers who reported that their village selected candidates through a more democratic nomination process also saw the electoral system as more competitive, another boost for the system's overall legitimacy (see Table 3). Thus 20% of MDN villagers saw the level of competition under the MDN systems as 'extremely intense' versus 11% of villagers in LDN villages. And when we combine 'extremely intense' and 'comparatively intense', villagers in MDN villages holding these views comprise 78%, while 52% of villagers in LDN villages held similar views ($p < 0.001$). Given that the Anhui elections were held two or three years after the Heilongjiang ones and after the reform of the electoral nomination system, it is possible that more democratic procedures make people see the electoral system as more competitive and fair.

Elections strengthen villager support for government policy. When asked to respond to the statement: 'After several rounds of elections, the villagers are more

Table 3. Perceived level of competitiveness in MDN and LDN elections, Anhui Province, 1999

Perception of elections	MDN villages	LDN villages
Extremely intense	20%	11%
Relatively intense	58%	41%
No change	5%	15%
Not very intense	5%	6%
Not intense at all	1%	1%
Don't know/No response	11%	26%
Total	100%	100%

Notes: MLA, $p = 0.001$. When we calculate the MLA value, we put the 'Don't know/No response' between 'No change' and 'Not very intense' category.
Source: Survey in rural China, Summer 1999.
Question: Was the level of competition in the most recent election more intense than the previous election?

supportive of government policy than before', some 23% of villagers strongly agreed with this statement, 43% agreed somewhat, 11% disagreed somewhat, and only 4% strongly disagreed (19% didn't know or didn't answer). Moreover, villagers who reported that their candidates had been nominated through more democratic systems were more likely to see a relationship between elections and support for government policy. Of villagers in MDN villages, 72% 'strongly supported' or 'relatively supported' this statement, while 58% of villagers in LDN villages held such a view (MLA, $p = 0.001$).

If villagers believed that elections brought bad influences, increased democracy could contribute to political or social instability, as some oligarchs assert. However, 61% of our villagers do not believe elections are harmful; only 11% feel this way, while 28% selected 'don't know'.

Would villagers be satisfied with good governance—without greater democracy—and could good economic development ameliorate aspirations for greater democracy? In response to the statement 'If the existing cadres are capable and trusted, there is no need for democratic elections', 12% agreed strongly and 24% agreed somewhat; yet, 33% disagreed somewhat, and 22% disagreed strongly (9% didn't know or had no response). Thus good governance alone is not sufficient for 55% of our villagers—they want democracy. Similarly, when asked to respond to the statement 'as long as village economic development is stable, there is no need to increase the level of democracy', 33% strongly disagreed and 32% disagreed somewhat. Only 7% agreed strongly, while 14% agreed somewhat (14% didn't know). Most villagers cannot be bought off by capable leaders and economic growth; they want democracy.

Elections, democratic values and economic development

As mentioned in our theoretical discussion, political scientists tend to believe that economic development, without significant inequality, is highly correlated with democratic development. As more rural inhabitants, particularly in the wealthier coastal or suburban areas, become more prosperous, might the demand for democratic procedures and greater political participation increase? To answer this question, we need to know if wealthier villagers held stronger democratic values.

We combined villager responses to four questions about democracy, elitism, and electoral politics to create a variable called 'the democratic idea' (see the Appendix for the list of questions and the villagers' responses to those questions). We stratified the responses into four categories, running from 'not democratic' to 'very democratic'. We also asked villagers to describe their income relative to other people in their village, selecting upper, upper-middle, middle, lower-middle and lower. Table 4 shows the cross-tabulation of these two variables.

Interestingly, the very wealthy (upper) are almost as non-democratic (38%) as the poorest or lower income group (41%), and comprise even a smaller share of the most democratic group (6%) than the poorest villagers (8%). The most democratic people are those who see their wealth as 'middle' or 'upper-middle', while those who see themselves as 'lower-middle' fall in-between. These findings are statistically significant.

Figure 1 presents the same data in a visual format. Note that across all four aspects of the 'democratic idea' we find a curvilinear relationship, where the poorest and richest

Table 4. Democratic idea by perceived level of wealth, in percentages

				Perceived level of wealth			
Democratic idea	Lower ($n = 250$) %	Lower-middle ($n = 435$) %	Middle ($n = 1,415$) %	Upper-middle ($n = 419$) %	Upper ($n = 102$) %	Total ($n = 2,621$) %
Not democratic	41	28	26	29	38	28
A bit democratic	42	50	47	41	43	46
Democratic	9	14	16	17	13	15
Very democratic	8	8	11	13	6	11
Total	100	100	100	100	100	100

Note: MLA, $p = 0.003$.
Source: Survey in rural China, Summer 1999.

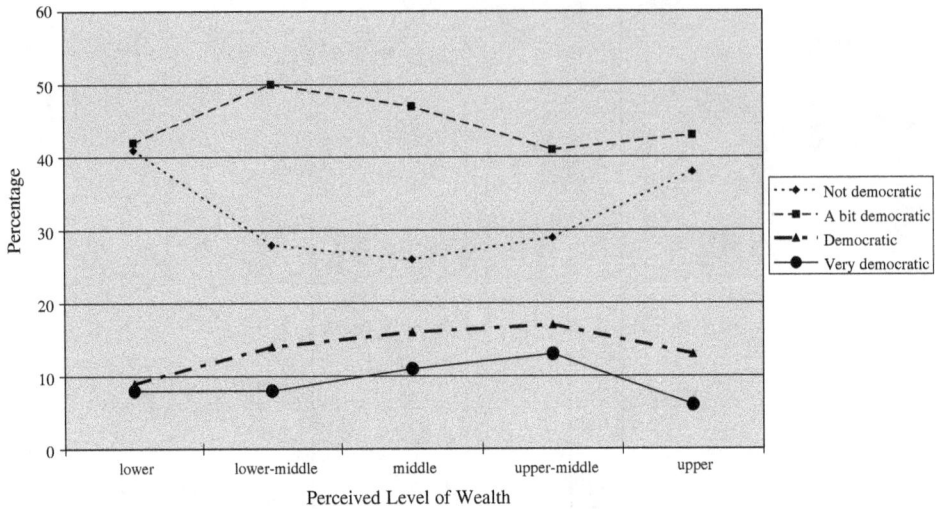

Figure 1. Democratic idea by perceived level of wealth, in percentages.

villagers in general are less democratic and the middle levels of wealth tend to be more democratic. This shape reflects our hypothesis in the opening sections of this paper. In particular, the 'not democratic' group shows the clearest curvilinear relationship.

The above findings employ the individual's wealth relative to villagers in their own village, rather than the village's overall wealth. But which communities are likely to be democratic—rich ones, poorer ones, or average ones? As mentioned above, Oi and Rozelle found a negative relationship between competitive elections and the level of industrialization. However, in their data, the incidence of contested elections decreased only in the wealthiest 10% of villages,[27] otherwise the level of economic development did not affect their measure of democratization.

Our data, though tentative, also suggest that richer villages, based on per capita income from village records, are less democratic. While 62% of villagers in wealthier villages reported that their most recent election had involved more candidates than positions, 72% of middle-income villages and 76% of poorer villages reported multi-candidate elections ($p < 0.001$). Similarly, while 64% of villagers in poorer villages saw the most recent elections as more competitive, only 44% of villagers in wealthier villages expressed such views.[28] Also, while speeches may not be that important in village elections, 26% of villagers in the poorer villages reported having had speeches, while only 21% of those in richer villages said that there had been speeches.[29]

---

27. Oi and Rozelle, 'Elections and power', p. 537.

28. It is worth noting that 41% of villagers in wealthier villages felt that there had been no change. Therefore, if their previous elections had been relatively competitive, this finding says nothing about the real level of competition.

29. Part of these results may be due to the fact that one of our Heilongjiang counties was significantly richer than the Anhui counties, but had held its elections between two and three years earlier. Therefore, the county affect may explain this difference. However, there was very little variation in voting rates among the four counties, suggesting that wealth, rather than locality, had some influence. Similarly, more of Heilongjiang's villages reported having speeches than Anhui's.

Table 5. Cadre attitudes towards democracy by village income per capita, in percentages

| | Village income per capita | | | |
Attitudes towards democracy	Poor (n = 108) %	Middle (n = 129) %	Rich (n = 123) %	Total (n = 360) %
Not democratic	16	13	25	18
Democratic	46	47	51	48
Very democratic	38	40	24	34
Total	100	100	100	100

Note: MLA, $p = 0.01$.
Source: Survey in rural China, Summer 1999.

Also wealth did not correlate with democratic values. When asked to respond to the statement 'so long as there is stable economic development, there is no need to promote greater democracy', villagers in richer villages were more likely to 'strongly agree' and 'agree' (24%) than people in poorer (17%) or middle-income villages (22%), and the finding was statistically significant ($p < 0.006$). Similarly, people in wealthier villages were more likely to believe that the wealthy should have more right to speak out on village affairs ($p < 0.001$)—what might be seen as an elitist view of democracy—and they strongly agreed with the statement 'because I know what's happened in the village, I have the right to participate in village affairs'. Here, 34% of villagers in wealthier villages 'strongly agree' with that statement, while only 22% and 17% of people in poor and middle-income villages, respectively, strongly agree. Again, the finding was statistically significant ($p < 0.001$), and again, middle-income villages were more democratic.

Cadres' attitudes towards democracy vary based on the village's per capita income (Table 5). Four questions assessed cadres' views on democracy and elections, and we broke their responses into three categories—non-democratic, democratic and very democratic. We also divided village income into richer, middle-income and poorer. In richer villages, 25% of cadres fell into the 'non-democratic' category, while only 16% and 13% of cadres in poor and middle-income villages held 'non-democratic' views, respectively. Similarly, only 24% of cadres in richer villages expressed 'very democratic' ideas, while 38% and 40% of cadres in poor and middle-income villages, respectively, expressed 'very democratic' values—a very big difference.[30] These findings suggest that richer villages breed less democratic cadres.

Finally, what kind of villages, and who within them, are most likely to demand good governance? We asked villagers: 'if you heard that village cadres were considering instituting an unfair measure (*cuoshi*), what would you do?' Based on their selection from a list of options, including collective or individual action, as well as no action, we gave each villager a total score. The individual scores varied based on their relative income, showing that richer villagers (62%) were much more likely to consider action than poorer (44%) or middle-income ones (55%, MLA = 0.00).

---

30. The relationship between these two variables was significant at the 0.003 level.

Similarly, when asked if they had taken actions to solve problems facing their village, richer villagers were again more active. Of the 14% of our entire sample who had taken some concrete action, richer villagers had acted more often (16%) than middle-income (14%) or poorer villagers (11%). The measure of linear association was 0.008. Therefore, perhaps it was the richer villagers—who are better connected, particularly with the local party leader—in poorer villages—where there were economic problems—who were most likely to consider taking action in response to unfair policies. This finding suggests that if cadres misbehave, wealthier villagers are most likely to challenge those actions. Still, although they are more likely to take action, remember that these richer villagers possess less democratic values.

Democracy and the emerging entrepreneurial class

The role of the middle class in promoting or supporting democracy is sometimes problematic. Barrington Moore argued that democracy depends on the emergence of a middle class,[31] while O'Donnell and others argue that in Latin America, the business community supported 'bureaucratic authoritarianism' and the repression of the working class.[32] Payne, however, found that Brazilian industrialists were agnostic about the regime type—they supported any regime that could insure political stability and stable investment rules.[33] Conversations between one of the authors and private business owners in rural China in the early 1990s yielded a strong antipathy towards democratization and political liberalization. However, the growing influence of the rural private sector and the emergence of a new middle class might abet democratic development. Newspapers, magazines and some scholars report that villagers elect entrepreneurs because they believe they are most capable of promoting the village's economy. Therefore, if they feel that they can gain political power through the electoral process, the local business elite may support elections.

Our localities, however, had few factory owners, with only 2% of our entire sample reporting that their family's main income came from wage labor. Still, interviewers in each village identified two entrepreneurs, yielding a total of 237 individuals, whose views we can compare with non-entrepreneurial peasants. These people were significantly richer than other villagers, both in terms of their self-identification of their level of wealth (their mean score of 2.4 versus a score of 3.2 for non-entrepreneurial villagers reflected their greater relative wealth) and in terms of the number of household appliances they possessed (mean of 4.4 versus 2.8).

But, do their views and attitudes about politics differ from the average peasant? They are much more aware of political phenomenon, discuss politics more frequently, and are more willing to voice their opinion on issues than average villagers. In fact, 28% of them report 'often' discussing political and economic issues, while only 14% of other villagers do so. This may be because they are more educated and more likely to have a member of the Communist Party in their family. They are also more willing than other villagers to discuss issues with the party secretary and to participate in the

---

31. Barrington Moore, *The Social Origins of Dictatorship and Democracy* (Boston: Beacon Press, 1967).

32. O'Donnell, *Modernization and Bureaucratic-Authoritarianism*.

33. Leigh A. Payne, *Brazilian Industrialists and Democratic Change* (Baltimore: Johns Hopkins University Press, 1994).

village representative assembly's meetings; but they are not more likely to discuss issues with the village director, perhaps due to his more limited influence.

In terms of values, they are no more democratic than other villagers, except for their response to one question—'as long as the village economy is stable, there is no need to increase the level of democracy'. The data in Table 4 above, about the relationship between the 'democratic idea' and level of perceived wealth, reflect the position of entrepreneurs somewhat, in that 47 of the 237 entrepreneurs, or 20%, declared their income as upper level, which placed them in the least democratic group. Still, 88 or 37% of them fall into the upper-middle income group, which was the most democratic cohort.

Compared to other villagers, however, entrepreneurs show greater support for good governance and political procedures that limit the local elite's ability to manipulate the local economy and intervene in private economic affairs. They are more likely than regular villagers to think that publicly displaying the village's financial records is good for economic development,[34] and to think that a contract between the villagers and the cadres improves villager–cadre relations.[35] Therefore, while they may not favor greater democracy, they reflect similar views to Brazilian industrialists who care less about democracy but more about good governance and political stability.

Yet villagers do not want entrepreneurs to serve as village director.[36] When choosing possible candidates from a list—villagers could choose more than one—only 7% selected entrepreneurs, less than those who selected normal villagers (*putong nongmin*) (8%) or cadres (17%). Also, when asked to respond to the statement 'entrepreneurs who are good at business and have money are the best candidates for village director', 71% of villagers 'totally disagreed' (38%), or 'disagreed' (33%), while only 13% 'relatively agreed' (9%) or 'totally agreed' (4%). Villagers see the agglutination of political and economic power as threatening to local democracy.[37] In these localities it will not be easy for entrepreneurs to break into local politics through the electoral process.

Democratizing the rural elite?

Have democracy and elections affected the local elite? Have elections led to significant turnover among elites and are the values of the new elite more democratic? And, do more competitive elections serve as a monitoring mechanism limiting cadre misbehavior?

Is there a 'power transition' underway?

To what extent have local elections led to a restructuring of power in the countryside? In our villages, elite turnover increased significantly between 1996 and 1999.

34. While a smaller percentage believe that it 'really speeds up economic development' (16% versus 18%), many more think that it 'speeds up development' (62% versus 47%). The Mantel–Hanzsel Measure of Linear Association was 0.02.

35. Of entrepreneurs, 76% believe that the charter has a 'big influence' or 'some influence' versus 65% for regular villagers. MLA = 0.00.

36. Baogang He, who studied elections in wealthier parts of China, particularly Zhejiang Province, found that 15–20% of village directors were entrepreneurs. See Baogang He, 'Village elections, village power structure, and rural governance in Zhejaing', *American Asian Review* XX(3), (Fall 2002), pp. 55–89.

37. Agglutination occurs when elites accumulate power on more than one dimension, i.e. political *and* economic power. See Robert D. Putnam, *Political Elites* (Englewood Cliffs, NJ: Prentice Hall, 1975).

Table 6. Getting re-elected, MDN and LDN village directors, Anhui Province, 1999

	MDN village directors		LDN village directors	
	No.	%	No.	%
Previous director, ran for office and re-elected	7	25.0	15	46.9
Previous director, ran for office but not re-elected	14	50.0	13	40.6
Previous director, did not run for office	7	25.0	4	12.5
Total	28	100	32	100

Note: Chi-Square test, $p = 0.173$.
Source: Survey in rural China, Summer 1999.

The percentage of village leaders taking office for the first time increased significantly year to year, from 37% in 1996 to 43% in 1997, reaching 53% in 1999.[38] Much of this turnover occurred in 1999 in our Anhui villages, where the introduction of more democratic nominations led 25% of cadres to decide not to run for re-election (Table 6). Also, when Anhui village directors ran again for office, they lost approximately 50% of the time. Rural elections are changing the people who hold political power.

Second, elections are pluralizing political authority in our villages. While the village party secretary in 1996–1997 was often also director of the villager committee, the 1999 election ended this phenomenon almost entirely. Thus in 1996 and 1997, the party secretary held both posts in 32% and 46% of the cases, respectively, but in 1999 the same person was elected to both posts in only one of 49 cases.[39]

But even though a clear division of labor and authority between the two top posts in the village emerged, an authoritarian leadership strata still held power, making the division of authority somewhat pro-forma. In Anhui, the director of the village committee was usually the deputy secretary of the village party committee. While in Heilongjiang in 1996–1998, 20% of people elected as director of the village committee were also the vice-party secretary, in 1999, 53% of the newly elected directors in Anhui were also vice party secretary. So, even with different people holding the two posts, key decisions would still be made in the party committee run by the village party secretary.

Are non-CCP members elected to the villager committee, a source of democratic values within the local elite? According to Jakobson, in 1997, 44% of village committee members nationwide were not party members. She also quotes Wang Zhenyao to the effect that 30–50% of village committee directors were not party members when they won the election, but were recruited into the CCP within a few weeks.[40]

---

38. In 1998, there were only three elections in the villages we sampled and in two of them the director of the villager committee was elected for the first time.

39. According to Jakobson, in 1997 only 2% of village directors nationwide were also party secretaries. Linda Jakobson, lecture at the Division of Social Sciences, Hong Kong University of Science and Technology, 2000. Perhaps our two Heilongjiang counties were unique. Recent reports, however, suggest that the CCP favors fusing these posts again because competition between these officials has created political instability. Personal communication, Kevin O'Brien, January 2004, Hong Kong.

40. Jakobson, lecture at the Division of Social Sciences.

In our survey, 25% of village committee directors reported that they had joined the CCP before becoming a cadre, while 54% of them had become a cadre and then joined the party. This latter group, then, was recruited into the CCP after attaining local elite status. However, the pattern for the village party secretaries was reversed: 48% of them had joined the CCP before becoming a cadre.[41] The finding suggests a different mobility track for party secretaries and village committee directors—with the former having much deeper roots in the CCP—which could lead to different values and attitudes.

The values of local cadres

Despite the different mobility tracks, village party secretaries and village directors held similar views on most issues, reinforcing the argument that a village-level oligarchy exists. On our democratic scales there were no statistically significant differences between these two groups. We would have hypothesized that on issues such as democratization or elections, their differing experiences should have led to different views. Nevertheless, since many village directors in our survey were nominated by local organizations or elected through only partially democratic procedures, their views may not differ so much from local party elites who may have influenced their selection. In fact, they were no more worried about losing office if they could not resolve local problems than the party secretary, suggesting that they felt well protected by the local power structure.

Still, elite turnover has had some impact on the values of local leaders. Cadres who simultaneously had held both posts were less democratic on a number of dimensions than cadres who held either the post of village party secretary or director of the village committee. In terms of their democratic predilections, of the 22 officials who had held both posts, 32% fell into the 'non-democratic category', while only 20% of party secretaries and 14% of village directors did so. Similarly, only 23% of those holding dual posts fell into the very democratic group, while 36% of party secretaries and 34% of villager committee directors did so. On the democratic process, these 'village emperors' were also less democratic. They were much more likely to believe that wealthier people should have more right to speak out on public affairs; they were less likely to disagree with the statement that 'if the economy is good then there is no need to promote democracy'; and, they were much more likely to agree that 'only people with special skills should have the right to hold office'.

Nevertheless, the most democratic group was the local non-party elite who were members of the village committee. As Table 7 shows, they were least likely to believe that the wealthy should have more say in public affairs or to believe that only people with special knowledge should have greater influence on decisions. Also, they were less likely to believe that good economic development mitigates the need for greater democracy (question 2). If these villagers move into leadership positions, the future local elite could become more democratic. Still, will they be able to enter the elite if they maintain those attitudes or will they not change those attitudes after they gain real power?

---

41. Unfortunately, we used the term 'cadre'—rather than village director—in the questionnaire, so it is unclear what was entailed in the term 'cadre'. If they held a village post before being elected village director, they might already have been a party member when they ran for village director.

Table 7. Attitudes towards democracy among different types of cadres

No.	Party secretaries (122) %	Village directors (97) %	Other cadres who are CCP members (103) %	Other cadres who are not CCP members (38) %
(1) *Wealthy people should have more say in public affairs than poorer people*				
Strongly agree	20	10	13	8
Agree	24	33	22	18
Disagree	21	24	35	32
Strongly disagree	33	31	30	40
(2) *As long as development of the village economy is stable, there is no need to increase the level of democracy*				
Strongly agree	4	4	3	3
Agree	5	4	8	3
Disagree	23	21	24	24
Strongly disagree	67	69	65	71
(3) *Only people with special knowledge and abilities have the right to speak at times of decision making*				
Strongly agree	24	12	18	16
Agree	25	32	36	21
Disagree	26	34	25	29
Strongly disagree	22	21	19	29

Source: Survey in rural China, Summer 1999.

Cadre attitudes towards elections, democratization and good governance

Central leaders frequently call on local cadres to be less rapacious and 'lighten the burden of the peasants'. Given that the state has raised this plea almost annually since 1978, a new mechanism is needed to monitor cadre behavior. According to Li and O'Brien, the Fujian provincial Bureau of Civil Affairs convinced the provincial Discipline Inspection Committee to support village elections 'when the commission realized that corruption tended to be lower where well-run village elections took place'.[42] If generally true, elections could decrease rural instability that results from cadre malfeasance.

In our survey, both villagers and cadres believed that elections had a positive effect on cadre behavior. In Anhui, 48% of villagers from more democratic villages believed that village elections decreased cadre haughtiness and rudeness, while only 41% of villagers in less democratic villages held these views.[43] Villagers from more democratic villages were more satisfied with the level of transparency of the village's financial records, with 64% of them being either 'very satisfied' or 'satisfied', while only 47% of villagers in less democratic villages held these views (MLA, $p = 0.001$). This finding occurred because villages that introduced direct nominations were also more likely to make their financial records public. That meant that 29% of citizens in less democratic villages were 'not satisfied' and 6% were 'extremely dissatisfied'.

This more favorable attitude towards how officials allocated village finances was reconfirmed by other questions. MDN villagers expressed greater satisfaction with how funds that they contributed to the village were used—44% being 'very satisfied' or 'satisfied'—while only 30% of villagers in LDN villages felt this way (MLA, $p = 0.001$). Importantly, 25% of villagers in LDN villages were flatly dissatisfied (the bottom scale on this question) as compared to only 15% of MDN villagers.[44] Still, villagers in MDN villages were not more likely to believe that elections could end the problems of 'random taxes or assessments' (*luan shou fei*) or prevent cadre corruption, a position echoed by Bernstein and Lu.[45]

Cadres say that elections make them more responsive to villagers' interests, a positive force for political stability. More than peasants, cadres believe that elections make them more likely to resist taxes and fees from the upper levels. While only 55% of villagers 'completely agree' (14%) or 'somewhat agree' (41%), 81% of cadres either 'completely agree' (31%) or 'somewhat agree' (50%). If true, however, cadre relations with higher-level officials become problematic if they respond to villagers' demands and protect the villagers' interests, a finding shared by Li Lianjiang.[46]

Ironically, elections may make it more difficult, not easier, for village directors to promote economic development. Cadres in MDN villages were more likely to have faced villagers who refused to contribute to development projects (36%) than cadres in less democratic villages (19%) (MLA, $p = 0.14$).[47] We also asked the village

---

42. O'Brien and Li, 'Accommodating "democracy" in a one-party state', p. 481.

43. Chi-square test, $p = 0.017$.

44. Nevertheless, it is worth reporting that 53.1% of villagers in MDN villages and 57.7% of villagers in LDN villages selected 'don't know' when asked who decides how the funds are spent in the village.

45. Bernstein and Lu, *Taxation without Representation in Rural China*.

46. Lianjiang Li, 'Elections and popular resistance in rural China', *China Information* XV(2), (2001).

47. We report this finding, even though it is not statistically significant. But given that we only have a total of 60 cases in Anhui, the value of the MLA is quite suggestive.

directors to agree or disagree—on a four point scale—with the statement 'Democratic elections make villagers more willing to contribute money to the village accumulation fund'. Directors in MDN villages tended to disagree with this statement (their mean score was 2.5), while directors in LDN villages were inclined to agree with it (mean score 2.1).[48] While the process of accumulating local capital may have become more democratic, democracy may not benefit economic development, despite the fact that local governments need capital to build roads and other infrastructure that promote economic development.

Conclusion

Like many other studies of democracy in rural China, this study will not make sweeping or definitive generalizations. Data from four counties simply do not permit that. Our findings remain suggestive. Part of the problem is that good indicators of democracy, stability, economic development or good governance are not easy to collect. Though few analysts confess to the limitations of their data, because it would call into question their findings, surveying rural China on political variables is costly and very difficult.[49] We, therefore, should not give up case studies, or in-depth interviews, although a research strategy involving case studies and surveys would be optimal.

Also, significant changes have occurred since 1999. Rural protests have increased dramatically, with land issues jumping to the forefront. Also, concern within the Chinese leadership over the conflict between two centers of power, the appointed party secretary and the elected—and therefore more legitimate—village director, has reportedly led to some backtracking on the electoral process. In some locations, the same person is again holding both posts. To that extent, our study catches rural China in a perhaps unique period of expanding democracy.

Still, democratic procedures based on our indicators were fairly well established, suggesting that democracy was strengthened in rural China in the late 1990s. As villages moved from having organizations or collectivities nominating candidates, increasing instead the role of individuals in this process, the democratic environment improved. Moreover, in villages with more democratic nomination systems, elections were also seen to be more legitimate, fairer and competitive.

But it is hard to say that wealthier localities are more prone to adopt democratic principles and procedures. Our data suggest that neither wealthier villagers nor villagers in wealthier villages are the strongest advocates of greater democracy or repositories of democratic principles; even though they are more likely to take action against cadre malfeasance. Similarly, cadres in the wealthiest villages were the least democratic of our entire sample. Instead, villagers in the upper-middle income bracket may be the most democratic citizens in rural China, while poorer villages were most active in trying to solve their problems.

---

48. Despite our small sample size of 60 villages, the finding was significant at the 0.08 level.
49. A conference at George Washington University, organized by Bruce Dickson, entitled 'Surveying China', addressed many of these issues, including the difficulty of finding good and reliable Chinese co-researchers, the high costs of surveys, getting local-level support for carrying out the survey, and problems of measurement.

One negative result of the electoral process was that elections made it more difficult for cadres to convince villagers to contribute to local projects, which may undermine economic development. Admittedly, local cadres often misuse local funds. But if they are disciplined by elections, then granting responsive or responsible officials the authority to create collective goods could promote the local economy.

Our data cannot confirm that elections constrain cadre misbehavior, though the direct nomination process in Anhui Province may have had that effect. Cadres said that elections kept them in line; but they knew the politically correct responses—that is how they got to be cadres. Moreover, few expressed great concerns that they might lose their jobs if they could not solve the villagers' problems. And, they are under great pressure to follow the directives of township leaders.[50] Still, elections may encourage them to resist the demands for fees and taxes from upper levels.

Finally, despite the increasing institutionalization of democracy, changes within the local elite suggest relative political constancy. While the people clearly favored more democracy, they were not really getting it. The old party secretaries, who also held the post of village director, were gone and a real division of authority emerged between the village director and the village party secretary. But as long as village directors are recruited into the CCP and are becoming the vice party secretary, the challenge to the CCP's authority posed by elections remains limited. We are not yet seeing the emergence of a *'dang wai'*, or the rise to power of any cohort of like-minded individuals outside of the ruling party who could coalesce into a stable opposition. Only if the non-party elite become village directors, all the while resisting pressures or blandishments to join the CCP, could this process materialize. But our data suggest that this type of major political transformation was not happening.

Appendix: Measuring the democratic idea

We asked villagers to respond to a series of questions which could tap into their democratic predilections. We made the following statement—'Only people with specialized knowledge and ability have the right to speak during periods of decision making'. Almost 45% of villagers disagreed with this statement—28% 'disagreed' and 17% 'strongly disagreed', while over 30% 'somewhat agreed', 12% 'strongly agreed', and 9% selected 'don't know'.[51] A second question confirmed the views of Li and O'Brien on the use of petitions by villagers as a means of political expression. In response to the statement 'If villagers disagree with local policies, they have the right to petition the higher levels', 81% 'strongly agreed' (41%) or 'agreed somewhat' (40.3%), while only 9% 'disagreed' (6.4%) or 'disagreed strongly' (2.4%).[52] Only 7% of villagers had no opinion on this issue. The third statement focused on whether poor people had the right to speak out on village-level policies. It stated: 'People with good

---

50. Bjorn Alpermann, 'The post-election administration of Chinese villages', *The China Journal* no. 46, (July 2001), pp. 45–67.

51. Selecting 'don't know' is a common choice in surveys in the PRC. In fact, one can study these responses to explain who is more likely to select this option. In many cases it reflects a lack of political awareness. See M. Kent Jennings, 'Missing data and survey research in China: problems, solutions, and applications', paper prepared for Conference on Surveying China, George Washington University, Washington, DC, 9–10 June 2000.

52. Even local cadres expressed strong support for the villagers' right to petition higher-level officials if they disagreed with 'local policies'. The question, though, is how they defined 'local policies'.

economic conditions have more right to speak out on village policy as compared to people with poor economic conditions'. Only 7% of villagers 'strongly agreed', and 18% 'somewhat agreed'. Instead, 35% 'disagreed somewhat' and 29% 'totally disagreed'. Some 13% either did not know or did not answer. Clearly, people in these villages do not think that the rich should dominate the decision-making process. Finally, villagers strongly disagreed with the argument often proposed by politically influential Chinese that Chinese people accept non-democratic politics if they can make money. This is a common reason given in Hong Kong for the slow pace of democratization. But in response to the statement 'As long as the village economy shows stable development, there is no need to raise the level of democracy', only 21% 'strongly agreed' (7%) or 'agreed somewhat' (14%), while 63% 'disagreed somewhat' (32%) or 'strongly disagreed' (33%). Finally, 10% 'didn't know'. Clearly, the oligarchs are wrong; even if there is good economic development, villagers in these communities still wanted more democracy.

Since each statement can be a good indicator of democratic values, those who 'strongly supported' any of the above statements received a score of -2 for each answer, while those who 'agreed somewhat' received a score of -1. Those who 'disagreed somewhat' received $+1$, while those who 'strongly disagreed' scored $+2$. By combining each person's score on all four questions, we gave them an overall score on the 'democratic idea' and positioned them on an anti- versus pro-democratic continuum.

Economic Development and the Implementation of Village Elections in Rural China

RONG HU

Based on survey data from rural Fujian Province of China, this paper shows that economic development, especially village collective revenue, plays an important role in village elections. With economic development and industrialization, collective revenues will increase and differentiated interests will develop among villagers. Village elections are institutional channels for villagers to articulate their interests. The research findings show that it is the collective revenue and the relative living standard of the village compared with other townships within the same county or district that arouse villagers' interests for participation and candidates' motives for campaigning, and thus enhance the implementation of elections. The paper concludes that village-level economic development is crucial for the implementation of competitive elections. With economic development, village committees will control more collective revenues, thus increasing the stakes villagers have in elections. This will result in greater participation by villagers in elections, and in more competitive elections. Increased competitiveness of elections will facilitate changes in the institutions regarding village committee elections.

There has been a longstanding debate about the relationship between economic development and democratization. Since most theories have focused on explaining democratization at a national level, there has been little systematic analysis of intra-national differences in the implementation of democratic reforms. This paper fills this gap by presenting evidence showing that in localities where economic development leads to higher government revenues, villagers participate more actively in newly instituted elections and competition between election candidates is more intense. Democratic reforms in these areas are more likely to become institutionalized rather than remain formalities.

Theoretical arguments

Theoretical arguments about the relationships between economic development and democratization can be traced back to Lipset, who proposed: 'Perhaps the most widespread generalization linking political systems to other aspects of society has been that democracy is related to the state of economic development'.[1] According to Lipset, two important factors related to economic development will enhance the likelihood of democracy in a country. First, economic development is associated with increases in education, which in turn promotes political attitudes conducive to democracy. Second, economic development alters the social structure by increasing the population of the middle-class, which is the main pro-democracy force in the society. Lipset's observations have generated a large body of research in comparative politics, which has been supported and contested, revised and extended, buried and resuscitated.[2]

The relationship between economic development and the village elections in rural China, which are the only grassroots elections under an authoritarian regime, is different from the national level democracies studied by social mobilization theorists. In other words, if relationships between economic development and village elections in rural China are to some extent similar to what has been suggested by mobilization theorists, the mechanisms and rationales behind them are totally different. First, the relationships studied by modernization theorists are macro-level phenomena and related to national states, while village elections are local-community level democratic practices. Second, mobilization theorists suggest that authoritarian regimes will begin the transformation process to democracies when per capita GDP reach $5,000–6,000. If making a comparison between village elections in rural China and residential committee elections in urban areas, we will find that the former is more contested, which seems to contradict mobilization theories, for the per capita GDP in rural areas is far below that in urban areas. Finally, mobilization theorists stress the importance of social structure transformation, arguing that with the increase of the middle class population, more people will receive higher education and they will become more interested in politics. However, the case in rural China is different. It is the increased collective wealth, not the transformation of social structure that directly arouses villagers' interests in participation. Furthermore, for national level democracy, it is important for voters to receive a basic level of education and to have some knowledge about domestic and foreign policies to make political participation more efficacious, while for grassroots democracy in rural China things are different. Although it is arbitrary to presume that there is no relationship between education and villagers' participation, the level of formal education is not a prerequisite for villagers to participate in local public affairs within a small community with a population of several hundreds to thousands. Uneducated villagers, even illiterates, know who will be more suitable to be their village leaders and who will represent their interests best and do things more fairly. So mobilization theories do not adequately explain what is happening in rural China.

In order to understand politics in rural China, we need to develop new theoretical arguments and explore the relationships between economic development and village

---

1. Seymour Martin Lipset, 'Some social requisites of democracy: economic development and political legitimacy', *American Political Science Review* 53, (March 1959), p. 75.

2. For a more recent review of the thesis, see Ross E. Burkhart and Michael S. Lewis-Beck, 'Comparative democracy: the economic development thesis', *American Political Science Review* 88(4), (December 1994), pp. 903–910; Adam Przeworski and Fernando Limongi, 'Modernization: theories and facts', *World Politics* 49(2), (1997), pp. 155–183; Edward N. Muller, 'Economic determinants of democracy', *American Sociological Review* 60, (December 1995), pp. 966–982; John B. Londregan and Keith T. Poole, 'Does high income promote democracy?', *World Politics* 49, (October 1996), pp. 1–30.

elections under a broader social and cultural context. Historically, peasants in China depended on landlords economically and on family and lineage networks socially. After the Communist Party took power in 1949, with the collectivization of land and the suppression of clan lineage, peasants became highly dependent on brigades and production teams under the Commune System.[3] Beginning in the 1980s, the process of de-collectivization began with the introduction of the household responsibility system. With the de-collectivization after the introduction of the household responsibility system, peasants became the most independent and autonomous stratum in Chinese society. Their political participation has been transformed from the so-called mobilized participation in the Commune period to autonomous participation in the present period.[4] When participating in elections and other public affairs, villagers will weigh costs and rewards and try to maximize their interests. Villagers spend time and energy to nominate candidates and compare candidates before voting. Candidates need even more time, energy and other resources to participate in campaigning. Therefore, only when villagers benefit more from the results than cost paid will they actively participate in elections; and only when candidates will be rewarded more when elected than they have paid into a campaign will they enthusiastically campaign.

As self-government organizations, village committees shoulder double tasks of implementing state policies, such as family planning and tax collecting, and enhancing public goods, including construction of village roads and schools.[5] Since the Organic Law on Village Committees passed by the standing committee of the National Congress in 1987, provincial laws on village elections have been promulgated. According to these laws, village committees are elected directly by villagers every three years. Although there are differences in the election procedures in different provinces, it usually requires great effort, energy, time and other resources both for organizers to hold elections and for voters to participate in elections. Take Fujian as an example, candidates nominated by villagers directly are called preliminary candidates (*chubu houxuanren*). The number of preliminary candidates nominated by villagers usually is several-times to ten-times the positions to be elected. The village committee usually has five to six members: one director, two vice-directors and two to three general members. The average number of preliminary candidates in each village was 7.2 for the village committee director, 16.3 for the vice-directors, and 33 for the two to three positions of general members in the 1997 election in Heshan Township, Xiamen.[6] These preliminary candidates must be nominated through a process called primary election (*yuxuan*), in which all village representatives vote to determine official candidates (*zhengshi houxuanren*). And

---

3. Jean Oi, *State and Peasant in Contemporary China: The Political Economy of Village Government* (Berkeley: University of California Press, 1989).

4. According to John Burns, peasants under the Commune System in Mao Era were mobilized to participate in politics aiming at implementing state policies. Rong Hu discusses villagers' political participation in village elections and insists that peasants' political participation has transformed from mobilized participation to autonomous participation. Johns Burns, *Political Participation in Rural China* (Berkeley: University of California Press, 1988); Rong Hu, 'Cunmin Weiyunhui Xuanju Zhong Cunmin De Zizhu Shi Changyu' ['The autonomous participation of villagers in village elections'], in Lianjiang Li, ed., *Cunweihui Xuanju Guangcha* [*Observations of Village Elections*] (Tianjing Renming Chubangshe, 2001).

5. Rong Hu, 'Cunming weiyunhui de zizhi jiqi yu xiangzhen zhengfu de guangxi' ['The autonomy of village committees and their relationships with township government', *Er Shi Yi Shiji* [*The 21st Century*] 50, (December 1998).

6. Interview, May 1997.

finally, this list of official candidates, usually more than the positions to be elected, will be published and voted on by all villagers aged 18 and above on the election day. In addition to the human and financial resources put into elections by the election committees, villagers must also spend a great deal of time and energy to nominate candidates, to compare and distinguish strong-points and weaknesses of each candidate, to participate in election conferences and voting, and even to campaign for some candidates. As for candidates, more resources are required for campaigning. In other words, election requires cost, both for voters and candidates.[7]

Therefore, to villagers, what can make the village committees so important for them that rewards from the results of elections will exceed the cost of their input into elections? To candidates, what can make their benefits from being elected and holding posts on village committees exceed their costs both for campaigns and for holding office? As the self-government organizations of local communities, village committees enjoy considerable power, which ranges from the distribution of land for building houses and construction of local schools, mediating disputes among villagers, providing certifications for villagers who migrate to urban areas for business or work, to collection of state taxes. If we compare village committees with resident committees in urban China, we will find the former is much more powerful. For in urban areas, under the planned economy, work organizations not only pay for their employees, but also provide housing, medical care, and other related welfare services for them.[8] Although reforms have tried to reduce their dependence, urban residents have been and still are highly dependent on their work units, and resident committees are less important for them.[9] Furthermore, villagers are also more autonomous than commune members in Mao's era. Under the commune system, peasants worked collectively in production teams and brigades, and they depended on collectives for grains.[10] After the household responsibility system, peasants were liberated from the control of collectives and became the most autonomous stratum in Chinese society. Therefore, as rational actors, villagers will weigh costs and rewards when they participate in election and rewards from the election results are most important for villagers' participation.

There are many factors that contribute to the impact of village elections on villagers' rewards; the most important factor is economic development.[11] The economic development level, especially village collective wealth, is directly related to how much villagers and candidates will be rewarded from the results of elections. In economically more developed areas, where village committees control more collective wealth and

---

7. For the classic discussion of election cost, see Anthony Downs, *An Economic Theory of Democracy* (New York: Harper Collins Publishers, 1957).

8. See Andrew Walder, *Communist Neo-Traditionalism: Work and Authority in Chinese Industry* (Berkeley: University of California Press, 1991); Yianjie Bian, *Work and Inequality in Urban China* (Albany: State University of New York, 1994).

9. For a discussion of the Residents' Committees, see Benjamin L. Read, 'Revitalizing the state's urban "nerve tips"', *The China Quarterly* no. 163, (September 2000), pp. 806–820.

10. Oi, *State and Peasant in Contemporary China*.

11. According to the Rong Hu, four important factors contribute to villager participation in elections: (1) incumbent village leaders' behavior: if leaders abuse their power during office terms, more villagers will participate in elections to vote against the incumbents; (2) election fairness: the fairer the election, the more efficacious villagers feel, and the more they participate in elections; (3) economic development: economic development will increase the competitiveness of elections; and (4) characteristics of local communities, which decrease the anonymity of voters, also contribute to high turnout under some occasions. Rong Hu, 'Cunmin Weiyunhui Xuanju Zhong Cunmin De Zizhu Shi Changyu'.

resources, villagers have a bigger stake in elections, and they participate in elections actively. In these areas, village committee members usually have more power and are rewarded more for holding positions, so more candidates will run for village offices and more resources will be put into campaigning.[12] On the contrary, in poor areas where village committees control less or even no collective wealth and resources, villagers' stake in village committees and their elections is low. Fewer villagers' care who will be their leaders and fewer villagers want to be elected to village committees to do these thankless jobs. Given such low participation from villagers and the high cost for elections, the complex election institutions cannot be implemented effectively and elections will inevitably become mere formalities in these areas. Therefore, the economic development level is crucial for the effective implementation of elections, and a certain amount of collective wealth is the prerequisite for successful elections. Only when village collectives control a certain amount of economic resources, no matter where these resources come from,[13] is it possible for villagers to get more rewards than costs from participation. Then they will actively participate in elections, and elections will be implemented effectively.

As a matter of fact, village election is an institutional mechanism to promote interests and to settle disputes among villagers. With economic development and industrialization, collective revenues will increase and villagers' interests will be sparked. Differentiated interests will develop among different natural villages, teams, clans, occupation groups and even age groups in an administrative village. These interests will need to be articulated through some channels and mediated via certain mechanisms. Village elections are such channels for villagers to articulate their interests, and village committees are such mechanisms to mediate interest disputes among fellow villagers.

Research design and variable measurement

Of the considerable research on village elections in rural China,[14] many have explored the relationship between economic development and village elections. For

---

12. According to Kevin O'Brien, in more developed villages, where many cadres broker semi-marketized relationships and sometimes operate highly profitable enterprises themselves, cadre spirit and energy are generally higher. See Kevin O'Brien, 'Implementing political reform in China's villages', *The Australian Journal of Chinese Affairs* 32, (1994), pp. 33–59.

13. Some village collective wealth comes from collective enterprises, some from compensation from the state for land confiscation, others from fees collected from villagers.

14. See, e.g. Tyrene Whyte, 'Reforming the countryside', *Current History* no. 91, (1992), pp. 273–277; Susan V. Lawrence, 'Democracy, Chinese style', *The Australian Journal of Chinese Affairs* no. 32, (1994), pp. 59–68; O'Brien, 'Implementing political reform in China's villages'; John Dearlove, 'Village politics', in Robert Benewick and Paul Wingrove, eds, *China in the 1990s* (Vancouver: UBC Press, 1995), pp. 120–131; Melanie Manion, 'The electoral connection in the Chinese countryside', *American Political Science Review* 90(4), (1996), pp. 736–748; Jean Oi, 'Economic development, stability and democratic village self-governance', in Maurice Brosseau, Suzanne Pepper and Tsang Shu-ki, eds, *China Review 1996* (Hong Kong: The Chinese University Press, 1996), pp. 125–144; Daniel Kelliher, 'The Chinese debate over village self-government', *The China Journal* 37, (1997), pp. 63–86; Tianjian Shi, 'Economic development and village elections', *Journal of Contemporary China* 8(22), (November 1999), pp. 425–442; Jean Oi and Scott Rozelle, 'Elections and power: the locus of decision making in Chinese villages', *The China Quarterly* 162, (June 2000), pp. 513–539; Kevin J. O'Brien and Lianjiang Li, 'Accommodating "democracy" in a one-party state: introducing village elections in China', *The China Quarterly* 162, (June 2000), pp. 465–489; Robert A. Pastor and Qingshan Tan, 'The meaning of China's village elections', *The China Quarterly* 162, (June 2000), pp. 490–512.

example, Lawrence argues that poor villages will take a leading role in the implementation process of village elections,[15] while O'Brien suggests that village elections are more likely to succeed in rich villages.[16] However, Oi proposes that there may be an inverse relationship between the level of economic development and progress in the implementation of the democratic village rule.[17] Epstein suggests that provinces with the middle level of economic development have developed their elections more successfully.[18] Shi further claims that the relationship between economic development and village elections is a concave curve: economic wealth increases the likelihood that a village will hold semi-competitive elections for people to choose their leaders, but its impact diminishes as economic wealth increases.[19]

Although these studies are helpful for our understanding of community politics in rural China, most of them are based on case studies, anecdotes or official archives, and only some have tried to analyze the relationship between economic development and village elections based on national-wide survey data. Shi did a survey in 1993–1994 and Oi and Rozelle based their analysis on a 1996 survey.[20] However, these studies, careful as they are, have noteworthy limitations. First, their measurements are too simplistic and problematic. For example, one important measure in Oi and Rozelle's study is the frequency of villagers' assembly meetings. Although stipulated in the Organic Law as the highest decision-making body in the village, villagers' assembly meetings are seldom held in practice,[21] for it is so difficult to assemble several thousand villagers aged 18 or above who live in scattered natural villages. Because of such practical and logistical problems, villagers' representative assemblies in many provinces have replaced villagers' assemblies. Therefore, it does not make any sense to use such a rarely assembled village body to measure elections. On the other hand, Shi measured elections by asking respondents whether their villages had held elections for them to choose leaders and whether these elections provided them with candidate choices, while Oi and Rozelle asked whether elections were contested as dependent variables in their regression analysis. These variables might have been adequate to measure village elections at the beginning of the implementation of the Organic Law more than ten years ago. However, they are too simplistic to measure the present electoral reality where contested election with multiple candidates is the common phenomenon in most provinces. Our survey data shows that all the 40 villages in our sample have implemented elections with more candidates than posts. Furthermore, Shi uses county-level data of economic development, per capita GDP in 1993 and economic development speed calculated from per capita GDP of 1982–1993, to explain village-level politics. As a matter of fact, disparities of economic development not only exist among provinces and counties, but also among townships and villages within a county. Although there are

15. Lawrence, 'Democracy, Chinese style'.

16. O'Brien, 'Implementing political reform in China's villages'.

17. Oi, 'Economic development, stability and democratic village self-governance'.

18. Army Epstein, 'Village elections in China: experimenting with democracy', in Joint Economic Committee, Congress of the United States, *China's Economic Future* (Armonk, NY: M.E. Sharpe, 1997).

19. Shi, 'Economic development and village elections'.

20. *Ibid.*; Oi and Rozelle, 'Elections and power'.

21. Wang Zhengyiao and Tang Jingsu, *Zhongguo Nongcun Cunmin Daibiao Huiyi Zhidu* [*Villager Representative Assembly System in Rural China*] (Beijing: Zhongguo Shehui Chubanshe, 1995).

some relationships between county-level economic development and village-level economic wealth, it is inaccurate to explain village election by using county-level data.

Second, these studies were based on nationwide survey data, without taking institutional differences among provinces into consideration. Although originated in two counties of Guangxi in the early 1980s,[22] village committees and their elections were stipulated by laws and implemented from top to bottom (*zi shang er xia*). After the Organic Law passed by the Standing Committee of the National People's Congress in 1987, provinces passed implementation measures in successive years. Since provincial level officials had different attitudes towards the Organic Law, it has been implemented unevenly among provinces.[23] Fujian and Zhejiang passed the implementation measures in 1988, Gansu, Guizhou, Hubei and Hunan in 1989, Heilongjiang, Liaoning, Qinghai and Shaanxi in 1990, Tianjin, Shanxi, Sichuang, Jiling and Xingjiang in 1991, Tibet in 1993, Jiangsu and Jiangxi in 1994, and finally Guangdong in 1998. It took more than a decade for provinces to promulgate implementation measures of the Organic Law. Furthermore, the differences also exist in the stipulations of election measures. For example, in the 2000 village elections in Fujian Province, it was stipulated that a single villager could nominate candidates and formal candidates were determined by primary elections (*yuxuan*) participated in by village representatives, without a process of qualification examinations (*zige shencha*);[24] while in the 2002 election in Guangdong, candidate qualifications were examined and it was stipulated that four kinds of persons would be deleted from the list,[25] such as villagers who violated family planning policies.

It is hard to make comparisons about how the electoral institutions have been implemented in different provinces, for the institutions per se vary so greatly. If we want to understand the real relationship between village elections and economic development and base our study on nation-wide survey data, we should take institutional differences of village elections into consideration and try to draw samples from provinces with similar election institutions or consider institutional differences as a control variable in the analysis. For example, although Shi and Oi drew samples from different provinces, they failed to take into account these institutional differences when they did their surveys.[26]

The data for this paper comes from a survey conducted in October–November 2001 in Shouning County and Xiamen Municipality of Fujian Province. Rather than drawing samples from different provinces, in this study we only make comparisons within one province. Even though there are differences in the implementation of the Organic Law in different counties and townships, the basic institutional settings are the same throughout the province. Besides the Organic Law passed by the national congress, the basic institutions of village elections consist of Implementation Measures of the Organic Law, Election Measures of Village Committees and related

---

22. About the origin and development of village elections, see O'Brien and Li, 'Accommodating "democracy" in a one-party state'.

23. See Kelliher, 'The Chinese debate over village self-government'; O'Brien and Li, 'Accommodating "democracy" in a one-party state'.

24. Interview, December 2000.

25. *Nanfang Ribao* [*South Daily*], (15 January 2002).

26. Shi, 'Economic development and village elections'; Oi and Rozelle, 'Elections and power'.

laws passed by provincial congresses, and administrative norms stipulated by provincial bureaus of civil administration. Therefore, the institutional consistence within one province is a solid basis for our comparison between different areas with different economic development levels in understanding how the same institutions are implemented differently.[27]

A multi-stage sampling method was adopted. First, Shouning County and Xiamen Municipality were chosen purposively. Consequently, five townships were drawn randomly from each area, and then four villages from each township. At the final stage, 25 villagers were drawn from each village. The total sample consists of 1,000 villagers, 40 villages and 10 townships. Out of the total sample of 1,000, some 913 villagers were interviewed successfully. Of the 913 respondents, 56.3% are male and 43.7% female; 24.4% are under age 30, 24.4% are from the age range 31–40, 23.6% from the age range 41–50, 12.9% are aged 51–60, and 11% are older than 61.

In order to correct shortcomings in existing research on village elections, more sophisticated variables are needed to measure the election. Variables in this study can be categorized into three sets: first, a dependent variable to measure elections in each village; second, two intermediate variables, villagers' participation, which is a dependent variable in Model 1, and election competitiveness, which is a dependent variable in Model 2, will be used as independent variables in Model 3; and third, independent variables measuring economic development, such as collective revenue and per capita income, and other predictors such as education and village distance to the county seat.

Let's examine the dependent variable measuring elections first. As mentioned above, Shi and Oi and Rozelle's measures of elections are too simplistic.[28] In order to measure the election, we designed a more complex and comprehensive scale, including nomination and determination of candidates and voting methods. We asked respondents: 'Were any of the following measures practiced in your village in the 2000 election?' Fifteen items listed in Table 1 followed this question. Of the 15 items, the following six items are related to the nomination process of candidates: (1) villagers nominate candidates directly (includes villagers nominating candidates individually or jointly); (2) the village Party branch nominates candidates; (3) township leaders nominate candidates; (4) the incumbent village committee nominate candidates; (5) villager representatives nominate candidates; and (6) a villager nominates oneself as a candidate. Of these six items, items (1), (5) and (6) are positive, which means that the more affirmative answers to these questions, the more open and fair the nomination process is. Items (2), (3) and (4) are negative questions. If more respondents give affirmative answers to these questions, the nomination process would be less open and fair.[29]

Candidates nominated by villagers are called preliminary candidates (*chubu houxuanren*). How official candidates (*zhengshi houxuanren*) are finalized from the

---

27. It might be interesting to explore how provincial institutions have been set up and why the Organic Law was implemented differently among provinces. But this is not the focus of this paper. We take institutions as a given in this study.

28. Shi, 'Economic development and village elections'; Oi and Rozelle, 'Elections and power'.

29. John Kennedy stresses the importance of nomination in village elections. See John Kennedy, 'The face of "grassroots democracy" in rural China', *Asian Survey* XLII(3), (May/June 2003), pp. 456–482.

Table 1. Items measuring village elections

Items	N	Percentage
(1) Villager nominate candidates directly (+)	22	55%
(2) The Party Branch nominates candidates (−)	5	12.5%
(3) Township government nominates candidates (−)	11	27.5%
(4) Incumbent village committee nominates candidates (−)	8	20%
(5) Villager representatives nominate candidates (+)	12	30%
(6) Villager nominates oneself as candidate (+)	2	5%
(7) Official candidates finalized by villagers' voting (+)	19	47.5%
(8) Official candidates determined by the Party branch (−)	2	5%
(9) Official candidates determined by township (−)	5	12.5%
(10) Official candidates finalized by villager representatives' voting (+)	5	12.5%
(11) There are more candidates than positions to be elected (+)	40	100%
(12) Villagers vote in election meeting (+)	40	100%
(13) Roving ballot boxes are used (−)	15	37.5%
(14) Fixed polling station is set up (+)	23	57.5%
(15) Secret polling both is set up (+)	20	50%

pool of preliminary candidates is a crucial juncture in the election *process*.[30] In Fujian, candidates were finalized through a process called 'democratic consultation' (*minzhu xieshang*) until the 1994 election, in which the election leadership group would determine official candidates by soliciting opinions of villagers and the township government. As a matter of fact, organizational intentions (*zuzhi yitu*) from the township government would prevail in this winnowing process. From the 1997 election on, a process called primary election (*yuxuan*) has been introduced and candidates are finalized by villager representatives' votes, which will increase the chance of villager-favored candidates to be placed onto the list of official candidates. In order to measure to what extent this stipulation has been implemented, we asked respondents these questions: (7) whether official candidates were finalized by villagers' voting; (8) whether official candidates were determined by the Party branch; (9) whether official candidates were determined by township government; and (10) whether official candidates were finalized by villager representatives' voting. If questions (7) and (10) receive more affirmative answers from respondents, the new stipulation regarding candidate finalization has been implemented. If questions (8) and (9) receive more affirmative answers, that means the new stipulation has not been implemented and villagers' will has not fully been expressed.

The last five questions in Table 1 focus on voting methods: (11) whether there were more candidates than positions to be elected; (12) whether an election meeting was held for villagers to vote; (13) whether roving ballot-boxes (*liudong piaoxiang*) were used; (14) whether fixed polling stations (*guding toupiaozhan*) were set up; and (15) whether secret polling booths (*mimi huapiaojian*) were set up. Roving ballot boxes, carried by election staff to collect ballots from door to door, have been used since the

---

30. See Jorgen Elklit, 'The Chinese village committee electoral system', *China Information* 11(4), (1997), pp. 1–13; Anne F. Thurston, 'Muddling toward democracy: political change in grassroots China', *Peaceworks* no. 23, (1998), United States Institute of Peace; Pastor and Tan, 'The meaning of China's village elections'; O'Brien and Li, 'Accommodating "democracy" in a one-party state'.

beginning of village elections in rural areas. Although this measure increases voter turnout significantly, it is also easy for election staff to cheat and manipulate the result. In the 1997 election, Fujian Bureau of Civil Administration stipulated that roving ballot boxes should be abolished and fixed polling stations should be set up. So we added items (15), (16) and (17) to our list to measure to what extent these new regulations were implemented in the 2000 election.

However, for our purposes of analysis, we want to know not only how many respondents answered our 15 questions affirmatively, but also how many villages in our sample practiced the 15 items listed above in the 2000 election. Because official statistics are usually contaminated by local bureaucrats and not so reliable, we prefer to deduce figures about villages. For differences of participation in and knowledge about elections among villagers, respondents from the same village might give different answers to the same question. Each question had three different answers: 'Yes', 'No', and 'Don't know'. Of the 20–25 respondents from each village, if more respondents answered a question 'Yes' than 'No', then we deduced that this village practiced this measure in the 2000 election. Otherwise, we deduced that the measure was not practiced in this village. Table 1 lists the deduced results, including the percentage and number of villages in our sample that practiced each election measure in the 2000 election. Of the 17 items, some were practiced by more villages, such as items (13) and (14), while others by fewer villages. Then we calculated a score for each village. As mentioned above, all the 17 items in Table 1 are divided into two categories: positive items, which are designated by ' + ', and negative items, which are designated by ' − '. If one measure with a positive sign was practiced, the village will get a score of one, and if the measure has a negative sign, the village will receive a score of minus one. The total score of each village is then calculated. Table 2 shows numbers and percentages of villages with different scores.

We assume that economic development influences implementation of election institutions partially through villagers' participation and competitiveness of elections, which are used as intermediate variables in the regression models. The more developed a village's economy, the more resources are controlled by the village committee, then it can be hypothesized that the villagers will have a higher participation in the election and that the election will be more competitive. Villager participation is a dependent variable in Model 1, while it is an explanatory variable in Model 3. We asked respondents to report whether they had participated in any of the 15 kinds of activities listed in Table 3 during the election. Some percentages are quite high, such as some 79.5% of villagers participated in voting, while others are lower such as only 6.1% of villagers nominated candidates. Each respondent's participation

Table 2. Numbers and percentages of villages with different scores

Scores	− 4	− 3	− 1	0	1	2	3	4	5	6	7	Total
Village N.	1	1	1	3	1	4	7	6	7	7	2	40
(%)	2.5	2.5	2.5	7.5	2.5	10	17.5	15	17.5	17.5	5	100

Table 3. Villager participation *(Have you participated any of the following activities during election?)*

Items	N	Percentage
Nominate candidates individually	56	6.1%
Mobilize other villagers to nominate candidates	21	2.3%
Nominate candidates with other villagers jointly	68	7.4%
Nominate oneself as candidate	16	1.8%
Participate in primary election meeting	111	12.2%
Mobilize others to vote for one's favored candidates	48	5.3%
Persuade others not to vote for one's opposed candidates	44	4.8%
Participate in voting	726	79.5%
Help to campaign for your favored candidates	55	6%
Give suggestions for improving election organizations	44	4.8%
Attend meetings for introduction of candidates	69	7.6%
Ask candidates questions on campaign speech meeting	30	3.3%
Attend campaign speech meeting of candidates	59	6.5%
Refuse to vote for improper election arrangements	29	1.9%
Persuade others not to vote for improper election arrangement	4	0.4%

score is calculated according to how many items he or she participated in, with a score of 1 for each item.

Another intermediate variable is election competitiveness. In order to measure election competitiveness, we asked respondents: 'During the last election, did any candidate in your village use the following methods to campaign?' This question was followed by nine items: (1) solicit villagers' support door to door; (2) invite fellow villagers to dinner; (3) ask clan heads to campaign for candidate; (4) mobilize relatives and friends to get support; (5) promise to do some real things (*bang shishi*) after being elected; (6) promise to take less fees from villagers after being elected; (7) promise to investigate corruption of the incumbent leaders after being elected; (8) promise to help villagers become rich after being elected; and (9) promise to spend candidates' own money to do public goods after being elected. Respondents' answer to each item of the question is listed in Table 4. The more campaign methods used by candidates in a village, the more competitive its election. Then we calculated a score for each respondent by adding up his or her affirmative answers to the nine items, with a score of 1 for each item. Of course, this is only the individual respondents' scaling of competitiveness of the election in his or her village. In order to get a village-level score, we calculated a mean of each village by adding up all respondents' scores and then dividing by respondents' number from the village. This village-level mean score, ranging from 2.09 to 5.25, represents the competitiveness of elections in the village, and is entered as a dependent variable in Model 2 and a predictor in Model 3.

We designed three variables as predictors in the models to measure the economic development level. The first variable is the annual per capita village collective revenue. The second variable is respondents' rating of the living standard of their village by comparing with other townships within the county or district. We asked respondents: 'How do you rate the living standard of villagers in your own village compared with villagers in other townships of your county?'

Table 4. Election competitiveness *(During last election, did any candidate in your village use the following methods to campaign?)*

Items	N	Percentage
(1) Solicit villagers' support door to door	393	43%
(2) Invite fellow villagers to dinner	220	24.1%
(3) Ask clan heads to campaign for candidate	274	30%
(4) Mobilize relatives and friends to get support	340	37.2%
(5) Promise to do some real things (*bang shishi*) after being elected	233	25.5%
(6) Promise to take less fees from villagers after being elected	63	6.9%
(7) Promise to investigate corruption of the incumbent leaders after being elected	87	9.5%
(8) Promise to lead villagers to become rich after being elected	220	24.1%
(9) Promise to spend candidates' own money to do public goods after being elected	75	8.2%

Five answers were provided: (1) much better, (2) a little bit better, (3) the same, (4) a little bit worse, and (5) much worse. Scores from 5 to 1 were given from 'much better' to 'much worse' in that order. The third variable is the annual per capita household income, which is the annual household income of each respondent divided by the number of family members. Some observers of Chinese rural politics use county-level per capita GDP to predict elections, while others emphasize the distinction between income sources.[31] We argue that explanation of village elections should be based on village-level data, especially village collective revenues.

Besides variables of economic development, villagers' education, distance from the county seat and percentage of out-migrant villagers are added to Models 1, 2 and 3 as control variables. Villagers' education is a continuous variable, measuring years of villagers attending school. Social mobilization theorists argue that education increases political participation. If this argument is applicable to rural China, respondents' education will increase participation in our models. Village distance from the county seat is added, for some observers argue that the presence of county officials facilitates elections. Finally, the percentage of out-migrant villagers is calculated in every village.[32] Since the household responsibility system was introduced to the countryside, many surplus laborers in poor rural areas have migrated to urban areas and richer villages to find jobs with private and foreign enterprises. Some observers have proposed that as out-migration increases, the amount of participation decreases.

---

31. Shi, 'Economic development and village elections'; Oi and Rozelle, 'Elections and power'.

32. We also calculate a percentage of in-migration in every village, which is not included in the models for its co-linearity with collective revenue (with a correlation coefficient of 0.561).

Findings

The results of regression models shown in Table 5 reveal that: first, villager's relative living standard greatly influences their participation in elections. In Model 1, villager participation is a dependent variable and the three economic development variables and other control variables, such as education and village distance from county seat, are entered as predictors. Of the three variables measuring economic development, only villager's rating of the living standard of their village influences dependent variables with statistical significance, which means that the relative living standard is crucial for villagers' participation. In other words, it is neither the household income nor the collective revenue, but the relative economic development level that motivates villagers to participate in local politics. If one village's relative development level in the county or district is high and villagers enjoy a high living standard, they will participate in elections actively. Otherwise, if one village's economic development lags behind in the county or district, villagers' interest in participation will wane.

It is interesting that the relative living standard has a such strong positive effect on villager participation (and election implementation in Model 3). The rating of living standard of the village is a complex index reflecting the economic development level of the village in comparison with other townships within the county or district. In the two areas we surveyed, respondents from villages with more convenient transportation and communication usually rated their living standard higher. For example, the two villages rated highest in Shouning County are Aodong village and Datong village, which are located at the suburb of the county seat, while the two villages rated highest in Xiamen are Tongxing village and Chuangdong village, which are in the vicinity of the district seat of Tongan. Thirteen percent of respondents rated their village's relative living standard as 'much better' and 56.5% as 'a little bit better' in Aodong village of Shouning; 8.7% of respondents rated their village's relative living standard as 'much better' and 34.8% as 'a little bit better' in Datong of Shouning; 28% of villagers rated their village as 'much better' and 68% as 'a little bit better' in Tongxing village of Xiamen; 30% of respondents rated their village as 'much better' and 50% as 'a little better' in Chuangdong of Xiamen. However, the relative living standards in villages far from the county seat and with poor natural resources were rated very low. For example, Kengdilin village and Cuntong village were rated the lowest in Shouning, and Xidong village and Aoxi village were ranked lowest in Xiamen. No respondents rated their village living standard 'much better' than other villages and only 4.5% rated it as 'a little bit better' in Kengdilin of Shouning; none of the respondents rated their living standard as 'much better' or 'a little better' in Cuntao village of Shouning. Similarly, none of the respondents from both Xidong village and Aodong village rated their living standards as 'much better' or 'a little better' than that of any other villages.

Furthermore, the rating of their living standard is related to per capita household income to some extent. The living standards of Aodong village and Datong village were rated highest in Shouning, while their average per capita household incomes are ranked fourth for Aodong (2,716.15 yuan) and fifth for Datong (2,423.2 yuan). The two villages with the lowest living standard rating in Shouning are Kengdilin village

Table 5. Regression analysis of factors influencing implementation of village election institutions (standardized coefficients in parenthesis)

Independent variables	Model 1: villager participation	Model 2: election competitiveness	Model 3: implementation of elections
Per capita collective revenue	−1.24E-04 (−0.041)	2.963E-04 (0.23)****	4.660E-04 (0.105)**
Relative living standard	0.292 (0.146)***	6.275E-02 (0.074)!	0.55 (0.186)****
Per capita household income	−1.52E-05 (−0.42)	−2.98E-07 (−0.002)	3.666E-05 (0.069)!
Education in years	3.794E-02 (0.084)*	2.905E-04 (0.002)	−5.23E-02 (−0.079)*
Distance from county seat	−1.81E-02 (−0.143)***	−2.09E-03 (−0.039)	−9.10E-03 (−0.049)
Percentage of out-migrant villagers	1.876 (0.105)**	2.523 (0.328)****	0.776 (0.029)
Villager participation		3.046E-02 (0.071)!	0.181 (0.123)**
Electoral competitiveness			1.097 (0.32)****
N	564	564	564
Constant	0.787*	2.76****	−2.061****
Adjusted R^2	4.8%	13.9%	21.3%

Significance level: $!P \leq 0.1$; $*P \leq 0.05$; $**P \leq 0.01$; $***P \leq 0.001$; $****P \leq 0.0005$.

and Cuntou village, and their average per capita household incomes also rank at the bottom of the 20 surveyed villages, seventeenth for that of Kengdilin, with an average per capita household income of 1,358.55 yuan, and twentieth for that of Cuntou, with an average per capita household income of 1,050.92 yuan. In Xiamen, the living standards of Tongxin village and Chuangdong village were rated highest, and their average per capita household incomes also rank as fifth (5,146.39 yuan) and first (15,540.2 yuan), while the average per capita household incomes in the two villages with the lowest living standard ratings also rank seventeenth and twentieth, 2,319.26 yuan for Xidong village and 1,495.37 yuan for Aoxi village. Despite the connections between rating of living standards and per capita household income, they represent different aspects of economic development. Respondents rate all villagers' relative living standard as a whole and the ratings for villagers from the same village are similar, while the gap of per capita income among different households is much greater. The coefficients of variation of per capita household income in each village is much bigger than that of living standards. For example, in Datong village of Shouning, the coefficient of variation of per capita household income is 106%, while the coefficient of variation of the living standard is only 36.81%; in Aoxi village of Xiamen, the coefficient of variation of per capita household income is 91.55%, while the coefficient of variation of the living standard is only 11.16%.

Thus, the higher the rating of the living standard, the more the economic opportunities in the village, and the more powerful the village committee will be. With more economic development opportunities related to or controlled by the village committee, villagers will be more interested in local politics and more candidates will participate in the campaign, which makes the election more competitive.

Second, collective revenue influences election competitiveness significantly. Of the three independent variables measuring economic development in Model 2, both per capita collective revenue and relative living standard have a positive and statistically significant effect on election competitiveness, and the former with a much bigger coefficient. However, per capita household income, which has a negative coefficient, fails to attain statistical significance, showing household income is not an important factor influencing election competitiveness.

Why does collective revenue enhance competitiveness among candidates so greatly? Collective revenue comes from enterprises owned by villages, rent of collective owned workshops, or appropriations from higher authorities. Usually, villages in more developed areas have higher collective revenue.[33] Cadres in rich villages can benefit from high collective revenue in the following ways. First, cadres from developed areas have higher salaries. For example, the monthly salary for each of the village committee members in Heshan Township of Xiamen is 1,000 yuan, while in poor mountainous villages of Shouning, only the village committee chairman and the Party branch secretary receive a subsidy of 200 yuan from township government each month.[34] Second, village cadres in rich areas have more chances to

---

33. However, some villages in poor areas may get a big sum of appropriation from higher government during some period. For example, Weishan village, a poor village in Xiqi township of Shouning county got 1,000,000 yuan appropriation from county government to build a road in 1997, which made the village election highly competitive. Interview, May 1997.

34. Interview, October 2001.

run their own profitable enterprises. The social networks and ties with government developed during their term of office are helpful to their own business. Third, there are more resources controlled by village committees in rich areas and village cadres are more powerful. And finally, it is much easier for village cadres to implement some unpopular policies of higher authorities, such as family planning and levying of agricultural tax. For example, in Heshan Township of Xiamen, village committees pay agricultural tax for every household with collective revenue.[35] Although it is more time-consuming and demanding to hold a position on the village committee in rich areas, the above rewards related to high collective revenue make the elections in developed areas highly competitive.

Third, collective revenue and living standards have a positive and significant effect on implementation of village elections. In Model 3, both per capita collective revenue and living standards have considerable effects on implementation of village elections with statistical significance. However, per capita household income's effect on the dependent variable fails to gain statistical significance.

Fourth, the more competitive the election, the better the elections will be implemented. In Model 3, besides the three economic development variables, more control variables, such as respondent's education, villager participation, election competitiveness, village distance from county seat and out-migration are included to predict implementation of elections. Of the four control variables, election competitiveness has the greatest effect, showing that the more competitive the election, the better the elections were implemented.

Fifth, the more villagers that participated in the elections, the better the elections were implemented. Of the independent variables in Model 3, villager participation has a considerable effect on the dependent variable, with the third biggest standardized coefficient, which shows that the more villagers participated in elections, the more effectively implemented were the election institutions.

Sixth, education's effect on villager participation and election competitiveness is limited. Social mobilization theorists argue that economic development enhances political participation by improving citizen's education.[36] Although villager's education influences villager participation slightly in Model 1, with a standardized coefficient of 0.084 at a 0.1 significance level, it has a negative effect on election implementation and fails to gain statistical significance on election competitiveness.

Seventh, county officials' presence facilitates villager participation. The effect of distance from the county seat is a dependent variable of Model 2. Competitiveness of election fails to gain statistical significance, showing village distance from the county

---

35. According to Kevin O'Brien, wealth and a flourishing collective economy may ease completion of state tasks, raise cadres subsidies, and soften villagers' resistance to state duties. I fully agree with O'Brien's argument. However, I don't think higher collective income will reduce incumbent's fear of electoral defeat.

36. Although considerable research suggests that higher education can make people more involved in politics, Shi finds that citizen education is only weakly correlated with political efficacy, weakly supports political change, and negatively influences support for economic reform. See Lipset, 'Some social requisites of democracy'; Gabriel A. Almond and Sidney Verba, *Civil Culture* (Princeton: Princeton University Press, 1963); Norman H. Nie, Bingham G. Powell Jr and Kenneth Prewitt, 'Social structure and political participation: developmental relationships, part I', *American Political Science Review* 63(2), (June 1969), pp. 361–378; Norman H. Nie, Bingham G. Powell Jr and Kenneth Prewitt, 'Social structure and political participation: developmental relationships, part II', *American Political Science Review* 63(3), (September 1969), pp. 808–832; Tianjian Shi, 'Cultural values and democracy in the People's Republic of China', *The China Quarterly* 162, (June 2000), pp. 540–559.

seat has no effect on competitiveness of the election. In Model 1, distance from the county seat has a negative effect on the dependent variable and with statistical significance. This shows that the presence of county officials, especially officials in County Bureau of Civil Administration, facilitates villager participation. In Model 3, distance from the county seat's influence on the implementation of elections fails to gain statistical significance.

Eighth, out-migration increases villager participation and election competitiveness. Differing from the assertion that out-migration will decrease villager participation, regression models in Table 5 show that out-migration has an influence on villager participation and election competitiveness with statistical significance. While out-migrant villagers may have less interest in village elections for their economic interests lie outside of the village boundaries, those who stay in the village may increase their interest for participation in elections. For the out-migrant fellow villagers, the more information from the outside that they may bring back every Spring Festival when they return home might stimulate renewed interest in the local election process. Furthermore, in villages with higher out-migration, villagers who stay home may also have some experience of out-migration and know more about the outside world, which will help enhance their effectiveness of participation and so they may more actively participate in elections as candidates.

Conclusions

The research findings show that economic development facilitates implementation of village elections. More concretely, it is the collective revenue and the relative living standard of the village compared with other townships within the same county or district that arouse villagers' interests for participation and candidates' motives for campaigning, and thus enhance the implementation of elections. Based on the above analysis, we may conclude that village-level economic development is crucial for the implementation of competitive elections. The more economically developed, the more collective revenues village committees control; the bigger stakes villagers have in elections, the more villagers will participate in elections, and elections will be more competitive. With increases in the competitiveness of elections, institutions regarding village committee elections, which are mechanisms for interest articulation and mediation among villagers and candidates, will be implemented more successfully.

Although our study focuses on the basic-level village elections and our conclusions differ from mobilization theories, it does not mean that our conclusions have no relationship with the democratization of the country. As a matter of fact, many observers have taken village elections as the starting point for bottom-up democratization.[37] As a developing country in the process of industrialization, China has the biggest agricultural population who live in the countryside. By participating in village elections, a huge number of rural residents will learn

---

37. For example, Mingxin Pei suggests that grassroots elections may be part of China's 'creeping democratization' and Sylvia Chan argues that villager's self-government may become a growth point for civil society. See Minxin Pei, 'Creeping democratization in China', *Journal of Democracy* 6(4), (October 1995), pp. 65–79; Sylvia Chan, 'Research notes on villagers' committee election: Chinese style democracy', *Journal of Contemporary China* 7(19), (1998), pp. 507–521.

democracy by practice. Village elections will help cultivate among Chinese peasants core democratic values, e.g. political equality, electoral legitimacy, peaceful competition for power, elite accountability, majority rule, minority rights, and political tolerance.

For those who are promoting democratization in China, our conclusions may have some implications. Besides village elections, there are still more direct elections in China, for example, people's representatives to county-level congresses and residential committees in urban areas. However, most of them are only formalities under an authoritarian regime. There are many factors that make these elections formalities. For example, manipulation from the Party, and lack of voter motivation and interest in these elections. In order to make these elections competitive, it is necessary to increase the importance of positions to be elected. For resident committees, interest seems, to a great extent, dependent on privatizing of government enterprises in which employees will become less dependent on their work units and care more about community affairs. For representatives to county congresses, the crucial issue is how they exercise the real power as the highest decision-making body at the county level as stipulated by the constitution. If the county congress is the real decision-making body, more people will compete to serve as representatives and more voters will participate in the elections to express their interests.

Economic Development and Village Elections in Rural China

TIANJIAN SHI

Many observers of Chinese politics suggest that there are certain relationships between economic development and village elections. Using empirical data gathered from a 1993 nationwide survey, this study examines whether economic development is associated in any way with successful elections in Chinese villages. The analysis reveals that the relationship between economic development and village elections appears to be a concave curve: economic wealth increases the likelihood that a village will hold semicompetitive elections for people to choose their leaders, but its impact diminishes as economic wealth increases. Rapid economic development may even delay the process of political development because incumbent leaders can use newly acquired economic resources to consolidate their power by: (1) making peasants more dependent on the village authority; (2) providing incumbent leaders with resources to co-opt peasants; and (3) providing incumbent leaders with resources to bribe their superiors to ignore the decisions of the central government to introduce competitive elections into Chinese villages.

Observers of political development in China usually suggest that there are certain crucial relationships between economic development and village elections. O'Brien, for example, argues that village elections are more likely to succeed in rich villages.[1] Oi proposes that 'there may be an inverse relationship between level of economic development and progress in the implementation of democratic village rule'.[2] Epstein, however, contends that provinces that are at the middle level of economic development with relatively strong agricultural and industrial sectors have developed their elections most aggressively and with the most success.[3]

Although the important issue—whether economic development will eventually bring democracy to Chinese society—has been touched by those China scholars,

---

1. See Kevin J. O'Brien, 'Implementing political reform in China's villages', *Australian Journal of Chinese Affairs* 32, (July 1994).

2. Jean C. Oi, 'Economic development, stability and democratic village self-governance', in Maurice Brosseau, Suzanne Pepper and Tsang Shu-ki, eds., *China Review 1996* (Hong Kong: Chinese University of Hong Kong, 1996), p. 140.

3. Amy Epstein, 'Village elections in China: experimenting with democracy', in Joint Economic Committee, Congress of the United States, *China's Economic Future* (Armonk, NY: M.E. Sharpe 1997), p. 419.

their studies did not provide a valid answer to this important questions.[4] This is because all their research on the relationship between economic development and village elections is based on case studies which, on the one hand, can help researchers to pinpoint political dynamics in different localities, but on the other hand, do not allow researchers to make a reliable assessment of that relationship which can be generalized to the whole country. This study is designed to fill this gap by using empirical data gathered from a 1993 nationwide survey to examine the relationship between economic development and village elections in rural China. The sample represents all eligible voters residing in family households at the time of the survey, excluding those living in the Tibetan Autonomous Region. The description of the sample is found in the appendix.

We begin this article with a review of the theoretical argument on the relationship between economic development and democracy. This is followed by an assessment of: (1) how many peasants in rural China had a chance to vote in village elections; (2) how many peasants had a chance to vote in semicompetitive elections; and (3) how many elections were semicompetitive. We conclude with a statistical analysis of the relationship between economic development and village elections in rural China.

Theoretical arguments

Social mobilization theory has been criticized as deterministic and has been buried again and again, but it is still used in various forms by students of Chinese politics.[5] According to the theory, economic development increases the desire and capability of people to participate in decision-making processes, and this in turn facilitates democratic transition. The theory proposes that three areas of social and political life vary with the level of economic development and also increase political participation. First, economic development increases the interaction between individuals and states, and in turn, increases in this interaction stimulate people to influence governmental decision making.[6] Second, economic development changes the composition of the population. As a nation develops economically, the shape of its social stratification structure is altered. That is, as greater numbers of citizens become members of the educated, white-collar class, the middle stratum expands

---

4. For such debates, see, among others, Gordon White, 'Democratization and economic reform in China', *Australian Journal of Chinese Affairs* 31, (1994); idem, *Riding the Tiger: The Politics of Economic Reform in Post-Mao China* (Stanford, CA: Stanford University Press, 1993); Barrett L. McCormick, 'Democracy or dictatorship?: a response to Gordon White', *Australian Journal of Chinese Affairs* 31, (January 1994); idem, *Political Reform in Post-Mao China: Democracy and Bureaucracy in a Leninist State* (Berkeley, CA: University of California Press, 1990).

5. For a recent reevaluation of the thesis, see Ross E. Burkhart and Michael S. Lewis-Beck, 'Comparative democracy: the economic development thesis', *American Political Science Review* 88(4), (December 1994), pp. 903–910.

6. As a nation develops, its government usually becomes responsible for more regulation and redistribution. Individuals' relationships with the nation-state now become critical. If taxes are collected and regulations to control the economy are imposed, individuals are very likely to respond by defending themselves against the state. For a discussion, see Myron Weiner, 'Political participation: crisis of the political process', in Leonard Binder *et al.*, eds., *Crisis and Sequences in Political Development* (Princeton: Princeton University Press, 1971), pp. 173–175.

and eventually becomes the majority class.[7] Finally, economic development transforms people's orientation toward political objects.[8] When people become more interested in politics, have more political knowledge, and feel more efficacious, they expect to have more input into the decision-making process in their society.

The theory in its original form, however, can hardly explain electoral reform in rural China.[9] Besides the fact that the pressure from the general populace has played only a limited role in electoral reform in rural China, other difficulties also prevent us from applying social mobilization theory to explain political reform in Chinese villages.[10] First, the per capita GDP in China is still far below the threshold for change. Empirical studies demonstrate that the transition to democracy usually happens when the per capita GDP reaches \$5,000–6,000.[11] The per capita GDP in China in 1994, even using the figures adjusted for purchasing power parity, is only about US\$ 2,500.[12] Moreover, the theory predicts that democratic change should occur in urban areas, but electoral reform in China has taken place in rural areas. Finally, according to the theory, increased wealth contributes to democracy by increasing the size of the middle class. Contrary to such a claim, electoral reforms in China have happened among peasants.

Responding to an overemphasis on the role of ordinary people in the transitional process, students of Latin American politics proposed that elites usually play a crucial role in this process. O'Donnell, Schmitter, and Whitehead argue that political elites can significantly influence democratic transitions.[13] They forcefully demonstrate that soft-liners in those countries played a crucial role in opening up of the authoritarian system.

Although the elite approach represents a major advance in our understanding of the process of democratic transition, it still leaves some critical questions unan-

---

7. Norman H. Nie, Bingham G. Powell Jr and Kenneth Prewitt, 'Social structure and political participation: developmental relationships, Part I', *American Political Science Review* 63(2), (1969), p. 362.

8. Among different aspects of psychological orientation toward social objects, some, such as cognition and feeling, are relatively easily influenced by changes in the social environment, while others, especially deep-seated norms, are more difficult to change.

9. Tianjian Shi, 'Village committee elections in China: institutionalist tactics for democracy', *World Politics*, 51(3), (April 1999), pp. 385–390.

10. All empirical research in China shows that electoral reform was introduced by mid-level officials and sponsored by mid-level officials in the central government. See O'Brien, 'Implementing political reform in China's villages'; Daniel Kelliher, 'The Chinese debate over village self-government', *China Journal* 37, (January 1997); Epstein, 'Village elections in China: experimenting with democracy'; Susan V. Lawrence, 'Democracy, Chinese style', *Australia Journal of Chinese Affairs* 32, (July 1994); Shi, 'Village committee elections in China'; Lianjiang Li, 'The two-ballot system in Shanxi: subjecting village party secretaries to a popular vote', *China Journal* (forthcoming); Lianjiang Li and Kevin J. O'Brien, 'The struggle over village elections', in Roderick MacFarquhar and Merle Goldman, eds., *The Paradox of China's Reforms* (Cambridge: Harvard University Press, 1999), pp. 129–144.

11. For the comparative study of the relationship between level of economic development and democracy, see, among others, Bingham G. Powell, Jr., *Contemporary Democracies: Participation, Stability, and Violence* (Cambridge: Harvard University Press, 1982). For recent literature on the relationship between economic development and political change, see among others, Adam Przeworski and Fernando Limongi, 'Modernization: theories and facts', *World Politics* 49(2), (1997), pp. 155–183; Burkhart and Lewis-Beck, 'Comparative democracy: the economic development thesis', pp. 903–910. Przeworski found that above a level of about \$6,000 in per capita GDP (in 1992 purchasing-power-parity US dollars—there is not a single case of a democracy reverting to authoritarian rule.

12. World Bank, *From Plan to Market: World Development Report 1996* (New York: Oxford University Press, 1996).

13. Guillermo O'Donnell, Philippe C. Schmitter and Lawrence Whitehead, *Transitions from Authoritarian Rule* (Baltimore: Johns Hopkins University Press, 1986), p. 3.

swered: why do some people in government perceive their options differently from others? More specifically, do changes in the demographic composition, attitudes, and perceptions of a population undergoing economic development influence the choices made by decision makers? If yes, how do changes in popular attitudes influence political elites?

Despite the fact that few scholars have tried to deal with these issues in a systematic way, students of Chinese politics tend to combine these two approaches in their study of electoral reform in rural areas. For example, O'Brien's analysis of the impacts of economic development on electoral reform focuses on both masses and elites, especially incumbent village leaders. According to him, economic development has positive effects on the successful implementation of Organic Law. Incumbent leaders who have brought prosperity to their villages have: (1) fewer fears of electoral defeat; (2) greater incentive to retain their position; and (3) enough money to co-opt villagers. Ordinary villagers also play an important role in this process. A profitable *collective* economy in the village may heighten villagers' interest in public affairs because they want to ensure that public funds are not misused or squandered.[14]

Differing from O'Brien, Lawrence and Oi argue that economic development is negatively associated with elections, and whereas Lawrence also emphasizes the role of elites, Oi focuses on township leaders. According to Oi: 'It was precisely because the village is so unmanageable, and performing so poorly economically, that local authorities felt the need to experiment with new forms of village governance'.[15] Ordinary peasants play no role in the process of electoral reform.

Oi observed that some of the most economically advanced areas lagged behind in carrying out political reform.[16] High levels of economic development, she believes, do not necessarily arouse enthusiasm for democratic reform among local officials. The key economic decisions in the wealthier places in rural China are usually made by a nondemocratically elected official—the party secretary. Because party officials adapted well to the economic reforms and led local development, they control the economic organizations and have more say on economic issues in the villages. Even if elections make village committees accountable to peasants, there is no systematic arrangement to subject a party secretary to the periodic scrutiny of peasants. Thus, although the current institutional arrangement may result in a stronger village economy, it reduces the power of the village committee.

Election experts in the International Republican Institute (IRI) argue that the provinces that are at the middle level of economic development with relatively strong agricultural *and* industrial sections are the ones that tend to succeed in village elections. As they see it, 'the development of local elections is dependent

---

14. O'Brien, 'Implementing political reform in China's villages', pp. 47–48.

15. Lawrence, 'Democracy, Chinese style', p. 67.

16. It should be pointed out that the dependent variable used by Oi is not identical to the one used by O'Brien and Lawrence. Whereas the research of the latter two scholars tries to explain the emergence of semicompetitive village elections, Oi tries to explain the establishment of the democratic governing process. For her, election itself is important, but more important is whether the institutional transformation provides villagers with a real opportunity to voice their opinion on the key issues facing them. Thus, her dependent variable is the '*democratic accountability* of local officials to peasants'. Oi, 'Economic development, stability and democratic village self-governance', p. 143.

on support from local and provincial officials'.[17] Indeed, they argue, the poorest and richest provinces have proceeded most slowly with the development of village elections and also generally with the most resistance.

In poor provinces, one might expect that frustration and lack of resources would lead ordinary villagers to make demands for improvements, but officials in those provinces usually do not see the value of village elections and pay little attention to improving transparency or competitiveness. Also, villagers tend to be concerned primarily with securing adequate food and shelter, not on improving local governance. In wealthier provinces, where one could argue that prosperity would lend itself to increased demands for popular control and autonomy, powerful local bosses have inhibited the development of competitive elections. A village committee chairman's economic success generally secures his reelection, giving rise to the development of boss politics. In recent years, local bosses have been cropping up in wealthy Chinese villages. Their success at building local factories, increasing prosperity, and implementing social programs, such as kindergartens and housing developments, helps ensure their continued reelection.

In sum, rather than adopting the traditional deterministic approach to their study of the relationship between economic development and electoral reform, students of Chinese politics now focus on the interaction between elites and peasants and argue that this complicated relationship determines the consequences of electoral reform in rural China. They also argue that economic development has certain impacts on the interaction between state and society. In the next section, we use survey data to test the relationship between economic development and village elections.[18]

The current state of affairs in rural China

From the previous discussion, we learn that different scholars use different dependent variables in studying the relationship between economic development and electoral reform in rural China. Our inquiry will be limited to the success or failure to introduce semicompetitive elections for local leaders in Chinese villages. This is not to say that other aspects of political reform, such as accountability of the party secretary or the supervision of the village assembly, are not important, but we do argue that introducing semicompetitive election into Chinese villages is the critical first step in political reform in rural China.

How many people in rural China voted for village leaders

We asked respondents in the 1993 survey to report whether their village had held elections for people to choose their leaders. If respondents gave a positive answer

17. Epstein, 'Village elections in China', pp. 418–419.
18. This paper does not intend to test the hypotheses proposed by the scholars cited above. First, none of them tried to make generalizations on the relationship between economic development and village elections in China. Second, the dependent variables in their studies are somewhat different from the one used in this study. For example, O'Brien uses up-to-standard in the implementation process of Organic Law as the dependent variable, of which having good elections was only one part. Oi's dependent variable is the establishment of the democratic governing process. Finally, the timing of their studies is different. While O'Brien tries to explain what happened in the first stage of the implementation process, Oi and Epstein explain what happened in the second stage of the implementation process.

Table 1. Percentage of people who reported that their villages had elections

If the village held any elections: *'During the past 5 years, were elections held in your village for people to choose the leaders?'*	
Answers	**Percentage (N)**
No	16.7 (433)
Yes	75.8 (1,961)
Not in the village	1.6 (42)
Do not remember	5.9 (152)
	100.0 (2,588)

Nature of elections: *'What kind of elections were they? Were they elections with or without a choice of candidates (deng'e xuanju haishi cha'e xuanju)?'*	
No elections	24.2 (627)
Plebiscitary elections	12.5 (325)
Semicompetitive elections	51.6 (1,336)
Do not know	11.6 (300)
Total	100.0 (2,588)

Source: 1993–94 Nationwide survey on political culture and political participation in China.

to this question, we asked them to report whether the election provided them with candidate choices. In Table 1, we report the frequency distribution of the answers to these questions given by respondents holding rural household registration.[19]

We learned that more than 75% of the respondents residing in rural China reported that their villages had held elections. Of the respondents, 16.7% reported that their villages failed to hold elections and 7.5% of rural residents either reported that they had forgotten whether their villages had held elections or refused to answer the question.

The next question asked whether the elections provided them with candidate choice. In the responses, 50.6% of peasants reported that elections in their villages were semicompetitive, and 12.5% of people reported that elections were plebiscitary. Among the respondents from rural China, 24.2% stated that their village did not hold an election for them to choose village leaders, and 11.6% claimed that they did not know whether elections were plebiscitary or semi-

---

19. Rural population in Chinese has two meanings. The first refers to those who hold rural household registration (*Chi nongcun huko deren*) and the second refers to people living in a rural area. Note that those who hold rural household registration may not live in a rural area (a typical case for people belonging to this category are those living in suburbs of big cities) and that those who live in rural areas may not hold rural household registration (especially retirees). We chose the type of household registration to differentiate the rural population from the urban one. The rationale for the choice is that only people who hold rural household registration have the right to vote for members of village committees.

competitive. In other words, only slightly more than 50% of people in rural China voted in semicompetitive elections for village leaders.

From individual voters to villages

Knowing the percentage of people who voted in semicompetitive elections is important, but for our purposes, even more important, is how many villages in rural China held elections for villagers to choose their leaders and how many of those elections were semicompetitive. There are usually two ways for researchers to get such data. First, they can rely on official reports and official statistics. Unfortunately, official reports on village elections were not available until 1996. Even when official statistics are available, however, it is not clear how reliable they are. The government does not provide information on how the data are collected, how different kinds of elections are categorized, and the distribution of different elections across different geographic regions. Experiences in both the Soviet Union and China have demonstrated that official data were usually contaminated by local bureaucrats.[20]

The second approach is using data on individual voters from a sample survey to deduce the figures. Although this method can avoid the contamination of government officials, it has two other problems. (1) Since villages are required by the authorities to hold elections for peasants to choose their leaders and the elections are required to be semicompetitive, peasants from villages that fail to hold elections or from the villages where elections fail to provide voters with candidate choice may lie to interviewers to avoid political trouble. (2) Reports of respondents in surveys can be inaccurate. This problem is more serious when respondents are asked to report on something that happened in the past.[21]

To avoid the first problem, we instructed our interviewers not to contact any local officials, including county, township, and village leaders before interviewing designated respondents in villages. The central office of the survey provided interviewers with a list of respondents in the village and instructed them to contact those respondents directly when entering the locality. These measures worked and

---

20. Students of political participation in communist societies have long noticed the flaw in official records of voter turnout. For example, Theodore H. Friedgut reported that more than one million voters in Moscow—close to one-fifth of the eligible population—were absent in the 1970 election although official records report voter turnout of more than 95%. See Theodore H. Friedgut, *Political Participation in the USSR* (Princeton: Princeton University Press, 1979). Studies based on emigré informants on political participation in the Soviet Union revealed that the actual turnout rate there was much lower than the 99% figure claimed by the authorities. See Rasma Karklins, 'Soviet elections revisited: voter abstention in noncompetitive voting', *American Political Science Review* 80(2), (June 1986), pp. 449–469. A more recent study reports that the 'Soviet scholars now admit privately that the turnout data may have been exaggerated'. See Donna Bahry and Brian D. Silver, 'Soviet citizen participation on the eve of democratization', *American Political Science Review* 84(3), (September 1990), pp. 821–841. According to their report, much of the well-accepted 99% voter turnout in communist societies was 'achieved' not by the ability of the regime to mobilize its citizens to vote but by its own bureaucrats cheating at various levels. Failing to mobilize private citizens to vote, bureaucrats in the Soviet Union, in an attempt to shift the burden of blame to please their superiors, helped ordinary people bypass existing rules and regulations. Shi found that officials in China engaged in the same technique to shield themselves from being blamed by higher authorities for failing to mobilize citizens under their jurisdiction to vote. See Tianjian Shi, *Political Participation in Beijing* (Cambridge: Harvard University Press, 1997).

21. John Zaller, *The Nature and Origins of Mass Opinion* (Cambridge: Cambridge University Press, 1992).

Table 2. Political fear of respondents in rural China

Fear of criticizing the Government: *If you criticized the government in conversations where you live or work, would you be concerned that someone would report you to the authorities?*

Answers	Percentage (*N*)
Completely unconcerned	1.2 (35)
Unconcerned	47.2 (1,223)
A little concerned	39.0 (1,008)
Very concerned	3.6 (94)
Do not know	8.0 (207)
No answer	0.9 (22)
Total	100 (2,588)

Fear of criticizing leaders of the country: *If you criticized the Party and state leaders in conversations where you live or work, would you be conconcerned that someone would report you to the authorities?*

Completely unconcerned	1.2 (33)
Unconcerned	43.9 (1,137)
A little concerned	40.0 (1,034)
Very concerned	4.6 (120)
Do not know	9.0 (233)
No answer	1.2 (31)
Total	100 (2,588)

Source: 1993–94 Nationwide survey on political culture and political participation in China.

our interviewers reported that respondents were usually candid in expressing their opinions during interviews.[22]

Fortunately, certain statistical techniques can be used to test the validity of the questions and provide a reliable assessment of the scope of political contamination. The survey included two questions designed to tap the scope of political fear in China. One asked if respondents fear criticizing the government and the other if respondents fear criticizing national leaders. Table 2 reports the distribution of these two questions. The data show that substantial numbers of people in China still fear criticizing the government and/or national leaders: about half of the respon-

---

22. We do have independent evidence to show that respondents were cooperative and outspoken. For example, when we conducted the pretest in 1990, many respondents asked our interviewers to bring their complaints to Beijing. After the actual fieldwork, our central office in Beijing received more than 300 letters from people in different areas reporting corruption or power abuse by local officials. More importantly, very few of those letters were anonymous. Had people been fearful of expressing their opinions, they would not have asked our interviewers to bring their complaints to Beijing, nor would they have written to our central office after the survey. Tianjian Shi, 'Survey research in China', in Michael X. Delli Carpini, Leonie Huddy and Robert Y. Shapiro, eds., *Research in Micropolitics: Rethinking Rationality*, Vol. 5 (Greenwich, CT: JAL Press, 1996), pp. 213–250.

Table 3. Zero-order correlation of political fear and elections in rural China

Variables	Report on elections	Report on nature of election
Fear of criticizing government	− 0.028 (0.185)	− 0.023 (0.263)
Fear of criticizing country leaders	− 0.023 (0.362)	0.040 (0.106)

Note: Data in parenthesis are level of significance (two-tailed test).
Source: 1993–94 Nationwide survey on political culture and political participation in China.

dents reported that they are at least a little concerned about possible political repercussion for criticizing the government and/or national leaders.

A more careful examination of the data shows that the problem may not be as serious as it appears to be. Among people claiming that they were concerned when criticizing the government, the majority were only 'a little concerned'. Less than 5% of respondents claimed that they were very concerned about possible political persecution when criticizing the government or national leaders.

It should be pointed out that even if a respondent is very concerned about political persecution when criticizing the government, such a concern may not necessarily lead him to lie to interviewers about the nature of elections in his village. Whether the answers of respondents to questions inquiring about elections are contaminated by political fear is an empirical question that can be tested by examining the correlation between political fear and the report of the presence of village elections. If political fear contaminates respondents' answers, we should find that fear of political persecution is positively correlated with: (1) the answers to whether the village held elections; and (2) whether the election was semicompetitive. If the fear of political persecution is not correlated with the answers to these two questions, we will be able to conclude that political fear does not influence the way our respondents answered these questions.

Table 3 reports the results of the tests. The analyses show that political fear does not significantly correlate with respondents' reportage about the presence and nature of elections. These findings clearly reveal that political fear did not make respondents in rural China lie to interviewers in the survey.

Ruling out that survey questions are contaminated by political fear is relatively easy. More difficult is identifying misreporting for non-political reasons.[23] Note that we used the Probability Proportional to Size (PPS) technique to draw the sample. Such a design requires us to interview between 2 and 17 respondents from each village.[24] That allows us to use different methods based on the answers of different respondents in the same village to calculate whether a village held elections and the nature of those elections. The results are summarized in Table 4.

First, we try to find whether a particular village held elections. The question has four response categories: yes, no, do not know (DK), or refusal. We first coded all

23. In fact, survey researchers even debate the meaning of conflicting reports by the same respondents in the survey. See Zaller, *The Nature and Origins of Mass Opinion*.
24. For PPS sample design, see Leslie Kish, *Survey Sampling* (New York: John Wiley & Son, 1965).

Table 4. Number of villages that hold semicompetitive elections for villagers to choose their leaders

	Majority rule	Majority-plus-1	Absolute rule
No elections	19.1 (62)	19.1 (62)	19.1 (62)
Noncompetitive elections	26.8 (87)	31.1 (101)	53.2 (173)
Semicompetitive elections	54.2 (176)	49.8 (162)	27.7 (90)

Source: 1993 nationwide survey on political culture and political participation in China.

the DK answers and refusals as no elections.[25] Then, we examined the answers of respondents from each village and found that people from the same village gave different answers to our interviewers: whereas respondents reported that there had been elections in their village, others reported no elections had been held.[26]

We then used two standards to deduce from the respondents' answers from each village whether a particular village had, in fact, held elections for peasants to choose their leaders. The first one is majority rule: if the number of respondents in a village telling us that their village held election exceeds: (1) the number of respondents telling us that their village failed to hold elections, plus (2) the number of respondents telling us they do not know if their village held elections, plus (3) the number of respondents who refused to answer the question, we categorize the village as having held elections for people to choose their leaders. Using this rule, we found that 267 villages had held elections, which represents 82.2% of the villages included in our sample.

Next, we used a more stringent standard—the majority-plus-one rule—to determine whether the village had held elections. According to this rule, for us to categorize a village as having held elections, the number of respondents in a particular village who gave positive answers to this question must be two more than the people who gave all the other answers. Using the second rule, we found that 244 villages, which represents 75.1% of the 325 villages included in our rural sample, had held elections for peasants to choose their leaders.

Finding out how many villages in rural China held elections for people to choose their leaders is important, but an even more important question is how many elections were semicompetitive; that is, were voters provided with candidate choices? To find out, we coded all villages that failed to meet the standard of majority rule as having had no elections. We then used three different methods to determine how many villages in rural China had actually held semicompetitive elections.

First we used the majority rule. The number of peasants in a particular village

25. The real situation could be much more complicated. While refusals might reflect the reluctance of respondents to reveal the truth that there had been no election in the village, the DKs may simply reflect respondents who really did not know whether there had been an election in their village.

26. Several reasons can make people in the same village give different answers to this question. (1) The respondent was not at home during election time and thus knew nothing about the elections; (2) the person was at home but had no interest in the elections; (3) the person knew about the elections but had forgotten about them; (4) there were no elections, but some respondents dared not tell the truth to interviewers; and (5) there were no election and respondents reported it faithfully to our interviewers.

who reported that elections in their village were semicompetitive must be at least one more than the number of peasants who reported that elections were noncompetitive for us to categorize elections in that village as semicompetitive. Using this rule, we found that elections in 54.2% of villages in rural China were, in fact, semicompetitive.

Next, we applied the majority-plus-one rule. To meet this standard, the number of peasants in a village who reported that elections were semicompetitive must be two more than the number of peasants who claimed that elections were noncompetitive, plus the number of people telling us they did not know the nature of elections, plus the number of people who refused to answer the question. Based on this rule, we found that elections in 49.8% of villages included in the sample were semicompetitive.

Finally, we used the most stringent standard—the consensus rule—to determine the nature of elections in those villages. To categorize elections in a village as semicompetitive, all respondents from that village had to report that the election in their village was semicompetitive. Using this method, we found that elections in 27.7% of villages were semicompetitive.

Of these three methods, we believe the majority plus one rule provides us with a reasonable balance. On average, we interviewed 5–7 persons from each village. In reality, the majority-plus-one rule allows only one of the five respondents or two of the seven respondents from a village to either report that elections in their village were noncompetitive **and/or** to give DK or refusal answers. In other words, most respondents must claim that elections in their village were semicompetitive for us to characterize elections in that village as semicompetitive. We therefore decided to use data deduced from this rule in the following analysis.

Economic development and village elections: empirical test

In this section we use multivariate techniques to study the relationship between economic development and semicompetitive elections in rural China. We chose logistic regression for our test. The dependent variable is whether a village has held semicompetitive elections. Three variables are used to predict the presence of semicompetitive elections in rural China. The first one is the level of economic development measured by the per capita GDP of the county in which the village is located. We use county-level data to measure economic development because the changes specified by social mobilization theory are unlikely to be brought about by economic development in a single village. We divided all the counties in the nation into three categories: poor counties whose per capita GDP ranged from 1,025 to 2,714 RMB, middle-developed counties whose per capita GDP ranged from 2,715 to 4,327 RMB, and rich counties whose per capita GDP ranged from 4,328 to 48,035 GDP. The poor counties are coded 1, middle-developed counties are coded 2, and the rich counties are coded 3.

The second predictor is the speed of economic development, measured by the ratio of per capita GDP of the sampling county between 1993 and 1982. The figure ranges from 0.75 to 27.73. We again divided our sampling counties into three categories: low-speed development counties (0.75–4.2), middle-speed development

Table 5. Logistic regression model for the relationship between economic development and the presence of semicompetitive elections in Chinese villages

Dependent variable	Model 1	Model 2
Intercept	− 0.359 (0.420)	1.322 (1.008)
Per capita GDP (1993)	0.019 (0.144)	2.508 (1.034)*
Speed of development from 1982 to 1993	0.008 (0.123)	− 1.213 (0.508)*
Distance to major cities or county seats	0.010 (0.006)	0.015 (0.006)**
Per capita GDP squared		− 0.590 (0.251)*
Speed of development squared		0.231 (0.109)*
− 2 log likelihood	446.787	433.752
Model chi-square	3.608	16.643
Degree of freedom	3	5
Significance	0.307	0.005

Note: The dependent variable is the presence of semicompetitive elections.
Source: 1993 Nationwide survey on political culture and political participation in China.

counties (4.21–6.69), and high-speed development counties (6.70–27.73). The low-speed development counties are coded as 1, middle-speed development counties are coded as 2, and high-speed development counties are coded as 3.

Finally, included in the model are the distances in kilometers between a village and its county seat. This variable tests the role of local officials. Some scholars argue that local officials play a major role in introducing semicompetitive elections in rural China, others believe that incumbent village officials play the more crucial role. If the success of village elections is determined by county officials, we should expect to find the distances between the village and the county seat negatively correlated with the presence of semicompetitive village elections. On the contrary, if incumbent village officials play a critical role, the distances between villages and county seats should have no significant impact on the presence of semicompetitive elections in rural China. We present the model on the left side of the Table 5. The result is simple and straightforward: economic development is not correlated in a linear way either positively or negatively with village elections.

On the right side of the table, we test the theory proposed by Epstein, who argues that the relationship between economic development and the success of village elections is curvilinear. For such a purpose, we add two new variables to the model: the levels of economic development squared and the speed of economic development squared. If the relationship between economic development and village elections is curvilinear, we should find that when the new variables are added to the model, the original variables and the squared ones should both have significant impact on village elections.

When the two new variables are entered into the model, each pair of variables has a significant impact on elections. While the per capita GDP has a positive impact on village elections, the per capita GDP squared has a negative impact on village elections. This result clearly indicates that the relationship between economic development and village elections appears to be a concave curve. Or to state the finding in a nontechnical way, economic wealth increases the likelihood that a village will hold semicompetitive elections for people to choose their leaders, but

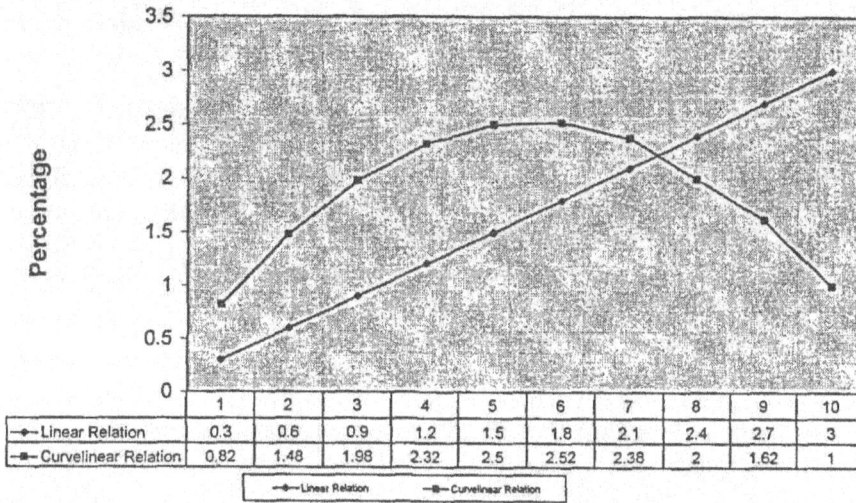

	1	2	3	4	5	6	7	8	9	10
Linear Relation	0.3	0.6	0.9	1.2	1.5	1.8	2.1	2.4	2.7	3
Curvelinear Relation	0.82	1.48	1.98	2.32	2.5	2.52	2.38	2	1.62	1

Figure 1.

its impact diminishes as economic wealth increases. This finding confirms Epstein's argument that the middle-developed counties in rural China are most likely to hold semicompetitive elections for peasants to choose their leaders.[27]

The relationship between the speed of economic development and village elections is also curvilinear, but the shape of the curve is different from the previous one. The relationship between the speed of economic development and village elections appears to be a convex curve, that is, a higher rate of economic development reduces the likelihood that Chinese villages will hold semicompetitive elections in an accelerated manner, that is, the higher the rate of economic development in a county, the less likely that elections in the villages located in that county will be semicompetitive. Finally, the distance between a village and country seat also influences village elections: the farther a village is from a county seat, the better the chance that elections in that village will be semicompetitive.

Discussion

Our analysis reveals that certain kinds of relationships do exist between economic development and political change in rural China, although such relationships are somewhat different from that suggested by social mobilization theorists. Rather

---

27. In Figure 1 we present two curves. The curve that represents the linear relationship assumes only one variable in the model. In the OLS model, $Y_i = a + \beta x_i$. For simplicity, we assume a equals 0. We then assume that the values of x_i range from 1 to 10, if β equals 0.3. If the value of x, that is, per capita GDP equals 1, Y will be 0.3%1. If the value of x equals 3, Y will be 0.3%3 = 0.9, etc. When GDP square is added to the model, we will have $Y = a + \beta x_1 + \beta x_2$. Suppose β for x_1, that is, the per capita GDP in the new model, equals 0.9 and β for x_2 or the GDP^2 equals -0.08. If GDP equals 1, we will have 1%0.9 + (-0.08%1) = 0.82; if GDP equals 3, we will have 3%0.9 = (-0.08%3^2) = 1.98. If GDP equals 6, we will have 6%0.9 + (-0.08%6^2) = 2.52. If GDP equals 10, we will have 10%0.09 + (-0.08%10^2) = 1. In the figure we also plot the data for this model. The value of Y in the second model first increases and then declines.

than being linearly associated with economic development, the relationship between electoral reform and economic development appears to be a curvilinear one, which seems to be in conflict with social mobilization theory.

Several reasons may help to explain the 'deviation' of the Chinese case. First, a number of empirical studies show that the transition to democracy usually occurs when the mean income of a country reaches between $5,000 and 6,000, and it becomes impregnable at the $7,000 level.[28] At the time of the survey, the mean per capita GDP in China was far below these figures. The level of development therefore has yet to reach the threshold at which the above political dynamic begins to operate.

Second, social mobilization theorists ignore the role of political elites in the process of transition. Recent studies have shown that political elites are important actors in this process.[29] Research on electoral reform in China has demonstrated that bureaucrats in the Ministry of Civil Affairs (MCA) and local officials played a key role in introducing semicompetitive elections into rural China. To understand electoral reform in China, we need to analyze the impacts of economic development, not only on the general populace but also on the interaction between state and society. While modernization theorists limit their inquiry to the changes brought about by economic development on demands, intentions, and resources for the general populace to participate in politics, it is also necessary to pay attention to the changes brought about by economic development on the attitudes and policy preferences of political elites in a society.

All political entities, whether a state, town, or village, rest on some mixture of coercion and consent. The consent of peasants used to be based on history and tradition. Economic development has a significant influence over the legitimacy of various political organizations. Before the reforms, peasants worked collectively for the people's communes to produce food, vegetables, housing, and other commodity goods. Although those materials were produced by peasants themselves, the communes controlled all of them and represented the state in distributing them to peasants. Such an arrangement blurred the nature of the relationship between individuals and the state, and many peasants believed it was the state that gave them those resources.

The de facto privatization in rural China after 1978 fundamentally changed the relationship between individuals and the state in the villages. Production is now organized by individuals, and peasants have regained control of the resources that they produce. Grassroots administration now depends on farmers to provide it with resources for its own operations, and public projects now usually rely on 'donations' for funding. As peasants changed roles from 'recipients' of resources to 'providers' of resources for local administration, they naturally demanded inputs into the decision-making process. A crucial but usually neglected consequence of this change is that the basis of the legitimacy of the grassroots organizations has gradually been altered. Legitimacy of village authorities is now heavily dependent

---

28. Przeworski and Limongi, 'Modernization: theories and facts'; Burkhart and Lewis-Beck, 'Comparative democracy: the economic development thesis'.

29. O'Donnell, Schmitter and Whitehead, *Transitions from Authoritarian Rule*.

on the performance of local officials. Economic development is not only testament to the previous performance of incumbent officials, but it also influences their ability to extract political support from both their superiors and subordinates.

In rich villages there are usually collective enterprises, many of which were established by incumbent leaders.[30] These enterprises can provide leaders with money to spend for various purposes. Even in places where development is largely based on private enterprise as distinct from collective enterprises, village leaders can extract money from those enterprises. First, since economic resources can increase the ability of incumbent leaders to accomplish various governmental projects, local officials are usually reluctant to replace them with other people. Second, incumbent leaders can use those resources to co-opt their protégés and persuade them either to ignore the requirements of higher authorities to hold elections or to tolerate them to turn the required semicompetitive elections into noncompetitive ones. Third, villagers in those places usually have little incentive to replace incumbent leaders because village leaders can use the newly acquired economic resources to trade for political support to offset the impacts of economic development on peasants. In 1996 the author visited a village in Zhaoyuan County in Shangdong Province. More than 90% of the people in that village voted for the incumbent leader, who has been the head of the village for more than 40 years. When the author asked voters why they voted for that person, the peasants in the village told the author that they did not need to pay anything to the government. The village used the profits earned by the collective enterprises to pay agricultural taxes on behalf of all peasants. In addition, each resident also received about 3,600 yuan per year from the village.[31] This might be an extreme case, but it is not unique, as similar situations can be found in many other villages. In 1997 I observed the elections in a rich village in Hebei Province. The incumbent leader, who was reelected, told the author privately afterward that in order to attract popular votes he had spent more than 200,000 yuan before the election to build roads and a primary school.

The political dynamics in poor areas is different. First, local officials may not be able to collect money for agricultural taxes and public projects. If the county is characterized as *qiongkunxian* (the officially impoverished county), not only will the government waive agricultural taxes but it will also provide peasants with various kinds of means of subsistence. Second, peasants in poor areas are concerned more about securing adequate food and shelter, especially to find a proper way to put their 'body and soul together', than about public affairs. Finally, people in poor areas may adopt different ways to pursue wealth. Because the opportunity in those areas is limited, those who want a better life tend to go to rich coastal regions in search of higher paying jobs, rather than trying to improve the governance in their own village.

The situation in middle-developed areas is different from both the rich and the poor areas. First, village authorities need to collect money from peasants to support the administration and to run public projects. When authorities ask for money from

---

30. Jean C. Oi, 'Communism and clientelism: rural politics in China', *World Politics* 37(1), (1984), pp. 238–266.
31. Interview with villagers in Zhaoyuan county, Shangdong Province, July 1996.

peasants, the latter will ask for the right to participate in the decision-making process. Second, it is not new to students of politics that rather than being generated by absolute poverty, the desire for change is more likely to be the product of a sense of 'relative deprivation'.[32] Such feelings are more likely to occur among people residing in mid-developed areas than in either the rich or the poor areas. People are more likely to ask why people in other places are wealthier than themselves; whether incumbent leaders are responsible for the economic stagnation; and, more importantly, whether replacing incumbent leaders can improve the economic situation in the village.[33] Because incumbent village leaders do not have the resources to co-opt villagers, they are less likely to be able to defend themselves against pressure from peasants to hold elections for them to choose their leaders. Third, village officials do not have sufficient resources to co-opt their superiors to resist change either. This explains why officials in counties of mid-level development have developed their elections most aggressively and with most success.

Conclusion

The findings of this article demonstrate that a fundamental change has occurred in rural China. After the authoritarian regime was opened up in the late 1980s, the changes in society brought about by privatization and economic development began to play a critical role in the process of political development in rural China. As occurred in other developing countries, changes brought about by economic development not only significantly influenced the attitudes of elements of the political elites toward political reform but also increased the peasants' resources and skills and enhanced their desire to get involved in the decision-making processes in their villages.

Nonetheless, economic development is not linearly correlated with political reform, as the social mobilization theorists suggest. Rapid economic development may even delay the process of political development. Rather than simply freeing people from political control, economic development in some places may help to consolidate the power of incumbent leaders by: (1) making people in those places more dependent on the village authority; (2) providing incumbent leaders with economic resources to co-opt peasants; and (3) providing incumbent leaders with economic resources to bribe their superiors to ignore the decisions of the central government to introduce competitive elections into Chinese villages.

Of course, these findings should not be interpreted as indicating that increases in wealth will not benefit political development in China. Political reform is a product of, among other things, interactions between elites and the general populace. Despite the fact that newly acquired economic resources may help incumbent

---

32. Ted Gurr, 'Causal model of civil strife: a comparative analysis using new indices', *American Political Science Review* 62(4), (December 1968), p. 1104. See also Joseph Greenblum and Leonard Pearlin, 'Vertical mobility and prejudice: a socio-psychological analysis', in Reinhard Bendix and Seymour M. Lipset, eds., *Class, Status, and Power: A Reader in Social Stratification* (Glencoe, IL: Free Press, 1953), pp. 480–491.

33. In fact, these questions are usually raised by villagers in mid-developed areas. Interviews of people from seven villages in Shangxi, Hebei, and Fujian Provinces, 1996–97.

village leaders consolidate their power at the current stage of economic development, economic growth may eventually break this equilibrium. For example,
generational replacement of local officials will make it more difficult for village
leaders to persuade them to resist required political reforms. Increases in the level
of education of peasants will eventually change their expectations about power and
authority. Thus, further economic development may make it difficult, if not
impossible, for village officials to co-opt their constituencies in the future. Although we do not know when the current equilibrium will be broken by changes
brought about by economic development, we know for sure that economic development increases both the ability for ordinary people to participate in politics and the
difficulties of incumbent officials in co-opting constituencies: it also changes the
attitudes of local officials toward elections. We are therefore confident that
the dynamic interaction of these factors will have significant influences over the
future of political development in rural China.

Appendix: sample design

The data come from a survey conducted in China from September 1993 to June
1994 in cooperation with the Center for Social Survey of the People's University
of China. The sample represents the adult population over 18 years of age residing
in family households at the time of the survey, excluding those living in the Tibetan
Autonomous Region. A stratified multistage area sampling procedure with proba-
bilities proportional to size measures (PPS) was employed to select the sample.
The Primary Sampling Units (PSUs) employed in the sample design are counties
(*xian*) in rural areas and cities (*shi*) for urban areas. Before selection, counties were
stratified by region and geographical characteristics and cities by region and size.
A total of 49 counties and 85 cities were selected as the primary sampling units.
The secondary sampling units (SSUs) were townships (*xiang*) and districts (*qu*) or
streets (*jiedao*). The third stage of selection was geared to villages in rural areas
and neighborhood committees (*juweihui*) in urban areas, a total of 551 villages and
neighborhood committees were selected. Households were used at the fourth stage
of sampling. Data analyzed in this paper include all villages in the sample, as well
as neighborhood committees in urban areas with more than 50% of residents
holding rural household registration.
In the selection of PSUs, the National Population Databook was used as the basic
material to construct the sampling frame.[34] The number of family households for
each county or city was taken as the measure of size in the PPS selection process.
For the successive stages of sampling, population data were obtained either from
the Public Security Bureaus of the regions or from the Statistical Bureaus of local
governments. At village and neighborhood committee levels, lists of household
registrations (*hukou*) were obtained from police stations in urban areas and
villagers' committees in rural areas.

---

34. Ministry of Public Security, *Zhongguo Chengxian Renko Tongji (Population Statistics by City and County of the People's Republic of China)* (Beijing: Map Publishing House of China, 1987).

Retired high school teachers were employed as interviewers for most surveys. Although most people in China read and write standard Chinese, people in many provinces in the South speak varying dialects, some of which are extremely difficult for Mandarin speakers to understand. To deal with this problem, professional interviewers from the National General Team for Rural Surveys (*guojia nongcun diaocha zongdui*) who speak local dialects were hired to interview in seven southern largely dialect-speaking provinces. Interviewers were given formal training before the fieldwork.

Before the interview began, we sent letters to all the sampling spots to check whether there were any changes in addresses. We then removed all invalid addresses from our sampling frame and thereby eliminated the majority of noncontacts. The project scheduled interviews with 3,425 people and 3,287 of the prospective respondents contacted by interviewers answered our questions, for a response rate of 94.5%. And the people who hold urban household registration are excluded from the analysis.

Direct Township Elections in China: latest developments and prospects

DONG LISHENG*

The first direct election of township government leader was held in Sichuan Province in 1998, following a decade of direct elections at the village level. There have since been experiments with four categories of elections at the township level: direct elections of government leader, deputies to the People's Congress, Party Secretary, and deputies to the Party Congress. Various indirect methods under different terms have also been introduced, which invariably increase the more active participation of ordinary voters. The assessments of these elections vary from total negation, serious doubts to enthusiastic praise. Suggestions for improvement focus on lowering the qualifications of candidates and allowing campaigning by candidates themselves. Following the latest amendment to the Constitution that extends the term of office of the township government from three years to five, four options for further reform are available. Except for one option, direct elections are proposed or at least possible.

Since the second half of 2003, the Chinese media has been reporting on the public recommendation and public selection (公推公选) of government leaders or Party secretaries at township and even county levels.[1] The first wave of publicity given to this issue was in the first half of 1999 following the first direct election of township government leaders in Suining City, Sichuan Province on the last day of 1998 and that of Shenzhen City, Guangdong Province between January and April 1999.[2]

---

* Dong Lisheng is Professor and Assistant Director of the Institute of Political Science, Chinese Academy of Social Sciences. He was a Visiting Research Fellow at the East Asian Institute of the National University of Singapore from August to October 2004.

1. 'Zhongguo shouwei gongtui gongxuan xianzhang changsheng' ['China has first county magistrate through the public recommendation and public selection process'], *Renmin Ribao* [*People's Daily*], (18 December 2003), p. 4; 'Caiji zhen gongtui zhixuan dangwei shuji' ['Caiji Town uses the method of public recommendation and direct election of the Party secretary'], *Xin Jing Bao* [*New Beijing News*], (12 April 2004), p. A14.

2. 'Gongxuan zhenzhang, Suining kai le xianhe' ['Elect township government head, Suining takes the lead'], *Chengdu Shangbao* [*Chengdu Commercial News*], (29 December 1998); 'Qusui zuimo yitian, wanyu gongmin maoyu canjia zhixuan' ['On the last day of last year, more than 10,000 citizens took part in the direct election under the rain'], *Huaxi Dushi Bao* [*Western China Metropolis News*], (3 January 1999); 'Shuidang xiangzhenzhang, renmin shuo le suan' ['People decide who becomes the town or township government head'], *Mianyang Ribao*, chengshi ban [*Mianyang Daily*, urban edition], (5 January 1999); 'Zhixuan xiangzhang' ['Direct election of township government head'], *Nanfang Zhoumo* [*South China Weekend*], (15 January 1999); 'Minzhu bu yunxu chaoyue falu' ['Democratization does not permit exceeding the law'], *Fazhi Ribao* [*Legal Daily*], (19 January 1999); 'Zhongguo diyige zhixuan xiangzhang changsheng' ['China has the first directly elected township government head'], *Fazhi Ribao* [*Legal Daily*], (23 January 1999); 'Dapengzhen jiang dansheng zhongguo shouwei minxuan zhenzhang' ['Dapeng Town will have China's first directly elected town government head'], *Yangcheng Wanbao* [*Guangzhou Evening News*], (28 April 1999); 'Zhongguo diyige minxuan zhenzhang shangwu changsheng' ['China gets the first directly elected town government head this morning'], *Shenzhen Wanbao* [*Shenzhen Evening News*], (29 April 1999).

Scholars have given a detailed account of the whole process of these experiments and discussed their significance to China's democratization.[3] However, the new developments since then have not been fully studied and the prospects for the popularization of direct elections at this level are not adequately discussed.

This paper will first trace the second round of elections at the much-reported Buyun Township and Dapeng Town, followed by an account of all kinds of experiments to date. Secondly, various methods used by these experiments will be analyzed. Thirdly, their implications and limitations will be discussed. Finally, the prospects of the direct elections will be examined against the various proposals for reorganizing town and township governments.

The latest developments since the first Buyun direct election

Immediately after their experimental direct elections of town or township government leaders between December 1998 and April 1999, the Buyun Township in Suining City, Sichuan Province and Dapeng Town in Shenzhen City, Guangdong Province became the focus of attention in China and abroad. In addition to other minor differences in procedures, the two experiments differed fundamentally in that the winner of the popular election in Dapeng was referred to the Town People's Congress for official endorsement. The very reason for doing so was that the organizers learned a lesson from the slightly earlier experiment in Buyun, which was criticized for violating the Constitution. It stipulates that the town and township government leaders are to be elected by the People's Congress at this level. The Guangdong and Shenzhen officials declared on many occasions that they would improve and popularize the new election methods in order to offer experience to China's political reform.[4] As the Buyun experiment was more innovative, the organizers faced pressure from higher authorities although academic circles gave them greater credit.

But three years later, when the new round of township elections were due to be held, the two places acted differently. In Dapeng Town, the methods as experimented

3. Li Fan *et al.*, *Chuanxin yu fazhan—xiangzhenzhang xuanju zhidu gaige* [*Innovation and Development—The Reform of the Electoral System for Town and Township Government Heads*] (Dongfang chubanshe [Oriental Publishing House], November 2000); Huang Weiping, ed., *Zhongguo jiceng minzhu fazhan de zuixin tupo—Shenzhenshi Dapengzhen zhenzhang xuanju zhidu gaige de zhengzhi jiedu* [*The Latest Breakthrough Achieved on the Development of Grassroots Democracy in China*] (Shehui kexue wenxian chubanshe [Social Sciences Literature Publishing House], March 2000); He Baogang, 'From village to township: will China move elections one level up?', *EAI Background Brief No. 126*, (29 June 2002); He Baogang and Youxing Lang, 'China's first election of the township head: a case study of Buyun', *Japanese Journal of Political Science* 2(1), (May 2001), pp. 1–22; He Baogang and Youxing Lang, 'Predicament in Buyun: a study of the first direct township election in China', *Twenty First Century, Hong Kong* no. 64, (April 2001), pp. 125–136; Joseph Y. S. Cheng, 'Direct elections of town and township heads in China: the Dapeng and Buyun experiments', *China Information* 15(1), (2001), pp. 104–137.
4. In the widely distributed publicity materials, Guangdong and Shenzhen governments claim: 'Dapeng reform is a new breakthrough in China's local political structural reform since the implementation of the direct elections of deputies to local People's Congresses in 1981. To certain extent, it signals the new orientation of China's development of democratic politics'. See Zou Shubin, Huang Weiping and Liu Jianguang, 'Shenzhen Dapengzhen yu Sichuansheng Buyunxiang liangci xiangzhenzhang xuanju gaige mingyun zhi bijiao' ['A comparison of the fate of the two electoral reforms in Dapeng Town, Shenzhen City and Buyun Township, Sichuan Province'], *Dangdai Zhongguo Yanjiu* [*Contemporary China Study*] no. 1, (2003).

with for the previous election were ignored. Instead the district Party organization department recommended a single candidate to the Town People's Congress. Traditional procedures were performed in contrast to the sensation aroused three years earlier. The electoral reform was quietly suspended. But in Suining City officials decided to continue with the reform. To avoid similar criticisms to those directed at the previous election, they modified the method in order to fit the current policy and legal framework of 'candidates nominated by the Party Committee to be elected indirectly (by the People's Congress) with the number of candidates equal to the positions under contest'. Therefore, they formulated the following method: 'the name of the winner of the direct election participated by all eligible voters is to be given to the Party Committee, which passes it over as the only candidate to the People's Congress for formal election'.[5]

In fact, that such experiments could be carried out in 1998 was due to the support or acquiescence of top policy-making bodies. But in October 2001, the Party Central Committee relayed to the whole country the 'Opinions of the NPC Party Core Group on Conducting Well the New Round of Town and Township Elections'. The document explicitly forbids the implementation of direct elections.[6] Notably, it was the organizers of the Buyun elections who continued with the reform three years later despite being criticized specifically after the first experiment, whereas, the Shenzhen officials, who are famous for 'keeping advance by shunning the red lights' on the economic reform front, immediately complied with the central decision. Some Shenzhen scholars have commented that the Dapeng experiment was a 'political show' directed by the officials without popular basis of support. Or it was not organized in response to the demands of the residents. On the contrary, the Buyun experiment was in every sense a direct election as Buyun reformers listened to and answered local residents' democratic demands, strengthened the opinion basis of the reform, and built enough momentum to resist the impediments. So they ensured the continuation of the experiment.

To a certain extent, the central and local authorities maintain a relationship that sometimes restrains each other while tending to persuade the other side to engage in the reforms that one prefers. This can partly explain what happened with the Buyun elections. After the second direct election on the last day of 2001, the Township People's Congress did not immediately convene to endorse the election result. This was due to the disagreement among higher authorities. Some demanded 'to return to the normal track of public recommendation'. However, the local reformers argued that if the result of this election was annulled, it would be difficult to explain to the voters. Only after the *Sichuan Daily* printed a photo of the election site on the election

---

5. 'Buyunxiang xuanmin gongkai zhixuan xiangzhang houxuanren shishi banfa' ['The Buyun Township implementation methods for the open and direct election of township government head by voters, Dec. 1, 2001'], *Zhongguo xuanju yu zhili wang* [*China Elections and Governance Website*], 28 October 2002 (accessed 9 September 2004).

6. Yang Xuedong, *Jubu chuanxin he zhidu pingjing: Sichuansheng Suiningshi shizhongqu 'gongtui gongxuan' xiangzhenzhang he xiangzhen dangwei shuji* [*Innovations in some Localities vs. Institutional Bottleneck: City Centre District, Suining City, Sichuan Province uses 'Public Recommendation and Public Selection' Method for Town and Township Government Leaders and Party Secretaries*), available at: http://www.chinainnovations.org/read.asp? type01 = 5&type02 = 3&type03 = 1&articleid = 127 (accessed 9 September 2004).

date was the impasse broken because it was regarded as a way of approval. Importantly, 40% of the towns and townships in Sichuan Province experimented with various forms of 'public recommendation and public selection' of leaders in 2001 and 2002.[7]

The more recent developments are that this method has been applied to other positions at the town or township level as well as to the appointment of higher level officials (Table 1). There are four categories of direct elections at the township level for: (1) government leader; (2) deputies to the People's Congress; (3) Party secretary; and (4) deputies to the Party Congress. In December 2003, the public recommendation and public selection method was used to appoint Peixian County Magistrate in Jiangsu Province,[8] the first such case in China. The province has also become the first in the country to use this method to appoint officials at the deputy director general level (副厅级). In 2003, the mayors of Baixia and Yuhua Districts of Nanjing City were appointed using this method.[9]

While direct election applies the principle of 'one person, one vote', the public recommendation and public selection method is either a kind of public opinion poll or a primary election attended by a few hundred cadres and some representatives of ordinary citizens. The latter, although modest in intensity, means an improvement to the current practice. The prevalent appointment system of township government leaders is dominated by the Party. More specifically, the county Party Committee decides the candidates. The list of names is passed to the Township People's Congress Presidium by the Township Party Committee. The deputies of the Township People's Congress normally vote to endorse the Party's recommendation.

A survey of the available reported cases show that the following six methods have been used as arranged in order of competitiveness and accessibility to ordinary voters.

1. *Direct election by all eligible voters.* In December 1998, voters in Buyun Township, Suining City nominated 15 candidates. The candidates had to possess the following qualifications: aged above 25 years old; with an education of high school or higher; living or working in the township. Each voter could nominate once only. A candidate had to receive the support of at least 30 voters, but the Party could nominate the candidate from the whole district rather than be confined to the township itself. The primary election was held on 15 December 1998 with 161 participants of township cadres, village Party branch secretaries, Village Committee chairpersons and clerks (文书), villagers' group heads and three villagers' representatives from each village. They voted for two final candidates—Cai Ronghui, a Village Committee chairman and Zhou Xingyi, a school teacher. The District Party Committee nominated Tan Xiaoqiu, a deputy

7. Lai Hairong, 'Township elections in Sichuan', presentation at Symposium on the Cases of Competitive Elections of District Level People's Congress Deputies in Shenzhen in 2003, available at: *China Election and Governance Website*, 9 October 2003 (accessed 16 September 2003).

8. 'China has first county magistrate through the public recommendation and public selection process', Renmin Ribao [*People's Daily*].

9. Xie Kai and Sun Aidong, 'Gedi gangbu zhidu gaige de bada liangdian' ['Eight bright points in the reform of cadre system in localities'], *Banyue Tan* [*Bi-monthly Talk*] no. 16, (2004).

Table 1. Summary of experiments

Date	Location	Types of elections
31 August 2004	Jintan County, Jiangsu	Party members elect township Party committee
2003–February 2004	Shuyang, Suyu counties, Jiangsu	Party secretaries & government leaders
18 December 2003	Peixian, Xuzhou, Jiangsu	County magistrate
2003	Nanjing City, Jiangsu	District mayor, *fu ting ji*
October 2002	Ya'an City, Sichuan	Party members elect deputies to county Party congress
October 2002–January 2003	Yichang City, Hubei	Party secretaries & government leaders
March–April 2001	Gongcheng County, Guangxi	Township government leader
17 December 2001	Chongqing City	Town PC deputies
December 1999	Xincai County, Henan	Township government leaders
April–May 1999	Linyi County, Shanxi	Township government leaders

Party secretary of the township. Thereafter the three candidates took part in 13 campaign rallies in ten villages and one neighbourhood committee. On election day, 31 December 1998, 54.95% of 11,347 eligible voters took part in the election. Mr Tan won with 3,130 votes or 50.19%. Mr Cai received 1,995 votes or 31.99% and Mr Zhou 1,017 votes or 16.03%.[10]

2. *'The three-ballot system'*. It took three months for Dapeng Town, Shenzhen City to complete the whole election process in early 1999. Eligible voters nominated 76 candidates, five of whom were decided as the primary candidates. All Party members, cadres, employees, workers and representatives of residents took part in the primary election, which produced one final candidate Mr Li Weiwen. He was officially recommended by the Town Party Committee to the Town People's Congress. The latter voted him as the new town government leader.[11]

3. *'The two-ballot system'*. Zuoli Town, Linyi County, Shanxi Province also used this method for the election of its town Party secretary and the People's Congress chairman. All eligible voters cast a vote of confidence. Based on the result of the opinion poll, the Party Committee nominated the candidates to the Town Party Congress or the Town People's Congress. The Party Congress elected the secretary and the People's Congress elected the town government leader.

4. *'The public nomination, public selection'*. Nanbu County and Suining City in Sichuan adopted this method. It is a combination of an examination system and a public opinion poll. The vacancies were advertised to invite applications. The top six candidates from the written tests received oral tests before an audience

---

10. Ma Shengkang, 'Buyunxiang liangci xuanju de gaikuang,bijiao ji sikao' ['A general account, comparison and re-thinking of the two rounds of elections of the Buyun Township'], paper delivered at the Symposium on the Election Law and Electoral System, 12 September 2002, *China Elections and Governance Website*, 12 September 2002.

11. Huang Weiping, ed., *The Latest Breakthrough Achieved on the Development of Grassroots Democracy in China*.

of 100-odd elites, whose composition was similar to those in (1) or (2). The top two were recommended to the Township People's Congresses for official election.

5. *Candidates were nominated by the People's Congress deputies.* The prevalent practice is that the PC deputies endorse the candidates nominated by the county Party Committee. This method was first used by the Mianyang City in Sichuan Province in November 1998.

6. *'The two nominations plus election'.* This was applied by Yangji Town, Jingshan County, Hubei Province in September 2002. It is similar to the Dapeng method, but the second nomination is made by the Villagers' Representative Assembly.

Comments and assessments

A closer look at these six methods reveals three basic approaches to reform. The first is the most radical experiment of introducing direct election to all eligible voters. It was implemented out of the confidence that rural residents are capable of rationally electing the township government leaders; the Buyun experiments testified to it. However, it faces two practical problems: (1) the direct election does not comply with the stipulations of the Constitution and the organic law of local government; and (2) there are no national or local relevant electoral rules, procedures and methods for administering direct township elections.

The second approach is a way of providing popular participation in the election of the township government leader within the existing legal framework. As used by Dapeng Town in Shenzhen and Yangji Town in Hubei, it has two serious flaws: (1) candidates nominated by all eligible voters undergo a primary election first before the final list is sent to the Town People's Congress. This kind of primary election has no legal basis and in practice manipulation of election results is possible; and (2) the rationale for allowing minority elites to rule over the majority selection (of candidates) is questionable.

The third method, also complying with the prevalent policy and law settings, incorporates the widely accepted civil service examination system and new requirements of respecting the right of knowledge of local residents about the candidates. Its merit lies in ensuring better qualification of candidates through the objective tests and increasing the involvement of local residents in the selection of officials. But it has at least three shortcomings: (1) potential candidates will have to satisfy several pre-requisites such as age, education and current administrative rank. According to these requirements, most candidates are eligible for promotion even if this method is not used while ordinary cadres and not to say ordinary citizens are actually excluded; (2) candidates have to sit for five or more rounds of tests organized by various relevant departments—the higher the administrative standing, the more rounds of tests the candidates have to undergo; (3) the oral test is loosely regulated but usually is decisive as the last step of the selection process. A lot depends on who the examiners are, what questions should be asked and what is the standard for rating or grading.

As both merits and shortcomings are apparent, it is understandable that these experiments have received differing assessments. Generally, it can be categorized under negation, questioning and praise. To be sure, those who negate the value of such experiments did so for different reasons. Some overseas Chinese democracy activists claim that township elections 'have been proved to be a hoax and nobody is bothered to mention it anymore'.[12] Another noted that in a highly centralized state like China, elections at such low levels of as the village and township mean that no matter who is elected, the result is no more than deciding who is responsible for transmitting the central documents. Further, that the central authorities agree to allow villagers to take part in elections is not intended as the first step toward democratization, but a measure to deal with the chaotic situation at the rural grassroots level after the dismemberment of the commune system.[13] From the other end of the political spectrum, some orthodox Party officials and theorists, as noted earlier, blame the direct township elections for violating the Constitution and weakening the Party leadership.

These reservations are directed at all aspects of such experiments. Some doubt the degree of actual participation of voters. They deplore the heavy control of the whole process by the authorities. According to them, some top leaders like Deng Xiaoping and Peng Zhen tried to turn township elections into a system that restrains the local cadres, bringing the initiatives of the ordinary people into play and implementing democracy among the people. But the promulgated laws and implemented system in recent years have deviated from their intention. The voters are given few choices. In the elections of the township People's Congress deputies, the township Party and government officials not only follow the will of the county Party Committee, but also play the role of election organizers (组织者), presiding officers (主持者) and arbitrators (仲裁者). They directly manipulated the elections to ensure that their preferred candidates were elected. The situation is not the result of the will of certain Party leaders but that of the institutional structure of 'the Party leading the government'. Restricting the power of the Party is a prerequisite for any innovations of the political system on China's mainland to be implemented. As long as the Party maintains the operational model of 'insistence in Party's leadership', any institutional renewal programmes will go nowhere.[14]

Some question the meaning or role of such elections in China's democratization. In some cases, the experiments were carried out not as a response to the popular demand for democracy, but as an attempt by some open-minded local Party departments and officials to present achievements. Worse if direct elections are resorted to as a way of shifting the burden and responsibilities of the higher authorities to lower levels, the promotion of democracy is no more than a by-product

---

12. Anhunqu, *Yangren de xingqu bu yinggai zuowei haiwai minyun zhuyao guanzhudian de qushe biaozhun* [*Foreigners' Interest Should Not be a Criterion of the Main Focus of the Overseas Democracy Movement*], available at: http://www.cdjp.org/gb/article.php/1517, 16 July 2004 (accessed 16 September 2004).

13. Hu Ping, *Ran women buyao zai tan cunmin xuanju* [*Let's No Longer Talk about Villagers' Elections*], available at: http://www.boxun.com/hero/huping/228_1.shtml (accessed 16 September 2004).

14. Zheng Yushuo and Yan Shenghua, 'Zhonggong dangzuzhi zai xiangzhen renda daibiao xuanju guochengzhong de juese' ['The role of the Party organization in the election process of the People's Congress deputies'], *Zhongguo renda xinwenwang* [*China People's Congress Website*], 19 March 2002 (accessed 17 September 2004).

rather than the aim. China has a multi-layer government structure. The direct elections have developed from the bottom up. To certain extent, this may not be the intentionally adopted strategy but a way of evading the responsibility for coping with the dire situation caused by heavy debts on the part of the township governments. Since the introduction of the divided tax system in 1994, the central government has amassed increasing financial resources while the financial situation of the county and township governments has been deteriorating. When the assets of these governments become liabilities, they tend to pass the responsibilities and burdens on to the lower levels and the society at large. The introduction of direct elections is for this purpose.[15]

Most researchers and some officials hail the experiments on direct township elections as an important step forward in China's democratization. According to them, if the village committee elections are a part of the democratization of the rural society, the direct township elections can be regarded as the beginning of the democratization of the state institutions.[16] Some see in it a new round of 'the rural areas encircling the urban areas'.[17]

They believe that the introduction of direct township elections will deepen the following three conflicts. The first is the conflict between subordinates and superiors. The elections change the appointment system into one that empowers the people; officials thus look to the people rather than to the higher authorities. The traditional contradictions between the two are intra-system in nature. The new ones are those between the hierarchical appointment system and the system of empowerment by the people. Once the citizens enjoy the right of direct elections, they will not relinquish it. Further they will demand to directly elect higher level officials.

The second is the conflict between rural and urban areas. Cities administering counties are expected to face the pressure for direct elections soon. In some provinces, one consequence of urbanization is the call for direct and competitive elections of neighbourhood committees as residents have got used to village committee elections.

The third is the conflict between the centre and localities. The current relationship between the two focuses on the division of power. The implementation of direct local elections will focus the conflicts on the sources of power. When local leaders are elected directly by the electorate, they are in a stronger position, backed by popular support, to face the centre. The centre will have to consider the political reform in order to consolidate its legitimacy. It took Taiwan three decades to upgrade local elections to the whole island. The mainland may need a much longer time.

Limitations of the experiments

As the experiments were often made by reform-minded officials rather than as a consequence of societal pressure, they tended to become the new Party way of controlling the cadres. The will and interests of citizens were not fully considered.

---

15. Lai Hairong, 'Township elections in Sichuan'.
16. He Baogang, 'From village to township'.
17. According to the official media and among academic circles, the first instance was the Communist Party's gaining of power on China's mainland by the guerrilla war in the countryside. The second instance was the launch of economic reform from the introduction of the household contract responsibility system at the end of the 1970s.

The selected townships were not representative in that they were stable without serious social conflicts, geographically remote or had a smaller population size. The Buyun Township completely met these conditions as the organizers intentionally chose it. It is most remote from Suining City, mountainous and inaccessible to public transportation. Its population size is about half the national average. The scholars who conducted field work in Dapeng Town found that Mr Li Weiwen possessed many of the qualities of a good official. Under whatever selection system, be it the appointment system, contractual employment system or various public recommendation and selection systems, he would have been guaranteed to become the town government leader. The election was without any uncertainties from the very beginning. This reduces the importance and meaning of the experiment.

Although the organizers of these elections tried to adopt the international practices of electoral administration, these elections were between the prevalent recruitment and appointment system dominated by the Party and internationally recognized free, open and competitive elections. Their shortcomings can be attributed to insufficient choices available to voters and the lack of competitiveness. More specifically, they have the following deficiencies.

The required qualifications for candidates were too strict. In addition to the specifications of the current legal framework, the local Party organizations raised the threshold in terms of age, educational attainment, birthplace and especially years of service at the immediate lower positions. For example, the township government leader candidate must have served as the deputy section chief (乡镇长候选人要求具有副科级两年资格), which means he or she already holds the rank of deputy head of the township government.

Primary elections are limited to 100-odd elites only. They are mainly township cadres, Party members, PC deputies, and some village cadres or villagers' representatives. The election campaigns were limited in scope and intensity. Except for some meetings held by the election organizers, the candidates usually were not permitted to interact with voters. At the meetings the exchanges between the voters and candidates were confined to speeches and a short question-and-answer session. There was no debate between candidates. Almost all issues regarding campaigns were not regulated such as the use of the media and the raising, distribution, disposal and supervision of campaign funds. Nor were the technicalities at polling stations as would be expected, including compulsory use of the booth for writing or marking the ballot privately, surrogate voting, helping the illiterate to cast a ballot and the safeguarding of mobile ballot boxes.

Competitive elections tend to be understood by election organizers as selection through examinations as used for civil servants. The purpose of competition to win the public trust and support is mistaken as the evaluation and assessment of the candidate's knowledge, expertise and capability. Accordingly the Party organization departments organize written and oral tests. In short, they confuse the recruitment of professional civil servants with the competition for public office by politicians.

There are many other flaws in these elections. For example, the candidates competing for the same position were nominated through different procedures. In the Buyun election, Mr Tan Xiaoqiu was nominated by the Party and was exempted from the primary election which the other two candidates nominated by the voters had to undergo. In Nanbu County in Sichuan, only the jury and deputies to the People's Congress attended the primary elections. The ordinary voters were not involved in this important step of the election process. In Dapeng Town, while all cadres, Party members and employees and workers took part in the primary election, each rural household could send only one representative. This violates the principle of 'one person, one vote' and is a discrimination against farmers.

Chinese scholars and officials have made many suggestions for improving the experiments. The most important is the direct election of township government leaders. The 1998 Buyun election model is preferred. Efforts should be made to achieve similar results as those from the Dapeng model. For this end, the priority is to convert the elections of township People's Congress deputies into real direct and competitive ones to avoid their rejection of popularly nominated candidates of township government leader. Since 1979 the election law has required the deputies to the People's Congresses at county and township levels to be directly elected. Therefore the intensity of improving this category of elections can be increased as it is officially and legally sanctioned.

Related to this is the proposal to change the role of the township People's Congress to that of a player of the primary election. However, such down-grading of its status and role is difficult to accommodate. The previous proposal for implementing direct elections of both the government leader and PC deputies remains the best option. As to the deficiency of the primary elections as experimented to date, the better solution is to increase the number of participants or put more candidates on the ballot.

The required qualifications of candidates should be reduced to a minimum. For instance, all local residents aged above 22 who are literate should be eligible. If such thorough reform is difficult to adopt immediately, steps should be taken to move away from the current stringent requirements. Some have suggested that the Village Committee chairpersons should automatically become the deputies to the Township People's Congress. If it is inappropriate to stipulate this in the law, they should be encouraged to stand for this category of elections. The total number of deputies can be reduced to facilitate more frequent meetings as well as proceedings of the sessions.

Another more innovative proposal is to introduce a kind of ticket system, under which pairs of candidates for the township Party secretary and the government leader contest in the elections. The specific procedure can include the following steps: (1) citizens or Party members freely register as candidates; (2) the Township Party Congress and the People's Congress meet separately to shortlist candidates to the required number; (3) the Party secretary candidates and the government leader candidates freely form pairs; (4) the pairs of candidates jointly conduct election campaigns; and (5) the voters elect a pair. The election of the deputy Party secretaries and government leaders could apply a similar method. There are at least three options. First, the Party Congress and the People's Congress hold primary elections separately and the Party secretary and government leader winning candidates choose other winners as their partners. Second, the secretary and leader candidates jointly nominate their running mates. Third, the newly elected secretary and leader nominate their deputies to the Party Congress and the People's Congress according to the 'principle of more candidates than positions available'.

The rationale behind this proposal is the prevalent tense relationship between the Party secretary and the government leader. The introduction of the direct election of the township government leader brings about the contradiction between the different sources of power of these two positions. The same happened earlier after the implementation of the Village Committee elections, which led to the introduction of 'the two-ballot system' to the election of the village Party branch secretary.[18] According to the researcher who raised this proposal, even the application of the two-ballot system to the elections of the Party secretaries fails to completely solve the conflicts between the two categories of office holders.[19]

Whether this is feasible and what impact it may produce have yet to be discussed and tested. But one outcome that can be envisaged is the intensification of campaigning and contests between candidates. In fact, for all types of experiments on the more direct township elections, candidates should have greater freedom to engage in more active campaign activities. They should be allowed to invite volunteers to assist them in campaigning. The raising and disposal of funds should be specified and regulated.

The prospects in the near future

The latest amendment to the constitution that extends the term of office of township government from three years to five has not put an end to the debate on the status of the township started a few years ago. On the contrary, the move has aroused greater public interest and attention to the issue. The prospects for the development of direct township elections hinge on it.

A summary of the various proposals for the reform of the township government, the lowest level in China's government structure, presents the following four options:

- Option 1, abolish the township government and turn it into the dispatched office of the county government.
- Option 2, merge townships, streamline offices and transform functions.
- Option 3, create smaller counties to replace the existing counties and townships.
- Option 4, implement township self-government.

When assessing these options, various factors have to be considered, but it is obvious that the last is preferred. Option 1 excludes direct elections. For Option 2, direct elections are proposed. In Option 3, direct elections are possible and in Option 4, direct elections are imperative. Each option has both its merits and demerits. Its implementation requires the removal of all kind of existing legal and administrative constraints.

In Option 1, the functions of the dispatched office of the county government include: supervising the implementation of the principles and policies of the Party

---

18. It was invented in Linyi County, Shanxi Provinve in the mid-1990s, under which all eligible voters rather than Party members cast a vote of confidence. Only Party members who received majority popular votes could stand for the election attended by Party members to become the Party secretary.

19. Wu Licai, 'Zhongguo nongcun xiangzhen de dangzheng fuzeren xuanju zhidu chuangxin ji gaige shexiang' ['Some suggestions on the institutional renovation and reform of China's electoral system of the town and township Party and government leaders'], *Dangdai Zhongguo Yanjiu* [*Contemporary China Study*] no. 4, (2003).

and the state laws; guiding and assisting the Village Committees or Neighbourhood Committees to facilitate self-governance; coordinating the counter offices of the county government bureaux; exercising some management authority over social affairs and providing a public service on behalf of the county government. The current administrative border of the township remains unchanged. While the Party and government offices will still be established, there are no local institutions of the People's Congress and the Chinese People's Political Consultative Conference.

Option 1 has the following advantages. (1) China's administrative hierarchy will be reduced by one level, resulting in savings of administrative expenditure, fewer government bodies and civil servants. (2) It will alleviate the financial pressure faced by the local government and the tax burden of farmers, helping ensure the smooth implementation of the reform of agricultural taxes. (3) It will reduce the over-stretched sphere of the government activities to fit better the need of developing the market economy. (4) It is conducive to the operation of the village self-government. (5) The implementation of the change will not interrupt the normal life of local residents as the administrative division is not changed.

The disadvantages include: it contravenes the relevant stipulations of the constitution and the organic law of the local government; it will make many civil servants redundant so it may meet with strong resistance; and it requires a large financial resource to resettle the civil servants at the initial stage of implementation.

Option 2 contains the following six points. (1) Small townships are to be merged. As a result, China's total number of townships will be reduced by one third to about 25,000.[20] (2) The functions of the township government should focus on social management and public service. Other functions as necessary under the planned economy should be removed. For example, the management of the collectively-owned assets should be transferred to the newly-established specialized body. The organization of production should be left to economic enterprises. The allocation of means of production should be left to the market. The provision of various professional services can be given to associations. (3) Local residents should be more actively involved in the management of local affairs. Direct election or, short of that, the public recommendation and public selection system should be applied. The transparency of government operation should be implemented. (4) Township government should have an independent finance under the principle of proportionality between the administrative responsibilities and financial resources. (5) The number of internal offices and staff should be reduced. In order to do so, the current practice of the township having identical number of offices to the county should be allowed to be overlooked. (6) The establishment of civic organizations should be permitted and encouraged to strengthen the societal capability of self-regulation and self-management.

The merits of Option 2 are obvious in that it does not have any legal impediments; the streamlining of government offices and personnel will alleviate the serious shortage of financial resources and reduce the tax burden of farmers; and it creates

---

20. The small townships are roughly defined as having a population size smaller than 30,000 in the Eastern China, 20,000 in Central China and 10,000 in Western China. After the merger, the population size will be increased to 80,000–100,000 in the East, 60,000–80,000 in the Centre and 20,000–50,000 in the West.

conditions for urbanization. Its pitfalls are not unique to itself but are familiar phenomena generated by the possible repetition of the vicious cycle of streamlining and expansion and the over-stretched administrative scope with difficulty in performing basic government functions.

Option 3 calls for the creation of smaller counties in the following three categories. (1) In Eastern China, the existing six or eight townships can become a county with a population of half a million. (2) In Central China, the existing four or six townships can form a county with a population of 300,000. (3) In Western China, a new county with a population of 200,000 can be set up by combining the existing two or four townships. Similar to the requirements as elaborated in Option 2, the new counties should be established under the principle of small but efficient government.

The advantages of Option 3 lie in the reduction of a level of government without laying off its civil servants. Its disadvantages are that its implementation involves a large scale change such as the re-demarcation of administrative boundaries. A full-fledged level of government tends to be bureaucratic and is hence detrimental to society's self-management and increasing the burden on farmers.

A prerequisite of implementing Option 4 is the clear definition of societal affairs and state or government responsibilities and its legalization. At least three steps have to be taken. (1) Abolishing the township government and transferring its public administrative functions to the county government. (2) Transferring its economic management and public service functions to the various civic organizations and professional associations. (3) Establishing residents' autonomous organizations for self-government under the principle of self-management, self-education and self-service. Within the autonomous organizations, the democratic election, decision-making, management and supervision should be instituted.

This is the most preferable choice as it will increase local democracy and alleviate state financial pressure and burden on farmers. But it requires profound changes in the local government structure and the relationships between the township and county as well as between the township and village, and alteration of internal power allocation at the township level. Likewise, the constitution and relevant laws need to be amended. The long authoritarian rule and tradition mean that if the county government has difficulty organizing and enforcing public management without the township level, disorder in society may occur. However, the experience of the village self-government in the past two decades proves that the wisdom and creativity of the rural residents should not be under-estimated. If democratization is a world trend, the township self-government based on direct elections should be pursued as an immediate goal.

Independent Candidates in China's Local People's Congresses: a typology

HE JUNZHI

Previous studies of China's local people's congress (LPC) elections have been preoccupied with the description of the new election law, the operation of that law, the control mechanism of local Chinese Communist Party (CCP) committees in the electoral process, electorates and selectorates, and the voting behavior in China's limited-choice election. Less scholarly attention has been paid to the emergence and implications of independent candidates in this electoral setting. Based on interviews, document analysis and observation, this paper defines the independent candidate, classifies them into four types, and describes the campaign process and specific outcomes in China's LPC elections. It is demonstrated that the development of independent candidates forms a realistic power locus in China's LPC elections, and to a large extent provides a functional substitution of opposition parties for exploring the change of authoritarian regime without opposition parties.

Introduction

Communist regimes have often been associated with non-competitive or non-selective elections. However, China's amendment to the election law of 1979 introduced a framework of semi-competitive elections into people's congresses at county and town levels. The implementation and political consequences of the revised election law have encouraged some Western scholars to analyze the changes in China's electoral politics. While relatively few scholars have researched extensively China's local people's congress (LPC) elections, such studies have already covered the description of the new election law,[1] the operation of the new

---

1. Alex Plavda, 'Elections in communist party states', in Guy Hermet, Richard Rose and Alain Rouquie, eds, *Elections without Choice* (New York: John Wiley and Sons, 1978), pp. 179–186; Andrew J. Nathan, *Chinese Democracy: An Investigation into the Nature and Meaning of 'Democracy' in China Today* (New York: Alfred A. Knopf, 1985), pp. 193–223.

election law,[2] the control mechanism of local Chinese Communist Party (CCP) committees in the electoral process,[3] electorates and selectorates,[4] and voting behavior in China's limited-choice election.[5]

While much of the focus centered around the semi-competitive electoral process itself, the candidates and their activities have received little attention in academic studies. For many scholars, the pre-selected candidates in the LPC election are merely puppets of the local CCP committees who dominate the control mechanism; yet since the amendment of the election law in 1979 another type of candidate in China's LPC elections has appeared. The independent candidate first emerged in 1981, was a sporadic presence throughout the 1990s, and rose to a great number in the 2003 county level people's congress election.[6] Many observers noted the great rise in the number of independent candidates in 2003. From then on many articles and books were published that reported and discussed the issue of independent candidates; some reporters and scholars even forecast that the rise of independent candidates in 2003 means a new hope for democracy in China.[7] Criticism of the existing unfair electoral procedures also brought on revision of the election law in 2004. Most of the new items changed in the 2004 election law are related to the production of candidates. For example, article 31 stipulates that the electoral committee must adopt a primary procedure to select the final candidates when agreement could not be formed by the traditional deliberative (Yunliang) procedure. Article 33 stipulates that the electoral committees must introduce the basic information regarding the candidates to the

2. Brantly Womack, 'The 1980 county-level elections in China: experiment in democratic modernization', *Asian Survey* 22(3), (1982), pp. 261–277.

3. Barrett L. McCormick, 'China's Leninist parliament and public sphere: a comparative analysis', in Barrett L. McCormick and Jonathan Unger, eds, *China after Socialism* (Armonk, NY: M.E. Sharpe, 1990), p. 134; John P. Burns, 'The People's Republic of China at 50: national political reform', *The China Quarterly* 159(3), (1999), pp. 580–594; Nina P. Halpern, 'Economic reform, social mobilization, and mobilization in post-Mao China', in Richard Baum, ed., *Reform and Reaction in Post-Mao China: The Road to Tiananmen* (New York: Routledge, 1991), p. 38.

4. Melanie Manion, 'Chinese democratization in perspective: electorates and selectorates at the township level', *The China Quarterly* 163(3), (2000), pp. 764–782.

5. Tianjian Shi, 'Voting and nonvoting in China: voting behavior in plebiscitary and limited-choice elections', *The Journal of Politics* 61(4), (1999), pp. 1115–1139; Jie Chen and Yang Zhong, 'Why do people vote in semicompetitive elections in China?', *The Journal of Politics* 64(1), (2002), pp. 178–197.

6. Min Jie, 'Zeng Jianyu, Jingxue Chulai de Daibiao' ['Deputy produced from election campaign'], *Zhongguo Qingnian Bao* [*China Youth Daily*], (14 January 2002); Li Fan, 'Cong Qianjiang Xuanju Shijian Kan Zhongguo Jicen Minzhu de Fazhan' ['Observing the development of China's grassroot democracy through Qianjiang people's congress electoral event'], *Renda Yanjiu* [*People's Congress Studies*] no. 4, (2004), pp. 24–27; Zou Shubin, Tang Juan and Huang Weiping, '2003 Nian Renda Daibiao Jinxuan de Qunti Xiaoying: Beijing yu Shenzhen de Bijiao' ['Collective effect in the campaign of people's congress elections in 2003, comparison between Beijing and Shenzhen'], *Renda Yanjiu* [*People's Congress Studies*] no. 4, (2004), pp. 18–23.

7. In terms of reporting the emergence of independent candidates in 2003, *Nan Fang Dushi Bao* [*South Municipal Newspaper*], *Nan Fang Zhou Mo* [*South Weekend*], *Fa Zhi Ri Bao* [*Legal System Daily*], *Xin Min Zhou Kan* [*New Civilian's Weekly*], and *Feng Huang Zhou Kan* [*Phoenix Weekly*] reported news and reviews. The monographs focused on this topic include Tang Juan and Zou Shubin, *2003 Nian Shenzhen Jingxuan Shilu* [*Records on Shenzhen's Campaigns in 2003*] (Xi'an: Xibei Daxue Chubanshe [North West University Press], 2004); Zou Shubin, *2003 Nian Beijingshi Quxian Renda Daibiao Jingxuan Shilu* [*Records on 2003's Campaigns at County and District People's Congresses Election in Beijing*] (Xi'an: Xibei Daxue Chubansh [North West University Press], 2004); Li Fan, ed., *Zhong Guo Jicen Minzhu Fazhan Baogao* [*Report on the Development of China's Grassroot Democracy*] (Beijing: Falu Chubansh [Law Presso], 2004). In 2006 and 2007, only one news item about an election lawsuit appeared in *South City Newspaper*, and seven cases about independent candidates were reported on the website of *World and China* (available at: www. World-China.org).

voters, and recommenders may publicize the candidates, though this could only be conducted at very small voters' meetings.[8]

Between 1 July 2006 and 31 December 2007, China's county and town level people's congresses experienced the first simultaneous elections after a revision of the constitution in 2004 that stipulated that both the tenures of the county and town people's congress should be five years. Despite the active involvement of news media and scholars on the emergence of independent candidates in 2003, few of them reported the activities of independent candidates in the election in 2006 and 2007;[9] but some evidence shows that the independent candidates increased in number in 2006–2007, compared to 2003: in Beijing, it is impossible to calculate the number, because they are all calculated as candidates nominated by ten or more people; in Shenzhen the number was about the same as in 2003; in Hubei's Qianjiang, there were 47 independent candidates, which is more than in 2003; in Wuhan there were 20, up from zero in 2003. There were also a good number of independent candidates in Shandong, Shanghai, and Zhejiang. In Wenling, Wenzhou, Shenzhen, and Wuhan, some independent candidates were elected.[10]

To explore the new trends of the independent candidates between 2006 and 2007, the author carried out a observation in Hongkou District People's Congress Standing Committee between 10 October and 10 December 2006, and interviewed some electoral officials, CCP officials, independent candidates, witnesses, and reporters in Quanzhou city, Shishi city, Qingliu county, Sanming city, and Fuzhou city in Fujian Province; Putuo district, Minhang district, and Pudong district in Shanghai; Hangzhou city, Wenzhou city and Lin'an city in Zhejiang Province; Chengdu city in Sichuan Province; and Chongqing Municipality under the direct management by the central government. Through the process of observation and various interviews, many independent candidates were found; some of them were interviewed directly, and others were found by local officials and witnesses. What becomes impressive is the fact that many independent candidates tried to be elected through public, or sometimes, secret campaign activities. Moreover, certain competitive dynamics even formed among rival independent candidates themselves.

Few researchers have focused on the different types of candidates and how they act. One reason for this is that it is very difficult to figure out who the candidates are and how they campaign in China's semi-competitive election system. This article will fill some of this gap in current research and increase our understanding of semi-competitive elections in an authoritarian regime without opposition parties. This study aims to explore this phenomenon with a focus on the dynamics

---

8. See Yang Xinnong, *Xianxiang Renda Xuanju Gongzuo Caozuo Chengxu Yu Fangfa* [*Procedures and Methods of Administration on County and Town Level People's Congress Election Affairs*] (Beijing: Zhongguo Minzhu Yu Fazhi Chubanshe [China's Democracy and Legal System Press], 2006), pp. 46–49.

9. In 2006 and 2007, only one news item about an election lawsuit appeared in *South City Newspaper*, and seven cases about independent candidates were reported on the website of *World and China*. See www.World-China.org in 2006 and 2007.

10. See Li Fan, 'Zhongguo jinqi jiceng renda daibiao xuanju qingkuang fenxi' ['An analysis of the prospects for Chinese basic-level people's congress elections'], in Li Fan, ed., *2006–2007 Zhongguo Jiceng Renda Daibiao Xuanju Shilu* [*Record of the 2006–2007 Direct Elections of Chinese People's Congress Representatives*] (Beijing: Shijie Yu Zhongguo Yanjiusuo [Institute of World and China], 2008), pp. 15–21.

that underlies the typology of independent candidates as well as their behavioral patterns. The first section defines dependent and independent candidates in China's distinctive electoral system, and compares their motivations, nomination styles and support resources. The second section classifies the independent candidates into four types: as idealist intellectuals, legal rights defenders, heads of state-owned sectors and grass-root elites. The third section describes the campaign processes and specific outcomes of independent candidates through three specific cases. The conclusion reflects on the implications for Chinese political development.

Defining dependent and independent candidates in China's LPC elections

It is important to note that the terms 'dependent candidate' and 'independent candidate' are not part of the official terminology of China's LPC elections. Most of the electoral staff and official government documents often employ the terms 'candidates nominated by organizations' and 'candidates nominated collectively by voters' in order to differentiate between the two kinds of candidates.

According to the election law, the CCP, all eight democratic parties, and official mass groups may nominate candidates collectively or individually; more than ten voters may also collectively nominate candidates. In practice, the CCP, all eight democratic parties and official mass groups always nominate candidates together. Those who are nominated by the CCP, all eight democratic parties, and official mass groups together are often named as candidates nominated by organizations; and those who are nominated by more than ten voters are often named as candidates nominated collectively by voters. This division is helpful to the electoral staff, because the candidates nominated by organizations are always supported by local CCP committees and governments, and the electoral staff should help them be elected. However, this typology is not helpful to academic analysis, because many candidates nominated collectively by voters are actually also supported by precinct CCP organizations, and it is the precinct CCP organizations that mobilize the party member voters to nominate some candidates. In order to understand the significance of the division between dependent and independent candidates, the nominating process of candidates in China's LPC election must be elucidated.

Candidates nominated by organizations and its problems

In general, the nominating process in China's LPC election can be best understood when divided into three stages. The first stage is the nominating process within the local CCP committee; the second is the nominating process of initial candidates; and the third stage is the confirmation of the final candidates. The next part of the article will illustrate the three stages and differentiate the independent candidates from the dependent candidates in this process. In order to predigest the scenario, the illustration will mainly focus on the process in the people's congress election at the county level.

In the CCP's system of nomenklatura, core leaders at the county level are managed by a superior prefect or a municipal CCP committee.[11] These core leaders are primarily comprised of members of the CCP county standing committee. Moreover, some important positions, like the chairperson of the county people's congress standing committee (CPCSC) and the chairperson of the Chinese People's Political Consultation Conference (CPPCC), for example, are also managed by a prefect or municipal CCP committee, even though they may not be a member of the Party standing committee. In order to govern the political system effectively, some of the core leaders managed by the superior CCP committee are often nominated as candidates for the position of delegates of the LPC. For example, if the superior CCP committee has an official in mind for the position of the chairperson of the CPCSC, they often deem that the person should be nominated as a candidate and elected to delegate first. About six months before the Election Day, the superior CCP committee often conducts a comprehensive evaluation of the county-level incumbent core leaders. After the evaluation, the superior CCP committee makes a decision to submit who stands as the candidates for county core leaders and who within them should be nominated as candidates for the deputes of county people's congresses. Only after the superior CCP committee decides who will be the candidates for core leaders, can it nominate candidates for deputies to county people's congresses from within the core leaders. Generally, the candidates for secretary and vice secretary of the county CCP committee, the head of the county government, the chairpersons of the CPCSC and the CPPCC, the head of county procuratorate and the head of the county court should be nominated as candidates for delegates of county people's congress.

After accepting the list of candidates from the superior CCP committee, the county CCP committee typically convenes a nomination meeting with other parties and official mass groups to add some candidates to the list. In practice, the pre-selected candidates of the following institutions are often added to the list: the head of particular county CCP departments, including the heads of the organizational department, the publicity department, the united front department, the head of the political and law committee and the head of the discipline and inspection committee; often also included are some department directors of CPCSC, along with representatives of eight democratic parties and official mass groups.[12] After the nomination meeting, the pre-selected candidates nominated by the superior CCP committee are incorporated with those selected by the county nomination meeting into a complete list of candidates, who are thus the candidates nominated by organizations.

---

11. On the nomenklatura system, see Melanie Manion, 'The cadre management system, post-Mao: the appointment, promotion, transfer, and removal of party and state leaders', *The China Quarterly* 102(2), (1985), pp. 203–233; and Melanie Manion, 'When communist party candidates can lose, who wins? Assessing the role of local people's congresses in the selection of leaders in China', *The China Quarterly* 195(3), (2008), pp. 607–630; John Burns, ed., 'Contemporary China's nomenklatura system', *Chinese Law and Government* 120(4), (1987–1988), pp. 2–134; Melanie Manion, *The Chinese Communist Party's Nomenclatura System* (Armonk, NY: M.E. Sharpe, 1989); and Melanie Manion, 'Strengthening central CCP control of leadership selection: the 1990 nomenclatura', *The China Quarterly* 138(2), (1994), pp. 458–491; Tao-chiu Lam and Hon. S. Chan, 'Reforming China's cadre management system: two views of civil service', *Asian Survey* 36(4), (1996), pp. 772–786.

12. Wei Naibin, *Renda Zhuren Gongzuo Gangwei Shang de Sikao yu Shijian* [*Reflections and Practices from a Chairman of LPC*] (Beijing: Zhongguo Minzhu Yu Fazhi Chubanshe [China's Democracy and Legal System Press], 1994), p. 281.

After accepting the list of candidates nominated by organizations from the county CCP committee, the county election committee typically should distribute these candidates into different precincts. Since all of the candidates nominated by organizations are pre-selected candidates for particular governmental positions, the election committee often faces a dilemma. On the one hand, the law stipulates that the candidates in every precinct should be greater in number than the total number of positions available. This of course means that even some pre-selected candidates may lose an election. On the other hand, the loss of pre-selected candidates in a given election means the failure of evaluation and nomination of the CCP committees, which is unacceptable for the leaders of the superior and county CCP committees. Furthermore, the defeat of the candidates nominated by the CCP committee might indicate a possible decline of the CCP committee's political influence. Since the county election committee is dominated by the CCP committee, it often faces pressure to try to ensure the election of the candidates nominated by organizations.

In order to avoid this predicament, a special measure was adopted in which candidates in every precinct are differentiated into two categories: candidates nominated by organizations and candidates nominated collectively by voters. For example, if a particular precinct has a quota of three delegates, it must have at least four candidates according to the election law. In this precinct, one or two candidates would be organization-nominated, with the rest collectively nominated by voters. If the candidates nominated by organizations are successfully elected to the county people's congress in the precinct, all three delegates' positions are awarded to the precinct. If, however, one candidate nominated by organizations loses an election in the precinct, the election committee will cancel the quota occupied by the candidate nominated by organizations. This, then, means that the precinct can only have two delegates. At the same time, the CCP organization in the precinct often also tries to persuade voters that the election of the candidates nominated by organizations will be helpful to this precinct for a political reward, because the pre-selected candidate may bring some political reward to the precinct in his or her upcoming position as one of the core leaders; even though the candidate lost in the election, he or she would still be one of the core leaders, which is pre-decided by superior and county CCP committees. For the voters, the cancellation of the quota means losing a delegate from the precinct; voting for the pre-selected candidate might bring some upcoming political reward. Furthermore, they can still choose two other delegates from the other three candidates.

Obviously, the candidates nominated by organizations have more opportunity to be elected to the county people's congress in this system. Moreover, it is easy for both the county CCP committee and the election committee to manage the election affairs and reduce the degree of competition. This system, however, always prompted the county CCP committees and election committees to increase the number of candidates nominated by organizations, and too many incumbent government officials were elected as candidates nominated by organizations. For example, in the first county people's congresses election after the amendment of the election law in 1979, there were only 49 voters in the second precinct of Wenjiang county CCP committee in Sichuan Province, but six of them were elected as delegates to the county people's congress, because most of the candidates nominated by organizations were elected in this precinct. There were only 45 government official positions higher than head of government departments in Luhuo county, Sichuan Province, but 38 of them were elected as delegates to the county people's congress, while in the other precincts in the same county, there were only two or three delegates produced from thousands of voters in each precinct.[13] Too many candidates nominated by organizations necessarily brought the reduction of the number of candidates nominated collectively by voters and decreased the level of competition among candidates. As a result, some voters expressed their grievances. In the first direct election at county level after the amendment of the election law in 1979, groups of students in Nankai University and Dalian Ocean Shipping College refused to choose the candidates and instead offered provocative remarks, such as Jia Minzhu (Pseudo Democracy), Pian Ju (Shell Game), on the ballot paper. A student in the history department at Nankai University even pasted a poster to urge the students 'Don't ballot for those whom we never met'.[14] In 1986, some university students in Wuhan municipality also pinned up a poster to protest the measures that assured the election of the candidates nominated by organizations.[15]

To inhibit an excessive increase in the number of candidates nominated by organizations, the offices of the CCP central committee and the National People's congress (NPC) standing committee published a notification to the local CCP committees and the LPC standing committees in 1986. This notification asked the local authorities not to increase the number of candidates nominated by organizations, and to respect voters' choice. Some people's congress standing committees even stipulated a limit to the number of the candidates that could be nominated by organizations. The Shanghai people's congress standing committee, for example, stipulated in 1995 in its detailed election rules that the number of candidates nominated by organizations could not surpass 15% of the total number of delegates from the county, district and town level people's congresses. Similarly, the Beijing people's congress standing committee limited the number of the candidates nominated by organizations to 20%.[16]

Although restrictions on the number of candidates nominated by organizations have been adopted by most people's congress standing committees, the number of CCP-supported candidates still occupies a large proportion of the total number of candidates because of the three-level electoral administrative system. In order to administer the county people's congress election, the county CCP committee always establishes an electoral affairs leadership group to lead the electoral committee. The head of the leadership group is often the secretary or vice secretary of the county CCP

---

13. Quanguo Xianji Zhijie Xuanju Gongzuo Bangongshi [The National Office of Direct Election at County Level], *Quanguo Di Yici Xianji Zhijie Xuanju Wenjian ziliao Huibian* [*Collection of Documents and Data on the First National Direct Election at County Level*] (Beijing: Falu Chubanshe [The Law Press], 1984), pp. 146–147.

14. *Ibid.*, p. 141.

15. Quaguo Renda Changweihui Yanjiushi [The Research Office of the NPC Standing Committee Bureaux], *Renmin Daibiao Dahui Wenxian Xuanbian* [*Selection of Literature on People's Congress*] (Beijing: Zhongguo Minzhu Yu Fazhi Chubanshe [China's Democracy and Legal System Press], 1992), pp. 179–183.

16. Wang Chongming and Yuan Ruiliang, *Zhong Hua Ren Min Gong He Guo Xuan Ju Zhi Du* [*The Electoral System of the People's Republic of China*] (Beijing: Zhong Guo Min Zhu Fa Zhi Chu Ban She [China's Democracy and Legal System Press], 1990), pp. 77–78.

committee; and the members include some vice chairpersons of the CPCSC, the heads of organization department, publicity department and the united front department of the CCP committee, the heads of the government office, civil affairs department and police station, the chairperson of the trade union, the chairwoman of the women's federation, and the secretary of the Communist Youth League. In the electoral process, the electoral affairs leadership group acts as a conduit from the CCP committee and the electoral committee, and most of the important decisions regarding elections are discussed and made in this electoral affairs leadership group and transmitted into the electoral committee. The chairperson of the electoral committee is often held by the chairperson of the CPCSC, and the members are delegates from the CCP, the eight democratic parties, the official mass groups, and relative administrative institutes.

The election administrative system and proportion structure of the delegates

In China's local people's congress election, the establishment of the electoral institutes, the partition of different precincts and the distribution of the quotas are highly dependent on the administrative system. According to the election law, it is the electoral committee that oversees the electoral affairs, but the electoral committee is merely a provisional committee, and all of the positions are held by the current government officials. Furthermore, the electoral committee does not send workgroups to precincts directly. It is the town CCP committee and the town government establishes individual electoral workgroups which are then led by the town electoral affairs leadership group. The county electoral committee can only guide the town electoral workgroups on technical but not political affairs. In the preparation stage of county people's congress elections, the county electoral committee only distributes the delegate quota to every town. It is the town electoral workgroup that divides the town into precincts, allocates delegate quotas to those precincts, and establishes the precinct's electoral sub-workgroups. In county level people's congress elections, several villages are often incorporated into a precinct by a town's electoral workgroup. And the members of a given precinct's electoral affairs leadership group and precinct electoral sub-workgroup are often appointed respectively by the town CCP committee and the town electoral workgroup, while the county CCP committee and electoral committee merely endorse those town level appointments (see Table 1).

Table 1. The election administrative system in China's county people's congress

	The CCP committee	Leadership group	Electoral institutes
County level	County CCP committee	County electoral affairs leadership group	County electoral committee
Town level	Town CCP committee	Town electoral affairs leadership group	Town electoral workgroup
Precinct level	Precinct CCP branch	Precinct electoral affairs leadership group	Precinct electoral sub-workgroup

This sort of electoral administrative system directly encourages the enlargement of the proportion of CCP-supported candidates in China's local people's congress elections. As a general rule, most people's congress standing committees have stipulated a limit to the number of candidates nominated by organizations at less than 20% of the total number of delegates; but this requirement only works at the county level nominating process. In other words, the county CCP committee only nominates less than 20% of the total number of delegates as candidates nominated by organizations to the county electoral committee, but the town CCP committee may also have its own predilection to nominate some local leaders, heads of villages and private entrepreneurs as candidates, because some of them might be more willing to make their voice heard on behalf of the town at the county people's congress, or because they would be more likely to deal with local issues with the town CCP committee.

At the same time, the stipulation of the proportion of the delegates' constituency also forces the town CCP committee and electoral workgroup to actively find some other suitable candidates. As mentioned before, the official document from the CCP central committee often stipulates a specific proportion for the county people's congress. The basic proportion structure is that the CCP members in the people's congress should ideally not surpass 65% of the total number of delegates; female delegates in every people's congress should ideally not be less than 25% of the whole; the minority groups and overseas Chinese should have some delegates, and some current delegates should be reelected.[17] For example, according to the election law, Hongkou district in Shanghai should elect 284 delegates as the members of the district (equivalent to county level) people's congress. Following the stipulation of the Shanghai Municipal People's Congress Standing Committee on the delegates proportion structure, the district electoral committee requires that 89 of the delegates should be non-CCP members, and 61 of them should be women and that the number and proportional structure be distributed to every electoral workgroup at the street office level (i.e. the town and township level), i.e. every workgroup gets a fixed proportional structure (see Table 2).

Once the workgroup further distributes the delegates quota to every sub-workgroup at the residential committee level (i.e. the village level), the proportional structure is further fixed. For example, there are 13 precincts under the management of workgroup 1; every precinct has one, two or three delegate quotas. When distributing the entire 27 quotas, workgroup 1 has to distribute the quotas of non-CCP delegates and women delegates into every precinct accompanied by the number of delegates. For example, of the three delegates' quotas of precinct number 9, one must be a non-CCP member, and one must be a woman, or the whole proportional structure would be damaged. In order to achieve the goal of this proportional structure, the sub-workgroup must try to avoid a situation where too many CCP members and men are decided on as candidates. If there is a woman who is a non-CCP member, it is very possible that the precinct electoral affairs leadership group or sub-workgroup will help her to be elected, because she can satisfy two qualifications at the same time. If this precinct was designated to produce a delegate from a minority group or

17. Government document from the Shanghai People's Congress Standing Committee: *Guanyu Zuohao Xianxiang Renda Huanjie Xuanju De Jidian Tongzhi* [*Some Notions on How to do Well on County and Town Level People's Congress Elections*], (12 July 2006).

Table 2. The distribution of delegates quota in Hongkou district, Shanghai, 2006

Workgroups (based on street office)	Number of delegates	Nomination style		Proportional structure	
		Nominated by organizations	Nominated by voters	Non-CCP Delegates	Women delegates
1	27	4	23	8	6
2	23	4	19	7	5
3	28	4	24	9	6
4	24	4	20	7	5
5	21	3	18	7	5
6	25	4	21	8	5
7	22	4	18	7	5
8	29	3	26	9	7
9	21	4	17	6	5
10	25	4	21	8	5
11	15		15	7	4
12	5		5	2	1
13	2		2	1	
14	4		4	1	1
15	5	1	4	2	1
16	5	1	4		
Reserved quota	3				
Total	284	40	241	89	61

Source: Hongkou District Electoral Committee, Shanghai, 2006.

Table 3. The number of delegates in different precincts in workgroup 1, Hongkou district, Shanghai, 2006

Precinct number (based on residence and work unit)	Number of delegates	Precinct number (based on residence and work unit)	Number of delegates
1	2	8	2
2	1	9	3
3	2	10	2
4	2	11	3
5	2	12	1
6	3	13	2
7	2		

Source: Hongkou District Electoral Committee, Shanghai, 2006.

overseas Chinese, some precinct electoral officials would have to find potential qualified people and mobilize them to be candidates. Otherwise it would be very difficult to fill the quota in this precinct (see Table 3).

Defining dependent candidates and independent candidates in China's LPC

Therefore, there are three groups of dependent candidates, that is, candidates exclusively nominated, supported or mobilized by the CCP committees or electoral committee to satisfy certain qualifications. The first group is constituted of those nominated by organizations; all of these candidates are pre-selected for some important positions in the county authority. The list of their names is directly transferred from the county CCP committee to the county electoral committee and distributed to different precincts by the county electoral committee. The second group includes those supported by the CCP committee at the town level, all of whom are supposed to act on behalf of the town. All of these candidates are nominated collectively by voters, but the voters who nominate them are mobilized by the CCP committee at the town level. The third group is made up of those who have some distinctive qualities, which may satisfy the proportional structure as established by the CCP policy. These candidates are also nominated collectively by voters, but these voters are mobilized by the precinct electoral affairs leadership groups. In each of these three cases of dependent candidates, it is not the individual candidate who seeks election to the delegate position of the county people's congress, but the CCP committees at county and town levels and the precinct electoral affairs leadership groups who see the need for their candidacy and support them to be elected to delegate positions.

Therefore, candidates nominated by organizations are not independent candidates. However, on the other hand, not all the candidates nominated collectively by voters are independent candidates, because some of the dependent candidates are also nominated collectively by voters. For this kind of dependent candidate, the voters do not nominate the candidate voluntarily, but they are instead mobilized by local authorities. Moreover, some of the candidates nominated by voters voluntarily may also not necessarily be independent candidates. According to the electoral law, there is only a need for ten voters to collectively nominate an initial candidate. This threshold needed to nominate candidates is so low that far too many initial candidates are nominated collectively by voters in every election. For example, in the author's records on observation, one precinct in Shanghai was given three quotas of delegates, but there were more than 200 initial candidates nominated by voters. Another example can be found in the Beijing county level people's congress election in 1993, where 284 delegate positions were available in the east city district (Dong Cheng Qu), but the initial candidates were more than 1,000 in number, and the final candidates were 414.[18] In the Dongcheng district case, more than 600 initial candidates had been removed before the final candidates were confirmed.

Thus the initial candidates nominated collectively by voters can be divided into three groups. The first group includes those who were supported by the local authorities. Although this type of initial candidate is nominated collectively by voters, it is the local authorities who mobilize the voters to nominate these pre-selected potential candidates. The second group is made up of those who have no desire to be elected as delegates, but for some reason are nominated collectively by voters. Because they are not the pre-selected potential candidates of the local

---

18. Liu Han and Zhang Mingshu, 'Woguo Zhijie Xuanju Zhidu De Tese Jiqi Xinfazhan' ['The character and new development of China's direct electoral system'], in Quanguo Renda Changweihui Bangongting Yanjiushi [The Research Office of NPCSC], ed., *Ren Min Da Biao Da Hui Cheng Li Si Shi Zhou Nian Ji Nian Wen Ji* [*Collection of Papers in Memory of the Fortieth Anniversary of the Establishment of People's Congress*] (Beijing: Zhongguo Minzhu Yu Fazhi Chubanshe [China's Democratic and Legal System Press], 1995), pp. 430–436.

authorities, and they have no desire to be elected as delegates, most of their names would typically be removed from the initial candidates list and they would not be included among the final candidates. While some of them may end up being final candidates, and even be elected as delegates, it is usually not a result of their own personal endeavor, but rather a happenstance. The third group is comprised of independent candidates. The independent candidates are those that have a strong desire to be elected as delegates; and it is they themselves who mobilize the voters to nominate them as initial candidates, to ensure that they become final candidates, and vote for them on the Election Day.

In China's distinctive voting system, there is another source of independent candidates. As mentioned before, when voting, a voter has four choices: endorsing a given candidate, rejecting a given candidate, abstaining from voting, or choosing other people whose names are not on the ballots (that is write-in candidates). When choosing others, however, voters should limit the number of write-in candidates. For example, if a precinct has three quotas for delegates, a voter can only add three names at the most onto the ballot; if a precinct has only one delegate quota, voters can only add one person's name onto the ballot. If more names are written in than the total number of allotted quotas, the ballot is treated as invalid. If the amount of votes for a given write-in candidate exceeds the number of votes for other candidates, the write-in candidate could be elected to a delegate position, even if he/she was not a final candidate. When independent candidates' names are canceled from the initial candidates list, they still have a chance to mobilize voters to vote for them by adding their names onto the ballot. Even when some independent candidates fail to be initial candidates, they can also adopt the same strategy to be elected to delegate positions.

In order to be elected as a delegate in China's distinctive nominating and voting system, an independent candidate only has two basic strategies in the present institutional arrangement. The first strategy involves three steps: mobilizing at least ten voters to nominate him/her as an initial candidate; mobilizing those who have a chance to decide on the final candidate to help his/her name be kept on the list of final candidates; and mobilizing voters to vote for him/her on Election Day. Because only a few voters have the chance to choose the final candidates from the initial candidates due to a established procedure set up by the local authorities, it is very difficult for some independent candidates to ensure that their names be kept on the ballots. In practice, many independent candidates fail in this procedure and later lose the election, but some of them are still able to mobilize voters to add their names onto the ballot. The second strategy employed by independent candidates is to directly mobilize the voters from stem to stem without considering the initial candidates and final candidates. Using this strategy, candidates bypass any attempts to make it on the initial or final candidates' lists, and instead rely solely on urging voters to add their names onto the ballots. When these candidates are elected, they are described simply as 'delegates who bounce from the ballot box'.

Another point that should be emphasized here is the CCP membership status of dependent and independent candidates. In China's local people's congress elections, not all the dependent candidates are CCP members, and not all the independent candidates are non-CCP members. According to CCP policy, the CCP member delegates at every level should ideally be not more than 65% of the total number of

Table 4. Three types of candidates in China's LPC elections

	Motivations	Nomination style	Support resources
Dependent candidates	Pre-selected by local CCP committees	Nominated by organizations or voters	Fully supported by local authorities
Intermediate candidates	None	Nominated by voters	Supported conditionally by voters
Independent candidates	To be a delegates of local people's congress	Nominated by voters or not as nominees	Supported by themselves and voters conditionally

delegates; some positions, like, for example, some vice chairpersons of the CPCSC, are presupposed to be held by non-CCP members. In order to satisfy the proportional structure of the delegates and find suitable candidates to hold the presupposed positions, the local authorities have to nominate non-CCP members as candidates and help them to be elected. While non-CCP members can often be nominated by local authorities, some independent candidates are CCP members. As is the case for their counterparts in other countries, their party membership does not predetermine their nomination or the support of their parties. In China's local people's congress elections, for academic analysis, only two standards but not the nomination style can be used to differentiate the independent candidates from the dependent candidates. One is the candidates' motivation and the other is the candidates' support resources. If the candidates are nominated and supported by the local authorities in the electoral process, they are dependent candidates. Those candidates who have a voluntary desire to be elected to delegate positions and who mobilize the voters to vote for them are independent candidates.

In sum, three types of candidates could be identified according to the candidates' motivations and support resources. The first type is the dependent candidate, who is supported by the local authorities and nominated by organizations or voters jointly; the second type is the intermediate candidate, who has no conscious desire to campaign but is nominated by voters jointly; the third type is the independent candidate, who has a strong desire to campaign and mobilizes the voters to nominate and vote for him/her (see Table 4).

Four types of independent candidates

In the 1980 local people's congress election, most of the independent candidates were university students. Throughout the 1980s and 1990s, only Yao Lifa and Zeng Janyu were openly defined in the media as independent candidates. When they joined the election as independent candidates, Yao Lifa was a government official in Qianjiang city education bureau, Hubei Province; and Zeng Jianyu was a worker in Luzhou city, Sichuan Province. In contrast, in the 2003 local people's congress elections, the independent candidates in Hubei Province included 11 teachers, five directors of village committees, five jurisprudent people, nine workers and 12 peasants; independent candidates in Beijing and Shenzhen included owner-occupiers, entrepreneurs, white-collar workers, university students, unemployed workers and lawyers. Compared to Shenzhen, most of the independent candidates in Beijing had been educated in law school, and included lawyers and law school teachers and students. Most of the independent candidates in both Beijing and Shenzhen had university educations and most of them were non-CCP members.[19] In the author's observations and interviews in 2006, heads of government departments, bankers, journalists, and heads of state-owned enterprises and public sectors were also all found to be independent candidates. It was noticeable that many legal rights defenders [Weiquan Renshi] for land, jobs and properties engaged in the local people's congress election as independent candidates. Moreover, some of the independent candidates' professional vocations overlapped each other. For example, some directors in village committees were also entrepreneurs in the countryside and some professors in law schools were also lawyers.

It was noteworthy that the independent candidates' motivations and campaign strategies were highly interrelated to their vocations. This interrelation was certainly understandable, because different vocations provided different resources and opportunities to each individual candidate. Based on these interrelations between motivations, strategies and vocations, most of the independent candidates can be sorted into four types.

The first type of independent candidate could be labeled as 'idealist intellectual'. The vocations of these candidates include university students, university teachers, and lawyers. Eight cases of intellectual independent candidates were identified by observations, interviews and sources from the media. Five of them were teachers, two were university students and one was a lawyer. One of the teachers and one student both had a strong desire to be elected to delegate positions, and tried to mobilize ten voters to nominate them at the beginning of the electoral process, because they wanted to achieve their own values of democracy and rule of law as delegates. Although it was very easy for them to become initial candidates, both of them ultimately failed to get themselves onto the finial candidate list. The other six candidates did not have any strong desire to be elected as delegates, but they were nominated by their colleagues and classmates. When their names were mysteriously left off the list of final candidates for no apparent reason, and when the electoral institutes left many of their questions as to why this had occurred unanswered, all six candidates were provoked by what they saw as unjust procedures and began to actively campaign. When campaigning, four of them leafleted and ran poster campaigns, and one university teacher in Shanghai mobilized students to vote for him by giving a lecture on the role of modern citizens and the electoral procedure. In the end, most of the intellectuals lost in the election, because they all faced an important institutional obstacle. Since they had failed to get themselves on the list of final candidates as a result of the local authorities having dominated the deliberative process, all of them lost their legal status as candidates, and they could no longer act as having legal candidate status. When they persisted in their campaigns, the local authorities had a lawful reason to stop them, and intellectuals' ideal of democracy and rule of law stopped them from adopting illegal campaign strategies in elections, because illegal campaign strategies breached their original intention for democracy and rule of law.

---

19. Zou Shubin *et al.*, '2003 Nian Renda Daibiao Jinxuan de Qunti Xiaoying'.

The second type of independent candidate is most easily identifiable as legal rights defenders. Their vocations include unemployed workers, owner-occupiers, peasants, and professional human rights activists. For most of them, they thought that their legal rights had been violated by managers of state-owned companies, property companies, and local government officials. When defending their rights by dealing with their perceived violators, they found that some of their antagonists were people's congress delegates. Therefore, they in turn sought to participate in people's congress elections, believing that their status as delegates would be helpful in reclaiming their lost rights. In eight cases of legal rights defenders, two owner-occupiers and one professional human rights activist were inspired by the fact that their antagonists, who were the bosses of property companies, were people's congress delegates. Two peasants hoped to be elected to delegate positions, so that the new status could help them prevent potential injustice treatment from their local governments. One professional legal rights defender had previously experienced an unsuccessful campaign and had studied the electoral law extensively for the following election. One unemployed worker and one owner-occupier had originally had no desire to campaign, but were ultimately mobilized by their colleagues, because they felt that if they were elected to delegate positions it would make it easier for them to negotiate with the local government. Since most of these activist candidates were residents in cities and countryside, most of the precinct level electoral officials were their contacts. Some of the candidates were able to get support in secret, because most of the electoral officials were members of the city residential committees or village committees, and they felt that these candidates would be competent delegates who could speak for them in the people's congresses. However, the electoral officials could not support them openly; in particular, when important dependent candidates were put into their precinct, some electoral officials even had to suppress the campaign activities of legal rights defender candidates. Since the legal rights defender candidates campaigned within their contact circles, they could adopt both formal and informal means of campaigning, like making open speeches, pasting posters, dropping in on residents, putting up banners, etc.

The third type of independent candidate could be labeled as heads of state-owned sectors. Their vocations included heads of government departments, public-sectors, and companies. In five cases of this type of candidate, two were heads of government departments, one was the head of a state-owned telecom company, one was the head of a state-owned bank branch, and one was the head of a state-owned TV station. For these particular independent candidates, becoming delegates would mean possible promotions, position guarantees, or even business extensions. For the heads of government departments, then, the status of delegate could provide more opportunities to access important figures, which could be helpful to their promotion; it could also help them evade supervision and regulation from the people's congress, because they themselves would be delegates of the people's congress and hold their current positions at the same time. For the three heads of state-owned institutes, becoming delegates would be helpful to their business extension by getting more resources from the governments, which could also help them be promoted to more important positions. However, as important local cadres, these candidates faced certain disadvantages. They were not able to campaign openly, because the campaign might influence the election of dependent candidates, which was not acceptable for the local authorities. Of course, these candidates also had some advantages, as they could easily mobilize their preexisting networks, including subordinates and staff from their work units, to vote for them. For them, the most important factor was where their precincts were located. If they were located in a precinct that had counterbalance competitors, the potential degree of competition would be high; yet if they were located in a precinct that only had small work units, they would be easily elected. Some of these candidates were very good at persuading the electoral committees to delimit their work units into a good precinct, so that their work units could have quantity advantages on votes. When their work units were incorporated into a precinct with residential districts, some of them might mobilize the residential voters by contributing to residential districts.

The fourth type of independent candidate is the grass-roots elites. In the author's fieldwork, this type appeared more often in the countryside. Their vocations mainly included private entrepreneurs and heads of village committees. As mentioned before, many heads of village committees are also private entrepreneurs. For all of them, becoming a delegate could increase their social status and prestige in their own local areas, and thus it would be easier for them to manage their businesses. For the private entrepreneurs, their would-be status as deputies could also provide more opportunities to access the local political leaders and government officials, and in turn they could get more resources and loans from the local authorities and could avoid random intervention from local government officials. Furthermore, delegates of a local people's congress have a special habeas corpus and could supervise local officials during their tenure as delegates, which would also be beneficial to their business. In ten cases, five of them were entrepreneurs, three of them were entrepreneurs and heads of village committees, and two of them were only heads of village committees. The distinctive scenario of grass-roots elites is that they use nearly all the possible means to campaign in the election, the most common however involved donating or promising to donate to commonwealth affairs, reciprocal bargaining, presenting gifts or banqueting voters. Many of them also mobilized their relatives and friends to help them collectively.

Campaign processes and specific outcome of independent candidates

One important difference between dependent candidates and independent candidates is that the dependent candidates do not campaign by themselves, whereas independent candidates have to. Since the dependent candidates are selected and supported by the local authorities, the failure of dependent candidates could potentially signal the weakness or ineffectiveness of the local authorities. Therefore, the main interactions in China's local people's congress election don't happen between dependent candidates and independent candidates, but between local authorities and independent candidates. Based on the cases on which information was collected in 2006 and 2007, three outstanding interaction patterns could be identified.

Coerced interaction

As a veteran in the election, Yao Lifa began campaigning as early as five months before the Election Day in 2006. In order to exchange ideas on campaign activities, Yao Lifa and five other potential independent candidates prepared to meet and discuss how to campaign before the election. When they met in Xiantao city, Hubei Province on 26 July, the Xiantao police station accused them of 'unlawful assembly' and detained them for several hours. When Yao Lifa finished printing leaflets, he began to mobilize his colleagues to campaign as independent candidates in his hometown. After he contacted more than 30 people, they met at a restaurant in Qianjiang to discuss how to defend their legal rights by campaigning in the people's congress election on 28 September. Only two hours into the meeting, they were told that policemen and government officials had already surrounded the restaurant. The participants in the meeting were then called away one by one by the government officials and the meeting was suspended.

Yao Lifa faced even more rigorous challenges from September onwards. In early September, he found he was being followed by three police vehicles and two motorcycles every day, he also discovered that the education bureau had sent special staff to follow him and that his telephone had been tapped by the local authorities. According to Yao Lifa, he was even warned not to campaign by a member of the mafia. On 23 October, he was also discouraged from campaigning by officials from the education bureau and the principal of his work unit. They told him to be careful, or he would be fired from the primary school where he was working. One of Yao Lifa's campaign volunteers, Liduan Pang, who lived in Changde, Hunan Province, left his home to help Yao Lifa on 8 October. During the time period from 11 to 27 October, when Liduan Pang copied down the names of voters from the voters' list and distributed leaflets for Yao Lifa, he was stopped by policemen on four separate occasions. He was also warned by policemen that he should not help Yao Lifa, and if he continued doing so, he would be detained. Another of Yao Lifa's volunteers, Guangmin Hu, also found he was followed by unidentified people.

When Yao Lifa tried to mobilize voters in his precinct to nominate him as an initial candidate, the voters were told that only females could be nominated as candidates in this precinct. Although he successfully mobilized 20 voters to nominate him as an initial candidate, his name did not appear on the list of final candidates, and voters were mobilized by the local authorities to withdraw their nominations. When he tried to mobilize voters to add his name on the ballot, he found himself the subject of many rumors, such as that he was a traitor, and was stopped by policemen many more times. On the Election Day, many policemen garrisoned the precinct and no one outside the precinct was permitted to observe the voting and counting process.

According to Yao Lifa, although he and 46 other independent candidates were trying to campaign legally, most of them lost the election because the local authorities helped the dependent candidates by hook and by crook. They attributed their failure to the unlawful means used by local authorities and tried to complain of their experience to the central government; but in the end, they received no response.[20]

Acquiesced interaction

Zhou was a banker and head of a state-owned bank branch, who was also a CCP member. When he was told of the coming election in 2007, he thought that becoming a deputy to the people's congress would help him enlarge the deposits and loans of his bank branch, while the new achievement of his bank on deposits and loans would help him be promoted in his bank system. In anticipation of becoming a candidate, he studied the electoral law and visited the electoral officials to learn the relative information in his precinct.

He was told that there were two delegates' quotas including one dependent candidate distributed to his precinct, and that the dependent candidate was ensured to be elected. Fortunately, he was also told that the other potential delegate could be occupied by a CCP membership of the male sex, and that his candidacy would not influence the proportional structure in his precinct. This meant that he had an opportunity to campaign for the delegate position, but not to challenge the dependent candidate. The main problem was that in his precinct, beyond his own bank branch, there was another bank branch, a residential district, and many other small companies. Although his bank branch had a large staff within the precinct, it occupied less than 10% of all voters in the precinct, and the head of the other bank branch also sought to be elected to the delegate position.

In order to win the election, Zhou convened a meeting with his core leaders' group in his bank. He told all of his subordinates of his intention and the situation, and asked them to brainstorm. The campaign strategies were produced at this meeting, and all of the participants began to help his campaign. As head of a bank branch, it was very easy for Zhou to mobilize at least ten voters to nominate him as an initial candidate, which the voters in his bank branch did immediately. In order to be elected to delegate, he and his colleagues needed to ensure success in two critical steps. First, they had to ensure that Zhou's name would be on the list of final candidates; and second, they had to mobilize more than half of the voters in the precinct to vote for him on Election Day.

In the precinct, only the delegates of big work units and some members of the residential committee could attend the deliberative meeting to decide who would be among the final candidates. To ensure that his name made the list of final candidates, Zhou and his team visited the residential committee and other small companies separately. Zhou himself, as was arranged by his friends, met the directors of the residential committee. He promised the directors that his bank branch could do some community work for the residential district and that he would speak for the residential

20. Sui Binbin, 'Yao Lifa Tan 2006 nian Qianjiangshi Renda Daibiao Huanjie Xuanju' ['Yao Lifa on Qianjiang's people's congress election'], in Li Fan, ed., *2006–2007 Zhongguo Jiceng Renda Daibiao Xuanju Shilu*, pp. 118–125; and Sui Binbin, 'Yao Lifa Tan 2006 nian Qianjiangshi Renda Daibiao Huanjie Xuanju' ['Yao Lifa on 2006 Qianjiang's people's congress election'], *Background and Analysis* 125, available at: www.world-china.org (accessed 25 July 2007).

committee in the people's congress. His team visited some important small companies and promised them favorable deposit and loan policies. After these endeavors, Zhou and his team successfully ensured his status as a final candidate. The only problem was that the head of the other bank branch was also successful in becoming a final candidate, and including the dependent candidate, there were three candidates campaigning for two positions in his precinct.

After further discussions with his team, Zhou decided to fulfill his promises in the residential district before the Election Day, as most of the voters lived within this residential district. Zhou appropriated a special fund for education to help the poor students in the residential district and asked the residential committee to help him perform a ceremony for the donation. On the day of the ceremony, he ordered all of his staff to attend the event with the uniform and emblem of his bank branch, and mobilize the residents to vote for him. He even hired professional artists to perform in the residential district, so that more and more residents in the residential district could know that the bank branch had set up a special fund for them.

Because Zhou was the head of the bank branch, and his colleagues knew that his campaign would be helpful for their performance of the bank, he easily mobilized his staff to join the campaign. At the same time, because his donation was beneficial to the residential district, Zhou gained the support of precinct electoral officials, who were in the residential district. He was also very careful in not challenging the dependent candidate, and therefore he was made to acquiesce by the local authority. Since all of Zhou's staff, most of the voters in the small companies, and the residents voted for him, in the end he was elected to the delegate position. Helped by the local authority, the dependent candidate in his precinct was also smoothly elected as a delegate.[21]

Competed interaction

Wenzhou was very famous for private companies in China, and entrepreneurs in Wenzhou have engaged in political campaigns on many occasions. Because electoral competitions have typically been very intensive, the county electoral committees found it to be useless to set up any proportional structure for delegates, and the town CCP committees were also very cautious to nominate any dependent candidates. Since the elections were without proportional structure, and the number of dependent candidates was decreased because the town CCP committee seldom nominated pre-selected candidates, more opportunities were available to independent candidates in the county people's congress elections.

Qiao, Wang and Lin were all private entrepreneurs in a village of P county, Wenzhou city, Zhejiang Province. In the P county people's congress election in 2007, their precinct was given two delegate quotas. When they began to campaign, all three adopted a traditional approach to mobilizing voters. They all banqueted voters in their constituency, and plied them with cigarettes and wine.

Soon Qiao and Wang decided to unite together to defeat Lin and help one another in the respective campaigns. The duo printed a lot of leaflets to publicize them and in

---

21. Interview with Zhou, Chongqing, 12 February 2007.

which they accused Lin of ignominious business operations. Their allegations irritated Lin and prompted him to print his own leaflets in which he made his own accusations of disreputable business operations regarding Qiao and Wang. Since Lin had been running a printing company, it was easier for him to print more leaflets and spread them out across the community. Facing Lin's rather serious disclosure, Qiao and Wang complained to the electoral committee that Lin had been using leaflets to launch a smear campaign against them. When the electoral committee investigated Lin's activities, Lin also accused Qiao and Wang of doing the same thing to him. Facing both sides' accusations, the electoral committee had to adopt a sweeping resolution, which stipulated that only leaflets with a stamp from the electoral committee could be distributed to voters, otherwise, the distributors would be punished.

At midnight before the Election Day, Lin suddenly ordered his staff to run all of his printers in his company to print a new leaflet for his campaign. In this leaflet, Lin promised all residents that he would invest 200,000 Chinese Yuan to build a new infrastructure for the village if he was elected as a delegate. He then made all of his staff distribute the new leaflet door to door in the village. Originally, he thought that midnight before the Election Day was a perfect time for him to mobilize voters, because his printing company could print enough leaflets quickly enough, while the other two entrepreneurs would not have enough time to respond, and at a time when electoral officials were already off duty. So his actions could be silently transferred to votes from the voters.

But Qiao and Wang quickly discovered Lin's new strategy. After an urgent discussion, Qiao and Wang mobilized all of their staff and relatives. For five hours until dawn, they drove cars and used loudspeakers to urge voters not to believe Lin's promise. When the precinct electoral officials prepared for voting at 10 o'clock on Election Day, they were told that Qiao, Wang and Lin had all violated the electoral law, as the law stipulated that no person can publicize or campaign on Election Day. After receiving the report from the electoral officials, the electoral committee decided to postpone the Election Day for three days, warning all three candidates not to do any campaigning during that time.

With this new situation, Qiao and Wang decided to negotiate with Lin. Eventually Lin agreed to step down from his candidacy, while Qiao and Wang paid all of Lin's expenses in the election. Finally, both Qiao and Wang won the election when it was eventually held.[22]

From a formal institutional perspective, it is very hard for independent candidates to win the elections. There are two institutional obstacles that the independent candidates have to overcome. The first obstacle is the process called determining the final candidates (确定正式候选人) and the other is the double majority (双过半) rule that determines the election winners. For any election to be valid there must be 50% plus one eligible voters participating in the election and the candidates must collect 50% plus one vote. Given such an electoral institutional arrangement, the more candidates there are, the more spread out the votes will be and the more likely it is that the election will fail. In order to get around that problem, all elections in China include an important process called determining the formal candidates.

---

22. Interview with a local government official in P county, Wenzhou city, Zhejinag Province, 18 April 2007.

When determining the final candidates, nearly every place uses deliberation (酝酿), i.e. discussion, bargaining, and consultation, to determine the final candidates. No matter how many independent candidates were first nominated by voters in a place, such a process may guarantee local officials the means to remove people they do not like from the ballot. As a result, no matter what kind of nomination methods are used, as long as the candidate nomination process allows for deliberation, local officials can often manipulate elections.

The cases in this paper show that the institutional obstacles in practice only apply for two types of independent candidates, the idealist intellectuals and legal rights defenders most often. For the other two types of independent candidates, the institutional obstacles often do not work very well. If the independent candidates are from the public sector, and if their engagement does not damage the proportional structure, and if they do not directly challenge the pre-selected dependent candidates, the electoral committees tend to tolerate their campaigns. In addition, institutional resources from the work units could help these independent candidates overcome the double majority threshold. In places where there are too many grass-roots' elites involved in elections and they form an intensive campaign situation, the local authorities seldom manipulate the electoral process openly. Furthermore, when the number of independent candidates, especially the number of idealist intellectuals rises to a certain level, the local authorities cannot manipulate the process arbitrarily. That is why there were about 20 university teachers and staff elected in Beijing in the 2006–2007 district people's congress election.[23]

Concluding remarks

The emergence of independent candidates is a new trend in China's local people's congress elections. This paper focuses on the typology of the new emergent independent candidates. The distinctive electoral system, and especially the combination of a party system and nomination practice, produces three types of candidates in China's LPC electoral process: dependent candidates, intermediate candidates and independent candidates. According to their motivations, campaign strategies and vocations, four types of independent candidates—idealist intellectuals, legal rights defenders, the heads of state-owned sectors and grass-root elites—can be identified. Based on three cases, multiple campaign processes and specific outcomes of the independent candidates are also described in turn.

The connections among the vocations, campaign strategies and results show that the variable of the candidates' professional vocations was very important in understanding their campaign process and ultimate destinies. The idealist intellectuals tended to adopt an altogether lawful strategy in order to campaign; the legal rights defenders faced far more unsympathetic regulations from the local authorities; the heads of state-owned sectors had more public work unit resources at their disposal; and the grass-roots elites tended to join the campaign by any and all possible means, whether fair or foul. In general, the heads of state-owned sectors

---

23. See Li Fan, 'Zhongguo jinqi jiceng renda daibiao xuanju qingkuang fenxi'.

from big work units and the grass-roots candidates from large companies had more opportunities to win the elections.

This case study also shows that the real political conflicts and competitions between candidates and between candidates and local authorities in China's semi-competitive election are from the emergence of independent candidates. Although the emergence of the independent candidates in general is sure to potentially challenge the pre-selected dependent candidates and local authorities, not all of the independent candidates challenge the latter in a given election. If the independent candidates do not influence the pre-ordained delegate structures and quotas, and do not directly challenge the pre-selected dependent candidates, the local authorities may tolerate the participation of independent candidates. If the local authorities perceive that the emerging independent candidates may potentially challenge the pre-established delegate proportional structures and quotas, and may defeat the pre-selected dependent candidates, they tend to hinder and obstruct their campaign by all means necessary. Especially when the local authorities resort to coercion, the fate of independent candidates can be calamitous, but if the local authorities avoid putting much emphasis on the delegate proportional structures and limit the number of pre-selected dependent candidates, the independent candidates may have more opportunities to campaign openly and ultimately win the elections. Therefore, the attitudes and responses of the local authorities to the independent candidates are also highly critical factors in understanding the campaign process and the specific destinies of the new emerging independent candidates.

Since the extant literature on China's LPC elections mainly focuses on the electoral institutions, control mechanisms and voting behaviors, this study could further seek to explain where the electoral institutions and mechanism could be fixed and where they could be more flexible. For researchers concentrating on voting behaviors, the author's research might further differentiate the high and low turnout and who tends to vote in elections. This study attempts to show that the flexibility of the electoral institutions and of the control mechanism might depend on which type of independent candidates emerge in specific areas, and the turnout and voting behaviors might also be related to the type and density of independent candidates.

When looking for the starting point and dynamics of the transition from an authoritarian regime, most of the literature concentrates on the emergence and activities of the opposition parties. This frame obviously meets problems when applied to China, because China prohibits the existence of opposition parties and direct elections only happen at county and town levels. Therefore no national opposition parties can exist, but the emergence, activities and destinies of the independent candidates can provide a new way to explore changes and transitions in an authoritarian regime. On the one hand, the emergence of independent candidates might inspire more independent candidates to participate in the election process and bring more competitive elections to China's local people's congress electoral system. On the other hand, the emergence of independent candidates might also bring more and more violence, bribes, and manipulation in local people's congress elections. This paradox could potentially prompt the central and local authorities to perfect the electoral rules in the long run, but might also prompt the local authorities to actively limit the independent candidates in the short term. In any case, the emergence of independent candidates may constitute a salient piece of evidence for the early stages of structural change, towards a new type of authoritarianism or democracy, in a country without opposing parties.

Index

Page numbers in *Italics* represent tables.
Page numbers in **Bold** represent figures.

INDEX

'women live inside, men outside' 106
Women's Federation of Qianxi County, Hebei
    114

Xin, Qiushui 54, 56; and Tan, Qingshan 81–
    99
Xu, Wang 62
Xu, Yong 62

Yang, Dali: and Su, Fubing 30, 38, 41
Yangmei village: concurrent office holding
    134–5; Party secretary Rong 134; secretary-
    chairman 134
Yao, Lifa: election campaign state hostility
    222–3; independent candidate (LPC) 218
yibashou 132
Yu, Zuomin 120

Zeng, Janyu: independent candidate (LPC)
    218
Zhangjia village: economic development
    company 123–4; VC chairman 124; VC
    challenges to VPB 123–4; VPB secretary
    123
Zhejiang prefectures 14
Zhongshan city: Town Party committees 127;
    village Party secretaries 128
Zhongshan municipality 119
Zhongshan Party committee: VC chairman
    129
Zhou: election campaign 223–4; independent
    candidate (LPC) 223–4; special fund for
    education 224
Zweig, David: and Chung, Siu Fung 136–56

For Product Safety Concerns and Information please contact our EU
representative GPSR@taylorandfrancis.com
Taylor & Francis Verlag GmbH, Kaufingerstraße 24, 80331 München, Germany

www.ingramcontent.com/pod-product-compliance
Lightning Source LLC
Chambersburg PA
CBHW081737270326
41932CB00020B/3306